D0004278

3 0600 00373 7443

WILLIAM DOUGLAS O'CONNOR

WILLIAM DOUGLAS O'CONNOR

Walt Whitman's Chosen Knight

Florence Bernstein Freedman

Ohio University Press

ATHENS OHIO · LONDON

Library of Congress Cataloging in Publication Data

Freedman, Florence B. (Florence Bernstein)
  William Douglas O'Connor: Walt Whitman's chosen knight

  Bibliography: p.
  Includes index.
  1. O'Connor, William Douglas, 1832–1889—Biography.
2. Whitman, Walt, 1819–1892—Friends and associates.
3. Authors, American—19th century—Biography.
I. Title.
PS2486.05Z65   1985   811'.3 [B]   84–25451
  ISBN 0–8214–0767–8

To my sons,
Jonathan, Eric, and Matthew,
who enabled me to be mother,
student, writer, teacher, and friend
without inner or outer conflict.

. . . William was a chosen knight—was selected of the select—as truly and grandly chivalric, in his own field of action, as any knight of feudalism, any lord or gentleman of the past. And not only so, but more humanly chivalric than any—more democratic. . . .

WALT WHITMAN (Camden, 5: 171)

CONTENTS

ILLUSTRATIONS

ABBREVIATIONS

Berg	Henry W. and Albert A. Berg Collection. New York Public Library, Astor, Lenox and Tilden Foundations.
Brown	Brown University Library: Harris Collection; Koopman Collection.
Camden	Horace Traubel, *With Walt Whitman in Camden*. 6 vols. Vol. 1, ed. Horace Traubel (Boston: Small, Maynard & Co., 1906). Vol. 2, ed. Horace Traubel (New York: D. Appleton, 1914). Vol. 3, ed. Horace Traubel (New York: Mitchell Kennerley, 1915). Vol. 4, ed. Sculley Bradley (Philadelphia: University of Pennsylvania Press, 1953). Vol. 5, ed. Gertrude Traubel (Carbondale: Southern Illinois University Press, 1964). Vol. 6, ed. Gertrude Traubel and William White (Carbondale: Southern Illinois University Press, 1982).
Chamberlin	O'Connor–Channing family letters (copies) and memorabilia sent to author by Katharine Beecher Stetson Chamberlin. Originals now in Library of Congress.
Columbia	Edmund C. Stedman and Daniel M. Conway Collections, Columbia University.
Comrades	Clara Barrus, *Whitman and Burroughs, Comrades*, (New York: Houghton, Mifflin Co., 1926.)
Correspondence	Edwin Haviland Miller, ed., *Walt Whitman: The Correspondence*. 6 vols. (New York: New York University Press, 1961).
Feinberg-LC	Charles E. Feinberg Collection of Walt Whitman, Library of Congress.
GWC	George William Curtis.
In Re WW	*In Re Walt Whitman, Edited by His Literary Executors*, Horace Traubel, Richard Maurice Bucke, Thomas B. Harned (Philadelphia: David McKay, 1893).
Journals	Clara Barrus, *The Heart of Burroughs Journals*, (New York: Houghton Mifflin Co., 1925).
LG/CRE	*Leaves of Grass: Comprehensive Reader's Edition*, Harold W. Blodgett and Sculley Bradley (New York: W. W. Norton & Co., 1965).
Life and Letters	Clara Barrus, *The Life and Letters of John Burroughs*. 2 vols. (New York: Houghton, Mifflin Co., 1925).
Pennsylvania	Collection of Walt Whitman. Charles Patterson Van Pelt Library, University of Pennsylvania.
Perry	Bliss Perry Collection. Berg, New York Public Library; and Harvard University.
Prose Works	Walt Whitman, *Prose Works 1892*, ed. Floyd Stovall (New York: New York University Press, 1963).
SHW	Sarah Helen Whitman.
Syracuse	William D. O'Connor Collection, George Arents Research Library for special collections, Syracuse University.
WDO'C	William Douglas O'Connor.
WW	Walt Whitman.
Yale	Collection of American Literature, Beinecke Rare Book and Manuscript Library, Yale University.

PREFACE

Throughout almost three decades of Walt Whitman's life the luminous and engaging William Douglas O'Connor played so important a part that the poet named him in his list of four "friends of my soul—stanchest friends of my other soul—my poems."[1] Whitman's correspondence and reminiscences are filled with letters to and from O'Connor and enthusiastic remarks about his loyal friend and brilliant advocate. Indeed, O'Connor is unique in the annals of American literature. No other writer, major or minor, devoted so much of his time and talent to the defense and dissemination of another writer's work at the sacrifice of his own.

Who was William Douglas O'Connor? He was a self-educated yet learned writer who participated fully in the actions and passions of his time. A skillful and principled fighter, he enlisted in the political causes of Abolition and Woman's Rights, and in the literary skirmishes to vindicate Edgar Allan Poe, to spread the praises of Victor Hugo, and to defend those who believed that Lord Bacon and a coterie of his followers were the authors of the plays falsely ascribed to the "peasant from Stratford." His most sustained and eloquent fight was for freedom of letters as exemplified in *Leaves of Grass.* Most important, he confirmed for Whitman the worth of the poet's vision and its unique expression. O'Connor was a student of art, a daguerreotypist, journalist, editor, poet, short-story writer, essayist, novelist, would-be inventor, responsible government employee, and friend extraordinary. A study of his life reveals a volatile man, whose "Irish bardic nature" (Whitman's phrase) made his spirit rise in elation and sink into melancholy, yet who "never needs a prod—is always afire,"[2]—a fascinating man to study and write about.

The book which follows is the result of many years of search and research, beginning in an undergraduate Whitman seminar where I learned from Emory Holloway of the first work written about Whitman, *The Good Gray Poet*. At that time, and for some time to come, little was known about the life of the man who had written it, apart from his connection with Whitman. As I continued my study of Whitman, I was intrigued by O'Connor and by the incomplete story of the quarrel which had severed the bond between the poet and his defender.

I found my first major source of O'Connor material when I learned from Charles E. Feinberg, who has shared his knowledge and collection with other Whitman scholars, that he also had O'Connor letters and scrapbooks (now in the Library of Congress). In his usual generous fashion he invited me to examine the material at his home in Detroit, and copy whatever I needed. I am deeply indebted to Charles Feinberg for his continuing interest in my work, which prompted him to send me copies of new materials as he acquired them, the most interesting of which was a love letter from Ellen O'Connor, William's wife, to Walt Whitman.

I was fortunate also in coming into contact with another most generous scholar—David Goodale.[3] In response to my "author's query" in *The New York Times*, he wrote that he had planned to write O'Connor's biography, and had collected all of his writings: short stories, poems, newspaper articles, and books. He had also assembled biographical data. Having given up the idea of writing the book, he sent it all to me with unparalleled generosity. Any expression of thanks must be inadequate.

David Goodale also knew of a descendant who was not known to me, Katharine Beecher Stetson Chamberlin, daughter of Charlotte Perkins Gilman and stepdaughter of O'Connor's niece, Grace Channing Stetson. On my behalf Goodale visited her in Pasadena and copied notebooks full of unpublished family letters and reminiscences, which Mrs. Chamberlin was willing to share with me but not to part with for photocopying. A three-way Chamberlin–Goodale–Freedman friendship ensued, at first through correspondence and later through a visit I paid to them in California. Later Mrs. Chamberlin generously sent me books, photographs and souvenirs. Among these are a lock of O'Connor's daughter Jean's hair, flowers (immortelles) from her funeral wreath, a planchette with which

Sarah Helen Whitman communicated with the spirit of Edgar Allan Poe, family photographs, and books autographed by O'Connor, including a volume of Tennyson's *In Memoriam*, which he gave to Sarah Helen Whitman with several of his own drawings tipped in. I regret that Mrs. Chamberlin died (in her late 90s) before this book was completed.

I greatly appreciate the help of William White, who willingly answered my questions about sources and bibliography, and encouraged me by publishing my articles about O'Connor in *The Walt Whitman Review* from 1963 to the present.

I am indebted to other friends as well. Malcolm Cowley encouraged me to undertake a life of O'Connor and made suggestions about the form it should take. Kenneth Neil Cameron advised me about the research methodology. Vasiliki Sarant helped in planning my initial presentation. Dr. Robert Leslie has frequently given me graphics for my Whitman collection. Marjorie Smiley, Maurice Charney, and Joseph Zimmerman read my manuscript and made valuable suggestions. I deeply appreciate their interest and help.

I am grateful for information, letters, and other documents from various other sources. The late Gertrude Traubel, daughter of Whitman's friend and executor Horace Traubel, while transcribing her father's diaries (which became *With Walt Whitman in Camden*, vol. 5) sent me relevant letters. Professor Herbert Harned of Yale University, son of Thomas Harned, Whitman's friend and executor, permitted me to examine his father's notebooks. Edwin Haviland Miller showed me Whitman letters before they were published in the *Correspondence* which he edited. C. Carroll Hollis, then of the Library of Congress, gave me new information and apprised me of related materials as they arrived at the Library even before they were catalogued.

The owners of the *Saturday Evening Post*, of which O'Connor had been an assistant editor, permitted me to examine the files in Philadelphia at a time when the magazine had suspended publication.

The General Services Administration of the United States made available to me the letters of recommendation presented by O'Connor when he sought government employment.

I acknowledge the special helpfulness of the librarians Barbara D. Hobson, Roger E. Stoddard, Rosemary Cullen, and Sherry O'Brien at Brown University, Lester G. Wells and Edward Lyon at Syracuse University, and Neda Westlake at the University of Pennsylvania, as well as the aid of librarians at the Berg Collection of the New York Public Library, the Morgan Library, the New York Historical Society, and the Huntington Library. Significant letters and other materials came from the collections of the following colleges and universities: Boston, Columbia, Dickinson, Duke, Johns Hopkins, Massachusetts Institute of Technology, Ohio Wesleyan, and Yale.

My editors at Ohio University Press, Holly Panich and Phyllis Sherman, have been most helpful at every stage from manuscript to published work.

I appreciate the work of Edna Kane Gronquist, Maxine Davis and Jeb Stuart in typing early versions of this book, and for the final manuscript I warmly thank Ruth Dropkin for her editorial acumen and Anne Goldstein for her word-processing skill.

I especially appreciate the encouragement of my late husband, Meyer Joel Freedman, and of my brother and sister-in-law, Edward and Esther Benton, as well as of my sons, daughters-in-law, and grandchildren, who have graciously accepted William Douglas O'Connor as an invisible member of the family.

Those who helped and encouraged me are not responsible for the book that follows, but I hope that they will like it. To them and to other readers, I would explain that I often yielded to the temptation to quote extensively from O'Connor's letters and writings (when summary and paraphrase would be the accepted mode) in order to convey directly the spirit of their author who, according to Whitman, "towers over all books: he is always a vital living man."[4]

NOTES

1. WW, *Prose Works 1892*, I.,283.
2. *Camden*, 2:240.
3. See Florence B. Freedman, "David Goodale (1910–1983): A Tribute," *Walt Whitman Quarterly Review*, II(1):40–41 (Summer 1984).
4. *Camden*, 1:466.

Always faithfully
W.D. O'Connor.

CHAPTER I

Presenting
William Douglas O'Connor

IN THE spring of 1860 William Douglas O'Connor, then twenty-eight years old, met the forty-year-old Walt Whitman at the publishing house of Thayer and Eldridge in Boston. Their meeting marked the beginning of a great friendship, the significance of which, in the lives of both men, has never been thoroughly explored.

The circumstance that brought them together was a happy one: The enterprising new firm of Thayer and Eldridge had offered to publish the third edition of Whitman's *Leaves of Grass* (the first two editions having been printed by the author) and had also invited O'Connor (then chafing under the restraints of being an editor of the *Philadelphia Saturday Evening Post*) to write a novel to be published by them. By mid-March 1860, Whitman was in Boston working with Thayer and Eldridge; O'Connor arrived at about the same time to discuss plans for writing his Abolition novel *Harrington* and to sign the contract for its publication.

The meeting at Thayer and Eldridge's between the handsome, enthusiastic William O'Connor, of Irish descent and temperament, and the larger, quiet, graying Walt Whitman, though not recorded by anyone present, must have been electric. O'Connor had known and admired Whitman's work since the appearance of the first edition of *Leaves of Grass* in July 1855. He had also seen and appreciated Whitman's poem "A Child's Reminiscence" which had appeared in *The Saturday Press* in 1859.

The friendship which grew from that first meeting was to be quiescent until December 1862, when William and Walt met again in Washington. After that it was the focal point of their lives, affecting the writings of both. Interrupted in 1872 by a quarrel and estrangement, it was resumed ten years later when both were past the peak of their literary powers and in failing health.

In later years Walt Whitman made puzzling statements about William Douglas O'Connor, his friend and defender: "I wonder what *Leaves of Grass* would have been if I had been born of some other mother and had never met William O'Connor," the sixty-nine-year-old poet said to his young friend Horace Traubel.[1] A strange pronouncement, for O'Connor had not been part of Whitman's life during the writing of the first three editions of *Leaves of Grass*. Why did Whitman couple the central role of his mother and that of O'Connor whom he did not meet until he was forty years old?

The aging poet also expressed the wish that O'Connor's letters about him be made into a book. "William's letters should be published—the *Leaves of Grass* letters; they would make a marvelous book—an eloquent book. It's of no importance that they should have been written about me; it's of every importance that they should have been written by William."[2] The poet was probably referring to letters by O'Connor printed in *The Round Table* in 1866 and 1867, in *The New York Times* in 1866 and 1867, and in the *New York Tribune* in 1876 and 1882. He may also have had in mind unpublished letters sent to newspapers, such as letters to the *Boston Transcript* in 1866 and to the *Tribune* in 1882.

In 1889, however, when Whitman spoke of publishing the letters, O'Connor's views of Whitman and his poetry were available in print. His eloquent monograph, *The Good Gray Poet* (which bestowed upon Whitman the sobriquet by which he continues to be known), first published in 1866, had been reprinted with a lengthy introductory letter in Richard Maurice Bucke's *Walt Whitman* in 1883.

Furthermore, between the publication of *The Good Gray Poet* in 1866 and the day in 1889 when Whitman expressed the wish that O'Connor's letters be published, the poet had received the recognition and appreciation lacking early in his career. Two biographies had appeared, as well as an English edition and a Danish translation of *Leaves of Grass*. Edmund Clarence Stedman had devoted a chapter to Whitman, as he had to Bryant, Whittier, Emerson, Longfellow, Poe, Holmes, Lowell, and Bayard Taylor in his *Poets of America*, published in 1885. (Emerson, however, had left Whitman out of his anthology *Parnassus* in 1874, while including, together with many famous English poets, the well-known Americans Bryant, Whittier, Lowell, and Holmes, and the less distinguished Felicia Hemans, Frank B. Sanborn, Julia Ward Howe, Edmund Clarence Stedman, Bret Harte, and Nathaniel P. Willis. Edgar Allan Poe was also among those excluded.)

During this period three more editions of *Leaves of Grass* had appeared, as well as the prose *Democratic Vistas*. Articles about Whitman had been published in England, France, and other European countries. As recently as 1886 Ernest Rhys had published a new English edition of the *Leaves*.

Why did Whitman want O'Connor's ephemeral letters to the newspapers to be published? Was this desire a form of appreciation for all O'Connor had done for him? Was it grief for his friend who was then dying? Or might it have been a sense of guilt that in O'Connor's wholehearted devotion to Whitman and his work, he had failed to fulfill the promise of his own earlier years?

A third puzzling statement appears in Walt Whitman's preface to O'Connor's posthumously published *Three Tales*. Here he wrote of "William O'Connor, my dear, dear friend, and stanch (probably my stanchest) literary believer and champion from the first and throughout, without halt or demur, for twenty-five years. . . ."[3] Yet there had been a quarrel between Whitman and O'Connor, followed by an estrangement of ten years, ending in reconciliation in 1882. How could this friendship be characterized by the poet as having been "without halt or demur"?

The book Whitman desired was not printed, and in the vast literature about Walt Whitman written in the past half century the man he considered so central to his life has been mentioned only briefly. Recently this negligence has been partly remedied by the publication of a book about O'Connor, containing a biographical and critical exploration, and the reprinting of most of his writings about Whitman.[4] A full-scale biography is still needed, however, not only to tell the story of an unusual friendship and to suggest possible solutions to Whitman's puzzling statements about O'Connor, but also to call to life a brilliant man who was representative of and participant in social and literary movements of mid-nineteenth-century America.

O'Connor's verve, imagination, exuberance, erudition and unselfishness were appreciated by his contemporaries. Friends also remarked on his good looks and charm. John Trowbridge, a well-known novelist and biographer, wrote that O'Connor was "strikingly handsome, with a winning graciousness of manner that gave to his gay volubility an indescribable charm."[5] Others who were struck by O'Connor's good looks, eloquence and erudition were William Dean Howells, Wendell Phillips, John Hay, and Charles Sumner. Walt Whitman described him as "one of the most graceful of men" and likened his walk to "the movement of a beautiful deer—a fawn; his body swung along with such strength and his step was so light, his bearing was so superbly free and defiant."[6]

The grace of his walk was seen differently, however, by a more critical acquaintance. Rebecca Harding Davis wrote in *Bits of Gossip* (published after O'Connor's death), "He was a little man, who always wore a high hat, and walked on tiptoe, and talked in superlatives and hurled defiance at the slave power with every breath. . . ."[7] (O'Connor's widow took exception to this, writing to Horace Traubel that "her abuse of William O'Connor is even more inane (than her "silly and abusive notice of Walt") . . . it is *personal spite*." Besides, she averred, William never had a tall hat.)[8] Rebecca Harding Davis, however, sounded the one sour note in a chorus of praises.

The warmest tribute came from Walt Whitman. During his last years in Camden, he talked often of O'Connor to his young friend Horace Traubel—remarks sparked by the finding of an old letter in O'Connor's clear, bold hand, or by the receipt of a letter concerning William's failing health. "William would talk alive with a dagger in his heart. . . . Other men are more famous than William, but no man is greater than he is. . . ."[9] Whitman deplored the fact that Ernest Rhys had returned to England without having called on O'Connor. " 'After having seen Niagara, after having seen you,' Rhys said, 'I can fairly say that I have been to America to some purpose.' " Whitman commented, ". . . twenty thousand Niagaras could not make up to me for one O'Connor."[10]

Two poems about O'Connor were published—one at the beginning of his career and the other after his death. The first was by Sarah Helen Whitman who, when he was not yet twenty years old, addressed him in her poem "To the Morning Star" as the "star of love and hope."[11]

After O'Connor's death Elizabeth Akers Allen ("Florence Percy") mourned him in "To the Author of 'Harrington' ":

> Who, once he had beheld it, could forget
> In all succeeding time, that brilliant face?
> Lit from within, like a young god's and yet
> Leading all hearts by winning human grace;
> In all that captivates, and hold, and charms
>   A man of men, with fame and heart and mind
>   Made to attract and elevate his kind.

The poem concludes:

> Now as above his grave the slow years roll
>   Only a few—how few! whose wound still bleeds
>   Remember that most rare and marvellous soul.[12]

This was William O'Connor as seen by his contemporaries— magnificent in service to others and vastly talented in writing. Why was he not able to become one of the great writers of his time? His friends advanced some reasons for his failure. John Trowbridge wrote: "It seemed as if such weapons of language and rhetoric should have made him our foremost man of letters, an American Hugo. Perhaps he was conscious of some defect of temperament that unfitted him for such a career. A certain heat and fury seemed necessary to move his mind to creative activity."[13] Perhaps he belonged to another time in history; Wendell Phillips, Boston statesman and orator, himself considered a "chevalier *par excellence*," wrote to O'Connor, "You ought to have lived in Sidney's day when knightly service was in fashion."[14]

Some friends criticized his devotion to Whitman. A "lifelong friend" (unnamed) wrote to Whitman's biographer, Bliss Perry: "He was a man of full and rich attainments and a genius—needing only a brake on his prodigal and affluent expression. He gave up the better part of his career to Whitman—whom he excelled in humanity, aspiration, and self-surrender."[15]

Perhaps the flaw was a lack of judgment in selecting the objects of his chivalrous protection. Myron Benton, in a letter to *The Critic* in answer to a review of O'Connor's posthumously published *Three Tales*, compared O'Connor's style to that of Henry James the elder—"a veritable Damascene blade." Referring to O'Connor's defense of Delia Bacon and her theory, however, he wrote, "He was not always level-headed. The windmill was not always distinguished from the castle."[16]

To O'Connor's friends and critics, however, one man's windmill was another man's castle. Benton chose as his windmill O'Connor's championship of Delia Bacon, which was praised by Hawthorne; the contemporary reader would see O'Connor's defense of the claim of Elizabeth Akers Allen ("Florence Percy") to the authorship of the popular poem "Rock Me to Sleep" in that light. John Burroughs disagreed with O'Connor's praise of Victor Hugo. Finally, to some the windmill was undoubtedly Walt Whitman's *Leaves of Grass*, which time has proved to have been a castle worthy of O'Connor's loyal and spirited defense.

To the student of O'Connor's life, it seems clear that circumstances cheated him of achievement and fame. He was born in poverty to the wrong parents, married a woman wrong for him (though she seemed an ideal choice at first) and, because of both admirable and self-defeating elements in his character, was doomed to drudgery instead of to creative satisfaction and accomplishment. Nevertheless, William O'Connor emerges from a study of his letters, his writings, and his friendships as a selfless friend of writers and an eloquent advocate of the cause of freedom of letters.

NOTES

1. *Camden*, 2:114.
2. *Camden*, 3:563.
3. WW, in *Three Tales*, p. vi. For full text of Preface, see Appendix A.
4. Jerome Loving, *Walt Whitman's Champion: William Douglas O'Connor* (College Station and London: Texas A&M University Press, 1978).
5. John Townsend Trowbridge, *My Own Story, With Recollections of Noted Persons* (Boston and New York: Houghton Mifflin Company, 1904), p. 376.
6. *Camden*, 3:76.
7. Rebecca Harding Davis, *Bits of Gossip* (Boston and New York: Houghton Mifflin Company, 1904), p. 214.

8. Ellen O'Connor Calder to Traubel, 18 November 1904 (Feinberg-LC).
9. *Camden*, 4:70–71.
10. *Camden*, 1:162.
11. Sarah Helen Whitman, *Hours of Life and Other Poems* (Providence, Rhode Island: George H. Whitney, 1853), pp. 93–95; and *Poems* (Boston: Houghton, Osgood and Company, 1879), pp. 99–100.
12. Elizabeth Akers Allen ('Florence Percy'), *The Sunset Song and Other Verses* (Boston: Lee and Shepard, 1902), pp. 46–47.
13. Trowbridge, *op. cit.*, p. 375.
14. Phillips to WDO'C, 17 May 1876 (Feinberg-LC).
15. Bliss Perry, *Walt Whitman: His Life and Work* (Boston and New York: Houghton Mifflin Company, 1906), p. 159 n. This friend was later identified as Edmund C. Stedman.
16. Myron Benton, "William Douglas O'Connor," *The Critic*, 20:184–85 (26 March 1892).

CHAPTER **II**

"Young Man Of Genius And Enthusiasm"[1]

IT TOOK wit and perseverance to overcome the difficulties of William Douglas O'Connor's childhood. He was born in Roxbury, Massachusetts (later a part of Boston), on January 2, 1832, of Irish and English parentage.[2] His Irish father, Peter D., who was a laborer said to have been descended from *The O'Connor* (a princely heritage), had run away to America at an early age, one drop in a wave of Irish immigration that was to wash over the big cities of the East and ebb into their brackish slums.

William was forced to leave home at the age of eight—speeded onward by a flatiron flung by his father.[3] Except for this dramatic incident, little is known of William O'Connor's family, childhood, and early youth.[4]

When he became a writer, William espoused several causes in poems, short stories, a novel, and critical articles and books. His first cause was the fight against the abject poverty he had known in his childhood, a situation which society did nothing to alleviate.

It may have been himself and his childhood home described in "What Cheer?," a story published in *Putnam's Monthly* in July 1855,[5] when he was twenty-three years old. Although the story is set in Providence, Rhode Island, its description of the life of the Irish in the slums may have come from his Boston childhood. He may have drawn on his own experience for the drunken Irish father, the proud mother, and the frightened little boy. Another child of the slums

10

appeared in his essay "The Grotesque."[6] Several of his stories depict the wide gulf separating the rich and the poor, and speak out against poverty, inequality, and injustice.

Whether or not the incidents and settings described by O'Connor are autobiographical, the scenes depicted are true to the experience of Irish immigrants to the United States in the 1830s, 1840s, and even later. Because of economic hardship and social unrest in Ireland, thousands emigrated to the United States and Canada; in 1827 the official count was 20,000 (with 30,000 considered nearer the actual figure). In each of the record years of 1831 and 1832, over 65,000 people left Ireland for America.[7]

The older inhabitants of cities like Boston viewed the newcomers with distaste and even alarm. Their gregariousness, which caused them to congregate in cities where their compatriots had settled, their gaiety, their improvidence, and their volatile temperaments set them apart from the more reserved, staid, and thrifty New Englanders. The saloon became the social club for men, providing conviviality and momentary forgetfulness of their hard lot. Drunkenness became so common that it was mentioned as a warning in *Advice and Guide to Emigrants going to the United States of America*: "It is a habit so peculiar to the lower classes of the Irish settled in the United States, that if a man be seen drunk in that country, it is generally inferred he must be an Irishman."[8]

Only their strong backs were welcome—and rewarded by wages of seventy-five cents per day. Yet despite the low wages and the poor living conditions, the Irish immigrants were on the whole better off than they had been in the old country. "In rural Ireland the average age at death was 19 years, and not a fifth of the population lived beyond 40. In the United States, the expectation of life at birth was approximately 40 years, and for those who survived the first 10, it was extended to 58, an age reached by less than 5 percent of the Irish at home."[9] The Irish poor, however, not knowing the favorable statistics, worked, starved, drank and brawled, and unable to discover or confront their enemies, fought with their wives, children and friends.

So it was that at the age of eight William Douglas O'Connor was on his own. Inadvertently he chose (or circumstances chose for him) the best city and the best decade in which to support himself by his own endeavors and to educate himself. Boston was the perfect city for anyone, no matter what his origin, who was interested in the life of the mind. It was so described by foreign visitors, who had the advantage of being able to make comparisons while being objective:

> Boston and its society has a peculiar character, different from all other cities in the world. It is the only one where knowledge and scholarship have the lead of society. A distinguished author, an eminent professor, an eloquent preacher, are socially equals of the monied aristocracy, which maintains its position only by its liberality toward literary institutions. The bankers and money-kings pride themselves in being connected, by family ties, with the aristocracy of intellect. Boston is therefore, for America, what the Court of Weimar once was for Germany—the center of literature and science. But there it was only the generous liberality of one prince which drew together the sages and poets of Germany into one brilliant constellation, which sank with his life. Here it is the spirit of the people—public opinion, the manners and the customs of the city—which encourage the development of talent by assigning to it the most honored position. . . .[10]

The year 1840 when O'Connor was forced from his home, was a good time in which to start out to improve one's lot. Symbolic of the year was the convention of Friends of Universal Reform in the Chardon Street Chapel in Boston—a convention described by Emerson as an assembly composed of "madmen, madwomen, men with beards, Dunkers, Muggletonians, Come-outers, Groaners, Agrarians, Seventh-Day Baptists, Quakers, Abolitionists, Calvinists, Unitarians and Philosophers."[11] People might laugh, but all these "isms" indicated faith in the perfectibility of individuals and society—to which goal there were many roads. For the very young William the first steps were toward self-support, the next toward self-education.

How William supported himself is not known; he later said that he had "grappled with difficulties from early boyhood"[12] but gave no details. William was undoubtedly able to find work. There were no laws against child labor. Extraordinarily handsome as a man, "with a splendid head, with rich curling hair, and the deep blue eyes of Ireland"[13] he must have been a beautiful child. The wit, charm, faculty for friendship, and genius for conversation which he showed in later years were traits that probably helped him through his difficult childhood and youth. The only allusions to his childhood in his letters were to its difficulties and to some of the books he had read.[14]

William attended public school for a time.[15] There is no record of his having been graduated. Such schools had been established only a few years earlier, their cause furthered by Horace Mann, who left the practice of law in 1837 to devote himself to public education, choosing to become "a circuit rider to the next generation."[16]

William's education came principally through reading. His chief source of books was undoubtedly the library of the Mercantile Library Association which had been established in 1820. He later addressed the Mercantile Library Association as "Alma Mater" in a poem by that title published in the *Boston Commonwealth* on March 31, 1854.

William was a rapid and avid reader with an extraordinary memory. His niece, Grace Channing, later recalled, "He never seemed to read; he merely turned the pages, and then laying down the book he would quote miles of it."[17] Some of the books he read were far beyond his years. He read the German poets Theodore Körner and Ferdinand Freiligrath in the translations of Dr. Charles Follen to whom he paid tribute in one of his letters. Dr. Charles Follen, a refugee from Germany who was a professor at Harvard, "left a great heritage of faith and aspiration among us, partly through his sweet and grand character, central in which was an immense devotion to liberty."[18] In later years O'Connor wrote to Ferdinand Freiligrath, who had translated some of *Leaves of Grass* into German, "as one whose boyhood was filled by your poems with many enchanted hours."[19] William's own first published work was a poem, "The Shadow on the Wall," which appeared in the *Boston Weekly Museum* December 22, 1849, before he was eighteen.

The novels of Dumas, read in his youth, also provided William and his friends with heroes to emulate. "Four romantic young men who had read 'The Three Guardsmen' took the names of the Guardsmen, and Mr. O'Connor was 'Aramis'. . . . Please remember that they were in their *teens* and Mr. O'Connor was the *poet* of the *quartet*."[20] George Bacon, who remained a lifelong friend, was "Athos." The influence of Dumas led William and his friends to study fencing with a Mr. Boulet, who had taught at West Point; he was the prototype for M. Hypolite Bagasse in O'Connor's novel

Harrington. O'Connor thought of himself as a fencer in his literary work, writing to Whitman when the 1882 edition of *Leaves of Grass* was in trouble with the censors:

> My old fencing master, Boulet (no better ever lived: He taught once at West Point;) taught me always to cover my breast with hilt and point, even in the lunge, and I think of his lessons when engaged in fence of another kind. I hope I have been both guarded and bold in this new encounter. . . .[21]

The youthful guardsmen left no written record of their adventures, but O'Connor must have talked of them. His niece recalled, "The adventures of D'Artagnan seemed to have rather had the edge taken off for me by my previous acquaintance with my uncle's. He had the advantage of being related in a voice which had not only no equal but no second in my experience. . . . Irresistible were those tales."[22]

During O'Connor's youth unschooled, ambitious young people could learn from lectures as well as from books; young workmen in Boston could attend lectures at the Mercantile Library Association and other places:

> Sir Charles Lyell and Agassiz were surprised, when they arrived in Boston in the forties, by the universal interest in education. Lyell had never seen such crowds of workmen listening on winter nights to learned lectures in geology and zoology, Shakespeare and Milton. Agassiz was present at an assembly of three thousand mechanics, brought together to form a library and listening for two hours with rapt attention to a lecture on the advantages of reading.[23]

The Mercantile Library Association provided William with his first opportunities to lecture and debate. At the age of nineteen he delivered a lecture on "The Past" as part of a "literary entertainment" somewhat patronizingly reviewed in the *Boston Daily Journal* on March 13, 1851: "The essays evinced habits of reflection, and a disposition on the part of their authors to break the fetters of trade, and tread in the flowery paths of imagination."

Through wide reading and listening to lectures in his boyhood and youth and voluminous reading throughout his life, O'Connor became an erudite man. Whitman spoke of his "monumental" knowledge of Elizabethan literature, saying "William is a man of broadest culture; he excludes no source of intellectual influence."[24] Senator Charles Sumner spoke of O'Connor's "curious learning and genius."[25]

O'Connor was also talented in art. While still in his teens he studied with the Boston artist Chester Harding, who was famous for his early portraits of Daniel Boone and Indian chiefs. William's other teacher was Albert G. Hoyt, the first president of the Boston Art Club. O'Connor occupied a studio at 22 School Street, of which he later wrote nostalgically:

> It was a magnificent room, occupying in its height two stories of the present building. All the windows were impenetrably draped with dark curtains, save only one, a square, filled with one large pane of glass. Through this slanted down a long shaft of clear and pure north-light, lighting only what lay within the angle of the broad beam, and leaving the rest of the chamber in warm dark shadow. All outward sound too, came muffled and remote to that luxurious silence. It was a real tower of dreams.[26]

It was not long before William had to leave his studio "tower of dreams." Whether he felt that his talent in art was insufficient, or whether (as occurred later with his writing) the need to earn a living interfered, the artist became a daguerreotypist before he was nineteen, never to devote much time to art again. Only a few of his sketches remain among his papers.[27] It was to pursue his career as a daguerreotypist that William left Boston for Providence, Rhode Island, in 1851.

Providence provided William with a source of income (for he went there to work for a daguerreotypist and soon took over the business himself);[28] the opportunity to have his poems published in the *Providence Journal*; a lady to worship—Sarah Helen Whitman; a dead poet to defend—Edgar Allan Poe; a literary friend and mentor—George William Curtis; a new philosophy—Spiritualism; and the inspiration to write short stories, one of which had its setting in that city, and another its model in the work of Edgar Allan Poe.

When O'Connor reviewed George William Curtis's *The Howadji in Syria* in the *Providence Journal,* a letter of appreciation from Curtis led to a lifelong friendship between them. Although only eight years William's senior, Curtis had already made a reputation as a writer. A native of Providence, Rhode Island, he had spent a year and a half at Brook Farm (where he trimmed the lamps). Later he spent four years in Europe and the Near East as a correspondent for the *New York Tribune. The Howadji in Syria* (1852) and the earlier *Nile Notes of a Howadji* (1851) were based on these experiences.

O'Connor's review was long and laudatory, quoting liberally and praising "the debonair humor, the subtle thought, the miraculous power of description, the keen perception, the exquisite use of language, . . ." Yet to O'Connor, Curtis was only a forerunner. He included a statement prophetic of his later interest in Whitman:

> We believe that in the dawn of the day now breaking, there is a light before which English literature begins "to pale its ineffectual fires." We can point with pride to Longfellow, and Bryant, to Poe and Mellville [*sic*], to Emerson, Curtis and Hawthorne, to them as representatives only of many that are, of more that are to be.

Thus, three years before the first printing of *Leaves of Grass,* it appears that the young poet-reviewer was awaiting a new native expression such as he was later to defend.

Curtis was moved to express his appreciation of so enthusiastic a review.[29] His letter of acknowledgment to O'Connor initiated a correspondence which was to last for many years, the letters abounding in literary advice, discussion of family matters, and even, at several points, arguments, when Curtis failed to concur in William's support of Woman's Rights and in his dedication to two of his heroes— Wendell Phillips and Walt Whitman.

Nevertheless, Curtis was a true friend and a valuable literary mentor. He read the manuscripts of O'Connor's short stories, advising him about possible publication, and often cutting them drastically. (It would appear that O'Connor sometimes restored the cuts.) Curtis was in a position to be helpful. He had many friends among editors and publishers. He helped to launch *Putnam's Monthly Magazine* and was its editor for a time. He also edited *Harper's* "The Editor's Easy Chair" and later became editor of *Harper's Weekly.*

Several of his books—*The Potiphar Papers* (1853) and *Prue and I* (1856) among them—were collections of his magazine sketches. His novel *Trumps* (1861) dealt with New York society and Washington politics.

The rest of O'Connor's contributions to the *Providence Journal* were poems signed "Aramis," six of which were published between September 18, 1851, and January 22, 1852. His favorite topics were politics and love. Two of the poems dealt with the state of the city and of the world. "To the City Fathers" appeared on October 28, 1851 and "To Athos" on November 25 of that year. In the latter, dedicated to George Bacon, the "Athos" to O'Connor's "Aramis" in their youthful adventures, he expresses his sympathy with the European revolutionaries, sadly surveying Europe in the aftermath of revolution, and mourning the death of the high hopes he and Athos had had in their youth. (The author was then twenty years old.)

> Thy pluméd dreams have met defeat—
> Thy destinies have met Decay—
> And cold between the shrouding-sheet
> Lies the dead Hope of yesterday.
>
> The hour is past—and to her breast
> France folds her pale and noble slain—
> The kite usurps the eagle's nest—
> The Barricades were piled in vain!
>
> The new Rienzi lives for Rome
> To find Rienzi's doom in store,
> And Kossuth leaves his shattered home
> An exile to the Pilgrims' shore;
>
> The German spirit sadly keeps
> The ashes of her fallen brave:—
> Weep Fatherland! for Freedom weeps
> Beneath the oaks on Körner's grave.

Six stanzas later William concludes with what Time has in store for Athos and for him:

> To thee, the fearless soul that sees
> The Future crowned in splendor rise—

To me, some gentle memories,
And sadder light within my eyes.

To me, beyond my faded flowers,
Beyond the storms that wildly rave,
Above the wrecks of broken hours,
The grander promise of the grave.

With the exception of the poem "To Athos," William seems far from ready for the grave. In most of the poems published in the *Providence Journal* as well as in some that remain in manuscript, William scatters his poetical favors among the ladies. In February 1851 "A Valentine" concluded with the words "for me and my Mary." In July 1851 the season called forth "A Midsummer Night's Dream—To Katie"; on September 18, 1851, there is a poem "To Mabel" and on December 20, 1851, "Aves: for Mrs. J—S—." There are also two undated poems among his manuscripts—a short verse "To Daisy" and an elaborate narrative poem, "The Tourney—a Valentine" in which he addresses Louise.

In October 1851 appeared "About the Goblet—For Helen." Unlike Katie, Mary, Daisy, and their fellow dedicatees who remain unknown, Helen was to hold an important place in William's life and affections, for she was Sarah Helen Whitman, a poet, known as the "seeress of Providence" and "Poe's Helen." To "Aramis" Sarah Helen Whitman was a princess in need of rescue—a pale, ethereal, veiled, restless spirit, who lived in a red house on Benefit Street, hallowed by the memory of Edgar Allan Poe, who had wooed and won and lost its mistress within four months in the fall of 1848.[30] Helen was to continue to think of herself as Poe's love, but to Poe's biographer (Hervey Allen in *Israfel*) she was one of *three* women he was interested in toward the end of his life. When, within two years of Poe's death, she met William O'Connor, Helen saw in him a startling resemblance to Poe, though O'Connor was still in his teens and Poe had been nearly forty. It was consoling to have a young poet-friend who could appreciate Poe with her and join in defending his memory. Shortly after they met she wrote a poem to him, "To the Morning Star."[31] In her later letters she addressed him as "Aramis," "Ariel," and the more prosaic "Wilhelm."

To the impressionable young artist-poet Helen must have appeared like a creature from another world. Although forty-eight years old when they met, she was ageless. It was said of her,

> . . . she herself was set to music; she was herself a poem. . . . As she came flitting into the room, and gave you her small, nervous hand, you saw a slight figure, a pale eager face of fine spiritual expression and irregular features, the dreamy look of deepset eyes that gazed over and beyond, but never at you. Her movements were very rapid, and she seemed to flutter like a bird, so that one of her friends asserted that she was in process of transformation, either to or from the condition of a lapwing. . . .[32]

In Helen's home William became acquainted with Spiritualism, a popular belief at that time—an idealistic philosophy which was expressed at times in table rappings, séances, and communications from the spirit world. (Even Horace Greeley, whose wife was a confirmed Spiritualist, was impressed by its philosophy, though he wrote to Helen that he was often perplexed to find that the spirits came so far to say so little of importance.)[33]

The house on Benefit Street was a fine setting for Spiritualism, and its mistress was well cast for the role of seeress. The sitting room was bathed in a dim rose glow from lampshades lined in rose or scarlet and inverted so that the room was in shadow while the paintings on the wall were illumined. Helen, who did not conform in dress to the prevailing modes, wore a white veil over her head, carried a fan, and seemed to flutter and float in draperies.

Through Helen, William came to an intense appreciation of Edgar Allan Poe and a desire to protect his reputation and to vindicate him against attack. Three years later he gave to his future wife a volume of Poe's poetry with an accompanying sonnet (never published) in which he expressed his sympathy with "my pale, dead poet."[34] Ten years later, when O'Connor was an editor of the *Saturday Evening Post* he published an article on Poe in "Notes on Books."[35] Later, an article he wrote about Poe remained unpublished because he insisted, against the editor's wishes, on including in it praise of Walt Whitman; another contemplated article was never finished. O'Connor seems to have been more perceptive than most of his contemporaries in his criticism of Poe, writing:

. . . it might have been little that he dwelt in the land without being one with the nation, but he lived on the globe without belonging to the world. How could one unrelated by such a combination of traits to the secular men and things around him, escape the penalty of his irrelation?[36]

William addressed two poems to Helen. "About the Goblet: For Helen," which appeared in the *Providence Journal* on October 16, 1851, is a long, fanciful, delicate poem of ninety-two lines, in rhyming couplets arranged in stanzas of varying lengths. Six months later, when William was living in Lynn, Massachusetts, he had a prevision of Helen's death, which he expressed in his poem "Helena." The manuscript of the poem has in it a curious anagram of the name Sara Helen Poer (Helen thought that her maiden name "Power," if spelled "Poer," showed that she and Poe shared a common ancestry.) Under the name were two phrases created by transposing the letters; "O a Serene Harp" (an unsuccessful anagram) and "Ha! Seraph Lenore" (a variation on Poe's "Ah, Seraph Lenore"). These phrases, however, were not incorporated into the poem, which began,

> Room for a spirit—a spirit of light!
>   Her raiment is white;
> She floated like music, away on the night
>   To the palm-shadowed land;
> Welcome her, Lord of the Seraphim bank—
>   Welcome her there:
> For the roses of innocence bloom in her hand—
>   O she was fair![37]

Perhaps it was William's loneliness in Lynn that caused him to have this despairing dream. Helen's death was not to occur until twenty-six years later.

William and Helen remained friends until her death, corresponding regularly, and probably seeing each other whenever he came to Providence. Helen admired William's critical acumen. At one time she suggested to the young John Hay that he send his poems to O'Connor for comment.[38] Correspondence about the poems led to a friendship which was to continue when O'Connor and Whitman lived in Washington. After Helen's death, William's brother-in-law,

William Francis Channing, who was Helen's executor, consulted him about the arrangement of poems for her posthumous volume, and returned to him hundreds of his letters which Helen had kept.[39]

The influence of Poe and the presence of Helen can be seen not only in the poem "Helena," but also in the short story, "The Knocker," originally entitled "A Tale of Spiritual Rappings," centering on a supernatural and unexplained mystery.[40] Paul and Helen Barry, each an only child, were both orphaned in childhood, as their parents had been. The narrator, their friend, was at their home celebrating their child's seventh birthday. The narrator's feeling for Helen is probably based on the author's feeling for Sarah Helen Whitman. It is a Platonic love for Helen who is the

> graceful image of First Love—the pure seraph that changed with maturer years into a quiet and tender memory, and hallowed its object forever. Our love had never been confessed; never dreamed of consummation. It was the highest form of an unimpassioned devotion, it was spiritual, pure, and adoring. The old tale of the sculptor inspired with a divine passion for the holy beauty of the statue, was a symbol of my love for her. But no; mine was even more shadowy.

The scene at the Barrys' home is pleasant and charming—the child nestling on the narrator's lap, Helen playing the piano, Paul reclining in a chair nearby—when suddenly a silence falls:

> As if that silence was ordained that it might flash upon my brain—clear and strange as if an unearthly voice had spoken it—a singular thought, lighting up a wide range of recollections, revealed them to me, bathed in the wild colors of fatality. I can not determine how these instantaneous mental transitions, which seem to know no intermediate process, are effected. Some bold metaphysicians have thought that there are ideas which are resolved in the mind by mental processes so subtle that they escape cognizance. It may be that this thought, which burst up like a colorless flame, irradiating things long known to me with the pallid tints of supernaturalism, was the residuum left by such mental chemistry. . . .

The narrator recalls that Barry's ancestor had been a Huguenot, "who had, by some wild sin, entailed the curse of a male descent and

perpetual orphanage on the line until the offense was expiated. . . ."
He supposes, however, that the doom had been revoked. "A female
child had been born to the house of Barry; she had outlived her infancy and was not an orphan. . . ."

After that visit the narrator went away for seven months. When he
returned, he found that Paul, the father, was away and the child ill.
Mysterious rappings, which began when the child first fell ill, sound
at intervals. The narrator, who learns that the father has died in
another city, watches the increasing sadness of the mother with an
inexplicable feeling of pleasure:

> —I thought that the face wore a singular—an indescribable look.
> Its supernatural beauty seemed to vail [sic], and half reveal,
> another face within, whose features were those of withered age—
> old and worn, and seeming to look through the outward counte-
> nance. At times—particularly when her eyes were downcast—this
> appearance of age was more strongly visible; the face wore a se-
> cret, blind, meaningless expression, as if the lineaments of another
> blended with, and partially confused it. In a word, it impressed
> me as if the countenance was introverted; or as having somewhat
> the appearance of the back of a transparent mask, where the fea-
> tures appear semi-neutralized. With the same placid, happy feel-
> ing, I thought that all this was but the work of a deep inward
> agony, changing her beauty to premature decay.

The coincidences, the rappings, the peculiar fate of the protagonists—none is explained. Just before the child's death, which
ends the story, there is a crescendo of madness, written in a style
reminiscent of Poe's.

> The ticking of the clock began to excite me. So slow, so monot-
> onous; it numbed my brain; it grew louder, beat by beat. Formless
> things, with a terrible smoothness to their surface—with a terrible
> silence in their motion, began to whirl and dilate in my mind,
> revolving with an awful velocity, but silently—silently; and I
> grew giddy with their dreadful speed, and although marble-calm
> without, became frantic within, and longed to burst out in shrieks
> and wild raving. . . .
> I stood, and looked, and listened to the faint respiration of the
> child. Timing with its low breathing—timing with the gigantic
> eddying sweep of that tremendous lunacy of size and motion in

my mind, I still heard the ticking of the clock, the low word that left no echo on the air—Death! death! It grew louder—louder— with no accompanying increase of quickness, but steady and slow, till it seemed to swell into a roar, and stunned my brain with the appalling thunder-strokes of that word—Death! death!

Curtis praised the story with some reservations.

> . . . I consider it a remarkable success in a difficult line.—For it is not enough that the story be possible to produce that weird and ghostly mood in which yours puts one. There is always the greatest fascination in the merging of not only the natural but the more ordinary and commonplace circumstances in the supernatural. It is along that glimmering line that Hawthorne treads. Poe did it, too, but more maliciously, and the German Hoffman loved that shadowy splendor.[41]

Lest the young author be too pleased at being included in such splendid company, Curtis delivers a warning against the morbidity of this kind of writing, saying, "Yesterday poor Wm. North killed himself. He was a victim, in a sense, of this same tendency." Despite this criticism Curtis helped to place "The Knocker" in *Harper's*. Inveterate editor, he suggested a change in name to "*The Family Curse: A Story of Roxbury Neck*, by the author of *Loss and Gain: A Tale of Lynn*." O'Connor evidently disagreed with the change, for on April 12 Curtis informs him that he has written to retain the original title.

Another short story, "What Cheer?," had its setting in Providence, although it was probably written after William left that city. In contrast to "The Knocker" it is a realistic story of social protest. Place is important, as it was to be in his later stories. The street he describes had its original in Jail Lane and the tavern keeper was a man named Todd.[42]

"What Cheer?" begins with the recollection of Roger Williams who founded the State of Rhode Island and the city of Providence, "thus giving to the Republic one town, which, in name at least, remembers God." In that city stands a building on which is carved "the unselfish and rebuking legend—'What Cheer?'" The narrator muses, "What cheer for the wild disordered world? What cheer for the nineteenth century of Christian advancement, and Christian knowledge? What cheer for the twentieth yet to come, and for its generations yet unborn? What cheer for the suffering and the poor?"

It is these last who are at the core of the story. Its protagonist, referred to as the "dark student," had learned from society not nobility and aspiration, but "to conceal the splendid dream of a heroic possibility, by a confusion of glittering gauds and greeds, and a siren whirl of illusions." He was infected with the "prevalent disease of self," which led him

> to cherish his own individuality above all things; never to abandon the presence of his own personality, to bow down in worship to the gigantic I . . . to nourish self with all rare culture of art, literature, music, and social intercourse, for the development of self alone; . . . to account self the center of the Universe, and to forget the circumference.

Absorption in self and disillusion with society have led the "dark student" to the point of suicide. He is interrupted by a cry from one of the houses in a nearby alley. It proves to have been the cry of an Irish woman whose husband has committed suicide. Their child, "a very small, stunted, dirty boy, barefooted and ragged," had gone for help to Ginn, the owner of a nearby tavern, who, it is revealed later, had been supplying the family with food while the father was out of work. The "dark student" accompanies Ginn and the child to the child's home in a filthy tenement.

The description of the tenement may have come from William's childhood experiences:

> Timmy goes ahead, and they follow him up the cavernous gloom of the dark, crazy stairs, slowly groping their way on tiptoe. The boards creak beneath them at every step. The darkness is close and thick around them. Horrible smells, with one dense, sickly odor of greasy boiled cabbage above them all, fill the stifling air. Up one flight into a thicker darkness, where the smells are stronger; five uncertain steps along the corridor, holding by the clammy banister; around a corner up three stairs; around another, where they both stumble upon more stairs; up these, and they pause at length, with no definite idea of the shape and extent of the place where they stand. The house is strangely astir tonight. Subdued movements and deadened tones, which attended their groping ascent, with inarticulate sounds, gruff, muffled voices,

and low whispers, now reach them as from a pit below, all
blended in one vague sense of a hideous life, awake and moving in
the wretched dwelling.

The contrast is drawn between the jaded cynicism which has led
the student to contemplate suicide and the real problems of the
poor. The father had committed suicide out of some "unutterable,
savage, and frightful rage at the life which he had never known how
to command and turn to profit or to honor. . . . He was a poor,
besotted, brutalized Irish laborer." His wife had clung to him even
though beaten and abused. The student wonders, "Why didn't she
apply for relief to somebody? Why didn't she go to the City and
represent that she was in want?" "Why didn't the City go to her?"
Ginn replies.

> Supposin' she didn't want to be bundled to the poor-house?—
> that's all the City'd do for her. Supposin' she had a streak of pride
> and didn't want to be a pauper. Why didn't the City fix things so
> that her husband could get work, and why didn't they shut up the
> rum shops, and indict a man who lets such a house as this, which
> ain't fit for no decent hog to live in, though poor folks have to?

The story ends with the student's realization of what the life of the
poor is like and his determination to look after this family; he has
awakened from the "baleful dream of self," and renewed "his early
vows of service to humanity." If this change of heart occurs in the
readers of the story and in others, the answer to "What Cheer?" will
be, "the star of the Human Commonwealth is in the sky."

A passage of particular interest in "What Cheer?," in view of
O'Connor's later devotion to Walt Whitman, is the description of the
sleepers in the city. [43] If this had been written after *Leaves of Grass*
appeared, it might have been considered evidence of Whitman's
influnce, but "What Cheer?" appeared in the same month as the first
edition of *Leaves of Grass*, and had been written and accepted for
publication some time earlier.

> He [the "dark student"] thinks how quietly the sleeping multi-
> tudes lie beneath the dark and silent sea of sleep which floods the
> town. He sees, as in a dream, the numerous strange faces of the
> sleepers, young and old, beautiful and ugly—faces that are brown

and wrinkled, or fair and smooth—holy, evil, sensual, delicate, sullen, queer, lovely, and mournful faces—all in the one horizontal position, all with closed eyes, all shadowed, smoothed, and softened by sleep. He thinks of the bright, living faces that looked into his own that day with smiles and greetings—all composed, changed, and quiet in their slumber. He remembers his mother, who sleeps in the home beyond the evening hills. He sees her grave and placid countenance, with all its reverend wrinkles smoothed with rest. He sees his young brothers and sisters in their childish, innocent repose. . . .

The "dark student" thinks about his own death—in images that again are somewhat Whitmanesque:

. . . To look up at night, filled with an abiding sense of rest, and be conscious of the gentle weight of earth reposing on the coffin-lid. To watch the worms, the mystic roots and fibres of the herbage, the gem-like dew glittering on their tops, and above them all, the broad and hollow dark. . . . To lie there till the bones are dust, the moveless dust shut in by the confining clay, goes slowly around with the gigantic revolutions of the whirling globe—while stars and suns wax and wane, and the great ages waste away; full of rest, and without change, while the roaring mob of life, and all the solemn joys and miseries of earth, sink and swell unheard forever. Around and around with the big world—a little heap of wise and happy dust, lying movelessly beneath the grass-grown surface!

Curtis tried to help O'Connor place "What Cheer?" after cutting it severely, objecting to the subjugation of the story to the general remarks, "so that the tale itself seems to be an illustration of certain speculations, instead of being trusted itself to make all the speculations dramatically evident."[44] From the published version it would appear that O'Connor restored some of the cuts, for the criticism is still valid.

"What Cheer?" was the third of O'Connor's stories to appear; two other stories, probably written later (since they had their settings in Lynn and Boston), having been published: "The Sword of Mauley" in *Harper's* in January 1855, and "Loss and Gain: A Tale of Lynn" in *Harper's* in December 1854.

O'Connor might have been pleased that a reviewer in the *Spring-*

field Republican mistakenly thought that "What Cheer?" was the work of the author of *The Potiphar Papers* (George Curtis), and equally pleased that the *Providence Journal* recognized it as the work of "Aramis." He received commendatory letters from James Baldwin, the editor of the *Boston Commonwealth*,[45] and from Dr. William Francis Channing, son of William Ellery Channing and an Abolitionist, who expressed his admiration of O'Connor's philosophy of life and of his humanity. The letter concludes, "You stand at my side in your aspirations. May the time come when the sympathy of large action together as well as personal nearness, may make us still more truly friends."[46] This wish was to be realized, for O'Connor was to join with Channing in Abolition activities, and later to become his brother-in-law and lifelong friend.

Not all reactions to the story were favorable, however. A reviewer in the *New York Courier and Inquirer* disliked both *Putnam's* and the story, saying that the magazine aims to be "amazingly American, and dreadfully Democratic, and frantically Free-Soil, and teetotally anti-liquor, and rabidly progressive."[47] These alliterative animadversions probably did not bother O'Connor, for they accurately described his aims in the story. They were to continue to be among the themes of his later stories, essays, and novel, and some of them were to be the guidelines of his activities throughout his life.

O'Connor left Providence early in 1852. His brief stay there had been inspiring and productive. The last poem written there was "To the North Star," printed in the *Providence Journal* on January 19, 1852. His poem, "Helena," written in April of that year, was signed, "Aramis, Lynn, Mass." Among the poems written in Lynn were "The Lost Land," "A Valentine" (which ends "For me and my Mary"), and "A Midsummer Night's Dream—to Katie." After he left Lynn, the *Providence Journal* published his poem, "Resurgemus," (September 23, 1853). Its title was the same, except for a difference in spelling, as Sarah Helen Whitman's, "Resurgamus," published in her volume, *House of Life*, in 1853.

Although William stayed in Lynn but a short time, the city made a profound impression upon him. He not only continued to write poetry there, but he also used Lynn as the setting for one of his most powerful short stories, "Loss and Gain: A Tale of Lynn." Longer and more complicated than the earlier stories "The Knocker" and "What Cheer?," its plot revolves about the ethical hazards of the life of trade and the physical hazards of the life of the sea—the twin occupations of the city of Lynn.

O'Connor's plot structure, which he used here as well as in "The Sword of Mauley," has to do with lovers kept apart by the evil deeds of an ancestor and finally brought together in a happy ending when the ancestral crime has been expiated. In this story the lovers are May Martin and Gervayse Phillips, forbidden by May's father, a fishing-boat Captain, to marry; Gervayse's father, Squire Phillips, had cheated the captain, and he feared that the curse of the father's misdeed might fall on the children. The problem is resolved after much unhappiness when Gervayse rescues the Captain's young son after a wreck at sea, and brings him home to find that the Squire had apologized to the Captain for his wrongdoing. The story ends with the marriage of the young couple, the marriage of the narrator and Gervayse's sister, and the death of Squire Phillips.

In the descriptions of the city and of the people, and in the recreation of their various speech patterns, the story belongs to the genre of regionalism which was to become popular in American letters.

> . . . Look at Cap'n Bugbee, and his burly figure suggested Cape Cod, and a whole fleet of seaboats, from a fishing-dory up to a merchantman. Hear him gruffly mumble a whole beach of tumbling surges. His big mouth reminded you of the gills of a codfish. I think he was born in canvas ducks and a pea-jacket. . . . It was impossible to imagine him, even in his celestial state, out of canvas ducks and a monkey-jacket. . . . As for the common idea of wings, in his case it is impossible—though I am not sure about fins.

O'Connor was able to hear and reproduce the dialect of the region. Cap'n Martin says: "That 'ere sea looks bright and blue today, Charley, but it's got a hungry maw. . . . That's the water kin bile right smart in cold weather, and cook your duff for you. Cape Horn arn't a suckumstance. 'Twont compare for stress of foul weather. . . ." Each character—the old aunt, Cap'n Bugbee, the little boy, and the lovers—speaks according to his origin and education. Only the speech of the "upper classes" sounds somewhat formal and stilted.

The hero, Gervayse Phillips, represents the ideal chevalier of O'Connor's young dreams: Perhaps he was named in honor of Wendell Phillips, who was O'Connor's hero.

I only noticed the same inexpressible delicacy and nobility of face and figure which had so often charmed me. The proud and graceful demeanor of the head, with its chivalrous fall of dark waving hair—the dark brilliant eyes, under the calm arch of the black brows, giving light and soul to the sun-tinted, august features—the broad, full chest—the piled muscle of arm and thigh, and the whole lithe, elegant outline of the elastic frame, unconcealed by close-fitting garments, made up an image from the days of the cavaliers. . . . It was the dream of gallant Richard Lovelace, with the graver grace of Philip Sidney, realized in the New England sunlight, beneath the Puritan shadow of the old High Rock. . . .

O'Connor's message of reform—this time against the unethical aspects of trade—is delivered by Squire Phillips, who explains why he wishes his son to become a physician rather than to enter the life of trade:

. . . God makes human nature noble, but the foul fiend of trade leads it into mean paths, thickly sown with pitfalls of temptation, and destroys it. . . . The principles of the counting-house are cold and mean, at best. . . . Study the character of our New England ancestry! Then look at the life and character of our people to-day! We are little better than a tribe of peddlers. What has wrought the change? The love of gain! It has absorbed each noble passion, every generous instinct. We are energetic at nothing but making money. The blood of the Puritans has been sopped up from our veins with banknotes. . . .

The young author manages to put in a few words about other causes in which he was interested. The Woman's Rights movement is alluded to as the narrator walked with May's Aunt Huldah: "Down by the hencoop the fowls recognized the mob-cap, and a yellow clucking hen, evidently schooled liberally on the subject of Hens' Rights, acted as chief spokesman, and petitioned for corn. Aunt Huldah, like a wise legislator, took it by handfulls from her ample pocket, amidst general satisfaction, and threw it in."

O'Connor also dramatizes Abolition sentiments in Cap'n Martin's description of the wreck of his ship off the Isle of Shoals some years before in which the Negro cook rescued the rest of the crew by jumping into a savage sea after the ship was wrecked, then succeeded in wedging himself into a ledge of rock with a rope tied about him which the men could grasp to get to safety. "He was a brave nigger, and we owed him our lives."

Harper and Brothers, in paying for "Loss and Gain: A Tale of Lynn," wrote: "The story is a capital one—is beautifully written." Curtis later forwarded their check for $85 in payment. The reviewers agreed: *The New York Times* of November 30, 1854 praised *Harper's* for its interest and readability, stating that in its fifth year it has a circulation of 140,000. The December issue, said *The Times*, "like every preceding number, improves upon its immediate predecessor," naming among other contributions, "one of the ablest and most powerful original tales, entitled, *Loss and Gain, A Tale of Lynn*, we have ever seen."

Curtis too wrote in its praise, "I wish I could have had such a tale when I helped rule Putnam. It is of the very finest magazine stories. . . . It is full of delicate humor and shrewd dramatic power. . . . To tell a story simply, gracefully, and dramatically, is the surest road to the most influential and permanent literary success. This is Hawthorne's gift. . . ."[48]

O'Connor did not stay very long in Lynn. It had been the inspiration of poems and a powerful short story, but it was in nearby Boston that ideals such as his were being put to the test.

NOTES

1. Nathaniel Hawthorne, referring to O'Connor in his sketch of Delia Bacon in "Recollections of a Gifted Woman," *Our Old Home: A Series of English Sketches* (Boston: Ticknor and Fields, 1863), p. 136.
2. Since no birth certificate has been found, the date of birth is based on the account in *Appleton's Cyclopedia and Register of Important Events of the Year 1889* (New York: Appleton and Company, 1890), New Series, Vol. XIV, p. 643. The copy for *Appleton's New Cyclopedia of American Biography* had been submitted by Rossiter Johnson to O'Connor for correction. (Johnson to O'Connor, 27 January 1888 and 16 February 1888.) The copy for the biographical sketch in the 1889 volume (after O'Connor's death) had been submitted to Ellen (Nelly) O'Connor (Johnson to Ellen O'Connor, 21 March 1890, Feinberg-LC). This sketch gives O'Connor's ancestry as Irish and English, although Sumner Kimball in his introduction to O'Connor's *Heroes of the Storm* speaks of his ancestry as Irish and Scottish. See also, Kimball's account of his death.
3. Information given to this biographer by Katharine Beecher Stetson Chamberlin, the stepdaughter of O'Connor's niece, Grace Channing. Within the family this episode was cited as evidence not of the father's cruelty but of O'Connor's ability to overcome difficulties.

4. His father's name (but not his mother's) appears on William's marriage license. The Roxbury, Mass. directory for 1849 lists Peter O'Connor, gardener, and the Lynn, Mass. directory for 1854 lists Peter O'Connor, laborer. In one of William's notebooks (undated) he lists Fred O'Connor of 66 Commerical St. in Boston and Newton, Mass.; Agnes O'Connor c/o Whedon in Colorado Springs, Colo.; and a P. E. O'Connor, with J. F. Manning, attorney, at 1424 New York Ave., Washington, D.C. and at 131 Devonshire St., Boston. (This information came from David Goodale.) In letters and reminiscences there are only a few references to these people: Grace Channing mentions a sailor brother with whom William had good times in their youth; Nelly writes of a brother who walked with Whitman in the rain, and in one letter, quotes Agnes O'Connor and a younger brother, Rod; after William's death she mentions a niece, Bertha O'Connor. Eldridge writes in 1886 that he has seen Fred in Boston. These are the few scattered jigsaw pieces from which it is impossible to reconstruct a full picture of William's family, childhood, and youth. Other references and correspondence may have been lost when his wife destroyed boxes of William's papers after his death, preserving those which she thought important. (Ellen O'Connor Calder to Anne Montgomerie Traubel, 19 April 1893.)
5. *Putnam's Monthly*, 6:8–24.
6. *Mercantile Library Reporter* 2:19–22 (December 1854).
7. William Forbes Adams, *Ireland and Irish Emigration to the New World from 1815 to the Famine* (New Haven, Conn.: Yale University Press, 1932), p. 160.
8. *Ibid.*, p. 4. Quotation is from P. B. Kelly, *Advice and Guide to Emigrants Going to the United States of America* (Westport, 1834).
9. Adams, *op. cit.*, p. 337.
10. T. and F. Pulsy, *White Red Black* (1853), quoted in Oscar Handlin, *This Was America: True Accounts of People and Places, Manners and Customs, As Recorded by European Travelers to the Western Shore in the Eighteenth, Nineteenth and Twentieth Century* (Cambridge, Mass.: Harvard University Press, 1949), p. 243f.
11. Ralph Waldo Emerson, *The Works of Ralph Waldo Emerson*, Standard Library Edition, 14 vols., (Boston: Houghton Mifflin & Co., 1883), vol. x, pp. 371–77.
12. WDO'C to Mrs. Caroline Dall, 15 January 1861 (Library, Massachusetts Institute of Technology).
13. Grace Channing, unpublished memoir (Chamberlin).
14. WDO'C to Freiligrath, 14 November 1868. Summarized in *Comrades*, p. 40.
15. Biography of O'Connor in Lamb's *Biographical Dictionary of the United States* (Boston, Mass.: Federal Book Co. of Boston, 1903).
16. Jonathan Messerlie, *Horace Mann* (New York. Alfred Knopf, 1971). Title of Chapter XII, pp. 251–79.
17. See note 13 above.
18. WDO'C to Traubel, 7 September 1888, unpublished letter (Feinberg-LC). An interesting account of Dr. Charles Follen is given in Samuel Eliot Morison, *Three Centuries of Harvard* (Cambridge, Mass.: Harvard University Press, 1936), pp. 234, 254. William Lloyd Garrison named one of his sons Charles Follen Garrison.
19. See note 14 above.
20. Ellen O'Connor Calder to H. L. Koopman, Librarian of Brown University, 19 February 1905 (Brown).
21. WDO'C to WW, 3 June 1882 (Feinberg-LC). Boulet taught at West Point from

1840 to 1842 (*United States Military Academy Centennial, 1802–1902*), p. 904.).

22. See note 13 above.
23. Van Wyck Brooks, *The Flowering of New England* (New York: E. P. Dutton and Company, Inc., 1936), p. 183.
24. *Camden*, 4: 364.
25. Wendell Phillips to WDO'C, 24 October 1874 (Feinberg-LC).
26. WDO'C to Louise Chandler Moulton, 24 August 1859 (LC). Mrs. Moulton's husband was the editor of "The True Flag," then housed where O'Connor had had his studio.
27. Some of his sketches are inked on the backs of American Express forms. His notebooks contain drawings, one a sketch of "The Dome" for a projected journal of that title, another an illustration for his story "The Brazen Android." There are also drawings tipped in to a volume of Tennyson's *In Memoriam* given to O'Connor by Sarah Helen Whitman. The only published drawing is an illustration for his poem "The Hermit," used as the first page of a brochure for the Washington Gymnasium, an athletic club of which O'Connor was a member of the Board of Directors in 1873 and vice-president in 1877–78 (Feinberg-LC). A pamphlet, "The Washington Gymnasium," 1873, was presented to David Goodale by Clifton J. Furness; the four-page folder of 1877–78 by Bliss Perry; and both given by David Goodale to the biographer.
28. George Bacon to Ellen (O'Connor) Calder (undated). ". . . William went to Providence 1850–1. I visited him two or three times while he was there. At first he worked for a daguerreotypist—after which he did the business himself" (Brown).
29. GWC to WDO'C, 8 June 1852 (Brown). Ellen O'Connor Calder gave the O'Connor-Curtis letters to Brown University of which Curtis was a graduate.
30. Edgar Allan Poe and Sarah Helen Whitman had met in September 1848; in October he had declared his love; a month later, despite misgivings, she consented to marry him. In December they drew up a marriage contract transferring Helen's estate to her mother (at the insistence of the latter, who suspected Poe of being a fortune hunter, though the fortune was a meagre one). The wedding date was set, but two days before it arrived Helen heard gossip that Edgar was interested in Mrs. Annie Richmond and that he had been seen drinking wine with friends—breaking a promise to her. There was a sad parting scene, with Helen languishing, ether-soaked handkerchief in hand, while Poe pleaded in vain for words of love from her. He was escorted from the house by their friend William Peabodie, whose account of the circumstances of the affair remained among O'Connor's papers with other material about Poe and his Helen.
31. Sarah Helen Whitman, *Hours of Life, And Other Poems* (Providence, Rhode Island: George H. Whitney, 1853).
32. Description by S. S. J. (Sarah S. Jacobs) found in the O'Connor papers (Feinberg-LC). Descriptions of SHW's house and appearance from an obituary signed EKC, among O'Connor's papers.
33. Greeley to SHW, April 1852, n.d. (Brown).
34. "To Ellen" (Feinberg-LC).
35. *Saturday Evening Post*, 4 February 1860.
36. Quoted in its entirety in Jerome Loving, "The Good Gray Poe: The Poe Reburial and William Douglas O'Connor's Forgotten Tribute," *Poe Studies* 10: 18–21 (June 1977).

37. Brown.
38. SHW to John Hay, 25 August 1858, in letter of introduction to O'Connor (Brown).
39. W. F. Channing, in a letter to C. Fiske Harris, 23 August 1878, wrote of Mrs. Whitman's high regard for O'Connor's critical judgment. It was O'Connor who had suggested that all her poems be published in one volume (Brown).
40. Published in *Harper's Monthly Magazine* 12: 57–73 (December 1855).
41. GWC to WDO'C, 10 November 1854 (Brown).
42. SHW in a letter to WDO'C, 7 July 1855, recognizes "Ginn" as Todd, and "Jail Lane" as a street in Providence (Brown).
43. "What Cheer?," p. 13.
44. GWC to WDO'C, 2 April 1855 (Brown).
45. The reviews mentioned above were enclosed in Baldwin's letter (Feinberg-LC).
46. Channing to WDO'C, 12 July 1855 (Feinberg-LC).
47. (Feinberg-LC).
48. GWC to WDO'C, 1 January 1855 (Brown).

CHAPTER III

Boston: City Of Contrasts

IN THE spring of 1853 William O'Connor, then twenty-one years old, returned to a Boston that was more than ever a city of contrasts. Not only were the old differences—between rich and poor, Boston Brahmin and Irish immigrant—still obvious; other contrasts had come to the fore—those between slave and free, Abolitionists and sympathizers with slavery.

O'Connor's short stories and novel show that he knew Boston well. His first story to be published, "The Sword of Mauley," begins with a description of an old mansion on a crooked street in the North End of the city—a proper setting for a story which goes back to Revolutionary times and had a strong element of the supernatural. Differences between neighborhoods are underlined in "The Ghost," a later story in which he described the houses on Beacon Hill:

> . . . long rows of Our First Giants, with very corpulent or very broad fronts, with solid-set feet of sidewalk ending in square-toed curbstone, with an air about them as if they had thrust their hard hands into their wealthy pockets forever, with a character of arctic reserve, and portly dignity, and a well-dressed, full-fed, self-satisfied, opulent, stony, repellent aspect to each, which says plainly, "I belong to a rich family, of the very highest respectability."[1]

In one of these houses Dr. Renton, a physician who is the protagonist of the story, lived. In contrast with this was the tenement house in which the poor lady who was his tenant and her sick child lived above a saloon in which a murder had occurred the previous night.

Of greater significance, however, and forming another strong contrast with Beacon Hill, was the area "vulgarly known as Nigger Hill," which is the setting of some of the action in O'Connor's novel *Harrington*. The novel takes place in the spring of 1852 when most of the Negro population of Boston lives there and where "the fugitives from southern tyranny" must take refuge.

Like Hawthorne, O'Connor varied the solid realism of his description of place with elements of the supernatural. In "The Sword of Mauley" the hero, Ernest, an artist (who occupies a studio very like that of the youthful author) is obsessed by the thought that the ghost of his grandfather, Colonel Mauley, is not at rest. A very old woman told Ernest that she had seen him after his death, his sword dripping blood, while his faithful housekeeper wiped the blood from the doorstep. Ernest loves Alice Bayne, the descendant of a man whom Colonel Mauley had murdered under cover of a battle in the Revolutionary war. Ernest dares not declare his love, for "I feel that there is a forbidding ban from the Past between us—that two dead ancestors confront each other in ghostly feud when we stand before each other." Ernest's obsession with his grandfather's ghost is reinforced by the sight of the old, rusted sword which hangs in his studio.

The eerie ghostliness and the sadness of frustrated love are leavened by humor—young, exuberant humor which sometimes verges on slapstick. The story ends happily with the discovery of a document, hidden in the scabbard, which shows that Colonel Mauley had repented and had made amends to his victim's family. This exorcises the ghost and enables the hero to declare his love for Alice, which she reciprocates.

"The Sword of Mauley" lacks the social and ethical commentary which almost overwhelms "What Cheer?" and "Loss and Gain: A Tale of Lynn." Its only serious discussion is about ghosts, Ernest maintaining despite the arguments of his realistic friend John that ghosts do exist. He alludes to the ghost of Hamlet's father, "no spectral delusion like the shade of Banquo—the creature of Macbeth's remorseful fancy—but a *real* ghost, seen as well by Horatio, Marcellus and Bernardo, as by the Prince." The story received praise from Curtis.[2]

Another ghost appeared in the last of O'Connor's short stories to be published while he was in Boston—"The Ghost." Here the ghost is central to the story, expressing its author's ideas about social justice which had figured prominently in "What Cheer?" and in "Loss and Gain: A Tale of Lynn."

"The Ghost," which he wrote in response to a suggestion by Curtis, is a typical Christmas tale, of which Dickens's "A Christmas Carol" is the most famous example. The Christmas story usually contained a hard-hearted villain, a victim with whom the reader could sympathize, and a change of heart caused by some supernatural intervention—on Christmas Eve, of course.

In "The Ghost" the villain was a wealthy physician, Dr. Renton, the victim a poor respectable woman tenant with a sick child; he is about to dispossess them on Christmas Eve. The ghost is the spirit of his dead friend, George Feval, a poet, whose haunting presence stirs Dr. Renton to reread and take to heart a letter Feval had written fifteen years before as he lay dying, adjuring his friend to be compassionate. The doctor's young daughter, Nathalie, called Netty (perhaps named for O'Connor's future wife, Nelly), also influences him to be generous by her loving concern for him and her sympathy for the woman, to whom she sends her Christmas money.

The message of that story—that Dr. Renton and others like him must become aware of their duty to their less fortunate fellows—is conveyed by means of the plot and made explicit in the letter George Feval had written, which is referred to and quoted in the course of the story, and is given in full at the end. The letter begins:

> Farewell—farewell! But, oh! take my counsel into memory on Christmas Day, and forever. Once again, the ancient prophecy of peace and good-will shines on a world of wars and wrongs and woes. Its soft ray shines on into the darkness of a land wherein swarm slaves, poor laborers, social pariahs, weeping women, homeless exiles, hunted fugitives, despised aliens, drunkards, convicts, wicked children, and Magdalens unredeemed. These are but the ghastliest figures in that sad army of humanity which advances, by a dreadful road, to the Golden Age of the poets' dream. These are your sisters and your brothers. Love them all. Beware of wronging one of them by word or deed. . . .

George Feval, whose ghost haunts Dr. Renton, appears to be a romanticized self-portrait of O'Connor. Renton describes him as:

> a genius,—that is, a person without an atom of practical talent. His parents died when he was near manhood. . . . Thrown upon the world, he picked up a scanty subsistence with his pen, for a time. I could have got him a place in the counting-house, but he would not take it; in fact, he wasn't fit for it. You can't harness Pegasus to the cart, you know. Besides, he despised mercantile life, without reason, of course; but he was always notional. His love of literature was one of the rocks he foundered on. He wasn't successful; his best compositions were too delicate, fanciful, to please the popular taste; and then he was full of the radical and fanatical notions which infected so many people at that time in New England, and infect them now, for that matter; and his sublimated, impracticable ideas and principles, which he kept to his dying day, and which, I confess, alienated me from him, always staved off his chances of success. Consequently, he never rose above the drudgery of some employment on newspapers. Then he was terribly passionate, not without cause, I allow; but it wasn't wise. What I mean is this: if he saw, or if he fancied he saw, any wrong or injury done to any one, it was enough to throw him into a frenzy; he would get black in the face and absolutely shriek out his denunciations of the wrongdoer. I do believe he would have visited his own brother with the most unsparing invective, if that brother had laid a harming finger on a street-beggar, or a colored man, or a poor person of any kind. . . .

In this description O'Connor was in a sense prophetic about his writings and about his future. Like the "best compositions" of George Feval, "The Ghost" was considered too fanciful. When it appeared in book form in 1867 (with illustrations by Thomas Nast), the reviewer in *The Nation*[3] liked everything about the story except the presence of the ghost and his usurpation of the book's title. Still it was popular. Later "The Ghost" was included in the volume devoted to *Mystery* in the *Little Classics* edited by Rossiter Johnson. Wendell P. Garrison, editor of *The Nation*, also wanted to reprint it in a new publication being contemplated.[4] Finally it was one of

Three Tales published after O'Connor's death, the other two being "The Carpenter" and "The Brazen Android."

O'Connor's time in Boston was not devoted entirely to the writing of short stories. However successful they were, they could not bring in enough money to support him. Fortunately he found a niche in Boston, even before any of his stories was published, working on the daily newspaper, the *Boston Commonwealth*, at first as a clerk and later as associate editor.[5] The offices of the *Commonwealth* were an ideal setting for a young man of spirit, for events were not only reported, but also plotted, there. Its editor, John Denison Baldwin, had had the broadest possible education for this post. He had been a teacher in the public schools to support himself while he studied law and then theology; he had taught himself archaeology, French, and German; he had served as a Congregationalist minister (after graduation from Yale Divinity School), leaving this field to enter politics as a member of the Connecticut Legislature. There he introduced the bill to establish the first Normal School in that State. He had entered journalism as owner and editor of the *Charter Oak*, a Free Soil paper in Hartford, Connecticut. After three years with that paper, he came to Boston to edit the *Commonwealth*. He later purchased and edited the Worcester *Spy*, and served in Congress for three terms (beginning in 1862).

While O'Connor was working on the *Commonwealth* in 1854, a famous journalist joined the staff. This was the uncompromising William Stevens Robinson ("Warrington") who had lost several earlier positions because of his Free Soil opinions.[6] Both Baldwin and Robinson were active Abolitionists. The *Commonwealth* was a center of Abolitionist activity, with Theodore Parker, Henry Wilson, and Charles Sumner, who were Baldwin's friends, frequent visitors.

Before O'Connor came to the *Commonwealth*, the Compromise of 1850 with its Fugitive Slave Law had made the rescue of fugitives (which had been going on for some years) more imperative and more dangerous than ever, for the rescuers were now acting not only against the Southern slave owners, but also against the federal government. The new Fugitive Slave Law made the return of escaped slaves to their owners the law of the land, to be enforced by federal marshals. It provided that fugitive slaves were not to be tried by a jury nor to testify in their own defense. Whoever tried to help or hide a fugitive or to prevent his arrest was subject to a fine of 1,000 dollars and six months' imprisonment. Federal marshals received ten dollars for the apprehension of a Negro suspected of being a fugitive slave and sent back if he was proved to be so; five dollars if he was not. This led Wendell Phillips to say that the price of a South Carolina Negro was now fixed at a thousand dollars and that of a Yankee's soul at five.[7]

According to O'Connor's own account, he "took an active part in the famous fugitive slave cases of that time."[8] When the Fugitive Slave Law was enacted on September 28, 1850, anti-slavery Bostonians promptly organized a Vigilance Committee, whose purpose was to protect fugitives and the "colored inhabitants" of Boston and vicinity from any persons trying to enforce that law. The directors of the Committee, elected at a meeting in Faneuil Hall, included Henry Bowditch, Charles Ellis, Lewis Hayden (a Negro lawyer), Thomas Wentworth Higginson, Samuel Gridley Howe, Ellis Gray Loring, Theodore Parker, and Wendell Phillips.

The Vigilance Committee soon attracted 250 members. They attempted to alert fugitive slaves to their danger and to try to free them if they were apprehended. These rescues were still going on when O'Connor returned to Boston. In view of his statement about his participation in Abolition activities and his detailed description of attempted rescues in his novel *Harrington*, it is likely that O'Connor was a member of the Vigilance Committee. Thomas Wentworth Higginson, a known participant, wrote of this novel:

> . . . no book of the period rendered with such vividness certain aspects of the fugitive-slave excitement in New England. One chapter in particular, "The Roar of St. Domingo," which was founded on an attempt by the colored people of Worcester, Mass. to mob a supposed slave-kidnapper, is something which no future historian of the *ante-bellum* period in this country can overlook. The book should be, and will be, reprinted some day, were it only as a historical document.[9]

Among the famous fugitive slave cases were those of William and Ellen Craft, "Shadrach," Thomas Sims, Solomon Northup, and Anthony Burns. William O'Connor based the first part of *Harrington* on the narrative of Solomon Northup, *Twelve Years a Slave*,[10] while using the Anthony Burns story for the framework of his plot. William was surely a witness to, if not a participant in, the attempted rescue of Anthony Burns which took place in 1854. When that effort failed, Anthony Burns was led through Boston to the harbor where a ship was waiting to take him back to the South and his owner. Fifty thousand spectators lined the streets. (Burns remarked to the sheriff that there surely were a lot of people out to see a colored man walk down the street.) Church bells tolled. The city was in mourning. From the windows of the *Commonwealth*, where O'Connor worked, flags mingled with dark folds were hung, while streamers of crape were stretched across the street.

But life was not all serious purpose. In Boston, O'Connor resumed his acquaintance with the group known as "The *Carpet Bag* Bohemians" in whose periodical his poems had appeared. Although usually associated with New York City and taverns like Pfaff's, a Bohemia also existed in Boston, which found its voice in the publication *The Carpet Bag*[11] and its leader in the genial person of Benjamin Penhallow Shillaber, its editor from 1851 to 1853.

In its own day *The Carpet Bag* was known chiefly for the editor's sketches about Mrs. Partington (a Yankee Mrs. Malaprop) and her nephew Ike, whose opinions and adventures (begun in the *Boston Post* when Shillaber was editor and continued in *The Carpet Bag*) finally filled four volumes. Mrs. Partington and Ike were said to have been the prototypes for Mark Twain's Aunt Polly and Tom Sawyer. Typical of Mrs. Partington's liberties with the language is her view of modern education: "For my part, I can't deceive what on airth eddication is coming to. When I was young, if a girl only understood the rules of distraction, provision, multiplying, replenishing and the common denunciator, they had eddication enough."[12]

The Carpet Bag is notable not only because of Shillaber; one issue, that of May 1, 1852, contained the earliest published work of three humorists: "The Dandy Frightening the Squatter" by sixteen-year-old Samuel L. Clemens, an essay by the seventeen-year-old Charles F. Browne, later known as "Artemus Ward," and drawings and text by G. H. Derby, who wrote as "John Phoenix" and "Squibob." *The Carpet Bag* also contained some of William O'Connor's poems.

Some years later when O'Connor was living in Philadelphia and editing the *Saturday Evening Post*, the memory of the *Carpet Bag* crew and their revels glowed in contrast to his drab life in Philadelphia. He wrote a nostalgic essay, published in the *Saturday Evening Post* of July 9, 1859:

> Once upon a time, in Boston, where, of course, all the people wear blue spectacles and white neckcloths, and where nobody ever laughs and everybody dresses in black crape—there dwelt, in the midst of the gloomy population, a crew of bold Bohemians, spirits of the morning sort, epicureans, gay hearts and light heads, guildsmen of Momus, followers of the Muse, true minions of the Sun and Moon. . . . [Among them he names Athos and Aramis.]
>
> What times they had! You can imagine. There was a paper called "The Carpet Bag," into which they put all the philosophy and poetry and farce they wrote on paper.

Of Shillaber he wrote:

> But who was he that moved, large and laughing, among these brave Bohemians, with a paternal air, even as big Papa Morel moves at the Cafe de la Régence among the Parisian chess-players? . . . Who was he, that portly and jovial man, with a temper as mellow as a prize pear, with a humor that streamed like autumn sun-shine, with household poetry in his brain and comic fancies fluttering from his lips, and a heart, like a central sun sending light and heat through all? Who but the intimate friend and reporter of Mrs. Partington and Ike. . . . Who in short was he but B. P. Shillaber?
>
> When he came into company, company rejoiced. . . . How the language was made to show its capacity, and flashed and snapped, and crackled and gleamed, with quips and jests, puns and repartees. Jokes sprang suddenly from the dullest subjects, like laughing Scaramouches from their boxes. And Shillaber was the soul of it all.

Aside from the *Carpet Bag* revels, O'Connor's life in Boston was that of the writer and activist. Although he was now a published poet and author, he did not forget the Mercantile Library Association, his acknowledged "alma mater." On December 1, 1854 his essay, "The Grotesque," appeared in the *Mercantile Library Reporter*.[13] In it he writes of the grotesque in nature—"the mandrake, for instance, which bears a crazy resemblance to the human body, and was once supposed to grow only in soil under the gibbets of criminals, or in the graves of the dead"; in man-made objects—"the form of household things—an antique pair of straddling andirons, in the dress of apish men, the bedizenings of fantastic women. . . ." The grotesque is found in art, not only in the work of mediocre old masters, but also in such ancient monuments as the Egyptian Sphinx, and the enormous idol-gods of the Hindu, but there "by the assimilation of the element of gigantic size it becomes sublime."

The last part of the essay reaches a crescendo in the description of the grotesque in humankind. Here he descants on the theme of some of his stories:

> You are a thinker:—Some day you meet in the filthiest street of the filthiest quarter of a great wicked city—say Boston—perhaps a child, in whom the nature of humanity has become blotted and transformed into a nature more low and fearful than the nature of the beasts. Born and bred, and nightly kenneled in some dark fetid den—the babe of wretched drunkards—nursed in squalid want and sin—cultured by the company of prostitutes, thieves, and stabbers—ragged, dirty, and diseased. . . .

The child's "precocious, villainous, unchildlike face . . . so surely predestinating a life of brutal violence and savage crime—that Shakespeare's tremendous image of the Bloody Child arises in your memory as its symbol, and assumes a new and fearful significance. . . ."

O'Connor continues: "The grotesque is most obvious in the strange Babylons men build so zealously and labor to enlarge (by annexation, for instance!) so strenuously, and call cities." He describes the denizens of the city who

> mince, saunter, amble, stalk, or swagger, probably grotesque to see, in all their diverse characters of apes, oafs, snobs, or zanies, by the lighted windows of the bazaar. Gently, gently, O man, these are your sisters and your brothers! The grotesque is on them, but as the demoniac mask that hides the features of a fallen divinity. . . .

The essay concludes with an admonition to the readers to trust that the day will come when the grotesque will be stricken away with all of which it is a symbol.

"The Grotesque" was probably well received, for William became the editor of the *Mercantile Library Reporter* in December 1855. He must have been proud to have reached this position in the institution to which he had turned for his education as a child and youth and where he had had his first experience of lecturing. The first issue under his aegis as editor contained a reprint of his poem "The Lost Land" and a pessimistic essay entitled "The New Year." In this essay he quotes from a new book, Walt Whitman's *Leaves of Grass* which had just appeared. O'Connor examines Europe in the wake of revolution (as he had done in his poem "To Athos").

> One dark, low-lying cloud of absolutism hangs heavily over Europe; and the denseness and closeness of that "stale and drowsy air—the air of slaves" slowly breeds the necessity for that tremendous flash of flame yet to burst with a stunning blood-roar, and leave Death and Ruin the sole victors among the blackened relics of an old civilization, and the corpses of the slain. (The quoted words are from *Leaves of Grass*.)

The author hears "the dying echoes of Sevastopol" as "the first faint mutterings of the thunderstorm of nations yet to come. 'When God gives a thinker to the world,' says Turgot, 'let the world beware'; God has given Victor Hugo, Mazzini, and Kossuth; they bide their time; let the world beware." He surveys the Italians groveling supinely under the Crozier, the French shouting "with fickle breath for Louis the Little," the Poles reaping "the bitter result of their own internal dissensions and jealousies," the Hungarians, "mute and weaponless," the Germans, "thoughtful, slow, suffering, vengeful, without the executive capacity in statesmanship which popular practice in governing alone gives a people" and the English, "blatant, boisterous, haughty, amidst the accusing crimes, miseries, and shame of a people fretted by abuses and misrule, and slowly inhaling the maddening ether of revolt that is abroad in the air. . . ." Nowhere are crowds sane, or crowns just.

He turns to the new world—"a prodigy of development unexampled in the world's history—but do prodigies live long?" Here he sees

> a union of states whose centrifugal tendencies grow stronger, and its centripetal weaker, day by day, a national fabric formed with-

out reference to the geometry of God—directly opposed to the moral law which pervades the universe and destroys whatever springs up in violation thereof; with a government policy which always sacrifices the Right to the Expedient—which crushes all weak races—Indian, Mexican, African—to gain power, area, gold . . . with a noisy vaunt of freemen in the hall, and an unblushing infamy of slaves in the dungeon. . . .

If there is to be any hope for the future, it will be up to the generation to come. Because he is writing for young merchants, he seeks young leaders in commerce "who will organize their wealth, their intellects, their executive power . . . to create a society" in which "no obdurate iron wall—such as Boston rears between the Black Sea and Beacon Hill, such as New York has between the Five Points and Fifth Avenue—on either side of which, in hate and scorn of each other, poor heathen and rich pagans dwell. . . ." This is the only hope for creating a Happy New Year. "The sword of the chevalier rusts in the scabbard, but the spirit that drew the sword lives in the van of the great human battle, and flashes a mightier weapon. . . ."

O'Connor was to continue to engage in that battle for the rest of his life. In his fight he was at first to have the encouragement and love of his wife, Ellen Tarr—and later her quiet and stubborn antagonism to a literary life for him.

NOTES

1. *Three Tales*, p. 1.
2. GWC, 16 November 1854 (Brown).
3. Issue of 21 November 1867.
4. Garrison to WDO'C, 21 February 1867 (Feinberg-LC).
5. WDO'C, *Mem.* Memorandum in O'Connor's handwriting (Berg). "He (O'Connor) was once employed in the counting room of the old *Daily Commonwealth*, and his bulletins were perfect gems of political sensationalism. I often thought they were of more service, as well as brighter, than the editorial articles." (W. S. Robinson, "Warrington," in a review of O'Connor's poem "To Fanny," *The Springfield Republican*, 27 January 1871.)
6. William S. Robinson, "Warrington," *Pen-Portraits* (Boston: Edited and Published by Mrs. W. S. Robinson, 1877), p. 530.
7. John L. Thomas, *The Liberator: William Lloyd Garrison, A Biography* (Boston: Little, Brown and Company, 1963), pp. 359–60.
8. See note 5 above.
9. Higginson in a letter to "The Critic," 9 April 1892, p. 216. He expresses the same

view in "Cheerful Yesterdays," *Atlantic Monthly* 79:354, though he does not
say here that it should be reprinted.
10. The title page adds, "A Citizen of New York, Kidnapped in Washington City in
1841, and Rescued in 1853, From a Cotton Plantation Near the Red River in
Louisiana." (Auburn: Derby and Miller; Buffalo: Derby, Orton and Mulligan;
London: Sampson Low, Son & Company, 47 Ludgate Hill, 1853).
11. Humorous weekly (1851–53).
12. Van Wyck Brooks, *The Times of Melville and Whitman* (New York: E. P. Dutton, 1947), p. 211n. Benjamin P. Shillaber, *Life and Sayings of Mrs. Partington*
(Reprint ed.; Upper Saddle River, New Jersey: Literature House/Gregg
Press, 1969).
13. *Mercantile Library Reporter* I(2):19–22. This and other articles from the *Mercantile Library Reporter* were located by David Goodale, who made them
available for this book.

CHAPTER IV

Ellen (Nelly) Tarr: Growing Up Poor In New England

WHILE IN Boston, in 1854, William met the lovely Ellen (Nelly) Tarr.[1] Small, slim, graceful, and vivacious, she shared William's enthusiasms for Woman's Rights and Abolition. Although there are no photographs of her at that time, later ones show large, brown eyes under arched brows, dark hair parted in the middle, smoothed over her ears and pinned in folded braids low on her neck. Of a photograph taken when she was sixteen (and the only one she liked), Walt Whitman said that she had an "aspiring" look. William and Nelly may have met because both were friends of Paulina Wright Davis of Providence, Rhode Island, or because they worked on similar papers—Nelly on Garrison's paper, *The Liberator*, and William on the *Commonwealth*, both anti-slavery papers.

By May 1854 they were in love, and William composed a poem for her, "To Nell—with a copy of the Poems of Edgar Allan Poe." The final draft was written on the back of a letter from the Mercantile Library Association, appointing William to a committee to superintend the checklists at the election of the Lecture Committee on May 5.

The romance progressed. In July 1855 William addressed Nelly's sister Jeannie in a poem accompanying the poems of Thomas Hood as one who will be his sister. In that month, it was through Nelly and

Jeannie that William saw and read a copy of the strange and wonderful new book, *Leaves of Grass*. (The volume had been brought to Jeannie by William Channing, who had been urged to read it by his friend Ralph Waldo Emerson.)[2]

Both Nelly and William had great independence of mind and sympathy for the same causes; they shared a willingness to give of themselves for friendship and for what they believed to be right. As time went on differences developed: William could give all to causes he believed in; Nelly drew the line at the point where her security (as seen in a steady family income) was threatened. Their likenesses drew them together and kept them close both physically and spiritually for ten years, and physically for another four; then their differences forced them apart—the final break occurring in the aftermath of a historic quarrel between William and Walt Whitman.

In contrast to the paucity of records of William's family, childhood and youth, the abundance of information about his wife, Nelly, presents not only a detailed account of her early years, but also a picture of the life of the New England poor in the 1830s and 1840s. Nelly was completely of New England, having been born in Portsmouth, New Hampshire, on February 22, 1830, and raised in Great Falls, New Hampshire, and in Boston and Lowell, Massachusetts. She was the seventh and youngest child and third daughter of Benjamin Tarr and Martha Dyer. Both grandfathers had fought in the Revolution—Seth Tarr (born in Massachusetts) as a second lieutenant, and Elkanah Dyer (born in Maine) as a private.

Much has been written of the traits of New England character—of the independence, thrift, nonconformity, industry, and reserve of its citizens. Nelly seems to have had all but the last. Instead of the traditional reserve, she had spontaneity, warmth, and charm—perhaps because as the youngest she was indulged by all. Her independence of mind showed itself in her work for Woman's Rights, among other causes. When, at the age of eighty-one, Ellen Tarr O'Connor Calder was asked why she was an equal suffragist, she answered that she "was one at birth, and had seen or heard no valid arguments against equal suffrage since."[3]

Perhaps Nelly became an equal suffragist when she and her older sisters, Martha and Mary Jane (Jeannie), envied the delightful freedom their brothers enjoyed; they were among "the Portsmouth boys" whose exploits were recorded by Thomas Bailey Aldrich, who celebrated Portsmouth (under the name of *River Mouth*) in his *Story of a Bad Boy* and *An Old Town by the Sea*. One of their adventures was told in the chapter "The Snow Fort on Slatter's Hill."

The dire poverty which Nelly experienced during her childhood left its mark upon her. When she was still a child, the Tarrs left Portsmouth for Great Falls. The father, Benjamin Tarr, then forty years old, had driven the mail stage coach between Portsmouth and Portland for years. Because exposure in all kinds of weather and long and late hours of driving had impaired his health, he was transferred to a shorter route which would take just a day at a time, one end of which was Great Falls. He therefore moved his family—his wife, three sons and three daughters (one boy had died in infancy)—from their Portsmouth house with its lovely old-fashioned garden to a little cottage in Great Falls. Even that cottage was to seem luxurious in retrospect, for it was their home for only one year; the father's health continued to fail and they had to move to one of the corporation boardinghouses, where the mother became the mainstay of the family.

Nelly's independence was a family characteristic. Her father, of Quaker stock, was a convert of the Reverend James Murray, founder of Universalism in America. During Benjamin Tarr's youth, the Reverend Murray had been pastor of a Universalist Society in Boston. In Great Falls, however, there were too few Universalists to have a church of their own, so the Tarr children missed the weekly social event that attendance at church and Sunday School represented in their small town. Their father explained that "he could not allow his little children to go to a church where doctrines that he cordially hated were taught." The children often overheard discussions between him and his Orthodox, Baptist, and Methodist friends, in which Bible texts were freely and aptly cited in support of different points of view. The sensitive Jeannie worried about him: "My father was one of a *very* small minority in his faith! What if he were mistaken and God instead of being the loving Father *he* believed in, should prove the stern and angry judge I so often heard Him depicted by the others! Angry indeed they seemed to think because my father believed Him *all* Love!"

The children seem to have had little joy out of their father's religion, despite its doctrine that God was love. "Sunday was kept with Puritanic strictness in our home. No work that could be done on

Saturday or left for Monday was allowed. No walks, no out-of-doors pleasant idling, no plays. Story books we had almost none and they were not *Sunday* books. What was left for children? Reading solemn books, and sitting in idleness."

Staunch as he was in his faith, Benjamin Tarr could nevertheless sympathize with others. Jeannie wrote, "It is a grateful remembrance to me to recall his outspoken indignation when the news came of the burning of the Catholic convent at Charlestown! Someone attempted to palliate that crime, but his mind and heart denounced it. He said in his Quaker traditions he had learned what intolerance and persecution meant." Nelly's brother Josiah later became a Swedenborgian. The Tarr family was clearly one in which it was a mark of distinction for the men to hold religious views different from those of the majority, but similar freedom was granted to the girls only grudgingly.

During their childhood the girls resented the favored position of the boys in the family. Their brothers were not only closer to the adored but distant father, but they also had other advantages. They could play outdoors, were dressed more warmly in the winter, could wear boots ("rubber overshoes were very rare and there were no boots for women and girls"), played with marbles, tops, kites, hoops and balls, and in winter, had sleds and skates. The only games for girls were jumping rope and playing tag, with no outdoor games in the winter; if they acted like "tom boys" they were frowned upon.

The men and boys worked hard, but the women and girls even harder. Every girl learned to sew when she was very young. Jeannie could not remember a time when she could not sew nicely. The crowning achievement of fine needlework was making a shirt for their father or brothers. The little girls also learned to knit and make rugs from rags. There were few if any "boughten" carpets in the village.

Another duty of the little girls was to bring water into the house in pails from the pump, which was a little distance away, or from the big cask set to catch rain water. They also brought in part of the wood and kindlings which the boys had split, and went on errands to the store. In the evening when the father and brothers could sit quietly or play checkers, the mother and girls were not permitted to rest. They were expected to sew or knit. Jeannie, the future suffragist, wrote,

I think with satisfaction of one energetic, young school teacher who lifted up her voice in remonstrance against the absurd and useless stitchery that was put into the shirts of the fathers, husband, brothers and sons. "I will not do it," she said; "I will read and study and improve my mind!" It was heresy then: she was in advance of her time.

Though the girls overheard discussions of politics, they could not participate in them. Jeannie recalled,

I heard politics discussed fully but only by the men, and as I found it very interesting to listen to these discussions, I wondered *why* there was always a laugh or a sneer at the idea even of a woman's being able to understand politics—especially as they were *expected* to understand and discuss theology to the extent at least of defending their own belief; for it was a matter of course, that even a young woman should hold some special faith.

There followed several years of poverty, family troubles, and hard work. The first tragedy was the death of the oldest brother, Benjamin. The solemn funeral was to be followed within two years by the deaths of the youngest brother George and the father.

But before the last two tragedies a few happy experiences intervened. They were the result of a move to Boston, where their brother Josiah had found work. There the father (having sold some bounty land he received because of his service as a Sergeant in the War of 1812) had a few days of freedom before taking a job, and showed the sights of Boston to his enchanted family. Though they lived in a small apartment, the city of Boston was theirs! Their first Fourth of July was a gala day—bells ringing, guns booming, and a military procession with the first bands they had ever heard. And fireworks on the Common in the evening!

Their father, though far from well, obtained a position in a ship chandler's store on Broad Street, and they moved to the upper part of a house on Belmont Street high on Fort Hill overlooking the busy Boston harbor. The task of carrying water and coal upstairs was more than compensated for by the wonderful view from their windows. They could look up from their sewing to see a changing panorama of shipping—Northeast gales tossing the ships; ice so thick at one time that a channel had to be cut down the whole length of it through which a majestic procession of ships passed. The girls continued their schooling for a while, and there were happy times until the youngest brother George became ill with rheumatic fever followed by consumption. Because of the extra expense the mother was forced to take in washing for a half dozen people. Before going to school on Monday mornings, Jeannie and Nelly picked up the bundles of wash, often crying because of the cold from which they could not protect their laden hands. The eldest sister Martha left school to learn the trade of vest making. Jeannie got extra work to do at home, trimming labels for jars of pickles and sauces put up at the store at which her father worked. Their pay was a mere trifle per thousand, but she "literally danced" as she went home with her first heavy pile of labels. The girls also earned extra money after school knitting cotton and linen edgings and insertings and making ginghams and sunbonnets for the neighbors' children.

Just a year after they came to Boston their brother George died at the age of eighteen. Soon after, the father's cough grew worse. Urged by his employers to give up work for a while, he took a trip to Maine to see his early home and his relatives. The mother was now the chief breadwinner. When Jeannie, having been promoted at school, had to choose between a new dress and new books, she chose the latter.

Times grew harder. The father was even sicker when he returned, and died just six months after the youngest brother, both of consumption. Soon after that, Josiah, who had been working in Connecticut, returned to Boston to be with his mother and the three girls. The mother took in boarders in addition to doing the washing and ironing for others. Martha's eyes gave out and she had to sit in darkness for six weeks. The mother sometimes went out as a nurse leaving the girls, then fourteen, twelve, and ten, to take care of the house and the work. Only Nelly could continue in school—but not for long. They still enjoyed their Sundays when they went to the School Street Church and heard Father Ballou and the Rev. E. H. Chapin, whom Jeannie considered the best orator she ever heard.

The spring after their father's death a friend who had been a Boston pilot and now had a cigar factory offered employment to Martha and Jeannie. There they stripped the heavy midrib from the leaves of tobacco and smoothed the leaves into piles for the wrappers of cigars, keeping the refuse for fillings. One of the men working there was William Legge who later married Martha Tarr. (There was a jingle in the family about three blue-eyed Williams who married three brown-eyed Tarrs, all in the month of October. William Legge was the first in 1844, William O'Connor the second in 1856, and William Channing the third in 1859.)

Jeannie, because of her talent for dressmaking, was apprenticed to a dressmaker the spring that she was fourteen years old. There she helped to make a white brocade gown for the prima donna who sang in "Moses in Egypt"—one of the early performances of oratorio in Boston. "And I learned what an oratorio was then for the first time, by hearing about it at this dressmaker's establishment."

Because of their brother Josiah, the girls' lives became more pleasant. He persuaded their mother to let him teach them whist and backgammon and even to take them to the Boston Museum where they saw their first exhibition of dancing, performed by Miss Adelaide Phillips. Occasionally they went to an evening lecture—once to an exhibition at the Institution for the Blind where they saw Laura Bridgman, then a very young girl; at another time they heard the wonderful young preacher, Thomas Starr King, who had been a schoolmate of their brothers in Portsmouth, and whose father had been their parents' minister. (Thomas Starr King later became a Unitarian minister in San Francisco and was influential in California's choice of the Union side in the Civil War.)

The brief interlude of pleasant social life was interrupted a year later when Josiah went into business in Lowell. Life was dull without him, and additional hardships came: The mother fractured her arm which was not properly set and never straightened; the additional burdens caused Jeannie to become weak and ill. Nevertheless, both Martha and Jeannie worked all winter in a large dressmaking establishment, and then, unfortunately, could not collect any of their promised pay.

Martha, not yet eighteen, had become engaged to William Legge, and Josiah, then in his mid-twenties, to Mary Delia Sawyer of Lowell. Despite Martha's reluctance to leave her fiance, the family moved to Lowell to be with Josiah. No more school for fourteen-year-old Nelly, who went into one of the factories while her two older sisters began dressmaking.

Luckily for Nelly, who desperately wanted an education, Lowell itself was like a school. The mills at Lowell had been conceived of by their founders, Francis Cabot Lowell and Nathan Appleton, as an industrial and educational experiment. There she met many young women of good New England families who had come to work in the factories in order to provide an education for their brothers. Some of them not only supported their brothers, but even had to pay the wages of the man their father hired to do the absent student's work on the farm. How these girls longed for an education!

> One winter someone suggested evening classes, in the school house. It "took." The days in the factory were long, there were no side walks, no lights in the streets except the lanterns they carried, no lights in the school-house, but each carried a lamp or a candle; *those* were *trifles* not to be considered where there was a chance to learn something of use. The hunger for learning was keen and the school room filled, chiefly by these young women.

They lived in boarding houses, supervised by respectable women such as Mrs. Tarr, and worked in mills where thread was converted into cloth entirely by machinery. The employment of intelligent girls was found to be economically advantageous both to the mill owners and to the girls and their families. (Astute businessmen, the Lowells, the Lawrences, and the Appletons were to become famous also as philanthropists.) At that time the only other occupations open to girls were teaching and domestic service. Factory work paid better than teaching and, unlike domestic work, enabled the girls to retain their sense of independence.

Like the other girls Nelly probably began with wages of 55¢ a week above her board of $1.25 per week.[4] She could look forward, with increased speed and skill, to as much as $4.00 per week above her board, though the average wage remained at $2.00. Though the mills did not use child labor, the youngest (girls in their early teens) worked as "doffers" or bobbin girls, changing the bobbins on the spring frames every three-quarters of an hour. All the operators worked an average of twelve-and-a-half hours per day, six days a week; in summer when the days were long they worked fourteen hours, fewer hours in winter when artificial illumination was needed. In addition to the usual holidays—free days but without pay—Fastday, which came some time in March or April, the Fourth of July and Thanksgiving, the mills added two other festivities that involved no time off. These were the "lighting up" and "blowing out" balls on September 21 and March 21—when lamps were kindled or extinguished.

Sundays were happy days. Like all New Englanders the Lowell girls were churchgoers and each could find the church of her choice, for by 1850 there were twenty-two churches in Lowell. Jeannie and Nelly attended Mr. Miner's Society.

Jeannie's account of life in Lowell describes the growing friendship between herself and her younger sister Nelly (their childhood rivalry and quarrels put aside), their new circle of friends, their social life, and the exciting ideas to which they, as well as the other Lowell girls, were exposed.

> Like every town of some size in New England at the time, Lowell had its Lyceum and Institute for the Diffusion of Useful Knowledge, where capsules of information were dispensed at a low fee, a season ticket for a series of twenty-five lectures costing only 50¢ in the 1840's. People who frowned upon the theater as an immoral pastime went freely to the lecture hall and surrendered themselves to the histrionics of the country's most gifted speakers, in the belief that they were being uplifted rather than diverted. For the country girls at Lowell, however, it must have been extraordinarily interesting to hear a talk by the former President of the United States, John Quincy Adams, to listen to the baroque periods of Edward Everett, or the golden voice of Ralph Waldo Emerson, uttering "his majestic intuitions of truth and justice." "The more original the speaker, and the more profound," wrote Theodore Parker, himself a lecturer of no mean ability, "the better he is relished."

Jeannie and Nelly met interesting young friends who influenced their thinking.

> In Mr. Miner's Society and especially at the evening socials, my sister Ellen and I met a circle of life-long friends—some very noble young men and women deeply interested in *ideas*, in *reforms.*
> Among the young men were several who had begun to study for the Universalist ministry and had become Socialists, Associationists, Transcendentalists, disciples of Graham, strict vegetarians! We read Brisbane and Godwin and the Harbinger. The young men were older, considerably older, probably an average

of ten years, and in a measure our leaders and teachers, but I had read Brisbane *first*, from my brother's bringing home his book. I was all ready for it. Ever since my childhood's frightened questionings and fears I had been in a condition of spiritual unrest. Socialism was the word that gave me hope. Association as I heard it in a course of lectures by Greeley and Brisbane, Allen and Rev. W. H. Channing and others that winter in Lowell and as promulgated by the Harbinger. One of our friends had made arrangements to live at Brook Farm just as the new building was burnt.

We were all hoping for a better wider life. Some of us were reformers to the degree of fanaticism. The young men thought it a matter of conscience to wear their beards and pretty long hair. Some of the parents of the young women regarded that wearing of long hair, unshaven faces, as an *almost* unpardonable offence.

One extremely strict vegetarian so influenced my sister of 15 years (Nelly) that for months she would eat *no* animal food. (Her health suffered, she grew thin and lost appetite and was irritable. It was very difficult to cater for one so strictly vegetarian and our mother was very indignant. Fortunately she did not continue the experiment long.) The influence of this circle of friends was essentially noble with these minor drawbacks. We read poetry; Shelley was our chief favorite, with admiration for Byron and on my part an enthusiasm for Motherwell that makes him still especially dear. We read Mrs. Child's letters and her *Philothea*; we read Emerson's essays. We formed classes to study phonography [a form of shorthand invented by Sir Isaac Pitman in 1837 and just beginning to be known]. We took long walks and came back with our stores of wild flowers. We went to the Lyceum lectures in winter.

Those few years, only two and a half, of life in Lowell were rich in growth in experience and in friendships. It was this circle of friends who renamed us. I became "Jeannie" and Ellen "Nell." Our family soon adopted the changed names.

When the Tarrs returned to Boston, the girls returned to the School Street Church, but soon left to hear Theodore Parker preach. Somehow Jeannie did not find there "the nutriment *my* spirit longed for." A friend from Lowell took them to the Saturday evening meeting of the Boston Union of Associationists. The next day they went to the Sunday afternoon services and heard Rev. W. H. Channing preach. Jeannie felt that here she was "indeed finding not husks, but bread." They became members of the Society.

It was in the face of strong opposition from our mother. She seemed bitter against the friends through whom we had come to Socialism. She made it very hard for us, so that many a time I gave up the meetings that were *more* to me than she could imagine. . . . I was then nearly twenty and my sister eighteen and we had the right on our side. Our brother had become a Swedenborgian with not a word of remonstrance or opposition from her. It was an object lesson in the difference between sons and daughters, boys and girls. She became by slow degrees reconciled to the change, or at least she accepted it.

Through the friends whom they met in the Union of Associationists, Nelly and Jeannie were offered an opportunity to go to Normal School at Newton, Massachusetts. Not having attended school in years they were afraid that they could not pass the entrance exam; after having passed successfully, they were afraid that they would not be able to compete with the other students, some of whom had received medals in the Boston Grammar Schools. But they soon lost their humility when they realized that their experience of hard work had given them habits of thinking and of self-reliance which the others had not acquired. All during her stay at Normal School, Jeannie spent her evenings in sewing for herself, Nelly and her mother. By boarding themselves, together with other schoolmates, they were able to save enough to go to Boston and attend services on Sundays.

When the Tarr sisters completed their Normal School training, Jeannie went to Attleboro to teach in the very week of her graduation. After a winter there she taught for six months in the Derby Academy at Hingham as substitute for the principal of the Girls Department. Then she returned to Boston where the Directory of 1853 lists her as an assistant in the Mason Street School for Girls. The following year she became an assistant in the Normal Department of the same school and a year later a regular teacher in the Girls High and Normal. Although begun so expeditiously, Jeannie's teaching career was not to last long. The years of ceaseless toil since childhood took their toll when Jeannie contracted tuberculosis in 1855 and had to quit teaching.

Nelly used her preparation as a teacher in a different manner—one that was to enable her to learn as well as to teach. She had the good fortune at about the age of twenty to become governess to the six children of remarkable parents in an unusual home, where she mingled with statesmen and writers who were leaders in the anti-slavery cause.[5] This was the home of Dr. and Mrs. Gamaliel Bailey in Washington, D.C.—a spacious house on C Street which became known as "an American *salon*." Dr. Bailey, a man of wide culture and ardent sympathies, had shipped to China as a surgeon-sailor, and later, helped fight a cholera epidemic out West. Then, eager to cure the social ills of slavery, he turned from medicine to journalism. In 1836 he joined James G. Birney, who had run twice for President on the Liberty Party ticket, in editing the *Cincinnati Philanthropist*, the first anti-slavery paper in the West. After a year he became the proprietor and sole editor. Although seemingly frail, he was coura-geous, refusing to be intimidated even though his office was mobbed and he was assaulted three times. His response was the es-tablishment of a daily paper, the *Herald*.

In 1847 he moved to Washington to become editor of the *National Era*, official voice of the Organization of American and Foreign Anti-Slavery Societies (a post which he held until his death in 1859). It was not long before he again had to face an angry mob. In 1848 a northern schooner, the *Pearl*, was captured in the Chesapeake with some seventy fugitive slaves escaping from the District of Columbia aboard. The Captain and his mate, Drayton and Sayres, were lodged in jail. When Dr. Bailey wrote in their defense, a mob came to attack him. The authorities asked him to pledge the discontinu-ance of his paper so as to insure his own safety. He refused. Facing the mob, he managed to get them to listen to him. He was so elo-quent that one of the mob jumped up and spoke in his defense, con-vincing his fellows to disperse.

Mrs. Bailey (Margaret Lucy Shands of Virginia), though Southern born, shared her husband's views and was partner in his endeavors. Encouraged by the hospitality, charm, wit, and radical thinking to be found at the Baileys, political and literary Washington flocked to their home every Saturday night and at other times as well. From 1850 to 1853, during part of which time Nelly Tarr was in the house-hold, among the frequent visitors were some who were to aspire to or hold high office in the future: two Vice-Presidents of the United States, Hannibal Hamlin and Henry Wilson; a presidential candi-date, Horace Greeley; a Secretary of State, Henry Seward; and a Secretary of the Treasury, Salmon P. Chase. Among the Senators who came were Wade, Corwin, and Giddings. Representatives Durkee and Doty of Wisconsin and Horace Mann of Massachusetts joined the group, as did Preston King of New York, and former Governor Cleveland of Connecticut. A colorful critic of the scene was the self-exiled Polish Count Adam Gurowski. Foreign visitors included Frederika Bremer, the Swedish author, and Louis Kossuth, the Hungarian nationalist. From the South came Moncure D. Conway, a young man of a slave-owning family who had "seen the light," but who met his first Abolitionist when "Grace Greenwood"[6] greeted him at the Baileys.

Writers who contributed to the *National Era* often joined the group: Mrs. E. D. E. N. Southworth, "Gail Hamilton" (Mary Abigail Dodge), as well as two whose fame was to outlive their time—John Greenleaf Whittier and Harriet Beecher Stowe, whose *Uncle Tom's Cabin* first appeared in the *National Era*.

According to "Grace Greenwood," evenings at the Baileys resembled a French *salon*, except that they were "more cosmopolitan and had a purer moral atmosphere." Writing almost forty years later (in 1890) "Grace Greenwood" remembered Nelly Tarr:

> Dr. and Mrs. Bailey were alike in their love of beauty, wit, and good, old-fashioned fun. Each winter they had as guests a succession of clever women and relays of pretty girls. Mrs. Stowe liked to visit this snug harbor from which her great venture set forth on its endless circumnavigation. It is a "far cry" from this time to that, but there are those still living who will remember, and with a glow of pleasure, the merry, yet intellectual, young ladies who did so much to render the Bailey *salon* so charming; poetic Annie Phillips, ethereal Eva Ball, graceful Nellie Tarr, witty Lizzie Ellicott, and demure Marion Scoble, with her surprising dramatic talent.[7]

After Nelly left the Bailey household, Harriet Beecher Stowe remained her friend. Years later Nelly told an interviewer that Mrs. Stowe was "a lovely woman—modest and shrinking and extremely susceptible. *Uncle Tom's Cabin* was prompted by a horrible murder, accompanied by torture, on the Kentucky border line. It affected her strangely and she was forced to write it down to rid herself of its horror."[8]

Nelly's absorption in the anti-slavery movement was to continue after she left the Baileys to work on Garrison's *Liberator* which she probably joined in 1853. At the same time, she was involved in another movement of the time—Woman's Rights—and in another interesting home—that of Thomas and Paulina Wright Davis in Providence, Rhode Island. When or through whom the Tarr sisters became acquainted with Mrs. Davis and involved in the Woman's Rights movement is not known. Jeannie was an early supporter of *Una*, the paper which Mrs. Davis established in 1853. Her name appeared in the list of subscribers in the third issue: "J. Tarr—one dollar." Both sisters visited the Davises frequently. Thomas Davis wrote of Nelly years later, "She has at different times spent many months in my family. I may say I have summered her and wintered her, and claim to know her intimately, and taken all in all I think she has but few superiors."[9]

The Davises became warm friends of Nelly and Jeannie, and later of their husbands, William O'Connor and William Channing—and through them, of Walt Whitman. Nelly Tarr was as fortunate in her association with them as she had been with the Baileys, for they were bright, charming and devoted people. Paulina Wright Davis, born Paulina Kellogg, was rich (having married a wealthy Utica merchant, Francis Wright, when she was twenty); she was unconventional, keeping Wright as her middle name when after his death she married Thomas Davis; she was attractive, slight and fair; she was an affectionate wife, a good housekeeper, a diligent needlewoman, and yet had the vision and found the time to become one of the organizers and most effective leaders in the Woman's Rights movement and to edit the periodical *Una*. (William O'Connor's poem, "To Jeannie, with a copy of the Poems of Thomas Hood," appeared in the July 1855 issue of that periodical.) Mrs. Davis had been an innovator in education, as well: When at one period she lectured to women on phrenology and physiology, she used a manikin as an illustration, causing some of her shocked auditors to bolt from the room, others to faint in their places.

In 1850 Paulina Davis was the chief organizer of the first National Woman's Rights Convention in Worcester, Massachusetts. Among the signatories to the call to the Convention were leaders in the anti-slavery movement—Wendell Phillips, William H. Channing, Bronson Alcott, William Lloyd Garrison, and Gerrit Smith. Evidently they were against slavery or inferior status whether based on sex or color. Garrison's *Liberator* was among the anti-slavery papers which always supported Woman's Rights. It welcomed *Una* upon its first appearance.[10]

Nelly's activity in the Woman's Rights movement appears to have been more extensive than Jeannie's, for she held office and prepared a report for one convention. In June 1854 she was elected secretary of the New England Convention. Her name appeared in the account of the Convention given in the *Liberator*:

> The New England Woman's Rights Convention assembled in Boston on Friday, June 9. It was the day on which poor Burns (Anthony Burns, the fugitive slave) was consigned to hopeless bondage; and though very many friends of the Woman's Rights movement stayed to see his sad surrender, still, at an early hour, the hall was literally crowded with earnest men and women, whom a deep interest in the cause had drawn together.[11]

The meeting was called to order by Lucy Stone; among the officers chosen were President, Sarah H. Earle; Vice-Presidents (eleven in all) including Dr. Harriet K. Hunt of Massachusetts and the Rev. Jehiel Claflin of Vermont, and Secretaries—Sarah Pellet, Miss E. M. Tarr. William L. Garrison, editor of the *Liberator*, was one of those who participated in the discussion. The article concludes: "Committees were appointed, from each of the New England States, to circulate petitions for securing a change in the laws regulating the property of married women and limiting the right of suffrage to men."

Before a petition to change the laws could be drawn up, however, it was important to know just what they were. Therefore a study of the laws of several states was to be prepared for the Convention of 1855. Nelly was to report on the laws of New Hampshire, her native state. It was at that Convention that the names of Ellen Tarr and William O'Connor appeared together for the first time. Nelly's report, as well as that of Mrs. Ann E. Brown on Vermont and a letter from the Hon. Francis Gillette of Connecticut, were read to the Convention by the eloquent William D. O'Connor.

The practice of having reports read by someone who spoke well, rather than by their authors, was due to a suggestion that the astute Susan Anthony had made several years before. At the Convention held in Syracuse in 1852, after straining to hear some of the papers, she said: "Mrs. President, I move that hereafter the papers be given to someone to read who can be heard. It is an imposition on the audience to have to sit quietly through a long speech of which they cannot hear a word. We do not stand up here to be seen but to be heard."[12]

The Convention of 1855 had a star-studded speakers list. At the morning session there were Mrs. Caroline H. Dall, Mrs. Lucy Stone Blackwell, Dr. William F. Channing (who was to become Jeannie's husband), and Thomas Wentworth Higginson, who averred that the time would come when it would be disgrace to a man not to be a Woman's Rights man. Other speakers during the day and evening were Wendell Phillips, Susan B. Anthony, William L. Garrison, and Ralph Waldo Emerson.

In Nelly's report she cited the pertinent laws of New Hampshire in detail, concluding, "Thus we see, that while, in law, the 'husband and wife' are considered as *one person*, that one is the *husband*—the wife is legally a *nonentity.*"

Despite O'Connor's gift for oratory and readiness to read the reports, the self-confident Paulina Wright Davis read her own paper on the laws of Rhode Island. William had had experience as an orator at the Mercantile Library Association meetings. Years later Walt Whitman said of him:

> William is in the best sense an orator—is eminently passionate, pictorial, electric. I'd rather hear O'Connor argue for what I consider wrong than hear most other people argue for what I think right. He has charm, color, vigor: he possesses himself of the field: He pierces you to the vitals and you thank him for doing it. I think he learned all that in the anti-slavery school, whether for good or bad I do not know—learned it all there, in the clash of clashes— won his spurs in the struggles of the abolition period.[13]

In this Woman's Rights Convention, however, William did not have to persuade his hearers; he had only to enlighten them with information gathered by Ellen Tarr and others. The Convention was sympathetic and ready to act. In view of the reports, Mrs. Davis proposed that memorials be presented to every State Legislature in the land, asking for women the right of citizenship. Petitions were to be circulated everywhere for signatures.

William's eloquent delivery may have contributed to this decision—but he was less effective in trying to persuade his friend Curtis to espouse the cause of Woman's Rights. Curtis argued,

> The ends to be accomplished by movements and conventions etc. are not those which seem to me of the highest moment in respect to women. . . . Women must conquer by pure womanliness. The victory is nothing if it proceeds from anything else. And what is purely womanly is determined by the subtlest instinct of the finest men, for themselves. . . . I must say I prefer Florence Nightingale to Miss Ernestine Rose. Let a woman be a woman—and not make falls because she is not allowed to command fleets. If she must command a ship, let her get a ship and command it, not go to Syracuse and say she ought to have a command. The proof of a right to do a thing, is doing it. . . . [14]

Nelly and William, however, disagreed with Curtis. They continued their interest in Woman's Rights throughout their lives, both remaining friends of Paulina Wright Davis and Susan Anthony. William included Woman's Rights doctrine in his short stories and novel, and pleaded the cause in appeals such as his report to the government on "Salaries of Clerks."[15]

Seven months after the Woman's Rights Convention (January 1856) Nelly and William were engaged. Alike in ideals, but different in background, they were to have a close and loving union for about a third of the years of their marriage.

NOTES

1. Ellen's own preferred spelling of her nickname is "Nelly." In a letter to Traubel (6 September 1908) she wrote that "Nelly" was the spelling William and Walt used (Feinberg-LC).
   The year of their meeting is mentioned in Ellen M. Calder, "William Douglas O'Connor's Award to Bacon," *The Conservator* VIII, 7 March 1897.
2. The source of information for this chapter is largely in Mary Jane Channing's reminiscence, "Sixty Years Ago," *The Youth's Companion*, 13 December 1894. Additional description of childhood and youth is found in her unpublished memoir.
3. Mentioned by M. J. Channing in her unpublished memoir. Also in Sara M. Algeo, "Equal Suffrage Notes," Providence *Daily Journal*, 23 July 1911 (Brown).

4. Hannah Josephson, *The Golden Threads: New England's Mill Girls & Magnates* (New York: Duell, Sloan and Pearce, 1949). Information about Lowell also taken from M. J. Channing's memoir.

5. James W. Stone, Treasurer to Republican State Committee, to S. P. Chase, 13 May 1861 (General Services Administration).

6. Pen name of Sara Jane (Clarke) Lippincott (1823–1904).

7. Grace Greenwood, "An American Salon," *Cosmopolitan*, February 1890, pp. 437–47.

8. Algeo, *op. cit.*

9. Letter of recommendation from Thomas Davis, Providence, R.I., to William P. Fessenden, 27 February 1865 (General Services Administration).

10. *Liberator*, 1 April 1853. *Una*, a woman suffrage periodical first published in Providence, R. I. in 1853; later printed in Boston where Caroline Dall became associate editor. The magazine lasted three years; subscription price: one dollar per annum in advance. *History of Woman Suffrage*, ed. Elizabeth Cady Stanton, Susan B. Anthony, and Matilda Joslyn Gage (New York: Fowler & Wells, 1881), vol. 1.

11. *Liberator*, 16 June 1854.

12. Katherine Anthony, *Susan B. Anthony: Her Personal History and Her Era* (Garden City, N.Y.: Doubleday & Co., Inc., 1954), p. 107.

13. *Camden*, 2: 11–12.

14. GWC to WDO'C, 7 September 1855 (Brown).

15. A memorial to the Congress, signed "Wm. D. O'Connor, secretary." Sent by William F. Channing to Thomas Davis (General Services Administration).

CHAPTER V

In Defense Of
Miss Delia Bacon's Theory

FROM 1856 until his death in 1889, O'Connor defended the Baconian theory of the authorship of Shakespeare's plays. The zeal and dedication with which O'Connor had written and acted for social justice and for the rescue of fugitive slaves, and which he was later to lavish on Walt Whitman's poetry, he also exercised on behalf of the proponents of the Baconian theory. Delia Bacon's essay, "William Shakespeare and His Plays: An Inquiry Concerning Them" in *Putnam's Monthly Magazine*,[1] was probably not O'Connor's first exposure to the theory, for Nelly later stated that he was a Baconian when they first met. In her article Miss Bacon expounded what came to be known as the Baconian theory (not because of Miss Delia but because of Sir Francis). She was the first American to claim that the plays attributed to Shakespeare could not have been written by the unschooled man from Stratford, but were the work of Sir Francis Bacon, Lord Verulam, or of a group of courtiers and wits under his leadership. Shakespeare, unschooled, untraveled, with little or no experience at court, a poacher, a money-lender—how could this man have acquired the knowledge which was the basis for the richly brocaded histories, the understanding of the subtleties of character of noble minds and of the varied philosophies reflected in the plays? How could he have expressed these in the imagery and with the grace of the Shakespearean writings? Even his will betrayed him: Careful to dispose of even his second-best bed (to his wife), he left not a single book to anybody. Since books were a rare and precious commodity, this indicated that he had not possessed any.

Some years later O'Connor wrote to Burroughs, "I will find it easier to believe that Barnum wrote Emerson's Essays than that the Stratford money-lender wrote Lear,"[2] and to Walt Whitman, ". . . what paralyzes all Shakespeare criticism . . . is the obstinate consideration of the work with that Stratford chucklehead and his chucklehead biography."[3]

O'Connor, who evidently believed that beauty was a sign of virtue, thought that even the contrast in the appearance of the two men was significant. The tinted Stratford bust shows "a fat fellow . . . blobber-cheeked, . . . a ten-per-center's forehead. . . . How different from the appearance of Sir Francis Bacon! . . . The broad tranquil brow, the mane of soft dark hair, the sweet jesting mouth and living eyes, the pure May bloom. . . ." What's more, Bacon's intellect, knowledge, and life fit him for the authorship of the Shakespearean writings, since he had lived abroad, ". . . been the companion and counselor of princes . . . seen the ways and learned the language of actors, sailors, gypsies, tinkers, grooms, as well . . . felt the whips and scorns of time. . . ."[4]

The true authorship of the plays was clear to the Baconians. Nevertheless, they had to prove two propositions: that Shakespeare could not have written the plays, and that Bacon did (either alone or as the guiding spirit of a group of authors). In order to find proof, the Baconians searched the plays for parallels between them and Bacon's published and unpublished works, and for clues, concealed within the plays or elsewhere, meant to be found by scholars of a later age. The first person to engage in this search was Delia Bacon.

Delia Salter Bacon was thirty-nine years old when she came to Boston to lecture. Born in Tallmadge, Ohio, on February 2, 1811, the daughter of Reverend David Bacon, one of the early Western missionaries, she was educated in the East, for a time at Miss Catherine Beecher's school in Hartford, Connecticut, where Catherine's younger sister, Harriet (later Mrs. Stowe) was a schoolmate.[5]

Delia Bacon was a woman of intellect and spirit. When not quite sixteen she was headmistress of a small school of her own in Southington, Connecticut. Later she headed schools in Perth Amboy, New Jersey, and Jamaica, Long Island. Though none of the schools lasted long, they exhibited remarkable ambition in one so young.

When she was only twenty years old, her short story, "Love's Martyr," won a hundred dollars offered by the *Philadelphia Saturday Evening Post* in a contest in which Edgar Allan Poe was an unsuccessful competitor. At about this time her book of short stories, *Tales of the Puritans*,[6] was published.

Before coming to Boston in 1850, she had achieved a reputation for scholarship and brilliance. Unfortunately she had also become the subject of scandal. She had invited a clergyman, Alexander MacWhorter, younger than herself, to visit her in her private parlor. Although he resided in the same boardinghouse, they had never been properly introduced. He showed her note of invitation to friends, and the gossip started. Delia and the young clergyman continued to see each other, but eventually the friendship ended—which compounded the scandal. Delia's reputation was so sullied that Catherine Beecher, her former teacher, was moved to write a book in her defense.[7] The author named no names, but those in the know were aware that the protagonists were Delia Bacon and Alexander MacWhorter.

At about the time of publication, Delia Bacon came to Boston, where she stayed until April 1851, lecturing before groups of women, fluently, without notes but with the aid of maps, charts, models and pictures. One of her friends who attended the lectures wrote of her, "I used to be reminded by her of Raphael's sibyls, and she often spoke like an oracle. She and a few of her class would often stay after the lesson and take tea with me, and then she would talk delightfully for the rest of the evening."[8]

Delia Bacon spent the summer of 1852 in England. After returning to New York and spending some time there, in 1853 she went to reside in England, to seek confirmation of her theory and to write a book about it. She was to remain there for five years, first at St. Albans, where Lord Bacon had lived when (as she supposed) he had written the plays, then at London, and finally at Stratford-on-Avon.

Delia Bacon had sent four chapters of a projected book to Emerson, who, after failing to interest a book publisher in them, sent them to *Putnam's Monthly*. All were accepted and the first, entitled "William Shakespeare and His Plays: An Inquiry Concerning Them," appeared on January 1, 1856, the issue[9] which contained as its first story O'Connor's "The Ghost." (*Putnam's* paid Delia Bacon $5 per page—its highest rate.) In her article, Delia Bacon advances the theory that the plays were the work of a group of "University wits." Although she does not name them she hints at Raleigh and Sidney, and shows by a reference to *The New Philosophy* that Bacon was the leader of the group. Hamlet's inserted speeches in the players' scene are to her an allegory of the production of the plays; in them she sees that the danger of censorship of radical political ideas caused the real authors to hide behind the name of the actor William Shakespeare.[10]

When *Putnam's* failed to publish the other chapters, some said the next one, scheduled for February publication, had been withdrawn at the request of friends of Delia Bacon, but O'Connor placed the blame on the Shakespearean scholar, Richard Grant White, who much later revealed his share in the matter. O'Connor may have heard about his intervention from his friend George William Curtis, who was one of the editors of *Putnam's Monthly* at the time. The editor of *Putnam's Monthly* later explained to Delia's nephew Theodore Bacon, that after setting the second article in type (with two more to follow), the editors decided that publication in book form would be more appropriate and that they would not interfere with the author's submitting it to Phillips and Sampson (a suggestion made earlier by Emerson) for publication as a book. The manuscripts were to be returned to Emerson. He, however, felt that after the publication of the first article in a periodical, he could not offer it again to Phillips and Sampson.[11] O'Connor was convinced that the cessation of publication left Miss Bacon "at the greatest disadvantage before the public, her introductory article having been just enough to arouse virulent opposition, without satisfying awakened curiosity."[12]

Another blow soon followed. Delia Bacon had written to Emerson, asking him to send the rejected manuscripts to her in England. Sophia Ripley was to take the manuscripts from William Emerson to deliver to his brother, Ralph Waldo Emerson. Before she reached the ferry from Staten Island to New York City, the manuscripts were lost under peculiar circumstances. Emerson[13] in a letter to Theodore Bacon and O'Connor[14] in a letter to Ignatius Donnelly differ in some details, but in the main their versions tally. Whether accident or plot, the manuscript was lost, and poor Delia had neither her entire manuscript, a publisher, nor enough money to live on. Nevertheless, she stayed on in England, living in simple lodgings, often unable to afford a fire, and writing while sitting up in bed for warmth.[15]

Delia Bacon's book, entitled *The Philosophy of the Plays of Shakespeare Unfolded*, was finally published in 1857 by Groombridge and Sons in England and Ticknor and Fields in Boston. Hawthorne had found the publisher, contributed 238 pounds of his own money for the expense of printing, and provided a preface in which he praised the author without supporting her theory. Disappointed by the coolness of his preface, Delia Bacon attacked him in letters which seemed to show a state of irrationality. Although Hawthorne said he never regretted having helped her, he wrote ruefully to Ticknor, whom he had persuaded to publish her book in America, "I never will be kind to anybody again as long as I live."[16]

After completing her book, Delia Bacon left London for Stratford-on-Avon, still seeking to penetrate the mystery. The strange epitaph on Shakespeare's tomb seemed to indicate to her that the secret of the authorship of the plays lay buried there. Otherwise why should he have written:

> Good Frend for Iesus sake Forebeare
> To digg the dust enclosed heare
> Blest be ye man y^t spares thes stones
> And curst be he y^t moves my bones.

Delia Bacon, ready to challenge the curse, but refused permission to open the tomb by the authorities at Stratford, haunted the graveyard and church. She never found the secret.

She could find no solace in the reviews of her book—all unfavorable.[17] "If any American ever wrote a word in her behalf," wrote Hawthorne, "Miss Bacon never knew it, nor did I. Our journalists at once republished some of the most brutal vituperations of the English press, thus pelting their poor countrywoman with stolen mud, without even waiting to hear whether the ignominy was deserved. . . . "[18] Neither Hawthorne nor Delia Bacon knew at that time of O'Connor's support of Delia Bacon's theory and admiration of her book. When her book appeared, O'Connor was an editor of the *Philadelphia Saturday Evening Post*, in which he published a favorable review on April 11, 1857. He returned to "The Shakespeare Question" on May 30 of the same year and wrote on "Sir Walter Raleigh" on March 27, 1858.[19] A friend of O'Connor's (unnamed) wrote to Ignatius Donnelly that O'Connor had championed Delia Bacon's cause in "uncompromising letters and editorials" in several periodicals at the time,[20] but only those in the *Saturday Evening Post* are known.

No word of praise came from Emerson. Although he had tried to place her book with publishers, and had taken an interest in the *Putnam's* article and the lost manuscripts, he had always urged Delia Bacon to provide proof of her theory. Instead she continued to present exposition and analysis without proof. When she wrote to him that her book was finished, Emerson greeted the completion with the same phrase he had used a month earlier in his famous letter to Walt Whitman, "I give you joy in the good news you send me of the ending of your work. What if it is only the beginning of another, it is also the pledge of the power to do it. . . . "[21] By 1857 Emerson's enthusiasm had waned. He wrote to a friend in Italy:

> Italy cannot excel the banks of glory which sun and mist paint in these very days on the forest by lake and river. But the muses are as reticent as Nature is flamboyant, and no fireeyed child has yet been born. . . . Our wild Whitman, with real inspiration, but choked with Titanic abdomen, and Delia Bacon, with genius, but mad, and clinging like a tortoise to English soil, are the sole producers that America has yielded in ten years. Is all the granite and forest and prairie and superfoetation of millions to know no richer results?[22]

Disappointed by the adverse criticisms in the press, foiled in her attempt to get permission to search Shakespeare's tomb, worn out by poverty and ill health, Delia Bacon began to behave strangely. Not long after her book appeared, the Mayor of Stratford-on-Avon, Dr. David Rice, a physician, wrote to Hawthorne that an American lady who had recently published a "Shakespeare book" was afflicted with insanity.[23] Delia Bacon's nephew, Marcus Hodges, came for her and took her to a sanitorium near Hartford, Connecticut, where she died in September 1859, at the age of forty-eight.

Hawthorne, sympathetic to Delia Bacon as a forlorn and half-mad lady, confessed that he had never read her book:

I believe that it has been the fate of this remarkable book never to have had more than a single reader. . . . But since my return to America, a young man of genius and enthusiasm has assured me that he has positively read the book from beginning to end, and is completely a convert to its doctrines. . . . [24]

The "single reader" was William Douglas O'Connor. In his *Hamlet's Note-Book* (1886) O'Connor explained why he had not published Delia Bacon's letters:

But for some who are dead and cannot answer for themselves, and some who are living and deserve consideration, I would publish the letters which Hawthorne gave me, that I might show the further distresses heaped upon her in a far country, where she still strove to recover ground, and toiled at her book, often without food or fire. [25]

O'Connor later sent these letters to Theodore Bacon. [26] Although he never wrote a book about Delia Bacon, O'Connor not only reviewed her book in the *Saturday Evening Post* but also tried to place her in the position he felt due her in his novel *Harrington: A Story of True Love*, published in 1860. [27] In the novel, O'Connor created a hero in his own image—John Harrington—who expressed O'Connor's views on Abolition, Woman's Rights, the destiny of the United States, as well as the authorship of Shakespeare's plays. John Harrington is an admirer of Lord Bacon, whose bust stands in his study. He alludes to Bacon when he is talking to his friend Wentworth, an artist, about the function of art:

No man can be a great painter, sculptor, composer, poet, whose heart is not deeply and firmly engaged in the life of his own time. It is the lack of interest and participation in human affairs which makes our modern artists mere imitators and colorists, and so much of modern art weak and pallid—a mere watery reflection of old models and forms of beauty.

Harrington goes on to say that Shakespeare was not engaged in the life of his time. It was Bacon who wanted a work "which is a science of man" and achieved it in the Shakespearean drama. [28]

In a note appended to *Harrington*, O'Connor speaks in his own

name about Delia Bacon's *The Philosophy of the Plays of Shake-*
speare Unfolded:

> I wish it were in my power to do even the smallest justice to that
> mighty and eloquent volume, whose masterly comprehension
> and insight, though they could not save it from being trampled
> upon by the brutal vision of the English press, yet lift it to the
> dignity, whatever may be its faults, of being the best work ever
> composed upon the Baconian or Shakespearean writings.[29]

O'Connor was criticized—even by an admirer—for including the
Baconian theory in *Harrington*. Robert Carter, editor of *The New*
American Cyclopedia, wrote to O'Connor that he did not like "Miss
Bacon's absurd vagary about Shakespeare," and although it was too
strongly interwoven in the book to excise it, he suggested that O'Con-
nor remove the note about Delia Bacon from the end of the book.[30]

It was some years after the publication of *Harrington* that O'Connor mentioned Delia Bacon again in print. In *The Good Gray Poet*, a
defense of Walt Whitman published in 1866, O'Connor names "Delia Bacon's splendid sibyllic book on Shakespeare" among the great
works of American literature.[31] Over the next two decades he
would, however, continue to make contributions to the debate she
started. These were acknowledged in Wyman's *Bibliography of the*
Bacon-Shakespeare Controversy, which included a portrait of
O'Connor as well as some remarks about him.[32] Further recognition
came when O'Connor was invited to join the Baconian Society in
England and to donate his writings on Bacon to the Shakespeare
Memorial Library at Stratford-on-Avon.[33]

Even in the last years of his life, despite a crippling illness and the
depression brought on by his daughter's death, O'Connor twice took
up battle in the Baconian cause. In 1883 he defended Constance Fea-
ron Pott's edition of *The Promus of Formularies and Elegancies* by
Francis Bacon.[34] Mrs. Pott, an Englishwoman, was a painstaking
scholar for whom Bacon's writings were so much a part of her daily
life that she kept a volume of his *Essays* (which she had requested as
a wedding present) on the table near which she sat when she had her
afternoon tea.

> As time went on, and in my happy little country home annual
> babies were added to the household, they were always with me at

this hour. . . . While they played and rolled about (five under six years of age), I could not do much, but I could catch a few refreshing ideas from my favorite author.[35]

O'Connor's *Hamlet's Note-Book* was written in response to a strong attack on the Englishwoman's work and on Baconianism by Richard Grant White, the Shakespearean scholar who had done so much to hurt Delia Bacon's book more than twenty-five years earlier.[36] Originally prepared for a magazine article titled "A Shakespeare Reviewer Reviewed," O'Connor's words were intended, as he wrote Whitman, "to take White's hide off."[37] The article remained unpublished—partly because the journal accepting it suspended publication, partly in deference to White's death in 1885. It emerged finally—in revised, book form as *Hamlet's Note-Book*—only because O'Connor realized that his rebuttal deserved the light of print when the attack on Mrs. Pott appeared in a posthumous collection of White's essays. Publisher after publisher had rejected the monograph. As O'Connor acknowledged in a letter to Whitman, "The last publisher to whom I offered it (Coombs, of New York) although I proposed to pay the cost of manufacture, wrote in reply that he would undertake it, push it with energy, and do everything for it in his power, if I would only consent that his imprint should not appear on the title page!!!"[38] In the same letter O'Connor says that Houghton had accepted *Hamlet's Note-Book* for publication.[39]

Critics did not take kindly to *Hamlet's Note-Book*, a book that pilloried their tribe. It is an uneven book—at times deft and incisive, at times blunt and heavy-handed. Burroughs was not at all enthusiastic, and Whitman, on receiving a copy, wrote O'Connor briefly and in general terms that he had been "looking it over the last hour."[40] O'Connor did not know that the poet had given it only that hour's cursory reading, confiding to Horace Traubel:

> I have very little faculty or liking for books which require charts, comparisons, references—close application—the observance of rules of logic: in the immortal words Swinton addressed to me in peevish humor: I have a damned ill-regulated mind.[41]

But there was balm for the wounds Burroughs inflicted in his criticism when Whitman sent O'Connor his article, "What Lurks Behind

Shakespeare's Historical Plays," published in *The Critic* on September 27, 1884. In it Whitman paid tribute to O'Connor and hinted at some connection between Bacon and the Shakespearean plays.

As usual, O'Connor himself was not completely satisfied with his work, despite some admiring letters from George William Curtis, Theodore Bacon, and the editor of *The Manhattan Magazine*, the last astonishing O'Connor for being "so unqualified in panegyric."[42] But as he explained to Bucke, he had first had to compress his material because it was meant to be a magazine article, and then to expand it into a book when he "was under nervous prostration and had no more head than St. Anthony when he carried his under his arm."[43]

In 1889 he again rallied to the defense of a Baconian—Ignatius Donnelly. Donnelly, like O'Connor the son of an Irish immigrant, had achieved popularity with the publication of two novels of the genus that has come to be known as science fiction. This versatile and complex man was journalist, editor, writer, and politician. In the course of his political career, changing parties but not convictions, he attained the offices of Lieutenant Governor of Minnesota, state senator, and congressman; he was the Populist candidate for the vice-presidency of the United States at the time of his death in 1901.

Donnelly's third book, *The Great Cryptogram*, purporting to demonstrate the true authorship of Shakespeare's plays, received a spate of harsh reviews. O'Connor was moved to defend the book not only because of his commitment to the Baconian theory but also because of his loyalty to Donnelly who had corresponded with him after seeing his name in Wyman's *Bibliography*. *The Great Cryptogram* had included a portrait and a flattering account of O'Connor.

In *Mr. Donnelly's Reviewers* O'Connor criticizes the

> gangs of ignorant and impudent men, self-styled reviewers who intercept a work on its way to the public. It would be difficult to name any cardinal book that upon its appearance was not belittled, censured or condemned by the literary authorities of the periodicals. . . . It is true that the intelligent critics who disparaged and reviled the entire galaxy, including Keats, Shelley, Coleridge, Wordsworth and Byron, closed up with astonishing unanimity in roaring eulogy on Alexander Smith, who certainly was a memorable geyser of splendid metaphors, but is now almost forgotten.[44]

Reviewers, he notes scornfully, had similarly attacked the works of Victor Hugo, George Sand, Darwin, as well as Buckle's *History of Civilization*, on all of which O'Connor comments eloquently. As for the poetry of Walt Whitman, he points out with chagrin that "the current criticism was . . . until recently, nothing but a storm of brutal pasquinades." In fact, he makes it clear, "No variety of books has escaped the injury of this fool system, which sets mediocrity or malignity to arbitrate over talent or genius."[45]

Turning to *The Great Cryptogram* as a case in point, O'Connor proceeds to cite the corroborative opinions of mathematicians, before answering the adverse critics. The deft parry and stunning rhetoric of *The Good Gray Poet* are missing here. A tired O'Connor indulges in statements like "Really the *non-sequitur* here is so gross as to suggest the *non compos*" about Clapp, his old-time friend. And of another reviewer, O'Connor was reminded of "the sonorous bell invented by a man in Pennsylvania, composed of a sheep's trotter hung in an old felt hat."[46]

He ends with what was a lifetime dream—by now a deathbed wish—that there were a critical journal which could be "an arena for discussion in which all that can be uttered, on every side of a theme, shall be expressed on the single condition of proper literary ability. . . . Such a journal is demanded by the democratic genius of this country."[47]

This last effort in defense of Bacon, *Mr. Donnelly's Reviewers*, was not published until after its author's death.

NOTES

1. Ellen M. O'Connor Calder, "William Douglas O'Connor's Award to Bacon," *The Conservator* VIII, 7 March 1897.
2. WDO'C to Burroughs, 8 August 1884 (Barrus collection).
3. WDO'C to WW, 1 April 1883 (Feinberg-LC).
4. *Hamlet's Note-Book*, p. 72. Despite O'Connor's opinion of Shakespeare's appearance as revealed in the bust, he was rather pleased that he was said to resemble the Chandos portrait of the bard. This resemblance was so noticeable that once when O'Connor entered a theatre, a monologist, improvising as O'Connor removed his hat, said, "With hat off he doth appear in brow and beard a Billy Shakespeare!" Piatt to Elliott, December 1911 (LC). Piatt attributes this anecdote to Stedman, who was present. Grace Channing, "Unfinished Account" (Chamberlin).
5. In addition to sources acknowledged separately, material on Delia Bacon's life

was found in Theodore Bacon, *Delia Bacon, A Biographical Sketch* (Boston: Houghton Mifflin Company, 1888) and Vivian C. Hopkins, *Prodigal Puritan: A Life of Delia Bacon* (Cambridge, Mass.: The Belknap Press of Harvard University, 1959).

6. Delia Bacon, *Tales of the Puritans* (New Haven, Connecticut: H. Maltby, 1831).
7. Catherine Beecher, *Truth Stranger Than Fiction: A Narrative of Recent Trans-actions Involving Inquiries in Regard to the Principles of Honor, Truth, and Justice Which Obtain in a Distinguished American University* (New York City: Mark H. Newman & Co., Booksellers, No. 199 Broadway, 1850).
8. Mrs. John (Eliza) Farrar, *Recollections of Seventy Years* (Boston: Ticknor and Fields, 1866), p. 319.
9. The editors of *Putnam's* prefaced the article with a disclaimer: "In commencing the publication of these bold, original, and most ingenious and interesting speculations upon the real authorship of Shakespeare's plays, it is proper for the editor . . . in disclaiming all responsibility for their startling point of view . . . to say that they are the result of long and conscientious investigation on the part of the learned and eloquent scholar, their author, and that the editor has reason to hope that they will be continued through some future numbers of the magazine."
10. Hopkins, *op. cit.*, p. 196.
11. Theodore Bacon, *op. cit.*, chap. X, *passim*.
12. *Hamlet's Note-Book*, p. 11.
13. Emerson to Delia Bacon, 23 June 1856 in Theodore Bacon, *op. cit.*, pp. 191–95.
14. WDO'C to Donnelly, 20 October 1887. Ignatius Donnelly, *The Great Crypto-gram: Francis Bacon's Cipher in the So-Called Shakespeare Plays* (Chicago: R. S. Peale & Company, 1888), p. 913f.
15. Mrs. John Farrar in Donnelly, *op. cit.*, p. 908.
16. Mark Van Doren, *Nathaniel Hawthorne*, The American Men of Letters Series (New York: William Sloane Associates, 1949), p. 213.
17. These appeared in *The Atheneum, The National Review, Punch*, and *The Leader* (18 April 1857); the last named survived among her papers.
18. Nathaniel Hawthorne, "Recollections of a Gifted Woman," *Our Old Home: A Series of English Sketches* (Boston: Ticknor and Fields, 1863), p. 136.
19. David Goodale called my attention to these articles.
20. Donnelly, *op. cit.*, 925.
21. Emerson to Delia Bacon, 5 August 1855 in Theodore Bacon, *op. cit.*, p. 83.
22. Emerson to Caroline Sturgis Tappan, 13 October 1857, in Ralph Rusk, *Letters of Ralph Waldo Emerson*, vol. V, pp. 86–87. See Florence B. Freedman, "Emerson Giving Joy: Summer of 1855," *Walt Whitman Review* 21:162–63 (December 1975).
23. Hawthorne, *op. cit.*, p. 135.
24. *Ibid.*, p. 137.
25. *Hamlet's Note-Book*, p. 11.
26. Theodore Bacon, *op. cit.*, note, p. 299.
27. *Harrington*. See "Note" at end.
28. *Ibid.*, pp. 215, 221.
29. *Ibid.*, p. 557f.
30. Robert Carter to WDO'C, 27 November 1860 (Feinberg-LC).
31. *The Good Gray Poet*, p. 42f.
32. William Henry Wyman, *A Bibliography of the Bacon-Shakespeare Contro-versy, with Notes and Extracts* (Cincinnati, Ohio: Cox & Co., 1882). Wyman

lists *Harrington* and the "Introductory Letter" to *The Good Gray Poet* in Richard Maurice Bucke, *Walt Whitman* (Philadelphia: David McKay, 1883).

33. James Gibson to WDO'C, 11 August 1884 (Feinberg-LC).
34. *The Promus of Formularies and Elegancies (Being Private Notes, circ. 1594, Hitherto Unpublished)* by Francis Bacon. Illustrated and elucidated by passages from Shakespeare. By Mrs. Henry Pott, with preface by E. A. Abbott, D.D., Headmaster of the City of London School (London: Longmans, Green & Co., 1883).
35. Donnelly, *op. cit.*, p. 932.
36. White's article, "The Bacon-Shakespeare Craze," appeared in the *Atlantic Monthly*, April 1883.
37. WDO'C to WW, 12 July 1883 (Feinberg-LC).
38. WDO'C to WW, 23 March 1886, *Camden*, 4: 414.
39. It appeared as a 78-page, hard-covered book, priced at one dollar; listed opposite the title page were two other books on the same theme published by Houghton.
40. WW to WDO'C, 17 April 1886, *Correspondence*, IV:26.
41. *Camden*, 2: 2.
42. WDO'C to WW, 7 March 1884 (Syracuse).
43. WDO'C to Bucke, 14 September 1885 (Feinberg-LC).
44. *Mr. Donnelly's Reviewers*, pp. 8, 9.
45. *Ibid.*, p. 11.
46. *Ibid.*, p. 61.
47. *Ibid.*, p. 101.

CHAPTER VI

Philadelphia: Pegasus Is Harnessed

IN JANUARY 1856, when *Putnam's* published Delia Bacon's article and O'Connor's story "The Ghost," William and Nelly were engaged.[1] This happy event was to separate him from his multi-faceted life in Boston—the lively companionship of the *Carpet Bag* Bohemians, the serious intellectual pursuits of the Mercantile Library Association, the dynamic activism of the Abolitionists, and even the creative world of the poet and short-story writer. He was to publish no more poems or short stories for the next four years. In the letter in which he told Curtis of his engagement, he asked about steady employment. Curtis answered, congratulating him upon his "happiness which I had long supposed," adding, "I am sorry to hear of the cares you mention," and warning him that "newspaper life is unmitigated slavery."[2]

William had been prophetic in his description of the fate of the poet in "The Ghost": The desire to become a "family man" forced him to express his love not in poetry or fiction, but in the search for a steady job.

O'Connor's next contribution to the *Mercantile Library Reporter* was to be his last. It was the first part of an essay on "Chivalry" in March 1856. In this essay he contradicts Edmund Burke's statement that the age of chivalry had gone, by saying that there never was an *age* of chivalry. There was an ideal of chivalry held by some during the brutal years of the age of feudalism. The chivalric order "was the virtue, valor, and benevolence of certain men, organized for the common good." Chivalry itself comprised "the same qualities unorganized." O'Connor ends the essay with some questions which he promises to answer in the next number of the magazine. Before that issue was to appear, however, O'Connor had left Boston to become an editor of the Philadelphia *Saturday Evening Post*,[3] where an unsigned article on Chivalry appeared on October 11, 1856.

The April number of the *Mercantile Library Reporter* contained a farewell to O'Connor by E. W. Foster:

> By the late departure of this gentleman for Philadelphia, whither he goes to assume the editorship of the Saturday Evening Post, the Mercantile Library Association loses one of its ablest and most talented members. . . . In the exercises of debate, Mr. O'Connor's abilities have been apparent in the ease and readiness of his extemporary speaking, and though he has been a prominent actor in many of the exciting debates connected with the Association, he has ever treated his adversaries with candor and fairness, and with that courtesy which noble merit unconsciously awards to an opponent.

The writer goes on to extol O'Connor's excellence as a writer, including the fact that he had contributed poems to the *Providence Daily Journal* "which attracted the notice of Mr. Longfellow, and which he warmly commended."

William's last service to the Mercantile Library Association was a lecture on "Heroism" on April 16. He exercised that quality soon after by leaving for Philadelphia. Pegasus, for the time being, was quite willing to be harnessed to the cart.

William O'Connor spent the six months from April to October 1856 alone in Philadelphia working to save enough money to establish a home for his bride-to-be. On October 22 they were married in Boston;[4] Nelly was then twenty-six and William twenty-four. Nothing is known of the ceremony, but it is tempting to believe that it might have resembled in some way the simple marriage ceremony of the hero and heroine in O'Connor's novel *Harrington*, written almost four years later—a novel which he later said had some autobiographical elements.

In the novel when the hero and heroine, Muriel Eastman and John

Harrington, are planning their "splendid" wedding, friends tease John, saying that he will undoubtedly be "married in his ordinary clothes, without a rag of a white kid glove, or an adornment of any kind whatever, or wedding cake, or cards, or guests, or anything."[5]

John responds seriously, saying that he would like a plain ceremony: "Marriage to me is so private and spiritual a sacrament that it seems a sort of profanation to make it public—or surround it with factitious embellishments." Muriel, Harrington's fiancée, surprises him by saying that they will be married in her parlor that very day, with no special arrangements or dress. She has invited Theodore Parker to marry them. Harrington is pleased. "If I am to have any minister to marry me, let it be Mr. Parker, it will be an added consecration." Muriel agrees with his wish for simplicity, saying that if she were in Pennsylvania she would choose "to stand up with John before our friends, avowing our love in the sweet and beautiful Quaker fashion, and sparing every other rite beside."

James Freeman Clarke, who performed the ceremony of the marriage of Nelly and William, was as fine a choice for them as Theodore Parker was for the characters in the novel. His earlier history was probably well known to them. After graduation from Harvard, he served as minister in Louisville, Kentucky, where he edited the *Western Messenger*, to which Emerson and Channing contributed. When he returned to Boston in 1841, he founded the Unitarian "Church of the Disciples." He also was an occasional member of the "Transcendental Club" which met at Emerson's home. Clarke had to leave Boston because of ill health. When he returned in 1854 he became deeply involved in the Woman's Rights and Abolition movements. In his later years he wrote an account of this period in his book, *Anti-Slavery Days.*[6]

Clarke may have known Nelly even before 1854, for he had visited the home of Dr. Gamaliel Bailey in the winter of 1851 when Nelly was there. In his autobiography he mentions some of the famous people whom he met there, among them Seward, Giddings, Chase, Hale, Julian, Slade, and Horace Mann. Unlike "Grace Greenwood," however, he does not say anything about the charming young ladies in the Bailey household.

Whether or not the O'Connors' marriage ceremony resembled the Harringtons', the Reverend James Freeman Clarke's blessing must have been for Nelly and William what Parker's was for their fictional counterparts—"an added consecration."

After the marriage, Nelly joined William in Philadelphia, where they were to spend almost five years, living at first at 1108 Wood Street and later at 2015 Cherry Street. Nelly was happy; her "inborn New England deep-rooted love of a stationary abiding place"[7] was satisfied in the quaint and quiet city of Philadelphia. Nelly loved housekeeping and felt that now she could use the domestic skills she had learned in her childhood in her own home, for the comfort of her handsome husband, and later for their two children, Jean, born in March 1858, and Philip, born in February 1860.

Almost thirty years later Nelly remembered Philadelphia as the place where she had been best able to exercise her domestic talents. Six months after William's death in 1889, she wrote to Walt Whitman: ". . . you know I did not live in Philadelphia five years for nothing! I have a great love of good housekeeping, care *too much*, I fear, for the trifles."[8]

William was a good husband and an adoring father—but he hated being in Philadelphia and working on the *Saturday Evening Post*. In Philadelphia, he complained, "there is no society or mental aliment for me."[9] He missed the companionship of those roistering "spirits of the morning sort," the *Carpet Bag* Bohemians, and that of the high-minded and heroic Abolitionists. There were, of course, occasional visits from friends such as George Curtis, who came to see the O'Connors when lecturing in Philadelphia.[10] Benjamin P. Shillaber, however, stirred by O'Connor's reminiscence of him in the *Post*, called only to find him away for the day.[11]

Another old friend who came to Philadelphia offered both intellectual companionship and a cause to be defended. On October 5, 1858, William Francis Channing married Nelly's sister Mary Jane (Jeannie). The newlyweds probably came to Philadelphia not only to be with their relatives, but also to escape the scandal their marriage had caused, for William had divorced his first wife on the grounds of incompatibility—a reason for divorce not recognized in Massachusetts.

William Francis Channing, twelve years O'Connor's senior, was the only son of the Reverend William Ellery Channing, "the impassioned little Saint who was the conscience of New England."[12] Although a doctor of medicine (having received the M.D. degree at the University of Pennsylvania in 1844) William devoted himself to science and invention. At twenty-one he assisted in the first geological survey of New Hampshire, and three years after he had become a physician, assisted in a similar survey of the copper region of Lake Superior. There were two instances of medical practice recorded, for it was Channing who dressed the wounds of his cousin, Thomas Wentworth Higginson, after the abortive attack on the Boston Courthouse in the attempt to rescue the escaped slave, Anthony Burns. He also was said to have treated Nelly and Jeannie for smallpox. As an inventor, Channing was known for the electric fire alarm, which he presented as a gift to the City of Boston. In 1865 he patented a ship railway for the cross-country transport of ships and in 1877 invented a portable electro-magnetic telegraph.

He had married Susan Burdick when in his twenties, and after some years of marriage and two children (one of whom died) he felt his marriage to be a failure and wished to terminate it by divorce. The laws of Massachusetts, however, did not permit divorce on the grounds of incompatibility. He therefore became a citizen of Indiana, where the divorce laws were more liberal, and some time later married Jeannie Tarr. At this time he was thirty-eight and she thirty. When he and Jeannie met is not known, but they were friends in 1855 when he lent her the first edition of *Leaves of Grass*.

Evidently the gossip attending William Channing's divorce and his marriage to Jeannie did not soon die down. More than three months after the marriage an editorial appeared in a Boston newspaper to which Dr. Channing felt he had to reply. His answer appeared in the *Boston Atlas and Bee* some months later—on November 11, 1859 when he and his wife were about to leave for the West Indies. The editorial had stated that Dr. Channing was "so far bewildered in the mazes of Spiritualism as to have abandoned his wife to find a spiritual affinity in another young lady" and that he had gone to Indiana to obtain a divorce so as to marry his new affinity. To this Channing replied that he is not a "Spiritualist" though he respects "the good and thoughtful" persons who are, and affirms: "My separation from my wife took place more than five years ago, from causes wholly confined to the union itself. No human being, either man or woman, interfered, or contributed in any way to bring about this result."

He goes on to explain that he went to Indiana because he found "that the laws of Massachusetts were oppressive in what was to me a matter of conscience." He felt that in Massachusetts marriage was a matter of physical union alone. Indiana, on the other hand, recognized that "it is the duty and interest of Society to release the parties to a permanently discordant marriage." Channing goes on to discuss marriage and divorce as matters of principle, and concludes after a column and a half: "I have acted from a conviction of right and duty, and am ready to abide the consequences."

That the Channings evidently suffered from the criticism of friends and foes alike is revealed in O'Connor's correspondence. George Curtis wrote him on November 26: "The question itself is not to be approached in a note like this. I only ask myself this,—if I had ceased to love my wife, and she still loved me, and knowing my feeling, was content to remain with me, have I no duty toward her, although I cannot in any just sense be her husband?" Curtis does believe in the purity of Dr. Channing's intention, concluding, "I hope he will hold on bravely to the path in which his conscience calls him to walk. Do you remember the first words of his father's book on 'slavery'? 'Not what is expedient, but what is right!' "[13]

It appears that Mrs. Caroline H. Dall, the Woman's Rights leader, in supposed friendship struck some blows against the Channings, then asked O'Connor to intercede. Three of his letters to Mrs. Dall refer to the matter:[14] In a long letter in which O'Connor refers to his review of her book for the *Post*, and takes issue with her remarks on Buckle in it, he tells of severing his connection with the *Post*, and adds:

> I hear from Dr. Channing and Jeannie. They are at the West Indies. Jeannie's health is very poor. I fear that she will be an invalid for life, though I still hope for her recovery. On their account, I have a bill against Mr. Greeley and Mrs. Grundy, which they shall pay with grief one of these days, if I live.
> I want to lecture one of these days on "Social Liberty." I have some choice bomb-shells which I shall explode to the rage and grief of "Society."
> Meanwhile, I see that Massachusetts has bowed to the justice of Dr. Channing's criticism by reforming her marriage laws.

In another letter, he thanks Mrs. Dall for her favorable view of *Harrington*, accepts her criticism of a minor point, and explains other matters which she questioned. He goes on:

After giving your message to William, I had a talk with him about his relations to you—the first understanding I have ever had on the subject. Shall I tell you what was said? It was painful—painful now to remember. I will not tell you unless you wish to hear. If you do, and if you can feel pleasantly toward me for telling you what is not pleasant, I will lay the matter candidly before you. . . .

Mrs. Dall, of course, wanted to satisfy her curiosity, but what she learned from O'Connor was hardly pleasant.

I think it best to tell you about William. The conversation I had with him ended by his showing me the letter you wrote him, and I here transcribe one passage from much of the same tenor:

"You have always seemed to me to think that you had a right to happiness—or the full play of *sensual,* psychical and moral attractions. On the contrary, *I* only feel that I am privileged to pursue *virtue—and to enjoy what consorts therewith.* I think self-denial and self-conquest the law of life, while *you* feel expansion and *infinite vegetation* in *pleasure,* not unaccompanied by nobleness, your normal condition. If you had never told me this, *I should have seen it in the lines of your face and the motions of your frame.*"

William heard from several sources that you had shown this letter to various persons. You could hardly have done him, a man of almost ascetic purity of life, greater injustice than to thus describe him in sharp antithetical contrast, as a radical voluptuary, nor could you have done him at that time much greater injury than to so exhibit him to others. I thought William mistaken in his feeling toward you, but I must say that when I saw this letter, I could not but agree with him.

O'Connor continues, pointedly, that "If your showing of this letter was meant as friendship, it was a friendship that performed the effects of enmity." O'Connor tempers that blunt remark by asking forgiveness if he has said anything that seems harsh or unkind—and goes on to talk about Mrs. Dall's writings and his own indecision about the future now that the publishers of *Harrington* have failed. In this last letter to Mrs. Dall on the subject of William Channing, O'Connor refuses to be the mediator between them, feeling that "any settlement of this painful difficulty, would be better effected between those immediately concerned, than by my intervention."

There is no record that O'Connor ever delivered the lecture against society that he had mentioned in his letter to Mrs. Dall. He did, however, deal with the subject in his novel *Harrington*. At one point O'Connor satirizes society gently: When his hero and heroine are married, the announcement "falling soft as a rose-leaf on the tail of that great Chicken Little, Society, Society ran around clucking as if the sky had fallen."[15]

The problem of marriage and divorce, however, is treated seriously and dramatically in *Harrington*. The subjugation of a wife, imprisoned in an unhappy marriage to a husband who is subtly cruel, is seen as a form of slavery. Lafitte, the plantation owner, taunts his unhappy wife: "I wanted you for one of my mistresses, and I got you at the little expense of a marriage ceremony . . . and they call it holy matrimony." Later he says,

> The beautiful social system makes you something like my slave, dear wife. I bring my negroes here, and I bring you here. None of you want to come, but you can't help yourselves, and so come you do. But my negroes cannot bring me here. No. Nor can you bring me here. No. Do my negroes run away? I set Dunwoodie's hounds after them, and run them down. Do you run away? That dear old Mrs. Grundy sets her hounds after you, and runs you down. . . . Well, go North to New York, for instance. Why their great Panjandrum up there, the "Tribune" man—what's his name— Greeley—he will tell you that you are living, and must live, in holy matrimony.[16]

No state would grant her a divorce except Indiana "the wicked, wicked state,"[17] and even there she would fail, for she has no witnesses to the unhappiness of her marriage.

At the denouement of the novel, both the wife and the slave are free. She has run away to Europe while her husband is in the North to seek his escaped slave, and the slave has been rescued by John Harrington, the hero, at the cost of his own life.

O'Connor's passages about the Channings in his letters and about marriage and divorce laws in *Harrington* failed to convince Mrs. Dall. In a biographical note on William Channing in the N.E.G.H. *Register* (Vol. XLVI, p. 179), she wrote: "He became conspicuous by divorcing his first wife for reasons not recognized by the laws of Mass. and when married a second time, went to R.I. in consequence, and later to California." (Actually the Channings went to California for reasons of their daughter Grace's health—but Mrs. Dall's implication that it was flight from scandal was probably deliberate.)

It remained for a twentieth-century writer, intent on seeing flaws in the armor of the St. Joans of the Woman's Rights movement, to give Mrs. Dall her comeuppance. Riegel in his *American Feminists*[18] points out that even in her youth, Caroline "complained continually of illness, and longed for the affection and love that she felt she did not receive." Her classmates nicknamed her "The Disappointment." She was as opinionated as she was unhappy. "She said later that she never asked an opinion from anyone else, but always told others, including her mother and father, the right answers." Although she always complained of being ill, she lived to be ninety.

Caroline Dall's unsympathetic view of William Channing and his divorce and remarriage may have stemmed from her own experience in marriage. Charles Dall, the Unitarian divine whom she fell in love with and married, later left her with two children and went to work first in Toronto and later in Calcutta. Yet she stressed the sacredness of the marriage bond and admitted no escape from "holy matrimony."

In addition to visits from Curtis, the Channings, and others, O'Connor partook of some "mental aliment" in Philadelphia through his correspondence with old friends.[19] His deep friendship with Sarah Helen Whitman continued through letters. He discussed literary matters with her, at one time expressing his delight with Walt Whitman's "A Child's Reminiscence" ("Out of the Cradle Endlessly Rocking") when it appeared in the *Saturday Press* in December 1859. He corresponded with Curtis and discussed work submitted for publication or review in the *Post* with him and other authors, among them John T. Trowbridge, Caroline Dall, and Louise Moulton.

One friendship, which was to continue throughout his later life, began at this time with an exchange of letters. John Hay, who was to be helpful to Walt Whitman in Washington, sent a letter of introduction written by Sarah Helen Whitman in August 1858. Having been unable to present it in person, he wrote from Warsaw, Illinois:

> I am very sorry to have been thus deprived of the pleasure of seeing you. It was a desire that I had for a long time cherished, first awakened on discovering the authorship of several articles which

had delighted me in magazines, and afterwards much increased by learning the estimation in which you were held by your circle of friends in Providence.[20]

On February 6, 1859, Hay sent O'Connor copies of his poems, "Last Night," "In the Mist," and "Parted." (He sent copies also to Sarah Helen Whitman and to Nora Perry, a well-known poet who was part of Helen's coterie.)

> I sent you a few copies of my rhymes as you did me the honour to request. I am sincerely distrustful of any praises that my friends have bestowed on the few efforts I have made in this direction. I have never seen very much in anything I have written, until either the politeness or the partiality of friends has first suggested it. With you, I am not personally acquainted. If you read the enclosed verses, you will judge them impartially. Is it asking too much to request that you will give me an opinion, not so especially with regard to their intrinsic merits (if they have any), as in respect to their availability for the use of periodicals or newspapers?

In this letter, John Hay reveals his nostalgia for the East, which must have seemed to O'Connor, exiled in Philadelphia, the echo of his own emotions:

> My connection, however slight, with friends in the East is about all that renders my life not utterly worthless. Hopes that bloomed in Providence have faded in wilderness, and I fear the future can only confer the pleasure of memory . . . I suppose in any case, the friction of this wild Western life, will wear the glory from former dreams, in a few years. The only *numbers* which are respected in this country are those preceded by the magical sign "$." In a year or two, if I live so long, I shall probably fall (or rise, if you will) to the level of the money-getting masses around me. When I have made my moderate "pile," I hope there will be enough soul left within me, to draw me back to the beaches and bays of the blessed Atlantic. . . .

Within a few years, John Hay was to return to the East, not to New England but to Washington, as assistant secretary to President Lincoln. There O'Connor met Hay and strengthened the friendship begun through letters.

Although in his black moods William said that he had no companionship in Philadelphia, he did make some new friends there, one of whom was to play a significant part later. This was J. Hubley Ashton, a young lawyer, who later moved to Washington after O'Connor did, entered government service, and became Assistant Attorney General. It was in this post that he was able to obtain a place for Walt Whitman in 1865 after his dismissal from the Department of the Interior by Secretary Harlan.

Letters from Ashton to O'Connor[21] show the closeness of their friendship throughout the Philadelphia days. At O'Connor's request Ashton read the manuscript of *Harrington*, offering advice on a legal point in the novel. When Ashton was in army camp, he wrote to both Nelly and William, saying she was the better correspondent. When O'Connor was in Washington in the summer of 1861, Ashton wrote asking him to have a photograph taken that he could show to his future wife, and delicately offering to pay for it, as he knew O'Connor, then looking for a job, was not in a position to make expenditures of this kind.

When little Philip O'Connor died in April 1862, Ashton wrote, "You rightly say that I can feel how bereft you and Nelly are, for I loved the little fellow dearly." "I am rarely attracted toward children," he continued, "but like you I scarcely looked upon him as a baby. Now that he is gone, I feel as if some friend nearly of my own age had left me."

Another friend in Philadelphia was Hector Tyndale,[22] who resembled members of the Bostonian circle in being a Free Soiler and a man of independent conscience. Although he did not consider himself an Abolitionist, it was he who escorted John Brown's wife when he thought she might be in danger; on the morning of Brown's execution Tyndale was shot at by an unknown assailant. It was he who received John Brown's coffin and insisted on opening it, for threats had been made that the body of an animal would be substituted.

When Fort Sumter was fired on, Tyndale was in Europe. He promptly returned and offered his services. He was commissioned a major of the 28th Pennsylvania Regiment in June 1861, and put in command of Sandy Hook opposite Harper's Ferry. He participated in 24 battles and 19 smaller engagements, and was made a Lieutenant Colonel in 1862 and later a Brigadier General of Volunteers. In the Battle of Wanhatchee he led a bayonet charge up a hill, which has since been known as Tyndale's Hill. In 1865 he was brevetted Major General of Volunteers. Three years later he was the Republican nominee for mayor of Philadelphia—and was defeated by 68 votes in a poll of more than 120,000.

Most of this colorful history lay ahead when he and the O'Connors met in Philadelphia in 1856. Tyndale's chief attraction was that he not only admired *Leaves of Grass* but even knew the author. Indeed, Hector's mother, Mrs. Sarah Tyndale, had called on Walt in Brooklyn on November 10, 1856, together with Henry Thoreau and Bronson Alcott.[23] Her son met Walt at the home of Mrs. Abby Price in Brooklyn. He is the "Major T." referred to in the following account by Mrs. Price's daughter Helen:

> At one time an evening was appointed (for Whitman) to meet Major T., of Philadelphia, and a number of others. We waited with some misgivings for his appearance, but he came at last. As soon as the introductions were over, he sidled off to a corner of the room where there was a group of young children, with whom he talked and laughed and played, evidently to their mutual satisfaction. Our company . . . were quite annoyed, and my mother was finally commissioned to get him out of his corner. When she told her errand, he looked up with utmost merriment, and said, "O, yes—I'll do it—where do you want me to sit? on the piano?"[24]

Tyndale had promised the O'Connors that he would arrange for them to meet Walt Whitman at his home, but Walt failed to come. Whitman explained in a letter to Mrs. Tyndale on June 20, 1857: ". . . Tell Hector I thank him heartily for his invitation and letter; O it is not from any mind to slight him that I have not answered it, or accepted the friendly call. I am so non-polite—so habitually wanting in my responses and ceremonies. That is *me*—much that is bad, harsh, an undutiful person, a thriftless debtor, is me."[25] Mrs. Tyndale answered reassuringly: "I think your judgment of yourself is rather severe. I have not changed my opinion . . . if (Emerson) or any one else expected *common* etiquette from you, after having read *Leaves of Grass* they were sadly mistaken in your character. Where etiquette, or what is *called* refined and exquisite taste *predominate*, I never expect to find much originality of character."[26]

Thus absolved from keeping his promises, Walt never did come to the Tyndales' to meet the O'Connors. They were so inured to disappointment that several years later in Washington, when Walt left his carpetbag at the O'Connors' with a promise to return, Nelly confessed that she still was "somewhat skeptical as to whether he would actually appear, as I had already learned of his elusive disposition, and of his dislike to be bound in any way. We had been promised by our friend Hector Tyndale of Philadelphia that we should meet him in that city, where he had often been looked for, on the strength of his vague assurances."[27]

Although the poet did not come to Philadelphia, his poetry had a place there in the discussions between William and Hector. Jeannie Channing recalled that in the winter of 1858 in Philadelphia, "I had frequent opportunities to hear Mr. O'Connor and Major Hector Tyndale talk over the poet. Both were enthusiastic, it seemed to me extravagantly so, in their estimate."[28] When Jeannie finally met Walt in Washington in 1866 she was annoyed at the poet's lack of appreciation of Tyndale's admiration of him.

> He . . . said, "Do you mean to say you believe Tyndale has any adequate idea of the aim and scope of my poems?" I think my wonder must have shown in my face, but to Walt it seemed the simplest thing in the world. No one could *over*-estimate his work and only a very few came near to seeing how great it is.
>
> This egotism was a matter of course. His faith in what was given him to write was absolute. . . .

It must be said in defense of Walt's attitude that by 1866 Tyndale had lost some of his earlier enthusiasm for *Leaves of Grass.* In a letter to Jeannie Channing about *The Good Gray Poet,* O'Connor wrote "that Hector did not like my pamphlet, thought it 'flashy' etc. . . . and that I entirely exaggerated Walt's eminence as a poet and that my interpretation of 'indecent' passages could not be sustained."[29]

In the Philadelphia days, however, Tyndale was still enthusiastic about *Leaves of Grass,* and he and Ashton in their conversation and Curtis, Hay, and others in their letters, relieved the tedium of O'Connor's life. O'Connor's work was more often frustrating than satisfying. The *Post* was arid in comparison with the *Commonwealth* on which he had served his journalistic apprenticeship in Boston.

Edmund Deacon and Henry Peterson, its editors and proprietors, were quite different in politics and personality from the wise Baldwin and the witty "Warrington" of the *Commonwealth*. Their spirit, according to Thayer and Eldridge (when they wrote urging O'Connor to leave the *Post*) "if not absolutely hunkerish and unprogressive, is so sycophantish and servile to the lowest average of public opinion as to make earnest men heartsick."[30]

With employers whose views were so different from his own, O'Connor was given little freedom. Writing for the *Post*, he said, was "like attempting beautiful chirography with the right arm lashed to the side, and four fingers of the pen-hand tied together." This was in explanation of his review of Caroline Dall's book, *Woman's Right to Labor with Low Wages and Hard Work*, which appeared on February 18, 1860: "Of course, it is not what I *would*, but what I *could*, say. Considering that the editor is dead against the Woman's Rights movement, and growls fearfully at all attempts to insinuate that abominable heresy into his paper, I consider this notice a success. . . ."[31]

In assuring Louise Chandler Moulton that he would try to review her book favorably, he qualified his statement with,

> Yet credit me only with the will, count not on the deed, for I have but little control here, and though I always know what I can write, I never know what I can get printed.
>
> What is it Shakespeare says in the sonnet?—"And wisdom tongue-tied by authority"!!! *Wisdom*! of course!!![32]

While preventing him from expressing his views freely in its pages, the *Post* also denied him the leisure to do any other writing. When he was invited to contribute a story to the first issue of the *Atlantic Monthly* (a most flattering invitation, since the leading writers of the day had been asked to contribute, among them Emerson, Motley, Holmes, Lowell, and Longfellow) he had regretfully to decline. He explained to Francis Henry Underwood, a founder of the magazine,

> I have been trying very hard to make Kosmos out of the chaos of a MS. tale I have for some time had on hand—a thing of shreds and patches it is, at present, existing only in stray sheets, scraps, and memoranda—but to save my life, I cannot get time enough to

build this little world of mine, I have to give so much to the affairs of this other world—the Post—of which I am in effect, the governor, and all the more so now, since the ostensible chief is away, and everything devolves on me. . . .[33]

He continues by hinting at how little he is able to say in the *Post* of what he feels most deeply:

And then, besides, when you do get a MS of mine, it is quite likely you will not like it, the revolution and the radicalism running so naturally to my pen, and my tales being my only present means of securing to myself the luxury of my individual views and opinions. . . .

This may have been "The Brazen Android" which O'Connor finally finished after he left the *Post*, and which was not published until after his death.[34]

Despite the strictures which irked him, O'Connor was able to give expression in the *Post* to some of his enthusiasms. On July 19, 1856, a year after the publication of the first edition of *Leaves of Grass* and a few months before the second edition, the *Post* presented without comment a lengthy passage from the Preface to the First Edition. (Aside from quotations given within the context of reviews of the book, this probably was the first lengthy quotation from *Leaves of Grass* in the press.) Titled "The Poetic View of America" and signed at the end, "*Leaves of Grass* by Walter Whitman," the passage consists of 47 lines from the Preface, beginning in its second paragraph with the sentence, "In the history of the earth hitherto the largest and most stirring appear tame and orderly to their ampler largeness and stir," and ending at the close of the third paragraph with, "It awaits the gigantic and generous treatment worthy of it." A copy of this passage in O'Connor's handwriting begins with two sentences which were left out of the *Post*: "The Americans of all nations at any time upon the earth have probably the fullest poetical nature. The United States themselves are essentially the greatest poem." It seems likely that this was the manuscript which O'Connor submitted to the *Post*, for the opening lines are more closely related to his title, "The Poetic View of America," than the lines with which the *Post* begins its excerpt.[35]

O'Connor also managed to write in support of Edgar Allan Poe in his review of Sarah Helen Whitman's *Edgar Poe and His Critics*, calling it "the first authentic movement in vindication" of the poet whose genius is being increasingly recognized in Great Britain and the United States. "One sad star, forever fixed—a growing orb forever, in the Southern galaxy, is the fame of Edgar Poe."[36]

Other reviews which may be ascribed to O'Connor include one of Robert Dale Owen's spiritualist *Footfalls on the Boundary of Another World*. He wrote to Sarah Helen Whitman that he had said all he could for it,

> . . . but I hope you will see Peterson's (the publisher's) editorial. It will show you that the age of superstition is not gone yet. Think of a sensible man in the 19th century, writing such stuff!
>
> Owen's book, by the way, has strong points, but it is tremendously open to criticism.[37]

In the same letter, O'Connor referred to Miss Dinah Maria Mulock's (1826-87) poems: "Many of them are beautiful—always exquisite in feeling, and some of them, such as 'Douglas, Douglas, Tender and True,' having sang through my soul like the night wind for years." Miss Mulock's poems are reviewed favorably in the *Post* on January 28, 1860.

Other books reviewed during O'Connor's editorship of the *Post* are: David Masson's *Life of John Milton*; Thomas DeQuincey's *The Avenger, Narrative, The Popes*; Herman Melville's *The Piazza Tales*; Lord Campbell's *Shakespeare's Legal Acquirements Considered*; and Lord Macauley's *The Life of Frederick the Great* and *The Life of William Pitt*; as well as poetry by William Motherwell, Sydney Dobell, and Anne Whitney. There were essays on Robert Burns, Sir E. Bulwer Lytton, Washington Irving, Sir John Suckling, and Sir Walter Raleigh. (Whitman later said that during this period in Philadelphia O'Connor steeped himself in Elizabethan literature.)[38]

Among the stories published serially was Dickens's *A Tale of Two Cities*. (Since O'Connor later wrote in disparagement of Dickens, it is possible that this was not his choice.) Many poems appeared in the *Post*, some anonymously. Of those signed, the authors include Christina Rossetti, Alfred Lord Tennyson, and "Florence Percy" (Elizabeth Chase, who later acquired two more names by marriage, and was known as Elizabeth Akers Allen). An item in the *Post* reveals that Florence Percy sailed for Europe with Mrs. Paulina Wright Davis and Paul Akers, the sculptor. (It was Akers's studio in Rome that was said to have been the setting for Hawthorne's *Marble Faun.*) Elizabeth Chase and Paul Akers were married; he died a year later. In 1865 Elizabeth married E. M. Allen, the ceremony taking place in John Burroughs's home in Washington in October.[39]

Two lengthy poems were written by O'Connor as editor: These were the customary "Address of the Carriers of the *Saturday Evening Post* to the Patrons" on January 1, 1857 and January 1, 1858. In the conventional farewell to the old year and greetings to the new, O'Connor expresses his political views with much the same emphasis which he had given in his essay "The New Year" in the *Mercantile Library Reporter.*

> Seek we still for hopeful gleams?—
> Asia lolls in opium dreams—
> Drugged—effete—or if astir
> Running mucks of massacre;
> And a savage darkness reigns
> O'er dear Africa's remains.—
> Dove of hope, oh, where for thee
> Resting place on the shoreless sea! . . .
> Joy and sorrow, the private woe,
> The public sin, the nation's throe,
> Saints in jail and knaves in sway,
> Work in the cause of the better Day. . . .

In the "Address" of 1858 O'Connor is freer in his rhythms and more explicit in his summary of the year gone by:

> . . . menaced from the outer vast
> By the missioned comet rushing past . . .
> (The old year) fatefully decreed
> That the nation's errands should not speed
> Through the interoccanic coil.
> Now the snickering mermen mock the toil . . .
> But the magic causeway still is planned,
> And the land shall yet accost the land! . . .

In the financial crisis of 1857 the Old Year

> Whirled the wealth of commerce out of sight,
> On each ledger perched the bankrupt sprite,

> And deranged, with shocks the engine feels,
> Trade's thick-millioned complicated wheels. . . .

O'Connor's concern for present conditions was also expressed in the essays he wrote for the *Post*. Even in the essay on chivalry—in a way a continuation of the essay he had written for the *Mercantile Library Reporter*—he related the ideals of chivalry to the present.[40] Of the first knights he wrote:

> Now it is quite evident that these noble men were, in a word, the Radical Reformers of their time; and, doubtlessly, had affairs been less desperate, they would have been treated as the Radical Reformers of other times have been treated—called "fanatics," "traitors," "seditious," "disorganizing," and promptly howled or hewed down. But it happened that circumstances were very strongly in favor of their enterprise.

O'Connor concludes in the vein of his story, "Loss and Gain: A Tale of Lynn":

> The military age has passed, and the monetary age has succeeded. Still the ancient feud between Right and Wrong goes on, but the weapons are changed. . . . The sword of the chevalier rusts in the scabbard, but the spirit that drew the sword lives in the van of the great human battle, and flashes a mightier weapon. . . . Let no man arrogate to himself the epithet of "chivalrous," who cannot show in his own example the valor and the virtue of the knights of old.

O'Connor had spent almost four years on the *Post* when the differences between him and the publishers came into sharp focus with the John Brown case in the latter part of 1859. On October 16, 1859, John Brown with twenty-one followers took possession of the arsenal at Harper's Ferry, planning to use it as a base from which they could free slaves by armed intervention. O'Connor's Abolitionist friends in Boston had contributed to his cause and encouraged him. John Brown was arrested and sentenced to be hanged on December 2, 1859.

O'Connor could not refrain from sympathetic comment in the *Post*. On December 3 he printed a paragraph, under a Washington dateline, which said that there were secret societies in various portions of Ohio and elsewhere whose members are bound by oath to rescue Brown and revenge him. On December 10, a dispatch from Charlestown, entitled "The Execution of John Brown," quoted Brown's request that no prayers be said for him by ministers who approved of slavery; but "that he would prefer to be accompanied on the scaffold by a dozen slave children and a good old slave mother, with their blessings on his soul, than all the eloquence of the whole clergy of the commonwealth combined."

Two weeks later another dispatch from Charlestown appeared: "Harper's Ferry. The Last Act in the Tragedy—Attempt to Escape—Final Execution, &c."

O'Connor also managed to give the anti-slavery point of view when, on January 7, 1860, the *Post* quoted verbatim the part of the President's message which referred to slavery and the slave trade, and summarized the rest. He followed this with an outright "anti-hack" and anti-slavery editorial[41]—and was dismissed from his job. The editors had other excuses than O'Connor's Radical Republicanism. The circulation of the paper had declined from about 90,000 to 30,000 during O'Connor's incumbency.

Having lost his position, O'Connor again faced the dilemma of whether to seek a steady income or the literary life of his dreams. The former was even more necessary than it had been four years earlier, for now there was little Jeannie, almost two years old, and a new baby, Philip, born that very month. In the letter in which he announces the arrival of the baby to Mrs. Dall, he apologizes for not having written to her sooner. " . . . my sky has been thick with cares, and, like Dogberry, 'I am a fellow who hath had losses'— losses, however, of the kind Mrs. Browning speaks of in the 'Lost Bower.' " He refers to the "general discombobulation" of things, and the great difficulty of writing for the *Post.*

> This pain, like some others, is over now, however, for my tasks here are drawing to a close. I have been in the *Post* for nearly four years, and now I am about to leave. What to do next, or where I am going, I know not. I hesitate between seeking another post as editor, or at once attempting a literary life in a better sense. The first involves a sure income, which is a great need, but it also involves slavery and suppression of myself. The second threatens pecuniary embarrassments, with only a doubtful glimmer of future emoluments but it promises culture and the activity of my best

powers. Were I alone, how promptly I could choose; but as it is, how cowardly and careful I must be!

My wish and aim is to get such work as shall leave me time for private study, for I have an idea to work out, perhaps I may never have a fair chance to do it. . . . [42]

He writes in the same vein to George Curtis, who begins his answer with congratulations and continues in light vein about his own child.

I hope you won't be disheartened when you forecast his schooling. One day my wife asked me why I was looking so doleful. I was obliged to tell the truth, "I was thinking what a time he'll have learning his irregular verbs."

That your wife is well as you could expect is not the least of the good news. It is a solemn time to every man who thinks, as well as feels. Give her my kindest love and congratulations and a kiss of welcome to the raw recruit.

Of future jobs Curtis writes like the young father he too now is:

—To have a son born and to lose your place at the same time, is a complication of affairs certainly. Of one thing I am pretty sure, and that is the value of some regular position for every man who must really live by his act. A man will find the chance-shooting in magazines, etc., too helter-skelter a life: and he can fire away in that manner more comfortably if he have not the nervous doubt of success hanging over him.

Curtis adds that there are few openings for permanent employment on magazines and weekly papers. The daily paper is slavery, and job writing in encyclopedias starvation. Yet he urges O'Connor to seek a steady income. "The honor and glory will not desert you for being a faithful servant:—and the little girl and boy will thank you. . . . " Unfortunately desirable posts were few and Curtis knew of no opening for him. [43]

William had to seek advice and help elsewhere. He hastened to respond to a letter he had received from a new publishing house, Thayer and Eldridge, just before his son was born. [44] The young publishers had written to O'Connor on February 6, expressing their interest in his work on the basis of his short stories in *Harper's* and

Putnam's and suggesting themselves as his future publishers on the basis of their success with James Redpath's life of John Brown.[45]

O'Connor answered on the 15th, writing of the "dull and sad routine of hack work in a newspaper office,"[46] of his desire to write a novel, and of his need of a regular income to enable him to do so. Their answer on February 23, coming after he had lost his job and had already learned that Curtis knew of no opening for him, must have seemed like a reprieve from the limbo of job hunting and a passport to a paradise where he could write as he wanted to. Thayer and Eldridge assured him:

> We are confident that arrangements can be made by which you can be secured a regular and steady income and yet have the requisite leisure and opportunity to devote your powers to the composition of an American novel. For this task we believe that you have singular and rare abilities and if written with the dramatic intensity and command of language which characterizes (*sic*) your magazine stories, we know that it would be in our hands a sensational book, and the results accrueing (*sic*) therefrom, such as to put you on the high road to permanent literary fame and pecuniary independence.

They go on to ask what he was earning at the *Post* so as to determine what to offer him as a drawing against his future royalties. They add some criticisms of the *Post* and encomiums of William which must have pleased him:

> We can imagine how uncongenial and irksome to a person of your spirit, who naturally are (*sic*) so outspoken and fearless, the connection with a paper like the *Post* must be! . . .
>
> When you went to Phila., your reputation in literary circles was brilliant, arising chiefly, to those who did not know you personally from your contributions to *Harper & Putnam*; and much was expected from you in your new position. But that paper has literally buried you alive.
>
> We know we can recall you to freedom and a literary career, with a large pecuniary benefit to both you and ourselves, in the manner we have thus briefly indicated.[47]

Flattered as he must have been, William still cautiously wrote to Curtis, the experienced author and editor, about the contract. "In general," Curtis replied, "do what the Bostonians ask. We must all begin by doing what we *can*. However, that needs to be talked."[48] The talk took place when William visited Curtis in mid-March, in the latter's new home on Staten Island, which William reached by quarantine boat.[49]

The contract with Thayer and Eldridge, dated March 24, provided that William was to write a novel within six months; it was to be a romance, of 384 pages, duodecimo, the title not yet determined. The publishers were to pay him twenty dollars per week from April 1 until two months after the book's publication. This amount was to be deducted from royalties of 10 percent on the retail price of the first 10,000 books and 5 percent thereafter. Thayer and Eldridge were to have first rights to continue publication after five years.[50]

Again O'Connor turned for advice to Curtis, who commended the contract as a just one. He nevertheless expressed caution about the future. "There is one thing that works against us—the fact that it is a Presidential year. My publishers tell me that will be bad for my *Trumps* which is about ready for the printer. . . . "[51] Curtis could not foresee that William's hopes would come to naught for another reason—the failure of Thayer and Eldridge immediately after the publication of his novel.

Although that failure aborted O'Connor's possible career as a novelist, his connection with Thayer and Eldridge had a positive effect on his life, for it was at their office that he met Walt Whitman.

Notes

1. Although the date is not known, there was a congratulatory letter from GWC in January (see note 2 below) and on April 24 Harriet Beecher Stowe concluded a letter to "Dear Nelly Tarr" with the words ". . . be sure to tell me all about our William." Sara Algeo, "Equal Suffrage Notes," *Providence Daily Journal*, 23 July 1911 (Brown).
2. GWC to WDO'C, 18 January 1856 (Brown).
3. Ellen O'C. Calder to Traubel, 8 August 1905 (Feinberg-LC).
4. Copy of marriage certificate, No. 3681, furnished by Health Department, Registry Division, City of Boston.
5. These and following quotations on marriage are from *Harrington*.
6. Clarke, *Autobiography, Diary & Correspondence*, ed. Edward Everett Hale (Boston & New York: Houghton Mifflin Co., 1891).
7. Ellen M. Calder, "Personal Recollections of Walt Whitman," *Atlantic Monthly*, 99:833 (June 1907).

8. Nelly O'Connor to WW, 29 November 1889 (Feinberg-LC).
9. WDO'C to Dall, 15 January 1861 (MIT).
10. GWC to WDO'C, 7 December 1860 (Brown).
11. Shillaber to WDO'C, 6 December 1860 (Feinberg-LC).
12. Van Wyck Brooks, *The Flowering of New England* (New York: E. P. Dutton & Co., 1936), p. 15.
13. GWC to WDO'C, 26 November 1859 (Harvard).
14. WDO'C to Dall, 14 February 1860; 7 December 1860; 15 January 1861 (MIT).
15. *Harrington*, p. 376.
16. *Ibid.*, p. 18.
17. *Ibid.*, p. 19.
18. Robert E. Riegel, *American Feminists* (Westport, Conn.: Greenwood Press, 1980—Reprint of 1963), p. 158.
19. WDO'C to Dall, 15 January 1861 (MIT).
20. Hay to WDO'C, 25 August 1858 (Brown). John Hay's biographer, William R. Thayer, is under the impression that Hay met O'Connor in Providence, but this letter controverts his opinion. W. R. Thayer, *The Life of John Hay*. (Boston & New York: Houghton Mifflin Co., 1908), I, 46.
21. (Feinberg-LC).
22. Appleton's *Encyclopedia*, 1887, vol. VI, p. 202 (with photo).
23. *The Journals of Bronson Alcott*, ed. Odell Shepard (Boston: Little, Brown, 1938), pp. 286–90.
24. Richard Maurice Bucke, *Walt Whitman* (Philadelphia: David McKay, 1883), p. 27.
25. *Correspondence*, vol. I, p. 42.
26. *Ibid.*, n. 2.
27. Calder, *op. cit.*, p. 826.
28. M. J. Channing, "Recollections of Walt Whitman," unpublished ms. (Chamberlin).
29. WDO'C to M. J. Channing, 18 February 1866 (Chamberlin).
30. Thayer and Eldridge to WDO'C, 6 February 1860 (Feinberg-LC).
31. WDO'C to Dall, 14 February 1860 (MIT).
32. WDO'C to Moulton, 24 August 1859 (LC).
33. WDO'C to Underwood, 20 August 1857 (Yale).
34. *Atlantic Monthly*, April and May 1891.
35. (Yale).
36. *Saturday Evening Post*, 4 February 1860.
37. WDO'C to SHW, n.d., but probably 1859 because of reference to Whitman's "A Child's Reminiscence" (Brown). Review appeared in issue of January 21, 1860. Robert Dale Owen, *Footfalls on the Boundary of Another World* (Philadelphia: J. B. Lippincott & Co., 1860).
38. *Camden*, 2:240–41.
39. *Life and Letters*, vol. I, 102 n.
40. *Saturday Evening Post*, 11 October 1856.
41. According to Nelly the *Post* had lost so many subscribers because of the anti-slavery position of Peterson, the editor, that the assistant editor had to be dispensed with. E. O'C. Calder to Traubel, 8 August 1905 (Feinberg-LC).
42. WDO'C to Dall, 14 February 1860 (MIT).
43. GWC to WDO'C, 17 February 1860 (Harvard).
44. William Thayer and Charles Eldridge had been clerks in the publishing house of Dayton and Wentworth. See chapter VII n. 1.
45. 6 February 1860 (Feinberg-LC). James Redpath, *The Public Life of John Brown* (Boston: Thayer and Eldridge, 1860).

46. WDO'C to Thayer and Eldridge, letter (not extant) mentioned in their reply (see note 47).
47. Thayer and Eldridge to WDO'C, 23 February 1860 (Feinberg-LC). In his unpublished autobiography, Thayer stated he was the sole author of this letter (LC).
48. GWC to WDO'C, 2 March 1860, unpublished letter (Brown).
49. GWC to WDO'C, 12 March 1860, unpublished letter (Harvard).
50. Holograph of contract (Brown).
51. GWC to WDO'C, 18 April 1860, unpublished letter (Brown).

CHAPTER VII

A Friendship Begun;
A Novel Written

THAYER AND Eldridge were enthusiastic and aggressive young publishers.[1] In their brief career of a little over a year, they published not only O'Connor's *Harrington* and a third edition of Whitman's *Leaves of Grass*, but also a Woman's Rights book, Lizzie B. Torrey's *The Ideal of Womanhood*;[2] two campaign biographies, a life of William H. Seward whom the radical Abolitionists favored for the presidency, and a hasty biography of Abraham Lincoln when he was nominated—both written by Richard J. Hinton and published anonymously; anti-slavery pamphlets by Hinton; and a life of John Brown by James Redpath with Hinton's assistance.

O'Connor and Whitman may have been surprised when they met their publishers and saw their quarters. William Thayer was only twenty-nine and Charles Eldridge twenty-one. Their office was a center of Abolitionist activity. Thayer wrote in his autobiography:

> The new fighting abolitionists in Boston formed a little society in the back part of our store where we had concealed, but ready for use, pistols and ammunition, knives and bludgeons. Our members wore around the neck under the collar a narrow black ribbon as a distinguishing mark. We knew each other as "Black Strings"![3]

Four days after their first letter to O'Connor, they wrote to Whitman that they were eager to become his first publishers. Although two editions of the *Leaves* had been published, in 1855 and 1856, both

101

had been printed by the author himself. The first edition had been copyrighted in the name of Walter Whitman, with the only identification of the author a photograph facing the title page and a line on page 29: "Walt Whitman, one of the roughs, a kosmos." For the second edition, Fowler and Wells had acted as Walt's agents but withheld their names from the title page and later renounced responsibility for the book.

Despite this history, the young firm of Thayer and Eldridge pleaded to become the publishers of the *Leaves* in an eloquent letter written by William Thayer with the approval of his partner on February 10, 1860:

Walt Whitman

Dr Sir. We want to be the publishers of Walt Whitman's poems—Leaves of Grass.—When the book was first issued we were clerks in the establishment we now own. We read the book with profit and pleasure. It is a true poem and writ by a *true* man.

When a man dares to speak his thought in this day of refinement—so called—it is difficult to find his mates to act amen to it. Now *we* want to be known as the publishers of Walt Whitman's books, and put our name as such under his, on title pages. If you will allow it we can and will put your book into good form, and style attractive to the eye; we can and will sell a large number of copies; we have great facilities by and through numberless Agents in selling. We can dispose of more books than most publishing houses (we do not "puff" here but speak *truth*).

We are young men. We "Celebrate" ourselves by acts. Try us. You can do us good. We can do you good—pecuniarily.

Now Sir, if you wish to make acquaintance with us, and accept us as your publishers, we will offer to either buy the stereotype plates of Leaves of Grass or pay you for the use of them, in addition to regular copyright.

Are you writing other poems? Are they ready for the press? Will you let us read them? Will you write us? Please give us your residence.

Yours Fraternally
Thayer & Eldridge[4]

William Thayer told more about this letter in his autobiographical memoirs.

It was so striking that Whitman, when visiting Ralph Waldo Emerson at Concord, Mass., gave it to him to read. The latter praised it, and said there was hope for freedom of thought and a free press when such a publishing house, as indicated, like T & E had its home in Boston, and dared to take up the defense for the poet who had been so savagely criticized.

Impressed by the letter, Whitman promptly opened negotiations with Thayer and Eldridge and in mid-March arrived in Boston. Two weeks later he wrote to a friend:

Thayer & Eldridge, the publishers, are a couple of young Yankees—so far very good specimens, to me, of this Eastern race of yours. They have treated me first rate—have not asked me at all what I was going to put into the book—just took me to the stereotype foundry, and given orders to follow my directions. . . . [5]

While Whitman was in Boston, William O'Connor arrived to sign the contract for his yet-to-be-written novel, and he and Walt met for the first time. William was already acquainted with Walt's work. He might have seen "Resurgemus" in *The New York Tribune* in 1850;[6] he had read and admired the First Edition of *Leaves of Grass* when it came out in 1855, as Mary Jane (Jeannie) Tarr Channing wrote years later.

I was spending the summer of 1855 with my friend Mrs. Paulina W. Davis. A letter from a Boston friend said, "I met Mr. Emerson the other day and almost his first words were 'Have you read the new poet?' I did not know of any new poet. He told me a man by the name of Whitman had sent him a most wonderful book. 'Get it at once and read it' he said; 'it is a revelation.' He was so enthusiastic in their praise and [undecipherable word] that I have got a copy; I think you and Mrs. Davis will be interested it it." We were interested in trying to discover what had so profoundly impressed Mr. Emerson, but did not greatly care for it ourselves. This was the very copy of Walt Whitman's poems that Mr. William D. O'Connor first saw and read. . . . [7]

In other notes Mrs. Channing wrote, "Neither Mrs. D. nor I found much to admire in the poems. The prose preface was extremely interesting to me. . . . "[8]

Nelly also wrote in later years of her reactions to this first edition of *Leaves of Grass*: "My own first impression after reading the quarto edition of *Leaves of Grass*, recommended by Emerson to the friend who gave it to me, was that the writer must be a pure man, or he would never have dared to speak so plainly of forbidden subjects."[9]

Before meeting Walt, William had also read and admired a more recent poem, "A Child's Reminiscence" (later called "Out of the Cradle Endlessly Rocking") when it appeared in the *Saturday Press*. On December 27, 1859, he wrote to Sarah Helen Whitman:

> Did you see Walt Whitman's poem, "A Child's Reminiscence," in the *Saturday Press*? What astonishing beauty—what weirdness— what reach of spiritual sight—what depth of feeling! Its sweetness melted my soul like one of Gluck's or Beethoven's symphonies. *Did* you see it, and *do* you feel its loveliness?[10]

And now, here in Boston, was Walt Whitman in the flesh! Six feet tall, broad-shouldered, with grizzled hair and beard, dressed in a hickory shirt with rolling collar open at the throat revealing his broad sunburned neck, Walt knew that he looked different from most Bostonians.[11] Although he was also quite different from the object of O'Connor's earlier hero-worship—the slim, elegant, scholar-activist Wendell Phillips—William was immediately drawn to the poet, writing to Sarah Helen Whitman:

> The great Walt is very grand and it is health and happiness to be near him; he is so large and strong—so proud, pure and tender, with such an ineffable bon-hommie [*sic*] and wholesome sweetness of presence, all the young men and women are in love with him.[12]

Their meeting came at a critical time in the lives of both men. The years preceding had been difficult ones. O'Connor had spent four frustrating years in the arid atmosphere of the Philadelphia *Saturday Evening Post*. The loss of this position had set the writer free, but posed a serious problem for the family man with two small children. Although his spirits were lifted by the prospect of writing a novel, he was still troubled by the uncertainty of whether he could accomplish his aims as a writer.

Before their 1860 meeting Whitman had undergone a serious emotional crisis which left him in a despairing mood. New poems in the 1860 edition, written between 1858 and 1860—especially those in the "Calamus" group—speak poignantly of self-doubt, love, and loss. The themes of love and death, present in the first two editions of *Leaves of Grass*, were expressed differently in this edition; here the love was individualized and the loss personal. He even feels that he may never write again. The final poem, "So Long!," suggests: "My songs cease—I abandon them," and he concludes,

> Remember my words—I love you—I depart from materials, I am
> as one disembodied, triumphant, dead.

No wonder that the lonely, despairing poet responded eagerly to the invitation of Thayer and Eldridge! The promise of a new edition was an affirmation of his belief in his poetry. When to this affirmation was added the friendship of William Thayer, Charles Eldridge, and William O'Connor, Walt's doubts about himself and his poems were diminished.

How much time William and Walt spent together is not known. It may be assumed that O'Connor, as an old Bostonian, had much to show his new friend. O'Connor may have participated in an adventure that would have delighted him as Abolitionist, adventurer, and knight errant. Frank B. Sanborn, one of a group which had aided John Brown, was to be arrested by a U.S. Marshal for his complicity in that affair. His friends had arranged for him to be arrested by the State of Massachusetts on a trumped-up charge, so that the U.S. Marshal could not take him. On April 4, the case was heard. His friends were fearful that the Massachusetts judge might nevertheless release him into the custody of the U.S. Marshal. Thayer wrote in his autobiography:

> Six of us went into the courtroom armed, and placed ourselves
> in position to shoot down any opponent and then hurry Sanborn
> to a carriage in waiting on the street below. In our crowd was
> Redpath, LeBarnes, Eldridge, myself, Hinton, and one other
> whose name I forget. At that time U.S. Marshal Freeman wanted
> to capture Redpath. I soon saw messengers flying about from the
> corner of the room where Freeman was. I called Redpath's atten-
> tion to it. "D—m him, let him come on," said Redpath, "I'll fix

him." But they did not molest him as, just then, Judge Shaw was giving his decision, and all eyes were fastened upon him. Wendell Phillips was on one side of Sanborn and Dr. Bowditch on the other. Redpath and I were posted at the middle of the back railing. Our purpose was to leap over, draw our revolvers, rush to Sanborn and drag him away. Mr. Phillips knew of the plot. Just before court session in the afternoon he came into our store. Seeing me loading revolvers, he asked, "Are you going to the courtroom?" I said, "Yes." He repeated the question, showing that he had feared my courage might falter. He quietly looked into my eyes and said, "I will be there!"[13]

If O'Connor was in Boston at the time, which seems likely, since he had signed his contract with Thayer and Eldridge less than two weeks before and had met Walt Whitman, he might have been the sixth member of the rescue group. It is known that Walt Whitman, although not a part of the group, was in the courtroom to see justice done. Sanborn later described his first sight of Whitman—from the prisoner's dock:

As I sat listening to the arguments of Andrew and Sewall in my behalf, and of Woodbury against them, and watched with admiration the dark, heavy judicial countenance of Old Judge Shaw— as striking as the ugliest and wisest of the English chancellors—I suddenly became aware of another face, no less remarkable, in the courtroom. It was Whitman's—he sat on a high seat near the door, wearing his loose jacket and open shirt-collar, over which poured the fullness of his beard, while above that the large and singular blue eyes, under heavy arching brows, wandered over the assembly, as some stately creature of the fields turns his eyes slowly about him in the presence of man.[14]

Perhaps William went with Walt on "a quiet Sunday afternoon" to hear Father Taylor preach to sailors in his "quaint ship-cabin-looking church."[15] They may have shared restaurant meals, at prices of which Walt complained to his brother Jeff—coffee at seven cents and beefsteak at nineteen cents.[16]

Walt and the printers worked expeditiously. By May 24 review copies had been sent out, and by June 14 the first issue was nearly all gone and the second printed and ready for binding. By mid-summer the publishers thought that the second printing would be exhausted within a month, and were planning both a cheaper and a slightly more expensive format for the next printing.

In the meantime O'Connor had left Boston to work on his novel at home in Philadelphia. Despite the alacrity with which he had accepted the assignment to write an "American novel," and despite the favorable terms, O'Connor found the process difficult. In reply to Sarah Helen Whitman who wrote expressing the hope that "the angel had touched his lips with a live coal from off the altar," he answered that he had not, "but that the Devil has put him on a particularly hot gridiron. Sitting on which he has written 321 pages of Ms. and expects to write the remaining 600 before October."[17]

While Whitman was in Boston he met other new friends besides O'Connor, Eldridge, and Thayer. Among them was John T. Trowbridge who had known O'Connor since the days of *The Carpet Bag*, for which he had written as "Paul Creyton."[18] Before Trowbridge met Whitman he had read and admired *Leaves of Grass*. On the day after he first became acquainted with the poems, he wrote to his sister:

> The only books that really feed my soul are the Bible and Emerson. Last night we had a reading at Mr. Newton's—a marvel and a monstrosity in the way of literature. The author is a sort of Emerson run wild—glorious, graphic, sublime, ridiculous, spiritual, sensual, great, powerful, savage, tender, sweet, and filthy.[19]

Years later, Trowbridge wrote:

> I was one of the earliest and most ardent admirers of "Leaves of Grass," with which I became acquainted soon after the first edition appeared in 1855—the thin small quarto, that astonished the critics by its uncouth typography, by the appearance of formlessness, almost of illiteracy, in its long irregular, ill-punctuated lines, most of all by its nonchalant treatment of a topic tabooed in modern polite literature as well as in polite society.[20]

In his first meeting with Emerson in 1857, Trowbridge said, "I have given up the fluent poets, and addicted myself to *Leaves of Grass*—I have become a Nebuchadnezzar, through Walt Whitman." To which Emerson replied, "Ah! I am glad to know that! It takes a strong stomach to digest that kind of food. Whitman is a man of extraordinary vigor. His prose—his letter and review of himself in the second edition—is as wonderful as his poetry. . . ." Emerson added: "I understand that Monckton Milnes (later Lord Houghton) has written highly commendatory letters. A gentleman had a letter for Whitman from Milnes; but feeling that Whitman had not used me well, he did not deliver it."[21] (This was a reference to Whitman's having quoted a line from Emerson's letter to him in the Second Edition—yet here Emerson himself does not seem to have taken umbrage.)

And now, here was Walt Whitman in Boston. A friend stopped Trowbridge in Washington Street, told him the good news, and escorted him to the stereotype foundry where the poet was correcting proof. The following Sunday Whitman visited Trowbridge in Somerville.

John T. Trowbridge, Charles Eldridge, and William O'Connor, all of whom met Whitman for the first time in Boston in 1860, were to meet him again in Washington several years later—the first as a helpful visitor, the second as a close friend, and the third as his champion and defender.

One who was to remain an adverse critic also appeared on the scene in Boston—Thomas Wentworth Higginson. Although he should have been dear to O'Connor as a cousin of William Channing and a prominent Abolitionist who was mentioned favorably by O'Connor in *Harrington*, he forfeited O'Connor's regard by disliking *Leaves of Grass*. Coming into the offices of Thayer and Eldridge and seeing a copy of *Leaves of Grass* on the desk, he said that the book always made him seasick, because he had first become acquainted with it on a voyage to the West Indies when he was recovering from *mal de mer*. He added that "if Walt's book represented health then he (Higginson) was diseased."[22] Higginson was to be the object of O'Connor's scorn in later years.

When Walt left Boston for Brooklyn after his book came out, the publishers and his new-found friends missed him. In August Thayer wrote:

> *We* too wish you could be with us in Boston, for we have *so* much to say; and our "fanatic" wants to get under the refreshing shelter of Walt's spirit; he does not ask Walt to talk, but only for the privilege of looking into those eyes of calm, and through them to enter

into that soul, so deep in its emotions, so majestic in all its thought-movements, and yet so simple and childlike. Yes, Walt Whitman, though men of the world and arch-critics do not understand thee, yet some there be among men and women who love thee and hold thy spirit close by their own.[23]

O'Connor, back in Philadelphia, worked on the novel from April through mid-September, right through "the dead heat of the Philadelphia summer," bursting with ideas, but pressed by the lack of time to explore them.[24] Dissatisfied with the novel when he finished it, O'Connor asked the publishers for time to rewrite, but they refused:

> We do not regard the want of time to re-write a good part of the book as any calamity. Many a fine work has been spoiled by too much artistic prinking and shearing. Gerald Massey has in the last edition of his works spoiled many of his finest poems in this way, and how Tennyson spoiled his "Charge of the Light Brigade" is still one of the chief sorrows of literature. Even Walt has hurt one or two of his own pieces by toning them. Better, far better, to be *crude and fiery*, than polished and dull.[25]

Fiery the novel certainly was, for its author was dealing with incendiary ideas: abolition, the rescue of fugitive slaves, woman's rights, reform of divorce laws, and the Baconian theory of the authorship of Shakespeare's plays. The title page read

HARRINGTON:
A STORY OF TRUE LOVE
By the author of "What Cheer," "The Ghost: a
Christmas Story," "A Tale of Lynn," etc.

Below this was a quotation from the Preface to *Morte D'Arthur* by Sir Thomas Malory, followed by the place of publication and name of the publisher. The next page held the copyright, by Thayer and Eldridge, and facing it the simple dedication:

I dedicate
this book
TO MY WIFE

There was no further clue to the identity of the author except the
initials *W.D. O'C.* signed to a note at the end of the book in which he
acknowledges his indebtedness for the sketch of the fugitive's flight
in the prologue

> to a couple of pages in the graphic and affecting narrative entitled
> "Twelve Years a Slave," by Mr. Solomon Northup, a free citizen
> of New York, who was kidnapped in that State and sold into bond-
> age in Louisiana, from which he was fortunately rescued and
> restored to his wife and children, after a dozen years of enforced
> servitude.[26]

The note continues with a brief reference to Delia Bacon's theory,
which the author had the hero, John Harrington, espouse, so "that
justice might be done to the great dead scholar in her grave."

Harrington opens with a lengthy prologue (68 pages) which introduces the slave-owner Lafitte, his wife Josephine, and his plantation, from which one slave, Roux, has escaped, and where Roux's
brother, Antony, is being subjected to harsh treatment. Lafitte treats
his slaves with brutality and his wife with subtle cruelty, neither they
nor she having any redress because of the laws governing slavery—
and marriage.

Antony runs away after undergoing the severe punishment of
"bucking" and having an iron collar affixed to his neck. His perilous
and frightening flight through the swamp ends in his capture and
delivery at gunpoint to a boat going back to New Orleans. As it nears
the city, the boat catches fire and in the confusion Antony is able to
jump into the river. There, seeing a brig marked "Soliman, Boston,"
he clambers on board and lowers himself into one of the hatches.
After days of starvation and despair, he is discovered:

> Recovering from their amazement, the sailors, with uncouth and
> profane ejaculations of horror and pity, lifted the inanimate body
> of Antony, disgusting even to their rude senses, and touching even
> to their rude sensibilities, out of the hold. They had hardly laid it
> on deck when the captain came rushing back again, shouting with
> oaths an order for look-out up aloft, with the hope of meeting
> some vessel bound for the city he had left that would take the
> slave back. Then giving the prostrate body a furious kick, he
> rushed away again, storming and stamping and swearing.

To Captain Bangham, good trade relations with the South and with the firm of Lafitte Brothers far outweighed the life of an escaped slave. As Antony lay in the hold he had wondered, "Who'll send me back after all I've gone through? Who'll be mean enough to do it?" The Prologue ends with the words, "Antony had received his answer."

Chapter One begins with a description of Boston in May 1852, where the fugitive from southern tyranny would discover two things—"first, that he must seek refuge with the people of his own color, in the quarter vulgarly known as Nigger Hill, secondly, that though they had once lived there in safety, neither he nor they could live there in safety any more."

And this was the case in Boston, a city built by fugitives, whose history the author traces. European seekers after freedom, including Kossuth, are still welcome. "But the fugitives from the South—the black Americans, men and women, who had fled thither for protection from a tyranny in no wise different from any other, save in its sordid vileness and abominable excess of cruelty and outrage—there was no safety for them."

Yet the Negro had contributed much to this country: "America has no distinctive music but her Negro melodies." Boston especially should remember that "one of the first five martyrs of her freedom and of the freedom of America, was a Negro—Crispus Attucks." Nevertheless, Boston had, for many years, paid her debt of gratitude to Attucks by treating the men and women of his race something after the fashion that Jews were treated in the Middle Ages. "They had their Ghetto at the west end of the town; there they lived by sufferance, despised, rejected, borne down by a social scorn which, to the noblest of them, was daily heartbreak, and which the lowliest of them could not bear without pain. . . ." O'Connor describes their "narrow range of humble employments" and lists the occupations open to them as well as the public places to which they were denied entrance:

> . . . excluded from the common schools, and allotted caste-schools where to learn anything was against nature; excluded from the colleges; excluded from the decent dwellings; excluded from the decent graveyards; excluded from almost everything. They were, however, freely admitted to the gallows and the jail.

But these, somehow or other, saw less of them than of the race that despised them.

Nevertheless, some progress had been made in the condition of the Negroes in Boston, because of that "heroic saint"—Emerson and the "saintly hero"—Garrison. And to Garrison's aid "gathered a little group of gentlemen and gentlewomen, writers and orators of marked power." Among them O'Connor names Abby Kelley, Lydia Maria Child, Mrs. Chapman, the Grimké sisters, Beriah Green, Theodore Weld, Edmund Quincy, Wendell Phillips, Theodore Parker, William Ellery Channing, John Quincy Adams, and Daniel Webster. Owing to their efforts, caste prejudices were breaking down. There were even one or two "colored" lawyers who had been admitted to the bar in Boston.

Then came the Fugitive Slave Law of 1850: "Suddenly over these struggling tides of light and darkness swept the black refluent surge of barbarism." And this law was passed with the endorsement of Webster! "The draft of a speech for freedom lying in his desk, he stood up in the Senate, spoke a speech for slavery, which was at war with every other speech of his previous life, and his game was made. He made it, played it, lost it, died, and lies cursed with forgiveness and buried in tears."

O'Connor goes on to describe the subsequent reign of terror in the northern cities, with thousands of Negroes fleeing to Canada, and those who remained, living in constant fear of kidnappers. Despite the heroic efforts of the Abolitionists and the Free-Soilers, fugitives were kidnapped. One of them—Shadrach—was rescued: "Ten or twelve gallant black men burst into the courtroom, and took Shadrach from his foes." But for another—Sims—rescue was impossible:

> The court-house was ringed with chains, under which the Chief Justice of Massachusetts, and other Judges, crawled to their seats. . . . Fifteen hundred Boston gentlemen offered to put muskets to their shoulders, if desired, to insure his being taken into bondage. "The Fifteen Hundred Scoundrels," Wendell Phillips christened this brigade of wretches, praying that bankruptcy might sit on the ledger of every one of them.

The first chapter of *Harrington* closes with a note of hope; though the torch itself was extinguished, the light of the torch still lives,

". . . and amidst the sordor and selfishness and cruelty of the period, it showed that the tradition and the promise of the Good Time Coming were immortal."

This note of hope leads to the introduction in Chapter Two of some of the protagonists and of the love story. The framework of romance which was to support O'Connor's ideas was a frail one. Yet it was necessary for the success of the novel that it live up to its subtitle: "A Story of True Love." Two pairs of lovers, John Harrington and Muriel Eastman, and Richard Wentworth and Emily Ames, become entangled by the false reports of a mischief-maker, Fernando Witherlee. All four are willing to give up their own desires on the altar of friendship. Thus Harrington is willing to surrender Muriel (who really reciprocates his love) to Wentworth, and Muriel to surrender Harrington to Emily (who really loves Wentworth). Everything is straightened out in time, culminating (after many pages and events) in the marriage of Muriel and Harrington, with the marriage of the other pair to take place soon after. Intertwined with this love story is the finding, secreting, loss, and final rescue of the slave Antony, in which the heroic Harrington loses his life only three days after his marriage to Muriel.

Harrington is truly a book of its time. Not only are real people and actual events woven into its fabric, but the fictional characters intermingle with the real. Two young clerks, who make a brief appearance in one of the scenes in the fencing studio (having taken up fencing because they had come upon the "heady wine" of Dumas), had been part of the mob of clerks and salesmen "who not long before had brawled down an orator of Dumas' own color—Frederick Douglass—at the Thompson meeting in Faneuil Hall." This leads the author to comment that Dumas would not have been safe in the "color-phobic" streets of Boston.

The leading characters attend the Anti-Slavery Convention presided over by Jackson and addressed by Garrison and Burleigh. On Sunday they go to hear Theodore Parker preach at Melodeon Hall; it is Parker who marries Muriel Eastman and John Harrington. Another real person is referred to when "Tugmutton," Roux's adopted son, says he wants to grow up to be a lawyer like the Negro William Morris.

The elements of Antony's escape, capture, and rescue are taken from several fugitive slave cases. The source of the flight through the swamp is acknowledged by the author to be Solomon Northup's account of his own escape. The name of the brig *Soliman* on which Antony hides shares its Turkish derivation with the *Ottoman*, on which in 1846 a slave named Joe was found secreted in the hold, lying naked upon the cargo, almost suffocated and half-dead with fear. The names of the captains—Bingham of the *Soliman* and Hannum of the *Ottoman*—have a similar sound. In the actual case, "The owner of the vessel had him carried back to New Orleans to preserve the integrity of his connection with the Southern market."[27] It was in reaction to this outrage that the meeting was held in Faneuil Hall at which John Quincy Adams presided and Theodore Parker gave his first anti-slavery speech.

There were, of course, other slaves who escaped by this method, including a "boy" belonging to F. C. Ewers, whose case was reported in the *Liberator* on October 31, 1856. (Like Antony, he was later rescued.) The tracing of Antony through a letter sent by Harrington which had been mailed in another city resembles a similar incident which led to the capture of Anthony Burns.

The climax of the novel is a rescue which had been twice proposed by the Abolitionists but never carried out.[28] Theodore Parker had proposed an attack on the boat which was to carry Sims back to his owner; a similar plan had been proposed by Captain Bearse for the rescue of Anthony Burns. In *Harrington*, the attack on Antony's captors and his rescue from the boat were carried out successfully by its hero, John Harrington, who was, however, mortally wounded in his heroic fight against seven adversaries. Antony and his brother Roux were then taken to Worcester (as the real fugitive slave Ellen Craft had been) in a closed carriage whose driver did not know the identity of his passengers.

Situations which seem impossible had their roots in reality. Muriel's mother, concealing the fugitives in her home, while her own brother, the merchant Lemuel Atkins, was trying to find Antony and return him to his owner, had its counterpart in at least one Boston home. It was the responsibility of George Hilliard, U.S. Commissioner, to restore slaves to their owners and punish those who had helped them—yet Mrs. Hilliard harbored fugitive slaves in the upper chamber of their house.[29]

Readers of *Harrington* may not only have recognized the real people and incidents in the novel, but may also have been able to guess the prototypes of the fictional characters. The fictional Captain Eldad Fisher of the *Polly Ann* resembled Captain Bearse, whose yacht, the *Flirt*, always stood ready to rescue slaves in the harbor. The French fencing master, Bagasse, was drawn from M. Boulet, the man who taught O'Connor to fence in his D'Artagnan-inspired youth. Harrington himself was probably a mixture of his ideal, Wendell Phillips, and his own idealized self—scholar, chevalier, hero. He expressed O'Connor's ideas—even his admiration of Lord Bacon, and like O'Connor, was said to be descended from the kings of Ireland. He also may have represented one of O'Connor's dreams which had not been fulfilled: After his marriage to Muriel, Harrington kept his own bachelor quarters so that he could continue his studies undisturbed. (This was a luxury which O'Connor might dearly have wished while writing his novel in great haste in a house with two-year-old Jeannie and infant Philip.)

Just as Harrington reflected O'Connor's ideas, Muriel reflected Nelly's. How much of her personality was based on Nelly's, however, is hard to determine. Harrington says of Muriel: "She has a rich, versatile, inclusive nature. You know that this union of feminine gentleness and manly spirit is not so uncommon." He calls Muriel the "fairy prince" when she is in her fencing costume, the "fairy princess" at other times. Perhaps she is the idealized Nelly—Nelly as she would have been if she had been rich and a member of Boston society. She was surely the author's ideal woman.

Muriel's ideas and beliefs, which are shown throughout the novel in her activities and conversation, are summed up in an amazing whole when her friend Emily teases her:

> Well, Muriel, you are the most astonishing Bostonienne I know. I should just like to analyze your mélange. Let's see now. In the first place, you defy fashion, insist on wearing dresses that show your shape, when all the rest of us are swaddled in half a dozen starched petticoats. . . . You won't wear low-necked dresses at parties. You don't waltz. You don't flirt. You don't care to be admired. You don't run after the lions. You pay court to all the taboo people, visit those who are voted out of good society, ask them to visit you. . . . Yes, and cry, "down with Mrs. Grundy." Then you cultivate the most miscellaneous and outlandish set of characters— authors and actors, and actresses, and reformers, and clergymen, and musicians and comeouters and people respectable and dis-

respectable all meet here, higgledy-piggledy, in the most hetero-
geneous mixture—the most chaotic—.

"Oh, no, Emily," Muriel interrupts, "not chaotic but cosmic. I accept them all as Nature accepts them all. Down with the walls!
That's my principle. No castes, no fictitious distinctions. Let fine
people of all sorts come together and learn to know each other. Democracy forever!"

"And then your studies," Emily continues, "perfectly omnivorous.
French, German, Italian, Latin, music, drawing, painting, moulding,
science, poetry, history, oratory, philosophy, Shakespeare, Bacon,
Dante, Plato, Goethe, Swedenborg. . . . "

Later Emily adds:

> There are your muscularities. You skate, you swim, you climb
> mountains, you ride horseback, you walk ten miles at a stretch,
> you saddle or harness your horse like a stableman, you catch up
> your horse's feet and look at the shoes like a blacksmith, you
> dance, you row, you lift weights, you swing by your hands, you
> walk on the parallel poles. . . . Yes, and fence with Wentworth
> and Harrington, besides turning the studio upstairs into a gymna-
> sium. Then you go on these tours, as you call them. You have a
> regular parish of Negroes and Irish people, and all sorts of forlorn
> characters, on whom you shower food, and clothes, and books,
> and goodness knows what else. And you go to theatres, circuses,
> operas, lectures, picture-galleries, woman's rights conventions,
> abolition meetings, political meetings of all sorts at Faneuil Hall,
> with the most delectable impartiality. Then you used to attend
> church at William Henry Channing's, which our best society
> thought horrid . . . and now Theodore Parker's, which they
> think worse still. And you have harbored fugitive slaves in your
> house, and helped them off to Canada. And you swallow Garrison
> and Parker Pillsbury—
> "—And adore Wendell Phillips," interposed Muriel.
> "Yes, and adore Wendell Phillips. And subscribe for the 'Common-
> wealth' newspaper . . . and Garrison's 'Liberator'. . . ."

Muriel assures her that many Boston ladies do the same; she is not
so original as Emily thinks. Later Muriel states her own philosophy:
"No effeminate culture for me. What I know or do, I will know or do
thoroughly and vigorously, or not at all." Her mother applauds this,

and says her father would have agreed. "There's no reason, he used to observe, why girls shouldn't be as vigorously trained as boys, and even supposing woman's share to be purely and simply that of a wife and mother, said he, she ought, on the most ultra conservative principles, to have every power and faculty fully developed that she may fitly educate her children."

"Good! Woman's rights doctrine, that," said Wentworth, playfully. "Muriel, do you vote?" he added, with a quizzical air.

"Yes," answered Muriel, so naively that Wentworth was taken aback. Then she explains that their servant Patrick asks her how he shall vote, and she tells him. That is her ballot. "But what do you think of the good sense of a community that allowing me capable of instructing a man how to vote, will not allow that I am capable of voting myself? What do you think of a country that denies to a cultured woman a right which it accords to the uncultured man who opens her street door?"

At the end of the novel Muriel is strong-minded even about her husband's death (of which both he and she had had premonitions) because he died in the cause they both believed in. To Captain Bangham, whose insistence on returning the slave was the ultimate cause of Harrington's death, she says:

> He is the light of life to me, but I yield him up with joy and pride. Can I feel one pulse of grief when I think that he dies for the inalienable rights of man? Can I remember that he dies to save a fellow-creature from cruelty and wrong, and mourn? Think! He was rich, and he dies for the poor; he was strong, and he dies for the weak; he was a freeman, and he dies for the slave. Is that a death to mourn? No! My soul is glad in him—my heart covers him with glory.

Thus Muriel is in every way a partner of Harrington—in ideas, in actions, and in sacrifice. O'Connor created Muriel, as he wrote to feminist Caroline Dall, who had not liked her, "at the head of Michelet—I mean that it was meant as the denial of the French invalid he paints as the model. . . . "[30] He confesses, however, that hers is the opinion of most readers. He had had but one letter praising Muriel—and that sent by Robert Carter, editor of *Appleton's Encyclopedia*, from a lady he did not name, but whom he characterized as "one of the most intelligent women of New England."[31] The lady agreed with O'Connor, writing, "Muriel is the woman Michelet ought to have described in *L'Amour*. That is real spirituality. . . . " The lady, while praising Muriel, criticizes the language of the ladies. "I think it would be impossible for Muriel and Emily to be so inelegant, brought up as they were. They use such phrases as 'Faith now! Bless me!' &c. which might be used by a fine woman who had risen from the lower classes, but are entirely out of the question in good society in Boston. As indeed unnecessary exclamations are everywhere."[32] O'Connor would probably have defended this mode of speech as did Wentworth, the artist, in the novel: "Slang is the picturesque of language, and we must talk picturesquely, or die."

Harrington turned out to be much longer than the original contract specified—558 pages in all. The story ends with the burial of John Harrington at the cemetery in Auburn, the sadness assuaged by a Whitmanesque augury of the future of America. After the burial Wentworth says of Harrington, "He was alone in nobleness," to which Muriel replies:

> No, not alone, not alone. This is America—America forming and emerging, with martyrs and heroes such as no land has seen. The Greek could die for freeman; but when died he for the helot? Oh, I see the heroes of all lands and times! They live and die for country, for ideas, for religions, but in America they live and die for man. Land of Lovejoy's grave, land of Torrey's grave, of the lovers for whose love the lowest was not too low, I read your golden augury! You prophecy the future; you herald the America uprising—the beautiful divine land of lovers and of friends! Shall it not come? Oh, graves of all who die that it may be, answer, answer, answer!

And the book ends with the assurance of a brighter future:

> It comes! It comes! Clear and sweet are your voices, oh, graves! Raging clamors drown the voices of the living, but clear and sweet are the voices of the dead, and it comes—the bright land comes—the land of lovers and of friends—it comes.

Not permitted to revise, O'Connor sent *Harrington* to Thayer and Eldridge. In October the impatient Curtis, who had been asking about the progress of the book all summer, was able to address

O'Connor (in a letter sent to him at the Smithsonian House in New York City) as "My dear Harrington."[33] In the same month an advance notice of the book, written by Sarah Helen Whitman, appeared in the *Providence Journal*. It promised that the book, by a writer "of singularly original genius . . . will be likely . . . to create a decided sensation."

Perhaps it was to celebrate the completion of the manuscript that O'Connor visited Pfaff's, famous rendezvous of the Bohemians.

> When O'Connor entered, Clapp, who was seated at the end of long table "giving his little senate laws," said, "I hear you've written a book, William. Is that so?"
> O'Connor admitted that it was.
> "Is it entirely original?" Clapp asks.
> "Why, of course it is," O'Connor replies indignantly.
> "Then we'll kill it," yelled Clapp and his fellow journalists in chorus.[34]

When *Harrington* appeared, the *Saturday Press* did not make good its threat. It praised the book for its vigor of moral enthusiasm, its humanitarian principles, its talent, pathos, power and brilliancy, but thought its ethics absurdly quixotic.

In the *Providence Journal* which had printed O'Connor's early work, a review by Sarah Helen Whitman was more favorable.

> It is not through its scholarly and beautiful elocution, its pomp of rhetoric and stamp of elegant culture—not through its finely touched and telling portraitures of the living orators and thinkers and actors of our day—not for its rare verbal opulence, . . . but it is through the tender, human sympathies, the noble heroic passions evoked in the heart of the reader, that *Harrington* enthralls the imagination and disarms criticism. Open to censure on so many points that we have not space even to touch upon them, we have in *Harrington* an earnest, high-toned, inspired book—a book profoundly interesting as a romance—noble in conception and design as a grand, heroic poem, superb in scenic effect as a gorgeous, tragic drama.[35]

Four months later (in March 1861), the *Atlantic Monthly* was largely adverse in its criticism, saying in part that it was "One of the most impossible books that man ever wrote. A book which one could almost prove never could be written, and which, as an illogical conclusion, but a stubborn fact, has been written, nevertheless."

An anonymous reviewer in the Boston *Wide World* in unconscious prophecy linked *Harrington* and *Leaves of Grass*, not because they emanated from the same publishing house, but because the reviewer considered them both "sensation" books. According to him, Whitman's poems were "prose run crazy . . . the veriest trash ever written, and vulgar and disgusting to the last degree," and *Harrington* was "another sensation book—an anti-slavery affair—one of the brood spawned by 'Uncle Tom'!"[36] Even William's friend Curtis had to temper his praise, writing:

> It is rich, exuberant, overwrought, melodramatic, fervid with passionate feeling and protest, morbid, gorgeous, full of fiery youth,—a book which you will be proud of and sorry for! I don't mean sorry in the ordinary way,—but merely that you plucked your golden fruit, green.[37]

All these reviews, whether favorable or adverse, might have promoted the sale of *Harrington*, but very soon after the book appeared, its publishers were in poor financial condition. For a while they were still hopeful: "The sale is dull at present," they wrote toward the end of 1860, "but if the country does not all go to smash we have no doubt as to a successful future for the work."[38] They ask O'Connor not to draw his eighty dollars that month as his draft could not be honored. Their hopes were not realized, and on January 15, 1861, they announced their bankruptcy. Later they wrote that they had assigned the plates to Horace Wentworth.[39] After attempting to promote the sale of *Harrington* through a pamphlet of reviews sent to their agents, and binding the prologue with a book by Lizzie Torrey on Woman's Rights, Wentworth and Company lost interest in it.[40]

Harrington was not completely forgotten, however. Edmund C. Stedman published an excerpt from it in his *Library of American Literature* in 1889, and it was the subject of an exchange of letters between John Benton and Thomas Wentworth Higginson in *The Critic* in 1892.[41]

O'Connor lost more than *Harrington* with the failure of Thayer and Eldridge. Another dream was shattered, for in the letter urging O'Connor to write for them, they had proposed a literary venture for the future. In "strictest confidence" they had told him that they planned to start a weekly newspaper "that shall be worthy of Boston—we think there is none such now—and to which the best intellects and most liberal spirits of the country shall contribute, such as Parker, Emerson, Mrs. Child, Higginson, and others. A paper which shall sustain with great ability radical views on the reformatory questions of the day, and combine these with the highest literary character."[42] They wanted O'Connor to contribute essays and tales and have a permanent connection with the establishment for that purpose. The paper never came into being. Charles Eldridge left for Washington, where he got a job in the Army Paymaster's office. William Thayer got a job in the post office in Boston, and later went out West and lost contact with Eldridge, Whitman, and O'Connor.

The failure of Thayer and Eldridge left O'Connor in the same situation and mood from which their first letter had rescued him. He spent the next six months in limbo—living in Philadelphia, hopefully listed in its directory as "author" instead of "editor," worrying about the need for more certain employment and working on a short story. The story was "The Brazen Android," an early example of science fiction, which was accepted in March 1861 by the *Atlantic Monthly* and paid for ($100 on account) the following month.[43] There was a long delay in publishing it, however, during which time O'Connor must have had his usual despairing afterthoughts. Almost a year after it had been accepted, he called it back for revision. Resubmitted by Nelly after William's death, "The Brazen Android" finally appeared in the *Atlantic Monthly* in April and May 1891 and was one of the *Three Tales* by O'Connor published that year by Houghton Mifflin Company.

In "The Brazen Android" O'Connor turned from the contemporary settings and semi-autobiographical incidents of his earlier short stories and novel to delve into medieval England. Yet here too he wrote of poverty and the need for social reform. He chose the thirteenth century when the darkness of the corrupt social system was being penetrated by a faint ray of the dawn of science. His characters were Friar Roger Bacon, Friar Thomas Bungy (*sic*), the wicked King Henry III, and the noble Simon de Montfort. Based on a legend about Friar Bacon, the story told of the invention and construction of a brazen head which could articulate words; with it Friar Bacon planned to admonish the king to listen to the counsels of Simon de Montfort, and so save England.

The story opens with a description of medieval London and the squalid homes of the poor:

> Light came dim, and sunshine dimly glimmering, into their darkened rooms. Summer heats made ovens of them. The old gray family of London fogs rose from the marshes north of the city walls, from the city's intersecting rivulets, from the Thames below, and crept in at every opening to make all dank and chill within. Down their squat chimneys swept the smoke, choking and blinding. Rains such as even rainy England knows not now soaked them through for weeks together. Cold, such as English winters have forgotten now, pierced with gripping blast and silent-shifting snow, to their shivering inmates. Foul exhalations from the filthy street hung around them an air of poison, or, rising from the cesspools, of which every house had one within, discharged themselves in deadly maladies. Lightnings stabbed their roofs or rent their walls, hunting for those they sheltered. Conflagration, lurking in a spark, upspread in dragonish flame, and roared through them devouring. Whirlwind swept through them howling, and tolled them down by fifties. Pestilence breathed through them in recurring seasons, and left their rooms aghast with corpses. Civic riot or intestine war stormed often near them, and brought them death and sorrow. Famine arose every few years, and walked through them on his way through England, leaving their tenants lean and pale or lifeless . . . while Science, builder of life that is holy, beautiful, and gay, was but a wondrous new-born child in Roger Bacon's cell, dreaming of things to come.

Yet science had difficulty in extricating itself from "the swaddling clothes of superstition." Although the mechanism by which the head of the brazen android is enabled to utter sounds is explained logically, there are hints of the supernatural in Dr. Malatesti, who taught the process to Friar Bacon. In Dr. Malatesti's view of mankind, O'Connor expresses his own darker thoughts while echoing some of Whitman's phrases:

I am the apostle of despair. I strip away the mask and show the man. Labor, labor to build the perfect realm; but the realm is made of men, and men are unchangeably bestial at the core. Wolf and snake, hog and harpy, are inextricably mixed in man, and virtue is nothing but a covering lie, itself the foulest vice of all. . . . Fair and white is the skin, but under the breastbone the hell-pool rages. Oh, may it rage forever!

(Evidently *Leaves of Grass* had become so much a part of O'Connor by this time that he echoed two passages without using quotation marks. In "Crossing Brooklyn Ferry" this line appears: "The wolf, the snake, the hog, not wanting in me," and in "Poem of the Road" (later, "Song of the Open Road") the line: "Smartly attired, countenance smiling, form upright, death under the breast-bones, hell under the skullbones.")[44]

When the brazen android finally speaks, it utters not the formula prepared by Friar Bacon, but original, cryptic phrases, heard only by a dull-witted servant who failed to call his master to listen. The android is shattered, but Friar Bacon is glad that he had not influenced the king by these means, for it would have meant playing on the king's superstition. "Better fail of good by truth, than win it by falsehood." Nevertheless, Simon de Montfort finally succeeds in bringing about needed reforms, and the story closes with a paragraph that sounded the keynote for O'Connor's later life:

For the good cause never dies, and it is never defeated. Its defeats are but the recoils of the battering-ram from the wall that is fated to crash in; its deaths are like those of the Italian story, where each man cloven in twain by the sword of the slayer springs up two men, mailed and armed to slay.

With "The Brazen Android" finished and accepted, O'Connor again took steps toward getting a job that would provide a steady income for his family. He turned toward Washington, D.C., as did many job seekers and office hunters in those troubled days. His friends Charles Eldridge and John Hay were already in Washington, the former as a clerk in the paymaster's office and the latter as assistant secretary to President Lincoln. O'Connor was to remain in Washington for the rest of his life—a life that would seesaw between fulfillment and frustration.

NOTES

1. Information about Thayer and Eldridge, their personal lives and publishing careers, is drawn from the unpublished "Autobiography of William Wilde Thayer," Indianapolis, Indiana, 1 November 1892 (LC). C. Carroll Hollis called my attention to this manuscript.
2. Lizzie B. Torrey, *The Ideal of Womanhood or Words to the Women of America* (Boston: Thayer and Eldridge, 1861). After the failure of Thayer and Eldridge, this book was bound by Wentworth and Co. with the Prologue to *Harrington*.
3. Further information about the "Black Strings" may be found in "The Black Strings of 1859," *The Sunday Journal*, Indianapolis, 20 August 1893, p. 9. Ruth E. Dickey, archivist of Indiana State Library, located this article for me.
4. (Feinberg-LC).
5. WW to Abby M. Price, 20 March (1860), *Correspondence*, I:49–50.
6. An indication of this is O'Connor's quotation of the phrase, "the stale and drowsy air" (in *The Mercantile Reporter*, January 1856), whereas in the First Edition of *Leaves of Grass* the line reads "its stale and drowsy lair." Walt Whitman, *The Uncollected Poetry and Prose*, ed. Emory Holloway (Garden City, N.Y. and Toronto: Doubleday, Page & Company, 1921), p. 27.
7. M. J. Channing, "Recollections of Walt Whitman," unpublished ms (Chamberlin).
8. *Ibid.*
9. Ellen M. Calder, "Personal Recollections of Walt Whitman," *Atlantic Monthly*, June 1907, p. 832.
10. (Brown).
11. "I create an immense sensation in Washington Street. Every body here is so like everybody else—and I am Walt Whitman!—Yankee curiosity and cuteness, for once, is thoroughly stumped, confounded, petrified, made desperate." *Correspondence*, vol. I, p. 50.
12. Fragment of an unpublished letter in SHW correspondence (Brown).
13. Thayer, *op. cit.*
14. Frank B. Sanborn, *Springfield Republican*, 19 April 1876 (LC).
15. WW, "Father Taylor—and Oratory," *Complete Works*, vol. VI, p. 111.
16. *Correspondence*, vol. I, p. 53.
17. SHW to a friend, Mrs. Freeman, May 1860, in Caroline Ticknor, *Poe's Helen* (New York: Charles Scribner's Sons, 1916), pp. 199–200.
18. See Chapter III, note 6.
19. Trowbridge to Mrs. Phelps, quoted in Rufus Arthur Coleman, *John Townsend Trowbridge*, Ph.D. dissertation, Boston University Graduate School, 1937, pp. 217–26. (Interlibrary loan to Hunter College, May 1963.)
20. *Ibid.*, pp. 294–96.
21. *Ibid.*, pp. 298–99.
22. Eldridge to Burroughs, 21 April 1892, in Barrus, *Comrades*, p. 302.
23. Thayer, mss. *op. cit.*
24. WDO'C to Dall, 7 December 1860 (MIT).
25. (Feinberg-LC).
26. See Chapter III, note 10.
27. John Weiss, *Life and Correspondence of Theodore Parker*, 2 vols. (New York: Appleton-Century-Crofts, 1864), vol. 1, p. 77.

28. Henry Steele Commager, *Theodore Parker* (Boston: Beacon, 1947), pp. 221, 223.
29. William Still, *The Underground Rail Road* (Philadelphia: Porter and Coates, 1872; reprinted New York: Arno Press and *The New York Times*, 1968), pp. 373–74.
30. WDO'C to Dall, 7 December 1860 (MIT).
31. Carter to WDO'C, 27 November [1860] (Feinberg-LC).
32. Carter enclosed letter he recopied from unnamed critic. 6 December 1860 (Feinberg-LC).
33. GWC to WDO'C, 19 October 1860 (Brown).
34. *Philadelphia Press*, 7 January 1887. This anecdote was told to the author of the article (unnamed) by "a gentleman who has a large acquaintance among the journalists and literary men of this country." WDO'C scrapbook (Syracuse).
35. 7 December 1860 (Syracuse).
36. Florence B. Freedman, "Whitman's *Leaves* and O'Connor's *Harrington*: An 1860 Review," *Walt Whitman Review* 9:63–65 (September 1963). The review is preserved in a WDO'C scrapbook (Syracuse).
37. GWC to WDO'C, 7 December 1860 (Brown).
38. Thayer and Eldridge to WDO'C, 1860, n.d. (Feinberg-LC).
39. Thayer and Eldridge to WDO'C, 23 January 1861 (Feinberg-LC).
40. Wentworth and Company to WDO'C, 3 May 1861 (Feinberg-LC).
41. Issues of 26 March 1892 and 9 April 1892.
42. Thayer and Eldridge to WDO'C, 23 February 1860 (Feinberg-LC).
43. James T. Fields to WDO'C, 7 April 1861 (Feinberg-LC).
44. LG/CRE, pp. 158, 163.

CHAPTER VIII

Washington:
The Magic Circle

❈ WILLIAM DOUGLAS O'Connor arrived in Washington on July 4, 1861.[1] The choice of Independence Day was ironic, for he was seeking a job which would undoubtedly take him away from his independent literary endeavors.

He had begun the search for a job two months earlier. For help in his application to Salmon P. Chase, Secretary of the Treasury, he had turned to his literary friends and to his associates in the Abolition Movement who were now influential in the government. Among those who wrote to Chase on his behalf were Robert Carter, George William Curtis, Senator Henry Wilson, and James W. Stone, treasurer of the State Republican Committee of Massachusetts.[2] Their letters, all dated between May 13 and May 16, 1861, antedated his own application, which was sent on May 20. All the letters spoke of O'Connor's marked literary ability and fine character. Curtis wrote most warmly that his "power and habit of tireless application, his absolute integrity, his self-sacrificing principle, and his remarkable abilities and accomplishments peculiarly fit him for the post. . . . If I were speaking for my brother, I could not be more sincerely anxious for the success of his application." Dr. J. W. Stone wrote about O'Connor's political background:

> . . . He is a radical, Anti-Slavery man of great genius, entirely reliable, alike in principle, character and ability.
> He is the author of "Harrington" and other works indicative of decided genius.

126

Dr. Stone goes on to say, "You may remember his wife who was Miss Ellen M. Tarr, and if not, Mrs. Dr. Bailey can remind you of her. She was, I think, for some years the governess of her admirably educated children."

None of these letters elicited a response, and O'Connor decided finally to go to Washington to seek a job in person. The day of his arrival was cloudy and warm, with the political climate as uncomfortable and uncertain as the weather. An extra session of Congress, called to deal with the crisis, began that day. Washington was rife with rumors and filled with apprehension. The following day news came that General Johnston had surrounded General Cadwallader's army at Martinsburg, and Washington feared invasion. On the 16th, there were rumors that General McClellan had possession of the Valley between the Blue Ridge and the Alleghenies, and on the July 22—a beautiful day—came the news of the terrible Battle of Manassas, followed closely by the arrival of trainloads of wounded.[3]

After O'Connor's arrival, John Hay lost no time in interceding for him. On July 5 Hay wrote to the Honorable Salmon P. Chase: "At your suggestion, I beg leave thus formally to call your attention to the application of Wm. D. O'Connor, Esq. for a clerkship in your Department." After referring to the letters of recommendation on file, he continued:

> Mr. O'Connor is a man of very remarkable genius, a consistent and laborious advocate of free soil, a capable clerk and of unblemished integrity. If you see fit to appoint him, you will confer upon him a favor for which he will always be grateful, and have the satisfaction of assisting a man whose great powers will never be applied to any but the noblest purposes.[4]

Still there was no answer from Secretary Chase. On July 23 O'Connor wrote again, calling attention to his application and adding the name of Senator Sumner to the list of his sponsors. On August 31 he wrote to the Assistant Secretary of the Treasury, George Harrington, of a specific opening in the Comptroller's office. (He may have had some temporary work as a copyist, because he suggests asking Mr. Ela about his capacity as a copying clerk.)

Striving so assiduously to attain what he did not really want, O'Connor must have been in a black mood during his first weeks in Washington. He wrote only a few lines to Nelly, neglecting even to give her his address. On August 3 his friend J. Hubley Ashton, then at an army camp, wrote that he was anxious to learn how O'Connor was faring in relation to a clerkship, and added: "I wrote to your wife the day I left for camp. She had had at the time of her last letter to me, but a line or two from you, and did not know the name of the street you were living in."[5]

It was not until October 9 that O'Connor, then living at 227 D Street, received a letter from George Harrington asking him to come for an interview. Nine days later he was appointed temporary clerk in the Treasury Department under the Lean Act of July 17, 1861, at a salary of twelve hundred dollars a year.[6] One of his letters of recommendation—from E. A. Stansbury—arrived after his appointment, its plea for an early decision "as Mr. O'Connor has a lovely young family entirely dependent on him" already granted.[7]

Two months later the lovely young family—Nelly and the children (Jeannie almost four years old and Philip almost two)—joined William. On February 1, 1862, O'Connor was appointed to a regular clerkship (third class) in the Treasury Department, Office of the Lighthouse Board, where he was to remain—rising in rank and with varying duties—overworked, frustrated, and often bitter about his job for the rest of his life. The early years, however, were years of enthusiasm and excitement. William Dean Howells, a journalist who was to become a novelist and editor of the *Atlantic Monthly*, met the young government clerk in Washington:

> It was on my second visit [to Washington] that I met the generous young Irishman, William D. O'Connor, at the house of my friend Piatt, and heard his ardent talk. He was one of the promising men of that day, and he had written an anti-slavery novel in the heroic mood of Victor Hugo, which greatly took my fancy; and I believe he wrote poems too. He had not yet risen to be the chief of Walt Whitman's champions outside the Saturday Press, but he had already espoused the theory of Bacon's authorship of Shakespeare, then newly exploited by the poor lady of Bacon's name, who died constant to it in an insane asylum. He used to speak of the reputed dramatist as "the fat peasant of Stratford," and he was otherwise picturesque of speech in a measure that consoled, if it did not convince. The great war was then full upon us, and when in the silences of our literary talk its awful breadth was heard, and its shadow fell upon the hearth where we gathered round the first fires of autumn, O'Connor would lift his beautiful

head with a fine effect of prophecy, and say, "Friends, I feel a sense of victory in the air." He was not wrong; only the victory was for the other side.

Who besides O'Connor shared in these saddened symposiums I cannot tell now; but probably other young journalists and office-holders, intending litterateurs, since more or less extinct. I make certain only of the young Boston publisher who issued a very handsome edition of Leaves of Grass, and then failed promptly if not consequently.[8]

Howells left to become consul at Venice before Walt Whitman arrived in Washington.

In April 1862 tragedy struck the O'Connors with the death of their little son Philip, probably of complications following a smallpox vaccination. (There was an epidemic of smallpox in Washington at the time.) This was a blow from which Nelly and William found it hard to recover. Fortunately, new interest and inspiration came into their lives the following December when Walt Whitman came to Washington. According to Jeannie Channing, "My sister (Nelly) said Walt's sympathy and friendship was (*sic*) beyond words helpful to her in that time of affliction" and that but for him "she did not know how she could have lived."[9]

During the interval between the failure of Thayer and Eldridge and his arrival in Washington, Whitman had returned to journalism, writing articles for the *Brooklyn Standard* and the *New York Leader*. The start of the war moved him to write a few stirring, but impersonal poems, two of which were published in 1861.

Walt Whitman reached Washington on December 18, 1862, en route to the battlefield in search of his brother George, who had been reported wounded in the battle of Fredericksburg.[10] Walt was penniless, for his pocket had been picked while he was changing trains at Philadelphia. Searching in the hospitals was no easy matter, for there were as many as fifty military hospitals in and around Washington. Churches and public buildings, such as the Patent Office, had been converted into hospitals; some of these held as many as a thousand soldiers; others were one-story wooden barracks, each of which held about sixty men.

While wandering through the city, he ran into Charles Eldridge and William O'Connor and told them of his plight. Eldridge could not refrain from saying that "any pickpocket who failed to avail himself of such an opportunity as Walt offered, with his loose baggy trousers and no suspenders, would have been a disgrace to his profession." But his friends were eager to help him, William supplying him with some funds and Charley with a pass to the front lines.[11] Walt left his carpetbag at the O'Connor house and departed for Fredericksburg. Nelly was away at the time, visiting in Boston. When she came home, even the presence of Walt's carpetbag did not assure her that he would return, for she remembered how he had failed to keep his promises to be at the Tyndales' in Philadelphia.

Walt did, however, come back to the O'Connors on December 28, 1862, after spending more than a week with his brother at the front.[12] It was at this time that Nelly met the poet whose work she had known since 1855 and of whom she had heard so much from her husband and from the Tyndales. The sight of the wounded on the battlefields, in the camp, and on the train was so pitiable that Walt wanted to stay in Washington in order to be of some help to them. He had acquired a list of possible places to board, but before he and William set out to look at them, William took Nelly aside and asked whether, if other places did not prove suitable, she would like to have Walt take a room in the house in which they lived and be their guest at meals. She readily assented.

When Walt returned with William, not having found lodgings, he rented "a werry little bedroom" for seven dollars a month on the second floor of the house at 394 L Street, in which the O'Connors had two larger furnished rooms on the third floor, for which they were paying twenty-five dollars a month (a price Whitman thought "*extra*ordinary"). Walt felt free to use their more spacious quarters; on the Saturday evening after his arrival he wrote to his sister-in-law, Martha: "Mr. and Mrs. O'Connor and their little girl have all gone out 'downtown' for an hour or two, to make some Saturday evening purchases, and I am left in possession of the premises—so I sit by the fire, and scribble more of my letter." On another evening, Walt stayed with little Jeannie when the O'Connors went to see Heron in *Medea*.[13]

In June Walt wrote to his mother about the O'Connors:

> . . . We have strawberries good and plenty, 15 cents a quart, with the hulls on—I go down to market sometimes of a morning and buy two or three quarts, for the folks I take my meals with—

Mother, do you know I have not paid, as you may say, a cent of board since I have been in Washington, that is for meals—four or five times I have made a rush to leave the folks and find a moderate priced boarding house, but every time they have made such a time about it, that I have kept on—it is Mr. & Mrs. O'Connor, (he is the author of "Harrington")—he has a $1,600 office in the Treasury, and she is a first rate woman, a Massachusetts girl—they keep house in a moderate way—they have one little girl, (lost a fine boy about a year ago)—they have two rooms in the same house where I hire my room, and I take breakfast (½ past 8) and dinner (½ past 4) with them, as they will have it so—that's the way it has gone on now over five months, and as I say, they won't listen to my leaving—but I shall do so, I think—I can never forget their kindness and real friendship and it appears as though they would continue just the same, if it were for all our lives. But I have insisted on going to market (it is pleasant in the cool of the morning,) and getting the things, at my own expense, two or three times a week lately. . . . [14]

Because of the kindness of the O'Connors, Walt's expenses were low; still he needed a regular income. Soon after his arrival in Washington he had obtained a job as copyist in the office of Major Hapgood, the Army Paymaster (possibly through Charles Eldridge, who worked there). He worked for a few hours each day, devoting the rest of his time to visiting the wounded in the hospitals. Whitman thought of trying to get more lucrative employment. For this, as O'Connor could undoubtedly tell him from his own experience, some patronage was needed. Walt therefore wrote to Ralph Waldo Emerson, confident of the friendship of the great writer who had responded warmly to the first edition of *Leaves of Grass*. Whitman had blazoned a sentence of that letter—"I greet you at the beginning of a great career"—on the cover of the second edition in 1856, and there was some question of the propriety of his having done so. Still he was evidently confident enough of Emerson's friendship to ask him for letters of recommendation to William Seward, Secretary of State, and Salmon P. Chase, Secretary of the Treasury. An indication of Emerson's continuing friendship was his prompt response, sending a letter addressed to each of these officials to Whitman, as he had requested. In the letters, which were almost identical, Emerson was laudatory but candid, the one to Seward stating:

. . . Permit me to say that he is known to me as a man of strong original genius, combining, with marked eccentricities, great powers & valuable traits of character; a self-relying, large-hearted man, much beloved by his friends; entirely patriotic & benevolent in his theory, tastes, & practice. If his writings are in certain points open to criticism, they yet show extraordinary power, and are more deeply American, democratic, & in the interest of political liberty, than those of any other poet. He is indeed a child of the people, & their champion.

A man of his talents & dispositions will quickly make himself useful, and, if the Government has work that he can do, I think it may easily find, that it has called to its side more valuable aid than it bargained for. . . .[15]

Whitman may have thought that Emerson's letters, with their references to eccentricities, would not be likely to gain him employment; the letter to Seward was probably never presented, the one to Chase some time later. A month after he received the letters from Emerson, Whitman tried to get help from Senators Charles Sumner of Massachusetts and Preston King of New York in obtaining a job in the State Department, but nothing came of his efforts. "Meantime," he wrote to his brother Jeff, "I make about enough to pay my expenses by hacking on the press here, and copying in the paymasters (sic) office, a couple of hours a day."[16] Whitman relied on his own meager resources and contributions from friends in Boston, Brooklyn, New York, and Providence to buy stationery, stamps, fruit, tobacco and syrups for his boys in the hospitals. The O'Connors' generosity helped him to stretch his income.

Walt stopped taking all his meals with the O'Connors in June 1863, when they moved to a more spacious apartment in the same street. During the hot summer, Nelly did not cook; the O'Connors took their meals in a family hotel nearby, while Whitman got his own breakfast and had dinner in a restaurant. He continued, however, to visit the O'Connors almost daily.

On October 6, 1863, Walt wrote to his mother: "My friends the O'Connors that I wrote about recommenced cooking the lst of this month (they have been as usual in summer taking their meals at a family hotel nearby.) Saturday they sent for me to breakfast and Sunday I eat dinner with them, very good dinner, roast beef, lima beans, good potatoes, etc. They are truly friends to me."[17]

Visits with the O'Connors afforded a pleasant contrast to Walt's daily life, for not only the hospital sights were sad, but also the scenes in the paymaster's office where soldiers were turned away for lack of funds. From these sad sights and sounds Walt found relief in the discussions, the games, and the banter at the O'Connors', night after night. A number of friends came to the O'Connors' in the evenings, to talk with their hosts, Charles Eldridge, and Walt Whitman. At various times the circle included Sarah and John Piatt, well-known poets at that time.[18] (John Piatt, who was also a clerk in the Treasury Department, later became librarian of the House of Representatives and American Consul at Cork.) Some of the regular visitors were Dr. Horatio Stone, surgeon and sculptor, Dr. Frank Baker of the Smithsonian Institution, Count Adam Gurowski, and Arnold Johnson, secretary to Senator Sumner. Others came when they visited Washington, among them John T. Trowbridge, the writer, Albert Brisbane, the Fourierist, Richard Hinton, biographer and journalist, John and William Swinton, writers, and beginning in 1866 Dr. William Francis Channing, his wife Jeannie (Nelly's sister) and their daughter Grace, who was two years younger than the O'Connors' daughter Jeannie.

It was in the fall of 1863 that John Burroughs, who was to be Whitman's earliest biographer and close friend, came to Washington, drawn by his desire to meet Whitman.[19] He had read Whitman's poems in the *Saturday Press* in 1859, and had paid a visit to Pfaff's in New York in the hope of meeting the poet there. In 1862 Burroughs's friend, E. M. Allen, had settled in Washington where he opened an army supply store. Walt had got into the habit of dropping in at Allen's store, and "between Walt and me has passed the bond of beer, and we are friends,"[20] Allen had written the envious Burroughs, and again, "Walt is much interested in you, and I sketched your history some to him. He would like to know you. . . . He sends his compliments and says if you ever come anywhere near him you must find him out and give him a call."[21]

The invitation was intriguing. Although at this time John Burroughs was beginning to write the nature essays for which he was to become famous, he was unhappy at work and at home. His meager salary as a school teacher was inadequate, and he was frequently separated from his wife Ursula for financial and emotional reasons. It was hard for him to live with her—or without her. His final decision to leave for Washington was prompted, according to the statement of one of his friends, by the recriminations following his awkward overturning of a spider (frying pan) of hot grease on the floor.[22]

Five months after receiving Allen's letter about Walt's interest in him, Burroughs arrived in Washington. Within a few weeks he wrote to his wife, "I have seen Walt and think him glorious."[23] During his first weeks in Washington Burroughs, not yet employed, "was sleeping on an army cot in Allen's store, washing out his socks and handkerchiefs, dining off a piece of pie."[24] He spent his days looking for work. But all this was worthwhile, for he was seeing Whitman, strolling with him through the woods near Washington, accompanying him on his visits to the hospitals, and talking with him of the soul and immortality.

After gaining and losing and regaining employment, Burroughs was able to send for his wife in the fall of 1864. He had become a clerk in the Currency Bureau of the Treasury Department, where he was to remain for ten years. A year later the Burroughses were able to get a house on Capitol Hill, which the O'Connors shared in 1868.

Although Burroughs saw a great deal of Whitman, he did not become part of the group which met at the O'Connors' until after 1865, when O'Connor's defense of Whitman, *The Good Gray Poet*, appeared. An earlier visitor was John Trowbridge, who had known O'Connor in the *Carpet Bag* days, and who had just completed his second anti-slavery novel, *Cudjo's Cave*. He came to Washington to write the biography of Salmon P. Chase, Secretary of the Treasury, who aspired to the presidency.

"I had at that time few acquaintances in Washington. One of the most prized of these was William Douglas O'Connor," wrote Trowbridge in his autobiography.[25] Trowbridge's account tells much of O'Connor:

> . . . He had turned aside from literature, in which we who knew him in the flower of his youthful promise had believed him destined to excel, and entered a department of the government, one of those vast mausoleums in which so many talents, small and great, have been buried, and brave ambitions have turned quietly to dust. His first employment was in the Treasury; in the Treasury, also, when I first knew him, was that other valiant friend of Whit-

man's, John Burroughs, who fortunately for himself and his readers, escaped O'Connor's fate. . . .

O'Connor was then in the prime of his powers, strikingly handsome; . . . I knew of his intimacy with Whitman, and when one day I found him at his office, and had answered his many questions, telling him where I was domiciled, one of the first I asked in return was, "Where is Walt?"—the familiar name by which Whitman was known to his friends.

"What a chance!" said O'Connor, in his ardent way. "Walt is here in Washington, living close by you, within a stone's throw of the Secretary's door. Come to my house on Sunday evening, and I will have him there to meet you."

On seeing him again at O'Connor's, I found Whitman but little changed, except that he was more trimly attired, wearing a loosely fitting but quite elegant suit of black,—yes, black at last! He was in the best of spirits; and I remember with what a superb and joyous pace he swung along the street, between O'Connor and me, as we walked home with him, after ten o'clock.

Trowbridge sharply contrasted "the fine, large mansion, sumptuously furnished, cared for by sleek and silent colored servants, and thronged by distinguished guests," and the old tenement opposite, where,

in a bare and desolate back room up three flights of stairs, quite alone, lived the poet. Walt led the way up those dreary stairs, partly in darkness, found the keyhole of a door which he unlocked and opened, scratched a match, and welcomed us to his garret.

Garret it literally was, containing hardly any more furniture than a bed, a cheap pine table, and a little sheet-iron stove in which there was no fire. A window was open and it was a December night. But Walt, clearing a chair or two of their litter of newspapers, invited us to sit down and stop awhile, with as simple and sweet hospitality as if he had been offering us the luxuries of the great mansion across the square.

Sit down we did (O'Connor on the bed, as I remember), and "drank delight of battle" over books, the principal subjects being Shakespeare and Walt's own Leaves of Grass. Over Shakespeare it was a sort of triangular combat,—O'Connor maintaining the Baconian theory of the authorship of the plays, and Walt joining with me in attacking that chimera. On the other hand, I agreed with O'Connor in his estimate of Lear and Hamlet and Othello, which Walt belittled, preferring the historical plays, and placing Richard II foremost; although he thought all the plays preposterously overrated. Of his own poems ("pomes" he called them) he spoke modestly, listening with interest to frank criticisms of them (which he always had from me), and disclaiming the profound hidden meanings which O'Connor was inclined to read into some of them. Ordinarily inert and slow of speech, on occasions like this his large and generous nature became suffused with a magnificent glow, which gave one some idea of the heat and momentum that went to the making of his truly great poems; just as his sluggish moods seemed to account for so much of his labored, unleavened work.

O'Connor was a man of unfailing eloquence, whom it was always delightful to listen to, even when the rush of his enthusiasm carried him beyond the bounds of discretion, as it did in the Bacon-Shakespeare business. Whitman's reasoning powers were not remarkable; he did not impress me, then or at any time, as a great intellect; but he was original, intuitive, a seer, and his immense and genial personality gave an interest to everything he said. In my enjoyment of such high discourse, I forgot the cheerless garret, the stove in which there was no fire, the window that remained open (Walt was a "fresh-air fiend"), and my own freezing feet (we all kept on our overcoats). . . .

Later Trowbridge, with Whitman's permission, gave Secretary Chase Emerson's letter of recommendation about the poet. Although Chase felt that Whitman's reputation prevented him from granting the request, he kept Emerson's letter. Walt was not to secure a regular government position for another year.

Another friend from Boston who turned up in Washington was Richard Hinton, Abraham Lincoln's first biographer.[26] Hinton had first met Walt Whitman and become acquainted with his poetry in 1855 in the *Knickerbocker* office in New York City when Whitman brought a copy of the First Edition of *Leaves of Grass* to be reviewed. Five years later it was Hinton who suggested to his publishers, Thayer and Eldridge, that they publish a new edition of *Leaves of Grass*. It was he who brought Whitman to Frank Sanborn's trial that spring.

An ardent supporter of John Brown, Hinton had agitated at the beginning of the Civil War for immediate emancipation and the recruitment of Negro troops. He had been appointed adjutant in the Federal Army, with the function of enlisting Negroes, was at the Battle of Antietam in September 1862 (either as a soldier or correspondent) and was wounded there. He was still in the hospital in Washington in December of that year, when Whitman, making his first visits to minister to the wounded, saw him and renewed their friendship.

During the war Hinton went out West, returning to Washington after the war ended. He was later correspondent for the *Boston Weekly Voice*, a labor paper—in whose columns he praised O'Connor's *Good Gray Poet* and urged Wendell Phillips to run for Congress, a course O'Connor supported.

A friend of Hinton who became one of O'Connor's and Whitman's circle was the irascible, swashbuckling, former Polish Count, Adam Gurowski, whose ardent democratic views had brought him to the United States.[27] (He was such an enthusiastic American that he voted seven times in the first election after he became a citizen.)[28] Gurowski worked as a translator in the State Department, and acted the part of self-appointed advisor on matters of the conduct of the war and foreign relations. He has been called "Lincoln's Gadfly." His appearance was sinister: sabre cut on cheek, green patch over one eye (or blue eyeglasses). Dressed in a sombrero and flowing cloak, he was the perfect figure of a conspirator. Indeed Lincoln said (whether seriously or in jest is not known) that if he feared assassination, it was from that man.[29]

O'Connor befriended Gurowski, helping him to edit his three-volume diary of the Civil War. Judging from the notes to O'Connor, with their misspellings and oddities of punctuation, this must have been quite a task. "My Dear Mystir," the Count addressed him in one note:

> I broke my nose at the door to your official cage, wishing to find out if you had any letters from N. York or Boston.
> I still hope that before long I shall go to work. I afraid you treat the subject to consciensciously. It is my prayer that you may look on it as being a schoolmaster correcting an exercise of a schoolboy. . . .

Yet the schoolboy did not always agree with the suggestions made. "I persevere about the heading," wrote the Count. "I prefer to let them stand. It is oukward, but this concession must be made to public stupidity." He signed the note, "Yours grateful Gurowski." On one occasion Gurowski asked O'Connor to intercede for a prisoner of war (without mentioning the Count's name), writing a letter on O'Connor's stationery of the Office of the Light House Board (October 3, 1864).[30]

Despite their friendship, O'Connor was the victim of at least one of the Count's rages: In August 1864, William wrote to Walt, then on a visit to his family in Brooklyn:

> The Count I have not seen for several weeks. The last time I saw him, he abused me frightfully—for the first time! I happened to say, very quietly, that the Rebels would probably repeat their raid into Maryland very soon. (A week afterward they did so and burned Chambersburg.) Whereupon the Count clutched his straw hat down upon his head with both hands, danced like a demon on the pavement, howled out "You *are* an *ass!*" and, in a word, behaved like a maniac. Indeed his conduct convinced me that he is a madman with lucid intervals. I seriously mean it. No one could burst into such tempests of rage and abuse on so slight an occasion and be sane. A few nights afterward he undertook to discipline the firemen with a pistol, during a conflagration, because they did not move quickly enough, for which freak he suffered fine and imprisonment.[31]

Gurowski shared O'Connor's admiration of President Lincoln—an admiration which Whitman had arrived at more slowly than they: "I did not enthuse at the beginning," Walt said,

> Now, O'Connor took to Lincoln unhesitatingly, at the first glance . . . never wavered: was warmly, even hotly, favorable, right along. There was Gurowski, too: he came to Washington: some of us grew to recognize his great keenness, his splendid intellect. I think Gurowski liked O'Connor on sight . . . liked me too, I believe . . . had the good sense to, as we used to say . . . he measured Lincoln at the first look: and said yes, yes, yes, from first to last. . . .[32]

Whitman and Gurowski were recognized as colorful literary figures of wartime Washington. An article by "Agate," correspondent of the *Cincinnati Gazette*, describes them both. In the *Milwaukee*

Sentinel of February 9, 1866, Whitman, O'Connor, and Gurowski, as well as Florence Percy and John Pierpont, are described in an article signed "S," dated Washington, and entitled "People Not Looked For." Of Count Gurowski, S. writes: "Count Gurowski may be said to have been Chief-of-Staff of the Gen. Dissatisfaction-at-home, while General Delay (McClellan) and General Defeat (Pope, et al.) were in the field."

Gurowski liked Whitman as a man before he recognized his worth as a poet. On November 24, 1863, Nelly wrote to Walt (then in Brooklyn) that she had met the Count who asked about Walt and said, "My Gott, I did not know that he was such a poet, tell him so, I have been trying everywhere to find him to tell him myself. . . . Tell him to write more poems."[33] The irascible Count approved of Whitman wholeheartedly, praising him in his *Diary* as the "incarnation of an American original genius." For the convenience of his readers Gurowski prefaced his *Diary* with three lists: *Praise*, *Half-and-half*, and *Blame*. Whitman was on the first of these, with Secretary Stanton, and Wendell Phillips. Abraham Lincoln, however, merited only "Half-and-half." In the course of the *Diary* Lincoln is criticized as having been "a great shifter" and "a political shuffler." "Everything he did was done by halves," wrote Gurowski. "He had not an atom of organizing or administrative capacity." Among those listed under *Blame* are G. T. Curtis (the judge who enforced the Fugitive Slave Law), Chief Justice Tancy, who had written the Dred Scott Decision, General McClellan, and all of President Lincoln's cabinet except Stanton.[34]

The circle of friends continued to meet at the O'Connors'. At the center of the circle were the four—Nelly and William, Charles Eldridge and Walt Whitman. It was almost as if O'Connor had found the musketeers of his youth.

For Walt the friendship with William was unlike any he had ever known. William was a writer, well-versed in literature, an enthusiastic, warm, outspoken friend. O'Connor not only provided friendship, but also a circle of like-minded, literary young people, a home in which the family-loving Whitman rejoiced, and an opportunity to read and discuss his poems. Here were people who were not jealous of his absorption in poetry, as the unknown lover in "Calamus" had been, but eager to hear and discuss it and to make plans to further its reception and appreciation in the United States and in the world.

Until this time, Whitman's friendships and literary acquaintances had been separate. His family had not understood or appreciated his poems; his friends had been men in many ways more akin to his family than to himself, working men, such as the street car coach drivers, who were drawn to him as a person but who did not know him as a poet.

Before he met O'Connor and his friends, the literary people whom Whitman knew were the group who gathered at Pfaff's Tavern in New York City. Brilliant and witty, they lacked the warmth that William showed. Henry Clapp, the leader of the group, liked Whitman's poetry and kept his name before the readers of the *Saturday Press*. He published "A Child's Reminiscence" (later titled "Out of the Cradle Endlessly Rocking") as well as more than a score of items by and about the poet: three poems, advertisements of the Thayer and Eldridge edition, parodies, and reviews both favorable and unfavorable. He might have continued to present Walt Whitman and his poems had not the *Saturday Press* suspended publication in 1860.

Clapp was known as "The King of Bohemia" and Ada Clare, the poet, as "The Queen of Bohemia"; in their court were Fitz-James O'Brien, a short story writer, George Arnold, a satirical poet, Thomas Bailey Aldrich, and some who were to remain Whitman's friends, such as E. C. Stedman and John Swinton. Yet among them, unlike John Swinton who "crossed swords with many a man there," Whitman was an onlooker. "My own greatest pleasure at Pfaff's," he told Horace Traubel, "was to look on—to see, talk little, absorb. I never was a great discusser, anyway—never. I was much better satisfied to listen to a fight than to take part in it."[35] There appears to have been one exception: "A great many years ago . . . I got into a regular row by defending the Queen. . . ."[36]

Whitman did not feel at home with witty and clever people. Years later he told Horace Traubel that when he saw Emerson at the Sanborns', with Bronson Alcott, his daughter Louisa and others present, he said very little: "No doubt I seemed very stupid to the roomful of company, taking hardly any part in the conversation; but I had 'my own pail to milk in' as the Swiss proverb puts it."[37] At the O'Connors' in Washington, however, he participated freely in the discussions—even in the arguments. These were serious young writers, many of them working as clerks while planning and hoping for careers in literature. Remembering those discussions, Nelly wrote:

> Whitman's evenings were usually spent with us at home, and with such friends as came to see us. I wish I had some record of the talks, discussions, arguments, that were nightly indulged in. No notes were taken, for all were engaged more or less in the melee. In those early days of intimate acquaintance no subject, whether under the heavens above or in the earth beneath, was ignored. Philosophy, history, religion, literature,—authors ancient and modern, language, music, and every possible question as to the conduct of the Civil War,—everything was discussed, and every side was heard. . . .[38]

The O'Connors' home provided more than a forum for the discussion of literary and political matters. It also provided Whitman with a family, a family who loved him not just as a son and brother, but as a man and a poet. Whitman said to Horace Traubel years later, when rereading one of Nelly's letters:

> It's not so much what's in the letter, Horace, as what it leads me back to, what it stirs up in me, what its tender indirections are. The O'Connor home was my home: they were beyond all others— William, Nelly—my understanders, my lovers: they more than any others. I was nearer to them than to any others—oh! much nearer. A man's family is the people who love him—the people who comprehend him. You know how for the most part I have always been isolated from my people—in certain senses have been a stranger in their midst: just as we know Tolstoy has been. Who of my family has gone along with me? Who? Do you know? Not one of them. They are beautiful, fine: they don't need to be apologized for: but they have not known me: they have always missed my intentions. Take my darling dear mother; my dear, dear mother: she and I—oh! we have been great chums: always next to each other: always: yet my dear mother never took that part of me in: she had great faith in me—felt sure I would accomplish wonderful things: but Leaves of Grass? Who could ever consider Leaves of Grass a wonderful thing: who? She would shake her head. God bless her. She never did. She thought I was a wonderful thing. But the Leaves? Oh, my, hardly the Leaves! But

she would put her hand in mine—press my hand—look at me: all as if to say I was all right though in some ways beyond her power to explain. I was saying our family is where we are loved— understood: by all the real tests the O'Connor family was my family: you, Rossetti, anyone that near to me, is my family. I have been giving you the letters—the avowal letters, we have called them: they are my family—the avowers: blood is thicker than water: but what does blood mean in a case like this? What do you think blood counts for with George? George is my brother: it may be said that I love him—he loving me too in a certain sort of a way. But would you say that George was capable of giving you any ripe views on Leaves of Grass? I would say, God bless George my brother: but as to George my interpreter, I would ask God to do something else with him. When I think of what my own folks by blood didn't do for me and what you fellows not of blood royal have done for me, I don't make much of the family diamonds or the inherited crown. Now, you must not set this down for a growl: it's not that: I never feel unhappy over what is unavoidable: I have no more right to expect things of my family than my family has to expect things of me: we are simply what we are: we do not always run together like two rivers: we are not alike: that's the part and the whole of it. My relations with Nelly and William were quite exceptional: extended to both phases—the personal, the general: they were my unvarying partisans, my unshakable lovers—my espousers: William, Nelly: William so like a great doing out of the eternal—a withering blast to my enemies, a cooling zephyr to my friends.[39]

William became that "withering blast" in 1865.

NOTES

1. "Duration of residence in the District—Since July 4th 1861" from Transcript of Death certificate, Health Department of the District of Columbia, No. 139746.
2. Memorandum in O'Connor's handwriting (Berg).
3. Elizabeth Lindsey Lomax, *Leaves from an Old Washington Diary*, 1854–1863 (New York: E. P. Dutton & Co., Inc., 1943), p. 162.
4. Hay to Chase (General Services Administration).
5. Ashton to WDO'C, 3 August 1861 (Feinberg-LC).
6. (Perry). Copy given to the author by David Goodale.
7. General Services Administration.

8. William Dean Howells, *Literary Friends and Acquaintances* (New York and London: Harper & Brothers Publishers, 1900), pp. 82–83.
9. MJ Channing, unpublished ms. (Chamberlin).
10. *Correspondence*, I:58.
11. Ellen M. Calder, "Personal Recollections of Walt Whitman," *Atlantic Monthly*, June 1907, p. 826.
12. *Ibid.* p. 825. John Piatt thought that Whitman had arrived in Washington on January 1, 1863, the day on which they met. (Barrus, *Comrades*, pp. 10–11.)
13. "Werry little bedroom" —WW to Martha Whitman. 3 January 1863. *Correspondence*, 1:63. "Heron in Medea"—WW to Nathaniel Bloom and John F. S. Gray. 9 March 1863, *Correspondence*, 1:83.
14. *Ibid.* p. 53.
15. *Ibid.* p. 29.
16. *Ibid.* p. 36.
17. *Ibid.*, p. 83.
18. John James Piatt, "Whitman in Wartime," December 1911, in Barrus, *Comrades*, pp. 10–11.
19. Barrus, *Life and Letters*, I: 83.
20. *Ibid.*, p. 71.
21. Barrus, *Comrades*, p. 6.
22. Barrus, *Life and Letters*, p. 82 n.
23. *Ibid.*, p. 85.
24. Barrus, *Comrades*, p. 8.
25. John Townsend Trowbridge, *My Own Story, With Recollections of Noted Persons* (Boston and New York: Houghton Mifflin and Company, 1904), p. 373.
26. C. Carroll Hollis, "R. J. Hinton: Lincoln's Reluctant Biographer," *The Centennial Review*, 5 (Winter 1961), 65–84.
27. Information about Gurowski was drawn largely from Leroy H. Fischer, *Lincoln's Gadfly, Adam Gurowski* (Norman, Okla.: University of Oklahoma Press, 1964).
28. Ellen O'Connor to WW, 10 November 1863 (Feinberg-LC).
29. Fischer, *op. cit.*, p. 117.
30. (Feinberg-LC).
31. *Camden*, 3: 339–40.
32. *Camden*, 3: 78–79.
33. Ellen O'Connor to WW (Feinberg-LC).
34. From a review in *The Nation*, 29 March 1866.
35. *Camden*, 1: 417.
36. *Camden*, 5: 227.
37. *Prose Works*, I, p. 279.
38. Calder, *op. cit.*, p. 827.
39. *Camden*, 3: 525–26.

CHAPTER IX

Parting And Reunion

THEIR FIRST parting after almost a year made the O'Connors and Whitman realize how deep their attachment had become. The affection of Nelly, Charley, William, and Walt was revealed in the letters that followed. On November 2, 1863, Whitman left Washington for Brooklyn, planning to spend ten days with his family. It was almost a year since he had been home; his brothers Andrew and Jesse were ill; his brother Jeff and his wife Martha had a new baby daughter, sister to the Manahatta Walt was so fond of. He wanted to retrieve the manuscript of *Drum Taps* and a copy of the 1860 *Leaves of Grass* in which he had been noting corrections and additions for a new edition, and to vote in the election. Since Walt could not afford the fare, O'Connor secured a pass for him from John Hay, ostensibly to enable him to vote.[1]

Nelly wrote a chatty letter a week after Walt's departure, asking about his family and his state of health, and telling about their friends and neighbors. She realizes that Walt could not possibly stay with his family only ten days, after such a long absence; "but we have been counting the days in the *very faintest* hope that you might come then."[2] Later in the letter she writes, "To tell you that we miss you *awfully* would not be news would it? You expected that, but I do have a most uncomfortable feeling of Goneness all the time, & I shall welcome you home here *very heartily*." She reminds Walt, "Don't forget the three things you were to bring for my especial benefit. The picture, letter and 'Drum Taps.' "

Walt responded on November 15 with a long letter to Nelly, filled with messages to Nelly's friend Mrs. Cooper, to William, and to

144

Charley. He assures Mrs. Cooper that he will stop to see her in Philadelphia. Of Nelly and the others he writes:

> I think about you all, & frequently. I have told my mother & sister
> about you all. I send my love to William. I feel that I have never
> had a better friend, & that no truer or warmer heart beats. Tell
> Charles Eldridge too I send him my love. I regret his not likely
> meeting me in New York to go around together. But, Charley, we
> will have it yet, dear comrade. . . . For all & sundry, & the year's
> most valuable kindness, from you three, what can I say, more than
> that I am sure I appreciate it.[3]

He goes on to tell Nelly about the trip, the election (which went
well),[4] news of the family, including the new baby, whom he would
like to name California. In writing of his mother, he says: "Nelly, I
have thought before that the real & best bravery is to be discovered
somewhere else than in the bravery of war, & beyond the heroisms
of men. . . ."

Walt writes of his visit with Charles Howells, a Washington friend
who had left his wife to go to New York to follow Stephen Pearl
Andrews, an Abolitionist and philosopher who wanted to establish a
new social order called Pantarchy. Andrews was the founder of a
Utopian colony on Long Island called Modern Times. Nelly had
begged Walt to persuade Howells to return to his wife, but Walt
was unsuccessful. He did call on Howells at 15 Charles Street (where
a huge placard, *Headquarters of the Pantarchy*, hung in the living
room). They had a long walk and talk, in which Howells discoursed,
with Whitman making an occasional dry comment. (Mr. Howells
later returned to Washington after his wife went to New York to
fetch him back.) Walt asks Nelly to visit his boys in Armory Square
Hospital, mentioning five of them by name. The close of the letter
must have pleased Nelly: "I shall probably stay five or six days
longer. I count on our all being together again. . . . Well, Nelly, I
will now bid you goodbye for present, my truly dear friend, & good
bye to the rest, & God bless you all."

Two days later Walt wrote to Charles Eldridge, "I feel to devote
myself more to the work of my life, which is making poems. I must
bring out *Drum Taps*. I *must* be continually bringing out poems—
now is the heyday. I shall range along the high plateau of my life &
capacity for a few years now, & then swiftly descend. . . ."[5]

On November 21 Nelly wrote again, this time to tell Walt that Mrs. Cooper (who had been staying with the O'Connors since Walt left) and Charley Eldridge were leaving that day for Mrs. Cooper's house in Philadelphia, where Charley was going to stay overnight. They wanted Walt to come to Philadelphia to meet them there. Mrs. Cooper evidently wanted to transfer the O'Connor circle to Philadelphia, at least for a while; Nelly wrote that she had been "coaxing, persuading, begging, entreating, commanding even William to go with them. . . . She wants me to go on also . . . ,"[6] but the O'Connors were not able to go.

Again Nelly expresses their feelings for Walt: "Dear Walt, we long for you, William sighs for you, & I feel as if a large part of myself were out of the city—I shall give you a good big kiss when you come, so depend upon it. . . ." Three days later Nelly wrote a longer letter, giving news of Mr. Howells, who had returned to Washington with his wife, inquiring about Whitman's family ("You are rich indeed in having such a noble, grand mother"),[7] telling of her meeting with Count Gurowski, and asking Walt on his way back to stop in Philadelphia to pick up a package for her at Mrs. Cooper's.

Nelly longs for his presence: "I wish that you were back here in your old room for my sake, for I miss you & shall." And "I count upon your return, and on our all being together much, very much this winter, and on some good talks, & good times reading your *Drum Taps.* You must publish that book. William often wishes for your return and wants to see you. . . ."

Walt stayed away for almost a month, returning on the night of December 1. His brother Andrew, who had been very ill during his visit home, died two days later, but Walt was not able to go back to Brooklyn for the funeral. Walt's presence restored the circle at the O'Connors'—almost a magic circle that was to hold its charm for nine years more before being broken by a shattering quarrel.

Walt continued to work as a copyist three or four hours a day, devoting the rest of his time to cheering the wounded in the army hospitals, and finding relief from his sad experiences, as well as his place as a poet, at the O'Connors' in the evening. There discussions of literature, politics, and the issues of the day raged. The men and women there were not disciples sitting at the feet of Walt, their master, but individuals of firm and often violent opinions, talking, arguing and shouting over ideas. Years later Nelly reminisced about those days: "Talks, morning talks at breakfast, and more fierce at night, growing more and more to be the custom, and certain pet topics upon which some violently disagreed. Mormon, slavery, denunciation of free love, etc. Stephen Pearl Andrews, the Apostle of Free Love. . . ."[8]

Sometimes the discussions began at breakfast, and continued while they, "lingered long over Emerson, Wordsworth, Tennyson, or any poet or author who was suggested at the moment. The talk about Emerson's 'Snow Storm' was a memorable one, with Walt and Mr. O'Connor regarding it as one of his most beautiful and finished poems, full of suggestions of home and seclusion."

Many mornings while they were still talking, they noticed a punctual colleague, Mr. Evans, walk by on his way to his office. It was suggested that O'Connor write a story called, "The Faithful Clerk. A Tale of the Treasury—Dedicated to the Nine O'Clockers, by a Half Past Tener (*sic*)."

In most matters Walt took the conservative view. Eldridge wrote of these conversations:

> . . . from 1863-1873 . . . we met at O'Connor's house every night for months at a time with hardly a break, and we talked of everything that the human mind could conceive. I have often wished that I had kept a diary, or at least a memorandum of these memorable conversations. Walt was then in the prime of his splendid manhood and O'Connor was the most brilliant talker I have ever heard or ever expect to hear.
>
> It will surprise some of Walt's admirers to learn that as revealed by his conversations, he was one of the most conservative of men. He believed in the old ways; had no faith in any "reforms" as such, and thought that no change could be made in the condition of mankind except by the most gradual evolution. I have never heard him give any countenance to the contentions of the "Woman's Rights" people; thought they were a namby-pamby lot as a whole, and he did not believe that woman suffrage would do any particular good. Susan B. Anthony was far from his ideal of a "fierce athletic girl." He delighted in the company of old fashioned women, mothers of large families preferred, who did not talk about literature and reforms. No man ever honored motherhood or true womanhood more than he did. Anything like free love was utterly repugnant to his mind, and he had no toleration

for the Mormons. In the early sixties there was an organization of free lovers in the upper part of New York City well known to those familiar with the Bohemian life of New York in those days. One of our circle was led astray, and abandoned his wife and children in Washington to join this unsavory crowd. Walt met this man once after this happened, and he gave him as severe a verbal castigation as ever a man received. As William O'Connor said, he actually "knouted" him. Words did not seem adequate to express his contempt for such a crowd and their practices. He was likewise very hostile to anything like anarchy, communism or socialism. At one time, after the war, Albert Brisbane, perhaps the ablest exponent of Fourierism in this country, spent the winter in Washington, and was often a visitor at O'Connor's, and met Walt. They had many talks together which I listened to, but Walt never yielded an inch of ground to him. He thought that any such ready-made plan for reorganizing society was ridiculous and not quite sane. Our form of Government he thought about as good as could be under present human condition. He was in favor, however, of strengthening the Executive branch, which he thought not quite powerful enough. He strenuously opposed the impeachment of President Johnson as an unwarranted attack on the independence of the Executive. In the headlong impetuosity of youth, I was warmly in favor of it, but the lapse of time has convinced me that Walt was right.

For the abolitionists he had no sympathy. While opposed to slavery always, he thought they considered the subject too all important and were incendiary in their methods. O'Connor and I, who were always ardent abolitionists, had many a "hot time" with him over this subject. Of the negro as a race he had a poor opinion. He said that there was in the constitution of the negro's mind an irredeemable trifling or volatile element, and he would never amount to much in the scale of civilization. I never knew him to have a friend among the negroes while he was in Washington, and he never seemed to care for them or they for him, although he never manifested any particular aversion to them. . . .[9]

Nelly O'Connor (then Mrs. Calder) corroborated these remarks in a letter to Bliss Perry on February 19, 1904. "Now I happen to *know* that every word of the statements by Eldridge is true, as again and again, during those heated discussions I have heard all and more. . . ."[10]

With William and Nelly long-time supporters of Woman's Rights, and together with Charley, confirmed and active Abolitionists, and other participants taking sides, the arguments were fierce indeed. Walt could be as violent in argument as the more volatile William. Nelly reported that Walt was not at all the calm, benign, patient man of his later years. Once the argument raged so vociferously that a policeman stopped to investigate the cause of the clamor he heard from the direction of the O'Connor house. It was only Walt, William, and some friends arguing the currency question.[11]

They often had discussions about words. Nelly wrote:

> Notwithstanding Whitman's fondness for coining words, and using many in uncommon fashions, he was, in a way, a great stickler for the correct use of certain words, one of which was "paraphernalia," which he insisted could be correctly used only in reference to a bride's belongings or trousseau. . . . We had many amusing discussions about words, and the best dictionary for final settlement of any vexed question, whether it should be Webster or Worcester. He used generally to say, "We'll see what Booby says,"—his pet name for either dictionary, but he did not readily allow either one to *settle* any point.[12]

At times the serious discussions were leavened by lighter interludes. Whitman liked to recite poetry, though his listeners thought his manner somewhat theatrical and artificial; his voice, clear and flexible in conversation, became stiff in recitation.

Sometimes the group played "Twenty Questions"—a game that Whitman had used as a teaching device when he was a young schoolmaster on Long Island. Once the object to be guessed was the white beard of Secretary Welles, at another time a Bible inscribed by Walt to the O'Connors. One New Year's Eve Walt arrived looking like Santa Claus and bearing the ingredients for punch, of which he later supervised the preparation. During the Christmas season, a policeman stopped Walt and asked him to remove his "false face," thinking it a Santa Claus mask. Assuring him that the only face was his own, Walt added quietly, "Do we not all wear 'false faces'?"[13]

Walt was part of the O'Connor family. Piatt found him helping Nelly hang window-shades ("an exasperating service at which he showed unusual good humor").[14] Nelly stitched paper to form the little notebooks in which Walt recorded his memoranda during the war, and darned Walt's socks.[15] She prepared special delicacies when the wounded men requested them. Walt pumped water for the O'Connors' breakfast from a pump at the corner of the street, and went with Nelly to the market to buy fruit for breakfast and for Walt to take to his boys in the hospitals. (Gurowski, meeting them once, approved of their errand.)[16] Walt, Charles Eldridge, William, Nelly, and Jeannie went to Mason's Island near Washington, at the invitation of Eldridge's superior, Major Hapgood, to witness the first paying of Negro troops. Nelly went with Walt to explore the older part of Washington, the Navy Yard district, and over the Eastern Branch into Anacostia. (A woman clerk in the Quartermaster's Office once said in a very offensive tone to O'Connor, "Well, I saw your wife sailing down the street with Walt Whitman the other day." Mr. O'Connor paid no attention to her.)[17] Sometimes the O'Connors and Walt went out after dinner into the woods of Georgetown and spent hours watching the rising moon and the attractive landscape.

These pleasant activities were interrupted for a short time in February 1864, when Walt visited the hospitals in Culpepper, Virginia, near the front line. Here, in a hospital for teamsters, Walt distributed (among other things) books which Trowbridge had sent him for the soldiers. The field hospitals were nothing but a collection of tents on the bare ground. They were heated by means of digging a long trench in the ground, covering it over with boards and earth, then building a fire at one end and letting it draw through to the other.

After about two weeks at the front in February, Walt returned to Washington and resumed his visits to the hospitals there. He began thinking of a visit home to see his family and friends and to bring out his book, *Drum-Taps*, but several months passed before he left Washington. During that time, Walt himself was frequently ill. Even when his own health was good, he felt depressed about the sights in the hospitals. He wrote to his mother on March 29, 1864:

> I feel as though I must have some intermission, I feel well & hearty enough, & was never better, but my feelings are kept in a painful condition a great part of the time—things get worse & worse as to the amount & sufferings of the sick, & as I have said before, those who have to do with them are getting more and more callous & indifferent . . . & then the agony I see every day, I get almost frightened at the world.[18]

Walt watched the troops parading on Fourteenth Street (where the O'Connors lived) on their way to war—"ranks after ranks of our dearest blood of men, mostly young, worn & sunburnt & sweaty. . . ." On one such occasion Jeannie O'Connor and a little friend stood on chairs waving their little flags as the men of General Casey's Division marched along. "Instantly on seeing them, the officers half halted and saluted the tiny flags, which spoke of intense loyalty to those men who were, many of them, on the way to their death." Not all of Washington was so loyal. Nelly heard one woman say that she had both a "Secesh" flag and a Union flag in her house, and was ready to wave to whichever army was successful.[19]

As the months of Spring 1864 passed, Walt became increasingly ill, depressed, and worried about the soldiers, the war, and his family at home. The house where he was living had been sold, and on May 21 he moved to a boarding house at 302 Pennsylvania Avenue, near Third Street. He did not like his third-story hall bedroom or the food that was provided there. Worrying more than ever about the men in the hospitals, a number of whom had become insane, Walt himself suffered from faintness, dizziness, head colds, and sore throat. The hospital doctor advised him not to go into the hospitals for a while because of his ill health. Walt had a friend take things to his boys for him.

In the third week of June, Walt went home again, this time to remain until January 1865. A severe sore throat kept him housebound for a while. Not until September did he write O'Connor that his health was fully restored, and that he was able to visit veterans' hospitals in New York City.

Just after Whitman left Washington, the city suffered a hot spell. O'Connor wrote to Whitman on July 2: "It was so lucky that you left when you did, for the three or four days succeeding your departure were fearful for dead heat, and I don't know how you could have borne them."[20] Nevertheless, William missed Walt dreadfully:

> Many thoughts of you have come to me since you went away, and sometimes it has been lonely and a little like death. Particularly at evening when you used to come in. But, on the whole, every feeling submerges in gratefulness and thankfulness that you were away from this great sultriness and where you can have the rest and help it was not our fortune to be able to give you here.

O'Connor's thoughts about the future reveal the substance of some of their discussions:

> I wonder what the future for us is to be. Shall we triumph over obscurities and obstacles and emerge to start the Pathfinder, or whatever the name of it is to be? I wonder if it is so written on the iron leaf. Shall you live to publish many great poems amidst recognition and tumults of applause? Shall I live to write my Shakespeare book and a score of gorgeous romances? Or shall we never meet, never work together, never start any Pathfinder, never do anything but fade out into death, frustrated, lost in oblivion?—
> "All the dawns promised shall the day fulfill,
> The glory and the grandeur of each dream,
> And every prophecy shall come to pass
> And all hope be accomplished."
> So says Master Robert Browning and so it may be.
> At all events I hope you will get well very soon and make preparations for eternity by publishing your Drum-Taps. . . .

Whitman responded on July 5: ". . . As to the future, & as to our meeting again, I have no doubt we shall meet again & have good times. . . . I have nothing new or interesting to write you. I intend to move heaven & earth to publish my "Drum-Taps" as soon as I am able to go around. . . ."[21] Walt's letter to William crossed Nelly's letter to him, written on July 5. William's phrase, "lonely and a little like death," is echoed in Nelly's letter:

> It will be two weeks tomorrow since you left us, and I have missed you terribly every minute of the time. I think I never in my life felt so wholly blue and unhappy about any one's going away as I did, and have since, about your going. I began to be really superstitious I felt so badly. I did not think that you were going to die, but I could not possibly overcome the feeling that our dear and pleasant circle was broken, and it seemed to me that we four should not be together any more as we have been. But now since you are so much better, I hope you will come back to Washington in the autumn to stay all winter, and I hope we shall spend a part of every day together, as we have so many days. Ah! Walt, I don't believe other people need you as much as we do. I am *sure* they don't need you as much as *I* do.
> William says it seems so desolate since you left. . . .

Nelly enclosed a picture of herself, deprecating it rather coyly:

> I got my picture last week, and they are rather bad, the front
> face, or rather three-quarter face, is hideous, William forbade my
> giving any of them away. The side face is—well, what do you say
> to it? I think it is *very* sharp, and I know I should not like anybody
> that looked like it, do *you*?[22]

On July 18 Nelly wrote that she was planning to go to Rhode Island with little Jeannic to visit her sister and brother-in-law, Jeannie
and William Channing. She hoped that Walt would be able to spend
a few hours in New York with her before the New England boat
sailed. He failed to come, however, and she wrote sadly from Providence on July 24:

> I was at the boat at 2 Wednesday afternoon and we sailed at 5. I
> *hoped* to see you, but feared you would not be able to go over. I
> was all the more sorry *not* to see you, as I inferred from it that you
> were too unwell to come over. . . . I long to hear from you. Wil-
> liam & Charley had each had two letters from you, & I not a word,
> don't you know I shall be jealous? And now this is my *third* epistle
> to you, so I shall claim a word from you *when* you are able to
> write. . . .[23]

Perhaps Walt was put off by Nelly's ardor, for his first answer to
her was a sentence in a letter to William in Washington, which he
asks William to send on to Nelly: "Nelly, my dear friend, you must
excuse me—I wished much to see you, too."[24] Nelly was hurt by this
roundabout answer to her letters:

> After seeing you every day, & so much of you those last days
> when you were sick, it seems doubly strange not to have had a
> word from you. You will not think me foolish if I tell you that it has
> hurt me a little, will you? You know what a foolish, absurd person
> I am, where I love as I do you, and knowing this, and now I having
> confessed, you will pardon. . . .[25]

She reminds him that she had sent her picture, and talks about having become a "lion" in the social group in Rhode Island because she
knows the poet Walt Whitman.

Nelly in Rhode Island and Walt in Brooklyn both escaped the siege of Washington during the summer of 1864. Not long after Walt left, the Confederates raided the city, and it seemed as if Washington might be taken. On August 2 John Burroughs wrote, "I was at the front during the siege of Washington and lay in the rifle pits with the soldiers, I got quite a taste of war and learned the song of those modern minstrels—the minie bullets—by heart."[26] Less than two weeks later, William wrote that he was drilling every day, and found the weight of the rifle and other accoutrements a strain in the hot weather.[27]

Nelly, with little Jeannie, had her day with Walt in New York City on the way back from Rhode Island. She refers to it in her letter of November 30: "I am glad that we had the day with you, it was some satisfaction to see you for even so short a time." She writes that there is a likelihood that Charles Eldridge will be transferred to Boston:

> How lonely we shall be with both you and Charley gone! I don't think of it any more than I can help.
> Every evening we talk of you, and wish you were here, & almost every evening we read from Leaves of Grass, read & admire. I don't believe, dear Walt, that you have in all the world, two heartier lovers & appreciators than William and Charley. . . .

Of course she asks about the publication of his poems.[28] Walt answered this letter within a week, saying that he intended to return to Washington that winter.

Much of the correspondence during Walt's long absence has to do with the preparation of his new book, *Drum-Taps*. He had evidently shared the poems as he was writing them, for William wrote that he had recited poems from *Leaves of Grass* and "numerous excerpts" from the new book to Miss Griffith, a young southern lady who had freed her slaves and moved North. William writes that he told her much about Walt, "painting you as the gigantesque angel of valor, compassion, and poetry that you are. . . ."[29]

In answer to Nelly's query about the publication of the poems, he writes: "About my book nothing particular to tell—I shall print it myself—also my new edition of Leaves of Grass—most likely shall do it in the way we have talked of, namely by subscription—I feel that it is best for me to print my books myself, (notwithstanding some very good objections to that course, but the reasons in favor are far stronger)—" And again Walt assures her of his love for her and William: "Dear Nelly, you & William have neither of you any idea how I daily & nightly bear you in mind & in love too—I did not know myself that you both had taken such deep root in my heart— few attachments wear & last throughout life, but ours must."[30]

On September 11 Walt had written to Nelly at Little Compton, Rhode Island. His health was improved, he has been visiting a hospital near his home where there are a couple of hundred soldiers, and he talks of some of their mutual friends. At last he acknowledges the picture she had sent him more than two months before: "Nelly, I was much obliged for the photograph—it reminds me of you & is good— how is dear little Jeannie?—& you, my dear, dear friend, how are you in health and spirits, & have you had a good time—O how I should like to see you all again—" He writes that *Drum-Taps* has not yet begun to be printed.[31]

In a letter to William in Washington written on the same day, telling more of his activities in New York with some of his old friends, Walt closes with avowals of friendship: "My dear friend, I often often think of you, & count on our being together again, may be quite soon—meantime goodbye & God bless you & I send you my best best love."[32] Another such avowal appears in a letter sent to Charley, to be shared with William: "I wish him to receive again my faithful friendship—while breath & sense remain I cannot forget what he has been to me—I love him dearly."[33]

William raises objections to Walt's printing the book himself, but assures him of his cooperation:

> I want very much to hear that "Drum Taps" are printing. I have many misgivings about your plan of getting out the book yourself. I wanted it to have a large sale, as I think it well might, and I am afraid that this sort of private publication will keep it from being known or accessible to any considerable number of people. Such a volume ought to make your fame secure and with a good publisher I think it would. How I wish Eldridge was in the field!
>
> Are you going to get it done by subscription? I want to know because I want to help as much as I can. The rascally Congress taxes me in September $50.00 in a lump, besides my normal income tax, so I shall not be able to do as well as I intended, but if

subscription is the order of the day, I mean to give as much as I
can. So let me know.[34]

The letters could not take Walt's place. In one letter William wrote
that on Thanksgiving he said, " 'I wish—' and stopped. 'What?' said
Nelly. 'I know,' chirped little Jeannie, 'he wishes Walt was here.'
Which was true—that was the unuttered wish."[35]

Despite the letters of friendship and longing, Walt stayed in
Brooklyn for more than six months, with *Drum-Taps* still not published. On January 6, 1865, he wrote William one of the few letters in
all his vast correspondence that deal with literary matters, and the
only one in which he discusses his feeling about *Leaves of Grass* and
Drum Taps. (For full version, see Appendix B.)

> Drum Taps is certainly more perfect as a work of art, being
> adjusted in all its proportions, & its passion having . . . indis-
> pensable merit. . . . The book is . . . unprecedently sad, (as
> these days are, are they not?)—but it also has the blast of the
> trumpet, & the drum pounds & whirrs in it, & then an undertone
> of sweetest comradeship & human love, threading its steady
> thread inside the chaos, & heard at every lull & interstice
> thereof—truly also it has clear notes of faith & triumph.
>
> Drum-Taps has none of the perturbations of Leaves of Grass. I
> am satisfied with Leaves of Grass (by far the most of it) as express-
> ing what was intended, namely, to express by sharp-cut self asser-
> tion, *One's Self* & also, or may be still more, to map out, to throw
> together for American use, a gigantic embryo or skeleton of Per-
> sonality, fit for the West, for native models—but there are a few
> things I shall carefully eliminate in the next issue, & a few more I
> shall considerably change.
>
> I see I have said I consider Drum-Taps superior to Leaves of
> Grass. I probably mean as a piece of wit, & from the more simple
> & winning nature of the subject, & also because I have in it only
> succeeded to my satisfaction in removing all superfluity from it,
> verbal superfluity I mean. I delight to make a poem where I feel
> clear that not a word but is indispensable part thereof & of my
> meaning.[36]

William sent this letter on to Charles Eldridge in Boston, who
wrote on January 22: "I thank you especially for the handsome copy

of Walt's letter, it seems to me a very noble and beautiful letter—so idiosyncratic, and every way worthy of him and the great fame which must one day crown his works. I shall carefully keep it as one of my choicest treasures."[37]

It was probably during Walt's lengthy stay with his family in 1864 and 1865 that he and William realized what the friendship meant to them. If Walt was to return to Washington, a job would have to be found for him. In writing on December 30, 1864,[38] about the possibility of a job in the Department of the Interior, William mentioned other efforts on Walt's behalf:

> Have been thinking of you constantly for months and have been doing everything I could to secure you a foothold here. For a long time, deceived (I must think) by Swinton's pretensions to influence and by his profuse promises, I hoped to get you either one of the New York State Agency Assistantships or the place of an Assistant Librarian in the Congress Library (the latter would be really a sinecure if the right one was got). But who follows Swinton follows a will-of-the-wisp, and though I followed him remorselessly every blessed day, for several weeks, and gave him neither rest nor peace, as the saying is, I got nothing except promises. Since I gave him up, I have been badgering Ashton, who is a man of another sort, as what he has done shows. The difficulty was to get the right thing. He secured for me some little time ago a place in the Post Office for you, but I declined it, because I thought it was not the proper place for you. I think a desk in the Interior would be first rate.

William tells Walt just how to apply for the position: Ashton had spoken to Mr. Otto, the Assistant Secretary of the Department of the Interior, and Mr. Otto asked that Walt write a letter of application to the Secretary of the Interior. William admonishes him:

> Now, dear Walt, do this without delay. The object of your writing the letter is to get a specimen of your hand. Pick out, then, a good pen and write as fairly as you can a letter formally applying for a clerkship. Then enclose a *copy* of this letter to Ashton, so that he can follow it in to the Secretary. The *first* letter you will, of course, mail to the Secretary direct. Do this as soon as you can. We shall fetch it this time. I have every confidence that you will get a good

and an easy berth, a regular income, etc., leaving you time to attend to the soldiers, to your poems, etc.—in a word, what Archimedes wanted, a place on which to rest the lever.

He assures Walt,

You are never forgotton. I read your poems often, I get their meaning more and more, I stand up for them and you, I expound, define, defend, vindicate, justify them and you with all the heart and head that I have whenever occasion demands.

The letter continues:

I got the Times with your long letter about the Hospital experiences, which I read with a swelling heart and wet eyes. It was very great and touching to me. I think I could mount the tribune for you on that and speak speech which jets fire and drips tears. Only it filled me with infinite regrets that there is not a book from you, embodying these rich and sad experiences. It would be sure of immortality. No history of our times would ever be written without it, if written with that wealth of living details you could crowd into it. Indeed it would itself be history. . . .

Walt's letter of application to Mr. Otto must have been written in his finest hand, for four days after it was sent, he received an answer from Mr. Otto, stating that after passing an examination, he would be appointed to a first-class clerkship; on January 24, Mr. Otto appointed him clerk in the Office of Indian Affairs at $1,200 a year.[39]

Concerned about Whitman's employment, O'Connor did not mention that he himself was then engaged in writing a memorial to Congress on the "Salaries of Clerks," which he presented in February 1865.[40] The memorial tells much of the way in which the O'Connors were living. (Their generosity to Whitman must have represented a sacrifice.) Clerks, representing the several bureaus of the Treasury Department, had appointed a committee of five including William O'Connor to draw up a plan for a temporary increase in wages needed because inflation had sharply reduced the purchasing power of their already low salaries. O'Connor, who was considered the best writer in the Department, was asked to compose the committee report.

The report, which is about 5,000 words long, begins by describing the wage scale, which ranges from the beginner's salary of $1,200 to the highest salary of $2,000, and states that the purchasing power of the dollar is less than half what it was in 1860 when this salary scale was adopted.

> On the highest of the salaries named, a man with a family must practice rigid economy to decently live in Washington. The hardest parsimony will barely enable him to live on the lowest. On two thousand dollars he must eat the bread of carefulness. On twelve hundred it must be the bread of poverty.

O'Connor, who was then earning $1,600, could have been writing about his own situation when he tells of how a clerk must live on such a salary, renting a few small rooms for himself and his family, or if he has a larger apartment or house, taking in boarders.

> "Cannot afford" becomes the dismal legend of their lives. They cannot afford respectable raiment, but must go patched and threadbare; they cannot afford a physiological diet; they cannot afford sanitary quarters; they cannot afford nourishment for the delicate; they cannot afford comforts for the well; they cannot afford medicaments for the sick. Pinned down by obligations incurred and means lacking, many of them cannot afford even to resign and seek better fortunes elsewhere. . . .

After discussing the life of poverty which the clerks lead, and asking for redress on these grounds, O'Connor stresses the responsibility of their positions, and the need for the best qualified men to perform these duties:

> What is the Treasury Department? It is, in one word, the banking and business house of the nation. What is the amount involved in its transactions? Not less this year than fifteen hundred millions of dollars. Who execute and administer this gigantic business? The Secretary and Assistant Secretary? The Heads of Bureaus? The Auditors and Comptrollers? No. They do much; their functions are vast, onerous, difficult; but not being omnipotent or ubiquitous—not even having the hundred eyes of Argus, nor the hundred arms of Briareus, they can only do a part, and it is by no

means the greatest part. Who, then, do the greatest part? The clerks.

O'Connor goes on to give in detail—with figures and amounts— some of the work in each bureau of the Treasury Department, in all its magnitude and importance to the nation, that is handled by clerks. He cites the particular duties and accomplishments of clerks:

> Every one of them performs in giant measure the duties of the commercial accountant. Everyone performs in addition the office of the jealous and relentless critic. Every one of them passes upon these accounts as a judge. Every one of them acts upon them as a chancellor.

Only men of the highest qualifications can perform these duties. Yet because of the low salaries there have been more than two hundred resignations during the fiscal year. Private enterprises offer higher pay. The Government must increase the pay, for the dearest thing the Government can buy is a cheap clerk. "To save two millions in salaries and lose ten millions in erroneous allowances is not economy."

Before concluding, O'Connor, ever mindful of Woman's Rights, stresses that he wishes this request for higher salaries to apply to women clerks as well as to men:

> The service these women render is a valuable one, and all that we have said respecting the cost of living in the city, applies even more cogently to them. Their expenses are, in most instances, nearly the same as those of the other sex, and their salaries are much lower. Some of them have little children to support. They are generally women whose fortunes have in various ways been broken by the war.

He ends by summarizing the proposal as a twofold one: the relief of distress and the recompense of public service which will "secure that order of talent in whose hands the public interests shall be safe, and whose work shall be lasting and splendid, like the Treasury halls."

O'Connor's appeal met with success. Armed with this petition, Secretary of the Treasury Fessenden was able to secure a 20 percent increase in salary for the clerks in his Department.

Dr. William F. Channing, without O'Connor's knowledge, sent a copy of this report to Hon. Thomas Davis (husband of Paulina Wright Davis), with a letter asking whether it was possible to gain for O'Connor a higher position: "I found the O'Connors pinched by the insufficiency of William's salary, which is of the second grade $1,600."[41] He asks Davis to intercede with Secretary Fessenden, who will be in office only until March 4:

> William O'Connor stands very high in the Department. He holds one of the best pens in the country, both in regard to elegance & facility of expression & legibility of hand. I believe Mr. Chase spoke of him as the best writer in the department. The selection of him by the clerks to draft their memorial shows their estimate of him. . . . *There is no man in the Treasury better fitted to conduct the most important correspondence of the department.* It is a post of this kind that I should seek for him.

It would appear that O'Connor did not acquire another position, but the raise in salary received by all the clerks benefited him.

For William all this was secondary to the glorious fact that Walt was back in Washington. From his room in the northeast corner of the Patent Office in the basement, Walt wrote to his brother Jeff that he worked from 10 A.M. to 4 P.M., mostly making copies of reports and bids, etc., to be sent up to the Congressional Committee on Indian Affairs. The work was easy, he was able to come late and leave early, and had plenty of time in the late afternoon for visiting the hospitals and the camps. Evidently he performed his work satisfactorily, for on May 1 he was promoted to a clerkship second class.[42] This was just a few days before the appointment of a new Secretary of the Interior, James Harlan, who was to have a marked influence on the lives of both Whitman and O'Connor.

NOTES

1. Charles I. Glicksberg, ed., *Walt Whitman and the Civil War: A Collection of Original Articles and Manuscripts* (Philadelphia: University of Pennsylvania Press, 1933), p. 138.
2. Ellen O'Connor to WW, 10 November 1863 (Feinberg-LC).
3. *Correspondence*, I: 182–84.
4. According to the *New York Times*, the election in Brooklyn resulted in victory for Union candidates.

5. *Correspondence*, I: 185.
6. (Feinberg-LC).
7. (Feinberg-LC).
8. (Yale).
9. Charles W. Eldridge, "Walt Whitman as a Conservative," *New York Times*, 7 June 1902. Eldridge also expressed this opinion in a letter to Trowbridge, 12 April 1902, in Rufus Arthur Coleman, *John Townsend Trowbridge*, Ph.D. dissertation, Boston University Graduate School, 1938. A rejoinder·by Horace Traubel, "Walt Whitman as Both Radical and Conservative," appeared 12 July 1902 (*New York Times*).
10. (Yale).
11. Ellen M. Calder, "Personal Recollections of Walt Whitman," *Atlantic Monthly*, June 1907, p. 829.
12. *Ibid.*, p. 830.
13. *Ibid.*, p. 831.
14. Piatt to Elliot, December (n.d.) 1911 (LC).
15. WW, speaking to Traubel, 14 August 1888. *Camden*, 2: 137.
16. Calder, *op. cit.*, p. 833.
17. "Mrs. Calder's Interview on Whitman and O'Connor" (Perry. Copy given to the author by Goodale).
18. *Correspondence*, I: 205.
19. Calder, *op. cit.*, p. 833.
20. *Camden*, 4: 366–68.
21. *Correspondence*, I: 236.
22. (Feinberg-LC).
23. (Feinberg-LC).
24. *Correspondence*, I: 239.
25. Ellen O'Connor to WW, 18 August 1864 (Feinberg-LC).
26. Burroughs to WW, quoted in Barrus, *Comrades*, p. 19.
27. WDO'C to WW, 13 August 1864 (Feinberg-LC).
28. Ellen O'Connor to WW (Feinberg-LC).
29. WDO'C to WW, 13 August 1864 (Feinberg-LC).
30. *Correspondence*, I: 244.
31. *Ibid.*, 240–41.
32. *Ibid.*, 242.
33. *Ibid.*, 243.
34. WDO'C to WW, 13 August 1864 (Feinberg-LC).
35. *Camden*, 2: 403.
36. *Correspondence*, I, 246–47.
37. Eldridge to WDO'C (Berg).
38. *Camden*, 2: 401–02.
39. *Camden*, 3: 470–71.
40. Committee Report reprinted several years later (Feinberg-LC).
41. Dr. W. F. Channing to Davis, 24 February 1865 (General Services Administration).
42. *Camden*, 3: 471.

CHAPTER X

A Defender Is Needed

THE FIRST few months of 1865 saw a resumption of Whitman's earlier stay in Washington—with the undemanding work which enabled him to support himself, the visits to the hospitals for a few hours each day or evening, and the circle of friends at the O'Connors'. One of his principal tasks in Washington at this time was to try to effect the release of his brother George, who had been captured in battle and was now in the prison at Danville, Virginia. Whitman enlisted the aid of John Swinton, editor of *The New York Times*, who succeeded in influencing General Grant to ask for the special exchange of two prisoners, one of whom was George Whitman.[1]

On the day of President Lincoln's inauguration, Whitman saw him riding to the Capitol "in his own carriage, by himself, on a sharp trot, about noon" and returning at about three o'clock, in his plain two-horse barouche, with his ten-year-old son at his side. The President

> looked very much worn and tired; the lines, indeed, of vast responsibilities, intricate questions, and demands of life and death, cut deeper than ever upon his dark brown face; yet all the old goodness, tenderness, sadness, and canny shrewdness, underneath the furrows.[2]

The weather, Whitman wrote, had been strange. "Indeed, the heavens, the elements, all the meteorological influences, have run riot for weeks past. Such caprices, abruptest alternation of frown and beauty, I never knew. . . ."[3] Although much of the daytime

163

was heavy, foggy, with interstices of bitter cold and some insane storms,

> some of the nights held superb beauty. . . . The western star, Venus, in the earlier hours of evening, has never been so large, so clear; . . .

A few weeks later Whitman went home to Brooklyn to see his brother George who had been quite ill. Walt extended his stay until the middle of April in order to print *Drum-Taps*. During this period William tried to get a job for Walt's brother Jeff in Washington, but succeeded only in getting him recommended as a draughtsman; Jeff had to decline because of lack of experience.[4] Walt, in turn, tried to do a favor for William—to get a copy of Victor Hugo's *Shakespeare* translated into English. (Eldridge had tried in vain to find the volume in Boston a few months earlier; when he found that he could order it at a cost of six or seven dollars, he had to decline. He had written William of his hope that an American edition would be published soon, so that "we can slake our thirst at the pure well of genius.")[5] Now Walt tried in vain to find a copy at Christern's, an importer of foreign books, and at Scribner's.[6]

Walt was still in Brooklyn when the terrible news of President Lincoln's assassination appeared in the newspapers:

> . . . we heard the news very early in the morning. Mother prepared breakfast—and other meals afterward—as usual; but not a mouthful was eaten all day by either of us. We each drank half a cup of coffee; that was all. Little was said. We got every newspaper morning and evening, and the frequent extras of that period, and pass'd them silently to each other.[7]

In the afternoon Walt rode the ferry to Manhattan and walked up Broadway, where stores and buildings were draped in black; there were only a few passersby, most of the men dressed in black. Later a crowd assembled in front of the newspaper offices to read the bulletin boards which displayed the latest news.[8]

Two days later Walt was back in Washington, a city of mourning, where the lilacs were in bloom. The strangely bright star in the western sky and the lilacs were to be woven into Whitman's elegy on the

death of Lincoln—"When Lilacs Last in the Dooryard Bloom'd."
The suggestion of the third symbol—the hermit thrush—came from
John Burroughs.[9]

The three symbols intertwine at the close of the poem:

> For the sweetest, wisest soul of all my days and lands—and this
>   for his dear sake,
> Lilac and star and bird twined with the chant of my soul,
> There in the fragrant pines and the cedars dusk and dim.[10]

During the sad days after the death of Lincoln, while Whitman
was writing his "Memories of President Lincoln," *Drum-Taps*, so
eagerly awaited by the O'Connors and the poet's other friends, was
finally printed in April 1865.[11] In it the poet came close to achieving
the feeling of unity of which he had written to O'Connor,[12] for most
of the fifty-three poems were about the war.

Walt hardly had time to rejoice in the fact that *Drum-Taps* was
ready for publication before he suffered a severe jolt. With the new
administration, Senator James Harlan of Iowa, former president of
Iowa Wesleyan College and an Abolitionist (whose daughter later
married Robert Todd Lincoln) became Secretary of the Interior. He
was not in office very long before the following notice appeared in
the *New York Herald* (May 30, 1865):

> The Secretary of the Interior has issued a circular to the heads of
> bureaus in the department, to report as to the loyalty of each of
> the employees under him, and also whether there are any whose
> fidelity to duty or moral character is such as to justify an imme-
> diate dispensation of their services.

Whether Secretary Harlan received an adverse report on the
moral character of the author of *Leaves of Grass* is not known. It was
said that the Secretary himself, foraging in Walt's desk, found a copy
of *Leaves of Grass* bound in blue paper; it was a copy of the 1860
edition with many emendatons and additions—the working copy
for a new edition.[13] In an age of reticence and prudery, it is not hard
to imagine the reaction of Harlan, who was also a former Methodist
minister, to some of the lines he read in the purloined book (although
they were but a small portion of the whole):

Through me many long dumb voices,
Voices of the interminable generations of slaves,
Voices of prostitutes, and of deformed persons,
Voices of the diseased and despairing, and of thieves and dwarfs,
Voices of cycles of preparation and accretion,
And of the threads that connect the stars—and of wombs, and
  of the father-stuff,
And of the rights of them the others are down upon,
Of the trivial, flat, foolish, despised,
Fog in the air, beetles rolling balls of dung. . . .

I do not press my finger across my mouth,
I keep as delicate around the bowels as around the head and heart.
Copulation is no more rank to me than death is.

To Secretary Harlan these and other lines from "Walt Whitman" (later called "Song of Myself") must have seemed both pornographic and blasphemous. The volume he read had only a few pencilled corrections—mostly in punctuation. Obviously the poet meant these lines to stand as printed. And there were many other passages, equally shocking to Mr. Harlan, throughout the book. The outraged Secretary lost little time in severing the author from government employment. Whitman promptly received an official notice, dated June 30, from the Department of the Interior:

> The services of Walter Whitman, of New York, as a clerk in the
> Indian Office, will be dispensed with from and after this date.
> > Jas. Harlan,
> > Secretary of the Interior[14]

Walt was distresssed. Not only did he need a job to enable him to stay in Washington and care for the soldiers, but he had liked the work in the Indian Office. In "An Indian Bureau Reminiscence" in *November Boughs*,[15] Whitman wrote about the experience he had had in the Bureau "until Mr. Harlan turned me out for having written *Leaves of Grass*."

> Along this time there come to see their Great Father an unusual
> number of aboriginal visitors, delegations for treaties, settlement
> of lands, &c.—some young or middle-aged, but mainly old men,
> from the West, North, and occasionally from the South—parties

of from five to twenty each—the most wonderful proofs of what
Nature can produce . . . .

Walt must have reveled even in their names. "There were Omahas,
Poncas, Winnebagoes, Cheyennes, Navahos, Apaches, and many
others." He had many talks with the interpreters who accompanied
the Indians, and would go to the hotels and spend an hour or two
with the Indians, talking informally with them through the interpreters, talks "sometimes quite animated and significant." Now with
the abrupt letter of dismissal, not only would all this come to an end,
but perhaps his stay in Washington, his marvelous talks with the
O'Connors and other friends, his work in the hospitals—the life he
had enjoyed—all might be ended.

Walt immediately took the letter of dismissal to William O'Connor, who in turn stormed into the office of J. Hubley Ashton, his old
friend of the Philadelphia days, who was now Assistant Attorney-
General. Years later Ashton wrote of the events following Walt's
dismissal:

> I remember as if it were yesterday the day in the summer of '65,
> on which O'Connor came down to my office from his room above
> in the Treasury Building, where the Attorney General's office was
> then located, with Secretary Harlan's letter to Walt in his hand,
> and his terrific outburst against the Secretary for his act of infamy,
> as he described it, when he put the letter on my table.
>
> Everybody who knew William O'Connor and has read "The
> Good Gray Poet" can imagine the scene in my office. I fancy that
> there never was before such an outpouring of impassioned elo-
> quence in the presence of an audience of *one*. The wrong commit-
> ted, as O'Connor said, was the ignominious dismissal from the
> public service of the greatest poet America had produced, an of-
> fence against the honor and dignity of American letters, and
> against humanity itself as consecrated in "Leaves of Grass."

Ashton agreed that the crime was a great one, and offered to intercede immediately with Secretary Harlan. Ashton stated:

> My great apprehension was, as I remember, not merely that he
> (Harlan) would refuse, as he did, to recall the dismissal of Walt
> Whitman, but that he would set his face against Walt's appoint-

ment to any place under the Government in Washington. If he had done so, it would have been difficult, and might have been impossible, for me, against his opposition, to secure for Walt such a vindication as he received by his appointment to the clerkship he held for several years in the Department with which I was connected.[16]

Four days after Ashton's interview with Secretary Harlan, Whitman set down what Ashton had told him of the interview. Written in his own hand, the notes were headed—"Interview between Mr. Ashton and Secretary Harlan, July 1, '65. (Made July 5th and July 8th, 1865 in Washington.)"

Interview between Mr. Ashton and Mr. Harlan took place, July 1st, 1865, at the Room of the Secretary of the Interior in the Patent Office. Mr. Ashton drove down there from the Attorney General's, about 10 o'clock a.m. and remained over an hour. The interview consisted of a most animated conversation. Judge W. T. Otto was present, but took little or no part in the discussion. The Assistant Attorney General asked why W.W. was dismissed; asked if he had been found inattentive to his duties, or incompetent for them. Mr. Harlan said, No, there was no complaint on these points. As far as he heard or knew, W. was a both competent and faithful clerk. Mr. Ashton then said, Then what is the reason? The Secretary said, W. was the author of Leaves of Grass. Ashton said, Well, is that the reason? The Secretary said, Yes. He then went into a sort of narrative, to the following purport. He was examining round the building, after office hours, and either in or on a desk he saw the Book. He took it up and found it so odd, that he carried it to his room and and examined it. He found certain passages marked; and there were marks by and upon passages all through the book. He found in the book in some of these marked passages matter so outrageous that he had determined to discharge the author, &c. &c. &c.

Mr. Ashton then went into a statement of the theory of the book—that a construction of that kind put upon the passages was not consistent either with the intention of W.W. or the rest of the drift of the book—That he knew the spirit and intention of the author, and they were noble, whatever merit, or deficiency of merit, there might be in the book. Mr. Harlan said: Well, he couldn't help that. He thought the author was wrong, was a free lover, deserved punishment, &c.

The Assistant Attorney General said: Mr. Harlan, I know something of W.W.'s life, and if you will listen to me I will tell you what it has been. He then described W.'s life throughout as manly, pure, and patriotic. Since the commencement of the War he had devoted himself to the care of the wounded and sick of our armies; had been to the front, had been on hand after all the great battles, labored actively, for nearly three years, in that field, and had actually ministered to, in direct contact with them, more than a hundred thousand cases of wounded and sick men, had indeed, sought his appointment so that he might be able to spend his leisure hours in the service of the maimed and sick, in camps and hospitals around Washington, and was now continuing quietly and faithfully at that work.

Mr. Harlan said after this: You have changed my opinion of his personal character, but I shall adhere to my decision dismissing him.

On the Assistant Attorney General commencing some remarks involving a change of that decision, Mr. Harlan said, "It's no use, Mr. Ashton—I will not have the author of that book in this Department. No, if the President of the United States should order his reinstatement, I would resign sooner than I would put him back."

He then went into a long and angry abuse of the book, its offensive passages, and of W.W., to which the Assistant Attorney General made no reply, but bowed and took his leave.

It is perhaps a main point of this transaction, and the getting of a full understanding of it, to know that the marked copy of Leaves of Grass which Mr. Harlan discovered after office hours he discovered by personally prying into the drawers of W.W.'s desk. Such a copy, marked all through (for corrections and elisions for future edition) W.W. had in one of his drawers. It contained special marks and peculiarities with pencil, to which Mr. Harlan directly and indirectly alluded in his account in his long and animated discussion; making it unquestionable that this was the copy Mr. Harlan found, took away, examined, and then returned. It lay in the drawer, with a lot of private letters and other articles such as a man puts in his private desk. It is due to Mr. Harlan to say that nothing else (at least as far as known) appears to have been abstracted from this private drawer.

This memorandum is made within a week of the interview above described, and, in order to have it right, a second and more minute account of the interview was obtained, before these items were jotted down.

Mr. Harlan said to the Assistant Attorney General: There is no need of any one's knowing either what W.W. was dismissed for, nor the particulars of this conversation. It would be best for you and me to confine the matter to ourselves.

The Assistant Attorney General said he was not willing to make any promise, on his part, to that effect; he said he should certainly tell W.W. as he thought he had a right to know what he was dismissed for.[17]

At Ashton's request, the Attorney General, James Speed, assented to Walt's working in his office, and, according to Ashton, "the result of it all was that the Government became the friend and protector, instead of the persecutor, of our poet." Ashton stressed the fact that "whatever benefit Walt derived from my intervention and action in respect to his dismissal by Mr. Harlan, was primarily due to the devoted friendship of William D. O'Connor."[18]

Whitman continued to work in the Attorney General's office until he left Washington in 1873. While he was there, Attorney General Henry Stanbery offered him the position of Pardon Clerk. Whitman felt that he had to decline, because, having met and talked with many applicants for pardon, he knew that he would have pardoned everyone—which was hardly the intent of the office.[19]

A few months after Whitman's dismissal, Judge Otto, Acting Secretary of the Interior, who had employed Whitman originally, passed by his desk in the Attorney General's office. According to notes made by Whitman that very day, September 29, 1865, Judge Otto said:

I was sorry to lose your services in our Department, for I considered them valuable. The affair (my dismissal) "was settled upon before I knew it." . . . He said that he had seen on Mr. Harlan's desk a volume of Leaves of Grass, in blue paper covers, & the pages of the poems marked more or less all through the book; . . .[20]

Walt Whitman was not the only clerk in the Department of the Interior dismissed on grounds other than economy. According to

O'Connor (in a letter written to Mrs. Abby Price the following January) Secretary Harlan dismissed all the women, about a hundred, employed in his Department, "on the ground that their presence there might be injurious to what he calls the 'morals' of the men": Harlan was a "Miserable, hidebound Pharisee," O'Connor continues, "on whom all the lightnings of Christ's invective would have stormed! . . . To think that at a time when throughout Christendom, the wise, the liberal, the just are struggling to widen woman's work and woman's wages and so save her from the abysses of miseries unspeakable, this creature should shut upon her the avenue of employment, turning out to starvation and winter and every bitter chance that can befall the poor a hundred of her sex, and for such a reason!"[21] This action, which aroused O'Connor, the advocate of woman's rights, probably received no public notice.

Whitman's dismissal, however, had been duly noted in his home town. The *Brooklyn Eagle* commented on July 12, 1865:[22]

> Our eccentric fellow citizen Walt Whitman has lost his position in the Interior Department at Washington under the general order discharging immoral persons, his "Leaves of Grass" being produced as evidence of his immorality. . . . Walt is personally a good-hearted fellow, with some ability, but he was bitten with the mania of transcendentalism, which broke out in New England some years ago, and still flourishes in that region. . . .

The editor of the *Eagle* admitted that

> during the war Whitman went to Washington and did humane service in tending the sick and wounded soldiers in the hospitals; he was rewarded with a clerkship in the Interior Department from which he has just been discharged. Walt, however, has been provided for elsewhere. He now occupies a desk in the Attorney General's office, where we suppose they are not so particular about morals.

Years later Walt told Horace Traubel that Harlan was a "despicable man—had a sort of penny-a-line character: was made for little issues, was set for small victories."[23]

On another occasion, however, Whitman was able to view Harlan more tolerantly—even half humorously:

> Don't ever assail Harlan as if he was a scoundrel: he wasn't: he was only a fool: there was only a dim light in his noddle: he had to steer by that light: what else could he do? . . . I have always had a latent sneaking admiration for his cowardly despicable act— . . . rooting in my desk in the dead of the night looking for evidence against me. What instinct ever drove him to my desk: He must have had some intimation from some one that I was what I was.[24]

In later years, Harlan would not admit that Whitman's dismissal was due to his authorship of *Leaves of Grass*. In a letter written in July 1894 to DeWitt Miller, who had inquired about the dismissal, Harlan stated:

> Whitman's Chief, Hon. Wm. P. Dole, Commissioner of Indian Affairs, who was officially answerable to me for the work of his Bureau, recommended it, *on the ground that his services were not needed*. And no other reason was ever assigned by my authority.[25]

This is the first mention of any action by Commissioner Dole, who was not referred to in Ashton's account of the interview with Harlan or in Whitman's notes of that interview. It is interesting to note that Commissioner Dole soon shared Whitman's fate.[26]

In 1910 Johnson Brigham, State Librarian of Iowa, preparing a biography of James Harlan, wrote to John Burroughs protesting the account of Harlan given in a "deluxe edition" of Whitman's work.[27] According to Brigham there was nothing secretive or underhanded in Harlan's character and therefore he could not have surreptitiously taken *Leaves of Grass* from Whitman's desk and read it. To Burroughs's response—"Harlan was guilty of a mean cowardly act. Probably it was the one thing by which he will be remembered"[28]— Brigham offers the counter claim that Harlan was one of Iowa's most important sons.

Years later, however, H. L. Mencken gave one of the verdicts of posterity:

> Let us repair, once a year, to our accustomed houses of worship and there give thanks to God that one day in 1865 brought together the greatest poet America ever produced and the damndest ass.[29]

Brigham hints that Whitman himself deprecated O'Connor's zeal; there is no evidence that this was so. Not only has no such statement been found, but Whitman is known to have admired O'Connor without reservation. He said to Traubel:

> To me William is self-justified in the truest sense of the word. He is intense, overwhelming—when he wrote the "Good Gray Poet," when he wrote the letter for Bucke's book, he was excited and indignant to a degree; but we must remember what it was that called forth his wrath—the consciousness of a great wrong: an inexcusable offense which demanded a corresponding emphasis of resentment. . . .[30]

Despite Ashton's successful intervention both in gaining Secretary Harlan's promise that he would not prevent Whitman's employment in another department of the government and in getting him a job in the Attorney General's office, O'Connor and Ashton were not satisfied. They wanted the case for Whitman, including what had transpired at the interview, to become part of the official record. There is a lengthy manuscript letter to Harlan in O'Connor's hand dated July 21, 1865.[31] Obviously it was meant to be signed by Ashton, since the letter is headed "Attorney General's office," and designates the writer as one "at whose instance Mr. Whitman was originally appointed to a position of responsibility in the Government," and as having made at the interview a formal request for his reinstatement in that position.

The letter reveals not only what Ashton and Harlan said during the interview, but also what Whitman at that time considered the intention of *Leaves of Grass* and the essence of his life and work. Although in O'Connor's handwriting, the letter was probably the joint work of O'Connor, Whitman, and Ashton. The style is formal and matter-of-fact, lacking O'Connor's rhetorical flourishes. The description of Whitman's intentions echoes the poet's writings. The letter does not speak in O'Connor's richly rhetorical manner.

There is no record that this letter was ever transcribed by Ashton and sent to Secretary Harlan. In any event O'Connor must have felt that the letter written for someone else to send, did not express fully all that he would have liked to say about Whitman and *Leaves of Grass*. Furthermore, while it praised Whitman and affirmed what had taken place at Ashton's interview with Harlan, it did not censure the Secretary as he deserved. There was more to be said, and to a wider audience—one which might be encouraged to read and appreciate *Leaves of Grass.*

Ten years had passed since the First Edition of *Leaves of Grass.* Two editions had followed; *Drum-Taps* was printed and ready for distribution. Whitman was preparing a new edition of *Leaves of Grass.* There had been a number of reviews of the first three editions, favorable and unfavorable; some recognition of the poet's unique quality by Emerson and a few of his friends, and publication of a few poems in the *Saturday Press.* But five years had passed since the Third Edition was published by Thayer and Eldridge. It must have seemed to O'Connor and others in the Washington group that their poet and prophet was honored only within their tiny circle. No new poems had been seen by the public. When they did appear in *Drum-Taps* and in a new edition of *Leaves of Grass,* how would they be received?

Who would speak for Whitman? And how would they be heard? There was no existing periodical that was sympathetic to Whitman and that would express the views of his admirers. To his friends Whitman was the foremost genius America had produced, whose poems, equal to those of the greatest masters of world literature, expressed the spirit of the new world—yet he was virtually unrecognized. And now, this indignity—dismissal from a minor clerkship because of his poems! To O'Connor neither Whitman's acquisition of another post in Government service nor an expostulatory letter to Secretary Harlan provided a satisfactory conclusion to the affair. What was needed was a letter to the American public and to writers overseas: The defense of Whitman could become a defense of freedom in letters. O'Connor had found another consuming cause.

NOTES

1. Actually George was released in a general exchange of prisoners. See Jerome M. Loving, *Civil War Letters of George Washington Whitman* (Durham, North Carolina: Duke University Press, 1975), pp. 17–25.
2. *Prose Works,* I: 92.
3. *Ibid.,* 94.
4. Thomas Jefferson Whitman to WDO'C, 15 March 1865 (Berg).

5. Eldridge to WDO'C, 19 April 1865 (Feinberg-LC).
6. WW to WDO'C, 7 April 1865, *Correspondence,* I: 257.
7. *Prose Works,* I: 31.
8. Charles I. Glicksberg, ed., *Walt Whitman and the Civil War* (Philadelphia: University of Pennsylvania Press, 1933), pp. 174–75.
9. Barrus, *Life and Letters,* I: 100.
10. *LG/CRE,* p. 337.
11. Gay Wilson Allen, *The New Walt Whitman Handbook* (New York: New York University Press, 1975), p. 112.
12. WW to WDO'C, 6 January 1865. *Correspondence,* I: 247.
13. Arthur Golden, *Walt Whitman's Blue Book,* Vol. 1, Facsimile (Oscar Lion Collection Rare Book Division, New York Public Library, 1968).
14. *Camden,* 3: 471.
15. *Prose Works,* II: 577–80.
16. Ashton to Eldridge, 13 June 1902 in Barrus, *Comrades,* pp. 27–30.
17. *Camden,* 3: 472–75.
18. See note 16 above.
19. Eldridge to Burroughs, 26 June 1902 (Berg).
20. Golden, *op. cit.,* transcription facing page lviii.
21. WDO'C to Price, 11 January 1866 (Yale).
22. Quoted by Gay Wilson Allen, *The Solitary Singer, A Critical Biography of Walt Whitman* (New York: The Macmillan Company, 1955), p. 347.
23. *Camden,* 2: 26.
24. *Camden,* 3: 476–77.
25. Barrus, *Comrades,* p. 26.
26. *Ibid.,* p. 33.
27. *Ibid.,* p. 30.
28. Burroughs to Brigham, 11 May 1910. *Ibid.,* p. 31.
29. H. L. Mencken, *Prejudices, First Series* (New York: A. A. Knopf, 1919), pp. 249–50.
30. *Camden,* 2: 240.
31. The "Ashton Letter" (Berg) is quoted in full among O'Connor's writings in Jerome Loving, *Walt Whitman's Champion: William Douglas O'Connor* (College Station and London: Texas A&M University Press, 1978), pp. 149–155. According to Eldridge, writing to Burroughs, 14 June 1902, Ashton wrote his record of Whitman's removal as a result of the personal appeal made by O'Connor, his old friend (Berg).

CHAPTER **XI**

A Champion Enters
The Lists

O'CONNOR'S *The Good Gray Poet: A Vindication*, triggered by Harlan's action but ranging far beyond it, was the first extended piece about Whitman as man and poet. Nelly O'Connor, in her introduction to a reprint of the book many years later, wrote:

> As soon as Mr. O'Connor realized what Secretary Harlan had done, he began to characterize the deed in terms which seemed to him deserved. Yet with all his wealth of language, I think that he could hardly characterize the act as fully as he felt that it merited. It was an outrage on literature, and, as such, no words could do it justice. He poured out the unqualified wrath of his pen, and after the vindication was printed he sent it to all the believers in untrammeled speech that he could reach. What one man could do he surely did in his generous and unstinted fashion.[1]

(Nelly does not tell the extent of William's generosity: the risk taken by a government clerk, wholly dependent on his job, in criticizing a high government official, the Secretary of the Interior, in a published diatribe.)

The Good Gray Poet: A Vindication, headed Washington, D.C., September 2, 1865, and signed William Douglas O'Connor, Massachusetts, was a forty-six page pamphlet filled with eloquent, even extravagant praise of Whitman as a man and poet and outrage at the action of Secretary Harlan. It presented an array of vignettes of the

176

great writers of the world describing their undoubted fate had they served under Harlan or his counterpart. The pamphlet serves not only as a vindication of Whitman but also of freedom in letters generally. The allusions reveal wide and perceptive reading, yet O'Connor averred that all were recalled from memory of reading done some eight or ten years earlier, there being in the nation's capital no library worthy of the name in which he could have refreshed his memory.

In style and structure *The Good Gray Poet* resembles a lengthy oration. Its outpouring of eloquence and hyperbole, which often seems extravagant on the printed page, would be impressive and persuasive in an auditorium. At a time when a single oration lasted as long as three hours, the forty-six page pamphlet might well have been the work of a master orator. (Wendell Phillips's speech on "Philosophy of the Abolition Movement" covered fifty-six pages and another on "The Boston Mob," fifty-nine pages when they were published.)[2] O'Connor skillfully uses the oratorical device of repetition of words, phrases, and sentence and paragraph structure to build to a climax, often followed by an ironic anticlimax. One such dynamic phrase, "Out with—" appears with slight variation at the end of each of a series of more than twenty paragraphs, each characterizing a great writer who would have fared ill under a man like Secretary Harlan; for example, "Out with Moses! The cloven splendour on that awful brow shall not save him! Out with Moses!"

Antithesis is another effective device: "When on grounds of taste, foes withhold detraction, friends may withhold eulogy," and ". . . to that long record of hostility, I am only proud to offer this record of affection." When, as is customary throughout the pamphlet, O'Connor drops from the height of an emotional outburst to a level, factual passage, the reader can almost hear the change in vocal level and intensity.

Several of the writer's friends sensed the oratorical quality of *The Good Gray Poet*. Wendell Phillips, though not in accord with O'Connor's opinion of Whitman, wrote, "If common events can so rouse and melt your nature, you ought to have been a speaker. Marry your style to a living voice and we talkers will all take back seats."[3] Whitman also discerned this quality in *The Good Gray Poet*. In reply to Traubel's comment that "it is so eloquent—vocal: when I read it I want to, I do, *hear* it," Whitman said:

Exactly: that's just it: that's what we all felt—feel. William is in the best sense an orator—is eminently passionate, pictorial, electric. I'd rather hear O'Connor argue for what I consider wrong than hear most other people argue for what I think right: he has charm, color, vigor. . . .[4]

The title of the pamphlet, *The Good Gray Poet*, a sobriquet which has become synonymous with Walt Whitman, was hardly the term most of his contemporaries would have chosen. The rough, licentious satyr might have been closer to their conception. The name, which was generally accepted, as well as the ideas about him in the pamphlet, were said to have influenced Whitman's conception of himself as man and as poet.

A critic has questioned O'Connor's authorship of the phrase,[5] but contemporary evidence proves that it was O'Connor's invention. O'Connor wrote to Moncure Conway on May 27, 1866, "Don't you like my name for Walt—'The Good Gray Poet,' I think that will stick."[6] He also referred to himself as author of the phrase in a letter to the *Independent* on November 9, 1867, in response to what he thought a scurrilous description of Whitman: "The term of The Good Gray Poet having been as is very well known, conferred upon Mr. Whitman by me . . . I naturally feel some personal interest in this allusion to it. . . ."[7] In a letter to *The Tribune* on March 30, 1876, Stedman supported O'Connor's authorship of the term, as did Frank Sanborn in a letter to the *Springfield Republican* on April 19, 1876. Sanborn wrote in part: "One of his eager young friends, William O'Connor, printed a warm defense of Whitman in which he termed him 'The good gray poet.' " (If there had been other claimants to this name for Whitman they surely would have come forward, for these letters were written at a time when O'Connor and Whitman were estranged.)

Years later Charles Eldridge affirmed O'Connor's authorship. In 1893 he responded to an article by DeWitt Lockwood in *The Californian*:

The title was also a subject of conference, and O'Connor has the sole honor of inventing it. It was suggested to him, he told me, by a line in Tennyson's "Ode on the Death of the Duke of Wellington"—"The good gray head which all men knew." . . .[8]

Ellen O'Connor (then Mrs. Calder), in Charles N. Elliot's *Walt Whitman, As Man, Poet and Friend,* affirms: "Mr. O'Connor gave Walt Whitman the name of the 'Good Gray Poet' by which he is known and always will be so known."[9]

In the pamphlet, perhaps in unconscious imitation of the First Edition of *Leaves of Grass,* O'Connor does not introduce the name of his protagonist until after some 800 words of description of the man as he might be seen in the streets of Washington—a man "tallying . . . the streets of our American cities, and fit to have for his background and accessories, their streaming populations and ample and rich facades, a man of striking masculine beauty—a poet—powerful and venerable in appearance; large, calm, superbly formed. . . ." As he had seen him some two hours ago, "rich light an artist would have chosen, lay upon his uncovered head, majestic, large, Homeric, and set upon his strong shoulders with the grandeur of ancient sculpture. . . ."[10]

Yet this poet, like the great of other ages in their time, walks unnoticed.

> But Dante stirs no deep pulse, unless it be of hate, as he walks the streets of Florence; that shabby, one-armed soldier, just out of jail and hardly noticed, though he has amused Europe, is Michael Cervantes; that son of a vine-dresser, whom Athens laughs at as an eccentric genius, before it is thought worth while to roar him into exile, is the century-shaking Aeschylus; that phantom whom the wits of the seventeenth century think not worth extraordinary notice, and the wits of the eighteenth century, spluttering with laughter, call a barbarian, is Shakespeare; that earth-soiled, vice-stained ploughman, with the noble heart and sweet, bright eyes, whom the good abominate and the gentry patronize—subject now of anniversary banquets by gentlemen, who, could they wander back from those annual hiccups into Time, would never help his life or keep his company—is Robert Burns; and this man, whose grave, perhaps, the next century will cover with passionate and splendid honors, goes regarded with careless curiosity or phlegmatic composure by his own age.

Still, there are some who have praised the poet: Alcott, Thoreau, Lincoln. "Sublime tributes, great words; but none too high for their object," and here, for the first time, O'Connor mentions the name of the man he writes of, "the author of *Leaves of Grass*, Walt Whitman of Brooklyn." An account of Whitman's dismissal by Harlan, and the circumstances as described by Ashton follows. A result of Harlan's action was "the scurrilous, and in some instances libellous, comment of a portion of the press." Denying Harlan's and others' allegations that Whitman was a bad man, a "free lover," or a rowdy, O'Connor tells of Whitman's blameless life and of his work:

> He has been a laborer, working successively as a farmer, a carpenter, a printer. He has been a stalwart editor of the Republican party, and often, in that powerful and nervous prose of which he is master, done yeoman's service for the great cause of human liberty and [the] imperial conception of the indivisible Union. He has been a visitor of prisons; a protector of fugitive slaves, a constant voluntary nurse, night and day, at the hospitals. . . .

O'Connor tells anecdotes of Whitman's great kindness and of the way in which people of all sorts are drawn to him.

> His intellectual influence upon many young men and women— spirits of the morning sort, not willing to belong to that intellectual colony of Great Britain which our literary classes compose, nor helplessly tied, like them, to the old forms—I note as kindred to that of Socrates upon the youth of ancient Attica, or Raleigh upon the gallant young England of his day. It is a power at once liberating, instructing, and inspiring. His conversation is a university. . . .

He writes of Whitman as a patriot, who has voted in every election, has nursed the wounded soldiers, who insisted upon putting his name upon the enrollment lists, that he might stand his chance for martial service—at a time when although forty-two or three years old, he looked like a man of sixty, and would have been passed over by the enrolling officers.

This panegyric comes to a climax in the lines ". . . his seems to me a character which only the heroic pen of Plutarch could record, and which Socrates himself might emulate or envy,"—then drops to the anticlimax of, "this is the man whom Mr. Harlan charges with having written a bad book . . . full of indecent passages."

O'Connor has counted the lines in *Leaves of Grass* and *Drum-Taps*. Of these 9000 lines, he has "culled eighty" on which "rest the whole crazy fabric of American and European slander and the brutal lever of the Secretary."

What Whitman has done, O'Connor explains, "is to mention, without levity, without low language, very seriously, often devoutly, always simply, certain facts in the natural history of man and of life; and sometimes, assuming their sanctity, to use them in illustration or imagery. . . ."

O'Connor imagines the great authors of the world condemned to clerkships under Mr. Harlan: Moses of the Book of Genesis, Homer of the Odyssey, Lucretius, Aeschylus, Ezekiel, Dante, Job, Plutarch, Herodotus, Tacitus, Shakespeare, Solomon of the Canticle of Canticles, Isaiah, Montaigne, Hafiz, Virgil, Swedenborg, Goethe, Byron, Cervantes, Victor Hugo, Juvenal, John of the Apocalypse, Spenser, Rabelais, Lord Bacon. Painters, sculptors and composers would also come under the ban: Phidias, Rembrandt, Mozart, and Michelangelo. In a succinct paragraph for each, O'Connor tells why he would have been dismissed by Secretary Harlan. O'Connor links them together as among "the demi-gods of human thought," "the light-bringers, . . ." "the liberators, the inspired inspirers of mankind; . . ." "There is not one of them that is not sacred in the eyes of thoughtful men. But not one of them does the rotten taste and morals of the Nineteenth Century spare."

Unfortunately Harlan is not alone in his views. Most of the great works are available to the nineteenth-century reader only in bowdlerized form. O'Connor quotes (without naming him) a writer whom he reveres who said that it was necessary to expurgate the old writers, but now that women have become readers, literature has sprung to a higher level, and there is no need for expurgation.[11] O'Connor, however, sees a different role for women, not "as expurgator or creator of emasculate or partial forms." Women will produce art "with sex, with truth, with universality, without omissions or concealments. . . ."

"Tell me not, then, of the indecent passages of the great poets!" thunders O'Connor. "The world, which is the poem of God, is full of indecent passages! 'Shall there be evil in a city and the Lord hath not done it?' shouts Amos."

Having considered the man Walt Whitman, and the poets and artists of old, O'Connor now turns to *Leaves of Grass* and hails it as "a work purely and entirely American, autochthonic, sprung from our own soil. . . ." Heretofore,

> in no literary form, except our newspapers, has there been anything distinctively American. I note our best books—the works of Jefferson, the romances of Brockden Brown, the speeches of Webster, Everett's rhetoric, the divinity of Channing, some of Cooper's novels, the writings of Theodore Parker, the poetry of Bryant, the masterly law arguments of Lysander Spooner, the miscellanies of Margaret Fuller, the histories of Hildreth, Bancroft and Motley, Ticknor's "History of Spanish Literature," Judd's "Margaret," the political treatises of Calhoun, the rich, benignant poems of Longfellow, the ballads of Whittier, the delicate songs of Philip Pendleton Cooke, the weird poetry of Edgar Poe, the wizard tales of Hawthorne, Irving's "Knickerbocker," Delia Bacon's splendid sibyllic book on Shakespeare, the political economy of Carey, the prison letters and immortal speech of John Brown, the lofty patrician eloquence of Wendell Phillips, and those diamonds of the first water, the great clear essays and greater poems of Emerson. This literature has often commanding merits, and much of it is very precious to me; but in respect to its national character, all that can be said is that it is tinged, more or less deeply, with America; and the foreign model, the foreign standards, the foreign ideas, dominate over it all. At most, our best books were but struggling beams; behold in *Leaves of Grass* the immense and absolute sunrise! It is all our own! The nation is in it. . . .
>
> . . . To understand Greece, study the "Iliad" and "Odyssey": study *Leaves of Grass* to understand America. Her democracy is there.

Leaves of Grass, he states, contains also a philosophy of life and of models of manly and womanly character for the future of this country. The poet expresses the essence as well as the mystery of human beings. When he deliberately emphasizes our most common attributes— "the great element of amativeness or sexuality," he is seeking "to rescue" it from "blackguards and debauchees . . . ."

O'Connor praises the language and the meter of the *Leaves*.

Whitman's use of the English language ranges "from the powerful, rank idiom of the streets and the fields to the last subtlety of academic speech." Borrowing from other languages, the poet has created a "daring composite defying grammar." Whitman's meter, equally "free" and "corresponsive to the thought," reflects "the vast elemental sounds and motions of Nature . . . ." O'Connor cites some of the poems for their perfect and vast music. If Whitman had never written any other poems, "When Lilacs Last in the Dooryard Bloom'd" would place him among the chief poets of the century, a poem "whose rich and sacred beauty and rapture of tender religious passion, spreading aloft into the sublime, leave it unique and solitary in literature, and will make it the chosen and immortal hymn of Death forever."

After his appreciation of the poems, O'Connor turns to criticizing the critics. He scolds them for the same judgments which "Voltaire not more ridiculously passed on Shakespeare." What was condemned "for rudeness, chaos, barbarism, lack of form," O'Connor maintains, may be the "magnificent wildness of a virgin world of poetry." O'Connor places Whitman beside Shakespeare, Aeschylus, Cervantes, Dante, Homer, Isaiah—"the bards of the last ascent, the brothers of the radiant summit."

It is only prudery which objects to some of the lines—"nothing but the horrible inanity of prudery, to which civilization has become subject, and which affects even many good persons." O'Connor cites examples of everyday prudery—pulling down the petticoat of an infant playing on the floor and "dressing in pantalettes the 'limbs' of the piano." This prudery is everywhere. Emerson has been criticized for using the word "spermatic," and Charles Sumner, in the debate on Louisiana, when he characterized the new state as a "seven months child, begotten by the bayonet, in criminal conjunction with the spirit of caste," was censured by the public prints and reminded that there were ladies in the gallery.

> It is not purity, it is impurity, which calls clothes more decent than the naked body—thus inanely conferring upon the work of the tailor or milliner a modesty denied to the work of God.

In contradiction to the feeling that "portions of the human physiology are base; that the amative feelings and acts of the sexes, even when hallowed by marriage, are connected with a low sensuality. . . . ," Walt Whitman has offered the conception of

> the individual as a divine democracy of essences, powers, attributes, functions, organs—all equal, all sacred, all consecrate to noble use; the sexual part, the same as the rest, no more a subject for mystery, or shame, or secrecy, than the intellectual, or the manual, or the alimentary, or the locomotive part—divinely commonplace as head, or hand, or stomach, or foot; and, though sacred, to be regarded as so ordinary that it shall be employed the same as any other part, for the purposes of literature—an idea which he exemplified in his poetry by a metaphorical use which it is a deep disgrace to any intellect to misunderstand.

O'Connor has a few more stings for the petty men who would criticize his poet:

> I know not what further vicissitude of insult and outrage is in store for this great man. It may be that the devotees of a castrated literature, the earthworms that call themselves authors, the confectioners that pass for poets, the flies that are recognized as critics, the bigots, the dilettanti, the prudes and the fools, are more potent than I dream to mar the fortunes of his earthly hours; but above and beyond them uprises a more majestic civilization in the immense and sane serenities of futurity; and the man . . . who has written to make his land greater, her citizens better, his race nobler; who has striven to serve men by communicating to them that which they least know—their own experience; who has thrown into living verse a philosophy designed to exalt life to a higher level of sincerity, reality, religion; who has torn away disguises and illusions, and restored to commonest things, and the simplest and roughest people, their divine significance and natural, antique dignity, and who has wrapped his country and all created things as with splendors of sunrise, in the beams of a powerful and gorgeous poetry—that man, whatever be the clouds that close around his fame, is assured illustrious; . . . And Time will remember him. He holds upon the future this supreme claim of all high poets—behind the book, a life loyal to humanity!

O'Connor returns to the description of Whitman's life. He describes the barracks-like hospitals in which Whitman walked, "in the spirit of Christ, soothing, healing, consoling, restoring, night and day, for years . . . he gives all his money, he gives all his time, he gives all his love." He describes hospital scenes which he himself witnessed, and could hardly bear to see. Yet Whitman went daily among these scenes, ministering to the men. O'Connor quotes Thoreau's saying of Whitman that "he suggests something more than human," and Lincoln's words, "Well, *he* looks like a *Man!*"

To those who would criticize the extravagance of his praise, O'Connor says,

> And if there be any who think this tribute in bad taste, even to a poet so great, a person so unusual, a man so heroic and loving, I answer, that when on grounds of taste, foes withhold detraction, friends may withhold eulogy. . . . To that long record of hostility, I am only proud to be able to oppose this record of affection.

As for the dismissal of Whitman by Secretary of the Interior Harlan, O'Connor states, "I denounce it as a sinister precedent; as a ban upon the free action of genius, as a logical insult to all commanding literature; and in every way a most serious and heinous wrong. . . ." Even though Harlan and he share the same political views and membership in the same party, O'Connor strongly condemns his actions and calls "upon every scholar, every man of letters, every editor, every good fellow everywhere who wields the pen, to make common cause with me in rousing upon it the full tempest of reprobation it deserves. . . ." In the spirit of "that old chivalry of letters, which in all ages has sprung to the succor and defence of genius," he proposes to send this message to Victor Hugo, John Stuart Mill, Francis Newman, and Matthew Arnold, for England, ". . . to Emerson and Wendell Phillips, to Charles Sumner; to every Senator and Representative in Congress; to all our journalists; to the whole American people; to everyone who guards the freedom of letters and the liberty of thought throughout the civilized world. God grant that not in vain upon this outrage do I invoke the judgment of the mighty spirit of literature, and the fires of every honest heart."

Had *The Good Gray Poet* been an oration, O'Connor would have had an audience, and would have known whether he had reached them. Since it was a written document he had to find a publisher before he could find an audience. O'Connor's impassioned defense had not as yet been heard beyond the small circle of admirers. The search for a publisher for *The Good Gray Poet* began immediately. O'Connor appealed to his friend George Curtis, who replied,

> The task you undertake is not easy, as you know. The public sympathy will be with the Secretary for removing a man who will be considered an obscene author and a free lover. But your hearty vindication of Free Letters will not be the less welcome to all liberal men.
> That a man should be expelled from office and held up to public contumely, because of an honest book which no candid mind can truly regard as hurtful to public morality, is an offence which demands exposure and censure. . . .[12]

Almost a month later when Curtis read the manuscript, he wrote again, disagreeing with O'Connor's argument, but offering to help place the book with a publisher:

> The rhetoric is gorgeous. Its estimate of the bard of course entirely outruns any present appreciation of him by that public which reads. . . .
> For my own part I read your lofty praise with admiration and shame that I could be so blind to so great a glory. I shall read the *Drum-Taps* with double interest. . . .
> For the substance of the work, you marshal a splendid array of "indecent" witnesses, and bravely accuse all the Great Gods of "nastiness." But I asked myself, as I read, two questions: First, is there no natural reticence about these sexual relations and organs,—and second, is the sense of various power in the greatest authors at all increased by their use of such allusions as metaphors or otherwise? Is it a prudery or an instinct which secretes the whole matter?[13]

Finally Bunce and Huntington of New York City agreed to publish the pamphlet, as a result of Curtis's efforts. It appeared in January 1866, priced at fifty cents, a sum O'Connor feared was too dear and would impede its sale. He also complained that the publishers had done nothing for the book.[14]

One of the first copies O'Connor sent was to Walt's mother, who commented on it some time later, after Burroughs's *Notes on Walt Whitman as Poet and Person* had come out. In a letter to her son,

Mrs. Whitman wrote: "you know i like . . . the good gray poet better than i doo borroughs book. O'Connor shows the spirit its wrote in, i should form an idea of the man if I had never seen him by reading his writings."[15]

Walt's sister Hannah Heyde wrote to her mother from her home in New Hampshire:

> My dear darling mother:
>
> I was very much taken with the vindication. I thought I would not have missed having it for anything in the world. I read it through the first night I got it. I know Walt was as good, but I liked the language, liked the way it was written better than anything I ever read. I would like to see Mr. O'Connor, I wish I could see a picture of him, the book done me good. I was not feeling real well, sort of down hearted. I was so much pleased with it, it made me feel cheerful and happy. . . .[16]

While O'Connor must have been pleased by the praise of friends, he was eagerly awaiting the response of the great writers of Europe whom he had addressed, for the envoy at the close of *The Good Gray Poet* was no mere rhetoric. He sent the pamphlet to all the people mentioned by name, as well as to writers and journalists of his acquaintance. Whether he sent it to all the Senators and Representatives is not known. (Bunce and Huntington sent fifty copies for distribution and asked for an additional list of people to whom they were to send copies.)

Among the responses from Europe which O'Connor kept were those from Matthew Arnold and Francis Newman of England. Matthew Arnold wrote:

> Mr. Harlan is now, I believe, out of office, but had he still remained in office I can imagine nothing less likely to make him reconsider his decision respecting your friend than the interference of foreign expostulators in the matter. I have read your statement with interest and I do not contest Mr. Walt Whitman's powers and originality. I doubt, however, whether here, too, or in France, or in Germany, a public functionary would not have had to pay for the pleasure of being so outspoken the same penalty which your friend has paid in America. As to the general question of Mr. Walt Whitman's poetical achievements, you will think that

it savours of our decrepit old Europe when I add that while you
think it is his highest merit that he is so unlike anyone else, to me
this seems to be his demerit; no one can afford in literature to
trade merely on his own bottom and to take no account of what
the other ages and nations have acquired. A great original literature America will never get in this way, and her intellect must
inevitably consent to come, in a considerable measure, into the
European movement. That she may do this and yet be an independent intellectual colony of Europe, I cannot doubt; and it is on
her doing this, and not on her displaying an eccentric and violent
originality that wise Americans should in my opinion set their
desires.[17]

To this O'Connor responded on October 16, 1866:

I can't agree that America must come into the European
movement, as you say, for, and I am sorry so many Englishmen
are blind to it, America has a movement of her own, the source of
her life, the secret of her power, and I think, if you will pardon me
for saying so, there is far more need and probability of Europe
coming into our movement, than we into hers. Democracy, true
or false, is the doctrine or principle in which this country has its
start, and her movement, in literature as in everything else, must
proceed and be sustained from it, and not from anything exterior
to it. As well expect that our flora and fauna should derive from
the influence of another zone, as that our letters, or any form of
our life, should find its inspiration and sustenance from the central
forces of foreign lands. . . .
    It may be, as you say, that in Europe as in America to write in
Shakespeare's grandeur of spirit and with less than Shakespeare's
daring, is an offence which has official penalties. I try to imagine
the man who belongs to England by his feet and to the Infinite by
his wings, expelled from some desk in the Elizabethan Custom
House which once stood on the banks of the Thames, for the publications of the twentieth sonnet, or the scenes of Troilus and
Cressida.

O'Connor writes in the vein of his pamphlet of the possible dismissal of Defoe, Burns, Landor, or Lamb:

It may be, as you seem to think, that these things could be done
in Europe with impunity. Unquestionably, Mr. Harlan is the man

that would do them. But if so not less clear is the duty of the scholar and man of letters, who knows, or ought to know that the greatest genius at least moulds its works without regard to conventions, solely in obedience to interior law, and practices its sweet and awful wisdom not less in its "indecencies" than elsewhere, always for the broad welfare of the race. That duty forever is to make any such Manworm plus Mr. Sycophant who ventures upon a course of this kind, feel if he be made of penetrable stuff, that he transcends his function when he attempts to play the censor to literature, and that neither the consciences nor the designs of geniuses are confided to his jurisdiction.

Free thought is the world's greatest interest, and there should be a spirit of free-masonry in men-of-letters strong enough to guard and avenge each other against their common enemy.

O'Connor responds to another point made by Arnold:

You gravely misread me if you think I claim that Mr. Whitman's work is unlike that of anyone else, pronouncing that a merit. But to me, as to you, that would be a demerit; nor has "Leaves of Grass" any such character.

As the author himself says, it "does not repel the Past" and it connects lovingly with precedents, as does America. My claim for Mr. Whitman is that his work is original in the only just sense of the word—as Homer and Aeschylus are original to Greece, despite their tap-roots in the Orient; as Shakespeare is original to England, though he derives so deeply from Spain, France, Italy, the medieval romance, the antique lore.[18]

The copy of *The Good Gray Poet* sent to Francis Newman of England (admired by O'Connor as the translator of Homer) shows by extensive markings that it was read carefully, but not entirely sympathetically. At the end of his copy, Newman wrote a summary of the letter of acknowledgment and "total and intense repudiation" he had sent to O'Connor.

The letter Newman sent, however, was more temperate than his notes. He wrote:

I heartily rejoice at your vindication of Mr. Walt Whitman. Your panegyric of him warms my heart. It is alike honorable to you and to him. I had heard with great pleasure of his beautiful patriotism displayed in the most arduous philanthropy. That Mr. Harlan's severity should come down on such a man, was truly unfortunate. Mr. Harlan evidently mistook the facts & (I suppose), like other men in power, is ashamed to confess his error. But the error was very natural: when (as you state) Mr. Whitman has remained unmarried to the age of 45, often dresses in what might seem *disguise*, and freely mingles with low & profligate persons, (for *their good*, as I have no doubt you truly explain,) and his book (you say) has been thought & called *lewd* by many critics. Mr. Harlan has already had cause to ask himself, whether to hold office under a traitor is not more out of harmony with the millennium than to have a licentious poet among one's subordinates.

Newman does, however, challenge the other major contention of *The Good Gray Poet*:

If your pamphlet limited its defense to Mr. Whitman, I should say no more; but you claim a right for men of "genius" to print what they please. Perhaps I imperfectly understand you; I am sure you have no understanding of me. Your principles seem to me distinctly to claim, that a man who thinks his "genius" impels him, shall be allowed to circulate poetry which others think polluting, or to paint pictures as obscene as he pleases, or appear in public as much undressed as he pleases. You forbid us to resent it. You seem even to claim a *right* to go naked in society.

Newman refers to a book by Robert Owen, in which he advocated nudity. "He was not mad, but only philanthropic & eccentric." Newman finds in O'Connor's pamphlet "plenty of contempt & sarcasm . . . directed against what are my own profound convictions; & I do not feel that they deserve any of your contempt. You are evidently a man of generous & energetic mind. Where you hold conclusions so vehemently I am not likely to revise them." Nevertheless, Newman continues the argument by stating that Greek corruption, which later spread to Persia and Rome, stemmed from the introduction of naked wrestling. "Naked statues of women were unknown, I believe, to Phidias; but the increasing depravity became common." Reluctantly, Newman would excuse certain things in past ages or in foreign cultures "which we not the less think to be gross."[19]

Despite his statement that he would not recur to this matter, Newman did write to O'Connor again in October, acknowledging the receipt of *Drum-Taps*, and characterizing it as "poetical prose." "To deny to Drum-Taps that in this extended sense it is poetry, would be unjust. But to the full idea of native poetry Form as well as Substance is needed; & to form it makes no pretense whatever."[20]

Several of the American writers to whom O'Connor sent his pamphlet did not accept it any more wholeheartedly than did the English. They disagreed either with his estimate of Whitman or with his views of censorship. Henry J. Raymond, editor of *The New York Times*, responded to *The Good Gray Poet* and to the request that he print O'Connor's review of the Fourth Edition of *Leaves of Grass*.

> I am a little puzzled by your proposition about *Leaves of Grass*. It is not a new book and has to encounter a good deal of prejudice. I am not blind to its merits, though I do not rate it so highly as you do. But there are sundry nastinesses in it which will & *ought* to keep it out of libraries and parlors: and I should not like to praise the book without branding them. . . .
>
> If you will pardon my hesitation I would be very glad to see your review and will print it if I can. Don't make it too long. Newspaper columns do not suffice to exhaust such a subject. What you said of W. *personally* in your pamphlet was as fine as anything I ever read. I would rather deserve all that than be emperor.[21]

John Swinton, former editor of *The Times* and friend of Whitman and O'Connor, concurred in all O'Connor said, but regretted that the exhausting labors of his position would prevent his doing much for the book or its subject. He admired the book's "wild rhapsodical eloquence, as well as its learning and earnestness. . . . You are the first who has said in print what I have long thought and often said in conversation." He refers to a poor article on Walt's "'Taps" (Drum-Taps) in *The Times*, but concludes, "Walt, however, has friends and admirers enough, and will, I am persuaded, have them through the ages."[22]

Wendell Phillips, whom O'Connor had admired as a prince among men ever since his youth in Boston, gave high praise to *The Good Gray Poet* while not completely agreeing with O'Connor's estimate of Whitman. He wrote in June 1866:

> As I promised you I have used my first summer leisure to read again your brilliant pamphlet. . . . Well I think still it is the most brilliant vigorous effort I know of in controversial literature. What is my judgment of Walt's book worth?—Nothing compared with yours. So if I yet think of that as I wrote you, still I revel & rollick in your breezy & flowing picture of a great poet all the same. Indeed Longinus like, you exemplify at any rate what you describe. It is one of those essays struck out in the heat of a great emergency which survive the occasion & take their places in living literature. WW himself I always respected & Redpath allowed me once to contribute to his resources. All that part of your book which appeals on the ground of his life went straight & hot as before to my heart.

Phillips wrote of his pleasure in O'Connor's references to the literature of the world:

> . . . finding so many things I never knew & so many I once knew & had forgotten was like a banquet after prison fare. . . . So I thank you—you've done me good—even if I am not wholly a convert to your critical opinion. . . . This "ill wind" blew *me* two delicious hours—& with it came evidence (pardon me the confession) of power I did not before accord to you—certainly not in such lavish measure. . . . At any rate when next you set your lance in rest we'll watch the career with all admiration & no fear. . . .[23]

Phillips never did become a "convert." In 1883 when he received Bucke's *Walt Whitman* with O'Connor's reprint of *The Good Gray Poet* and a new introductory letter by O'Connor, he wrote: "Don't blame me if I confess that, just glancing over the pages of your letter, I found myself more rapt with the racy and eloquent advocate as he bears me along in the hot current of his plea than with the good grey (*sic*) himself."[24]

The Good Gray Poet received mixed reviews. A few—mostly by friends—were favorable. Richard J. Hinton was responsible for at least two as "Richard" in the *Daily Evening Voice* and "R.J.H." in the *Milwaukee Sentinel*. In the *Daily Evening Voice*, official organ of The Workingmen's Assembly of Boston and Vicinity, on January 17, 1866, a paragraph on page 1 calls attention to the article by their

Washington correspondent because it "contains statements and observations of great interest to working men; and soldiers will appreciate its denunciation of the injustice which has been done by a U.S. official to one of the most humane of their friends."

The reviewer says of *The Good Gray Poet*:

> It is a marvelously eloquent production sweeping a wide range of scholarship and thought, making a noble and indignant demand for the righting of an act of contemptible meanness, and deserves to be read throughout the land, wherever men think, and courage, learning, and nobleness of spirit are honored.

After describing the contents of the pamphlet, "Richard" exhorts his readers:

> It is not a question as to whether one agrees with Walt Whitman's philosophy, or his own and friends' estimate of his poetical genius; but is . . . a question of freedom of thought, of manhood, of the independence of intellect. Let us be heard, oh VOICE, in defense of these and in censure of the bigotry which brings, as much as it dares, the spirit of the Inquisition into the 19th century.

The writer also mentions Harlan's dismissal of about 100 female clerks, giving as his reason "that the presence of women in the public departments leads to immoral conduct." A week later, "Richard" writes again to the *Voice* in answer to an unfavorable review in the *Boston Transcript*. The article concludes:

> So with the critics—the yelping pack all—sublime in their littleness, there is no room in their sphere for a grand free nature. Such a thing is a monstrosity. A genuine enthusiasm is to be corked down; it is not genteel. Its strong breath may disorder the thin voices that cover their respectable hypocrisies. Let them go to their rests in the tombs, all the Dryasdusts. Someday America will have a literature worthy of its grandeur. Then the great forerunner,— the seer who tallied the ages in a time hardly worthy,—will be duly honored.

The review of *The Good Gray Poet* signed "R.J.H." appeared in the *Milwaukee Sentinel* on February 9, 1866. In answer to Lanman's unfavorable article in *The Round Table*, R.J.H. writes that ex-Commissioner Dole, Whitman's immediate superior, has said that he was in every way competent.

In contrast to these favorable reviews, *The Round Table* on January 20, 1866 criticized the pamphlet adversely. (O'Connor thought that this review had been written by William Winter, but Burroughs thought that it was by Henry Stoddard.) Recalling O'Connor's earlier work, the reviewer wrote of *Harrington*, "We had the misfortune to read it, and still remember the dazed condition in which it left us, and which we can compare to nothing except, perhaps, a fevered dream of fireworks of a Fourth of July night." As to Harlan's dismissal of Whitman, the review states that

> the whilom preacher and president (of a college), not having the taste of Nebuchadnezzar, could not stand Mr. Whitman's "Leaves of Grass" . . . that the Hon. Secretary did a very foolish, as well as a very unjust thing . . . can hardly be doubted . . . but we do not agree with him [O'Connor] in his estimate of Mr. Whitman's genius; nor do we see the force of his multifarious illustrations of loose writing in the great authors of the world.

The reviewer ends by asserting that it is madness to class Whitman among the great creative minds of the world: "We beg to add that Mr. Whitman will be a Great Name when these writers are forgotten—but not till then. For when such works as *Leaves of Grass* are considered literature, chaos will have come again."

The Round Table's taste in poetry may be gleaned from the column adjoining the review of *The Good Gray Poet*, in which he quotes a "graceful poem" by John Esten Cooke, a Confederate officer. The first and last stanzas are as follows:

FROM THE RAPIDAN
1864

A low wind in the pines!
  And a dull pain in the breast!
And oh! for the sight of her lips and eyes—
  One touch of the hand I pressed!
· · · ·

Oh sunshine flitting and sad,
  Oh wind that forever sighs!

> The hall may be bright, but my life is dark
> For the sunshine of her eyes.

The Round Table's review was followed by an exchange of letters between Charles Lanman and O'Connor in which O'Connor made a point of correcting some errors of fact and of opinion. O'Connor does thank the reviewer for having written that the Secretary of the Interior "deserved and deserves to be pilloried in the contempt of thinking men for this wanton insult to literature in the person of Mr. Whitman."[25] Similarly, a review in the *Boston Transcript*, which praised O'Connor,[26] inspired him a few days later to send a long letter that the paper commented on but did not publish.[27]

O'Connor had written of Harlan, "Admitting that this were a little thing, a man, high in place, has wantonly violated the great principle of intellectual liberty, and the violation of that principle can never be a little thing," and ending with great force: "It is the first time in America that an author has been punished for his authorship: as far as I can have it so, it shall be the last."

The Good Gray Poet—its reviews and controversies—brought Walt Whitman into the public eye. Instead of apathy, there was partisanship. Trowbridge wrote: "He himself (Whitman) used to say that it was O'Connor's defense that turned the tide in his favor; meaning the tide of criticism and public opinion, which had until then set so tremendously against him. . . ."[28]

The pamphlet also confirmed in Whitman the *persona* he had created in his poems and prefaces, and his role as the embodiment and spokesman of America and democracy. In *The Good Gray Poet* he saw in the words of another not only his person and his intentions, but also his place in the galaxy of the great of all ages. There it was, in print, for all the world to see.

The Good Gray Poet was to be followed by letters to the press, reviews of *Drum-Taps* and the Fourth Edition of *Leaves of Grass*, and the placement of some of Whitman's new poems and articles in periodicals. The production of the English edition of *Leaves of Grass*, edited by William Michael Rossetti, was guided from the O'Connors' parlor.

Thus O'Connor's pamphlet was the opening salvo in the campaign waged by his friends for recognition of Walt Whitman and appreciation and understanding of his poems.

NOTES

1. *The Good Gray Poet: A Vindication* (Toronto, Canada: Henry S. Saunders, 1927) pp. vii–viii. Henry Saunders did the typesetting and binding of all 125 numbered copies of this edition, his printer doing only the press work. (Letter from Mrs. Frank Sprague to Saunders's niece, Silvia, copy given to F. B. Freedman by Mrs. Sprague.) A complete text also appears in Jerome Loving, *Walt Whitman's Champion: William Douglas O'Connor* (College Station and London: Texas A & M University Press, 1978), pp. 157–203.
2. Wendell Phillips, *Speeches and Lectures* (Boston: Lee and Shepard, 1884).
3. Phillips to WDO'C, June 1866 [n.d.] (Berg).
4. *Camden*, 2: 11.
5. Nathan Resnick, *Walt Whitman and the Authorship of the Good Gray Poet* (Brooklyn, New York: Long Island University Press, 1948).
6. WDO'C to Conway (Manuscript Division, New York Public Library).
7. A copy of this letter was sent to the author by David Goodale.
8. Barrus, *Comrades*, p. 312.
9. *Walt Whitman As Man, Poet and Friend, Being autograph pages from many pens, collected by Charles N. Elliot* (Boston: Richard G. Badger, The Gorham Press, 1915), p. 61.
10. *The Good Gray Poet*. Quotations are from the edition published by Bunce and Huntington in 1866.
11. WDO'C in a letter (18 February 1866) to M. J. Channing identifies this person as Wendell Phillips (Chamberlin).
12. GWC to WDO'C, 30 September 1865, in Bliss Perry, *Walt Whitman: His Life and Work* (Boston and New York: Houghton Mifflin and Company, 1906), p. 172.
13. GWC to WDO'C, 29 October 1865, *ibid.*, pp. 173–74.
14. WDO'C to M. J. Channing, 18 February 1866 (Feinberg-LC).
15. Louisa Van Velsor Whitman to WW. *Correspondence*, I: 340–41, n. 16.
16. Hannah Heyde to her mother, n.d. From C. J. Furness's typed notes of address given at MLA conference, December 1937. Sent to author by Goodale.
17. WDO'C, 16 September 1866, in Perry, *op. cit.*, pp. 177–79.
18. *Ibid.*, p. 179.
19. Newman to WDO'C, 24 April 1866 (Berg).
20. Newman to WDO'C, 16 October 1866 (Berg).
21. Raymond to WDO'C, 16 October 1866 (Berg) in Perry, *op. cit.*, pp. 176–77.
22. Swinton to WDO'C, 11 January 1866 (Feinberg-LC).
23. Phillips to WDO'C, 21 June 1866 (Berg).
24. Phillips to WDO'C, 1 August 1883 (Feinberg-LC).
25. WDO'C to Editor of the *Round Table*, 3 February 1866. *Round Table*, vol. 3, p. 76.
26. 17 January 1866.
27. Comment appeared 15 February 1866; letter (23 January 1866) was included in *In Re Walt Whitman*, pp. 149–57.
28. John Townsend Trowbridge, *My Own Story, with Recollections of Noted Persons* (Boston and New York: Houghton Mifflin and Company, 1904), p. 391.

1. Daguerrotype of William Douglas
O'Connor taken when he was living in
Providence R.I. *Library of Congress.*

2. Sarah Helen Whitman. *Courtesy
John Hay Library, Brown University.*

3. A drawing by O'Connor which was
tipped into the volume of Tennyson's *In
Memoriam* given him by Sarah
Whitman.

HARRINGTON:

A STORY OF TRUE LOVE.

BY THE AUTHOR OF "WHAT CHEER," "THE GHOST: A
CHRISTMAS STORY," "A TALE OF LYNN," ETC.

"Herein may be seen noble chivalrye, curtosye, humanyte, friendlyenesse,
hardyenesse, love, friendshype, cowardyse, murder, hate, vertue and synne.
Doo after the good, and leve the evyl, and it shall brynge you to good fame
and renomme."—Sir Thomas Malory: *Preface to Morte D'Arthur.*

BOSTON:
THAYER & ELDRIDGE,
114 & 116 WASHINGTON STREET.
1860.

4. Title page of O'Connor's *Harrington*, published by Thayer and Eldridge in 1860. *Courtesy New York Public Library.*

5. Title page of *Leaves of Grass*, brought out in the third edition by the same publisher in the same year as *Harrington. Courtesy New York Public Library.*

6. Walt Whitman in 1859, when he was editor of the *Brooklyn Times*, and first met O'Connor at the offices of their publisher. This engraving, from the portrait by Charles Hine, was used as frontispiece for the third edition of *Leaves of Grass. Courtesy Charles E. Feinberg.*

7. Frontispiece and title page of Solomon Northup's book, *Twelve Years a Slave*, which O'Connor acknowledged as the source of the prologue to his novel *Harrington.*

5

Leaves
of
GRASS.

Boston.
Thayer and Eldridge,
Year 85 of The States.
(1860-61)

6

7

SOLOMON IN HIS PLANTATION SUIT.

Solomon Northup

TWELVE YEARS A SLAVE.

NARRATIVE

OF

SOLOMON NORTHUP,

A CITIZEN OF NEW-YORK,

KIDNAPPED IN WASHINGTON CITY IN 1841,

AND

RESCUED IN 1853,

FROM A COTTON PLANTATION NEAR THE RED RIVER,
IN LOUISIANA.

AUBURN:
DERBY AND MILLER.
BUFFALO:
DERBY, ORTON AND MULLIGAN.
LONDON:
SAMPSON LOW, SON & COMPANY, 47 LUDGATE HILL.
1853.

9

8

10

11

8. Photograph of O'Connor probably
from the early 1860s. A drawing from
this likeness was used as frontispiece for
The Good Gray Poet, 1927
edition. *Library of Congress.*

9. Walt Whitman in 1863, when he was
living in wartime Washington. These
were the early days of his close
friendship with O'Connor. *Courtesy
Charles E. Feinberg.*

10 and 11. Ellen Tarr O'Connor: a
photograph she sent to Whitman on July
5, 1864, and one taken near the end of
her life. *Courtesy John Hay Library,
Brown University.*

12 and 13. Jean "Jeannie" O'Connor, daughter of William and Ellen, in a childhood portrait and as a young woman. *Courtesy Charles E. Feinberg.*

14. Jean O'Connor (on table) with her cousins Grace (on steps) and Mary "Mollie" Channing. O'Connor wrote to Grace about this picture: "You look demure, Mary very grave, and Jean Mephistophelean." *Courtesy Katharine B.S. Chamberlin.*

14

15. Whitman in 1872, the year of the quarrel with O'Connor. *Courtesy Charles E. Feinberg.*

16. Note by Whitman, dated 1882, which indicates that he and O'Connor have been reconciled. *Library of Congress, Feinberg Collection.*

Washington, D.C. Nov. 11. 1880. — Dear friend: I have been away and am just returned. As soon as I can, I am going to write you, especially about Stedman's article, which is about as I told you I expected, only better. I have a funny letter from him, (not yet answered) the tone of which is decidedly tremulous, and evidently in deprecation of the anticipated wrath of Achilles! How he could be chawed up! All his points (those of censure or objection) could be fatally turned on him. But the article is a great advance, and will help W.W's cause much. — Au revoir. Hope the reports I sent for came. Faithfully. W.D.O'C.

17. This postcard to Bucke shows that O'Connor had returned to the defense of Whitman in 1880.

18. O'Connor as photographed June 4, 1885. *Courtesy Charles E. Feinberg.*

18

THE HERMIT.

I.

It was a holy hermit spake
  To Edwin, standing meek and coy:
"Come now, and let us counsel take.
  My pretty little waggish boy.
Ford's Opera House was built to guide,
  And stands thy wayward steps to win,
To the Gymnasium t'other side,—
  My pretty little boy, go in!

II.

"Go in, my funny child, for there
  Are many baths, both hot and cold,
And magazines and journals rare,
  And exercises manifold.
There bathe, and read, and fence, and box;
  The health-lift try, the dumb-bells seize;
Haul hard upon the pulley-blocks,
  Or fly upon the big trapeze.

III.

"From dawn till ten o'clock at night,
  There's health and youth, a treasure-trove:
And what for all this pure delight?—
  Three dollars for three months, be Jove!
What's this to pay, should paper pass
  And specious specie be preferred?
My little Civil-Service ass,
  Three cents per diem and a third!

IV.

"Dost thou Potomac boating vaunt?
  Ah, when thou pay'st for it, thou'lt say
That Asia's broadest elephant
  Hath danced upon thy porte-monnaie!

And what, for all its greater cost,
  The greater good it does to thee?
By Charon! fifty dollars lost
  For what thou might'st have had for three!

V.

"And thou art feeling bad, alack!
  And thou art feeling weak and gone!
And thou dost patronize the quack,
  Or try the gin-and-tansy on!
Ah, me! the nostrums all are lies,
  Nor count old bar-keep as thy friend,
For know thou, Dryden says 'the wise
  For cure on exercise depend.'

VI.

"What makes in spring thy blood run fleet?
  And when the summer fervors fall,
What keeps thee strong to bear the heat?—
  Games in the cool Gymnasium Hall!
And lest these truths from thee should slip,
  Take this;"—and in his lightsome play
He gave young Edwin such a clip
  He made him see the Milky Way.

VII.

"So now," the holy hermit said,
  "Some sense being beaten into thee,
Bless thou the happy chance that led
  Thy steps beneath the greenwood tree.
For wisdom on thy early brow,
  Soon, like thy muscle, will appear;
So go and buy thy ticket now,
  And come, my lad, and have some beer."

II. If, superimposing one miracle upon another, the prophet Jonah could have absorbed the whale that had previously swal- lowed him, he would not have been a completer interfusion of sanctity and oil than was em- bodied in the suave saint of the Boston mail-bags on that holy Thursday. He blandly assured Mr. Chainey that no objection had ever been taken

19. Drawing and poem by O'Connor which appeared in a brochure, "The Gymnasium" (1877–78), for a club of which he was an officer.

20. A page of manuscript from O'Connor's "Tobey or Not Tobey," which was published after his death. *Library of Congress, Feinberg Collection.*

21. O'Connor with his niece Grace Channing (and dogs Nellie and Rover) on the porch of the Channing house in Pasadena, California, where he went in 1887 in hopes of restoring his health. O'Connor characterized himself in this photo as "The bogey of the piazza."

22. Whitman's inscription in a copy of *November Boughs* which he sent to O'Connor in his last illness. *Courtesy Charles E. Feinberg.*

> Wm D O'Connor
> from his friend the author.
> O how I should like to send
> you with this book the good
> bodily strength & perfect health
> of former times again —
> Meanwhile best love, memories,
> & prayers — Walt Whitman
> March 3 1889

CHAPTER XII

"Friend Of My Other Soul, My Poems"[1]

O'CONNOR WAS not content to rest his efforts after *The Good Gray Poet*. He was determined to keep Whitman's name and work before the public.

When *Drum-Taps* and its sequel *Memories of President Lincoln* appeared, O'Connor immediately wrote a review which he sent to *The New York Times*. It was not published; William Swinton, managing editor, wrote that it had arrived too late to appear.[2] A few months later John Swinton (his brother) wrote that had he been managing editor the review would have been accepted.[3] Some of O'Connor's views of *Drum-Taps* are expressed in a letter he wrote to Jeannie Channing: "It (*Drum-Taps*) is not in the tone of Leaves of Grass—the joyful thunder of young power; it is an episode of the civil war, vivid, but as such an episode should be, very sorrowful." The poems "do not set fire, they drop tears. . . ."[4]

O'Connor did help in the acceptance of *Drum-Taps* and its sequel by arranging to have a review of the book by John Burroughs published in *The Galaxy*. W. C. Church, editor of *The Galaxy*, had invited O'Connor to contribute to his magazine on June 13. O'Connor answered belatedly on August 24, saying that while he wished to become a contributor, he was too overborne with official labor. Instead he commends "to his gracious hospitality" an article by John Burroughs about Walt Whitman's *Drum-Taps*, praising the review for its "noble beauty and thoughtful eloquence."[5] (He did, however, submit and have accepted his poem, "Earl Mord," which was printed in the same issue as the Burroughs piece.)[6]

O'Connor was probably responsible also for a cautious mention of *Drum-Taps* by Curtis in *Harper's* "Editor's Easy Chair" in December 1865, probably written out of friendship for O'Connor. Curtis, never enthusiastic about Whitman, after a notice of some holiday "gems" by Jean Ingelow and Tennyson, writes of *Drum-Taps*, explaining that "if any reader is appalled by seeing that name (Walt Whitman) in so choice a company, let us not argue the matter nor express any opinion, but ask if there is no poetry in this wail upon the Death of Lincoln and in the Song of the Drum."

Not everyone was even grudgingly receptive. *The Nation* had an adverse review by the young Henry James, who said that *Drum-Taps* "exhibits the effort of an essentially prosaic mind to lift itself, by a prolonged muscular strain, into poetry."[7] O'Connor was particularly angry at *The Nation*, writing to Jeannie Channing: "That *Nation* is an infamous paper every way, with fifty thousand dollars of radical money in it, think of it abusing Sumner and maligning Phillips!"[8]

Soon after *Drum-Taps* and its sequel appeared, Whitman was ready to have his Fourth Edition of *Leaves of Grass* published. Based on the 1860 Edition (the famous "Blue Book" which Secretary Harlan had furtively examined) this edition had many changes in phrase, structure, and arrangement, as well as some deletions. It also contained six new poems. "Drum-Taps" and "Memories of President Lincoln" were included as annexes.

This was the edition that showed the effect of the O'Connors' friendship, which, together with the war experiences, had caused a change in the poet's mood. This is seen most clearly in his elimination of three poems of the "Calamus" group, which were never to be restored to *Leaves of Grass* as it grew and developed throughout the rest of the poet's life. The excised poems were those which expressed self-doubt and deep despair stemming from unrequited love. (He kept those which expressed love and longing unaccompanied by despair, such as "I Saw in Louisiana a Live-Oak Growing.")

One of the rejected poems was "Long I Thought That Knowledge Alone Would Suffice," with its lines

> For I can be your singer of songs no longer—one who loves me is
> jealous of me, and withdraws me from all but love.

Another poem left out of this edition was "Hours Continuing Long,
Sore, and Heavy-Hearted." In this he had written,

> Hours discouraged, distracted—for the one I cannot content my-
> self without, soon I saw him content himself without me. . . .

and

> Hours of my torment—I wonder if other men have the like, out of
> the like feelings?
> Is there even one other like me—distracted, his friend, his lover,
> lost to him?

In the third poem, "Who Is Now Reading This?" he wonders in despair whether his reader is puzzled by him:

> As if I were not puzzled at myself!
> Or as if I never deride myself! (O conscience-struck! O'self-
> convicted!)
> Or as if I did not secretly love strangers! (O tenderly, a long time,
> and never avow it;)
> Or as if I did not see, perfectly well, interior in myself, the stuff of
> wrongdoing,
> Or as if it could cease transpiring from me until it must cease.

Why did these poems no longer speak for the poet, while most of
the poems in the first three editions did? Whitman's change in attitude may have come from his experiences during the war years, his
tumultuous yearnings satisfied by his care of the wounded soldiers.
Yet if he had not had a change of mood and a change of feelings
about himself, it is likely that the sight of the carnage of war and the
wounded and dying young men would have increased his sense of
helplessness and despair.

The difference in mood and attitude was caused in large part by
his finally having found "lovers and avowers" of himself and of his
poems in William and Nelly O'Connor, in Charles Eldridge, John

Burroughs, and in the Washington circle of friends—with William as the central figure. In the past those who had loved him—his family and the unknown objects of his affection in "Calamus"—had not known or understood his poems or had been jealous of them. Here in Washington, beginning in 1862, he had found affirmation, validation, understanding and love, not only of himself but also of his poems. Except for showing poems occasionally to Henry Clapp, who had published a few in the *Saturday Press*, Whitman probably had never shared his work with anyone before it was published. Even now he did not read his own works to the men in the hospital wards, though he often read the works of others. A few literary people had admired his work—Emerson, Alcott, Thoreau, and Conway—but they paid single visits and did not form sustained, and sustaining, friendships. He was heartened by their approval—but they could not be thought of as friends.

In Washington the poet acquired a circle of literary friends (largely through O'Connor) who met to hear and discuss his poems and everything else which interested him. They not only understood and appreciated his writing, but also confirmed him in his role of the representative man and poet of his country, gave him confidence in his future, and defended *Leaves of Grass* in print. Their recognition dispelled some of his self-distrust and guilt. Years later he spoke of this group as "a small band of the dearest friends and upholders ever vouchsafed to man or cause—doubtless all the more faithful and uncompromising—O this little phalanx!—for being so few. . . ."[9] And of William O'Connor he said, "He's a withering fire to his enemies and a sustaining force to his friends. William has more right words for right places in him than any man I know of in America."[10]

Whitman said at another time that William often saw meanings in his poems beyond what he thought he had put there.[11] When he reviewed his poems in 1888 he wrote of their "unconscious, or mostly unconscious intentions."[12] Perhaps William and the others had brought these "indirections" and "intentions" to the light, helping the poet to develop and fulfill his stated role.

O'Connor felt close to the Fourth Edition of the *Leaves* because he had seen it grow. His review in *The New York Times* on December 2, 1866 was quite different in tone from *The Good Gray Poet* and the unpublished letter to the *Boston Transcript*. Both of these were oratorical in style and form and contentious in tone; this review was a critical essay, an explanation and appreciation. Despite its restrained tone, the *Times* editor (Henry Raymond) prefaced the article with what amounted to an apology, writing that they publish the review "not because we accept it as a just critical estimate of that book, but because it is written with very marked ability, and embodies the opinions of a very competent and accomplished writer." The editor points out that "while he sometimes soars aloft in the very highest regions of thought and song, Walt Whitman often wallows exultingly in unredeemed and irredeemable indecency and filth." He concludes, "with this partial protest, we submit the able and interesting review of our contributor."

In his lengthy review, O'Connor contributes new understanding of *Leaves of Grass* in general and of this edition in particular. He points out that "in this new edition the plan and theory of the author appear more distinctly and to greater advantage than before." He offers his own interpretations of the *Leaves*. While admitting to blemishes (which he will leave to others to point out) he claims that "this is the only book in our literature which aims at a distinctively national character and a high classic importance and performance. . . ." He refers to de Tocqueville's analysis of America, saying that what he had attempted in prose "Whitman has triumphantly cast in poetic synthesis."

Like Dante and Montaigne, he points out, Whitman "is the central figure of his own creation." He appears "not only physiognomically but also psychologically and physiologically. . . . There is perhaps, in poetry, no equal celebration of the human being in his completeness. . . ." And again, "There is an immense sense of space in the book. There is an equally immense spread of salient and worldwide scenery, and a sustained impression of time, as from birth to age and death."

He asserts that Whitman speaks for everyone. "The divine, the diabolic, the human, which are in all of us, are in him." The poem "seeks to express the cosmical character of the individual—yourself; the absolute miracle you are in all your parts from top to toe; . . . your centrality in the universe."

At times O'Connor adds his own ideas to those he finds in the *Leaves*. The discussion of Whitman's ideal woman is an example of this. Only the first line is pure Whitman; the rest is the O'Connor of *Harrington* and the Woman's Rights movement.

> This magnificent perfection of the male also included the female. . . . No more a toy, an invalid, a child, a fashion-plate, an odalisque, a gentle dependent, a delicate and charming subordinate, a caressed and courted being, without a flag or a land, she appears here adult; full grown; strong in her own right; powerful in womanly charms; manly and the equal of man; cultured, athletic and noble; crowned with the civic dignity; an American; a citizen; consubstantial with pride, the ambition, the love and glory of her country.

This review is of special interest because most of O'Connor's writings about Whitman were defenses against attacks, and therefore cutting and vituperative, distinguished by eloquence and invective. This review is a sober, analytical presentation of what O'Connor considered to be the unique place of the *Leaves* in American literature.

Whitman was pleased with it. He wrote to his mother on December 4, 1866, "The piece in the *Times* is by O'Connor. He grows stronger and stronger, and fiercer and fiercer in his championship of 'Leaves of Grass,'—no one can ever say a word against it in his presence, without a storm."[13] He added that Raymond, the editor, has received a number of favorable letters in response to the article.

The next step in the recognition of *Leaves of Grass* was a major one: In 1867 John Burroughs (with considerable help from Whitman) wrote the first biography of the poet, entitled *Notes on Walt Whitman as Poet and Person*.[14] Although Burroughs was more restrained and cautious than O'Connor, *Leaves of Grass* had shaken him; even while he was writing the biography of Walt, he wrote in his journal:

> The book is still a problem to me. I am delighted, and stunned, and ravished, and aroused, all at the same time: and I am unable to decide whether the fault, if fault there is, is in me, in my habits and training, or in the poems.
>
> I cannot rid myself of the impression that the poet is sometimes putting on airs, and is wilfully perverse and defiant. He need not have laid it on quite so thick, to begin with. The public made wry faces at his first poem, and he seems to have said, "If you make wry faces at that, I will give you something to make wry faces for," and so wrote the poems of procreation.

Yet for Whitman the man, Burroughs had nothing but love and respect. He tried to get at the essential quality of Whitman in some of the entries in his journals. "There is something indescribable in his look, in his eye, as in that of the mother of many children."[15]

After the publication of *The Good Gray Poet* a letter of praise came from John Burroughs. O'Connor then invited him to visit. "I never force an acquaintance or friendship, believing it an uncanny thing to do, but let it grow itself—and you must come to help grow this one! . . ."[16]

Burroughs was temperamentally so different from O'Connor that he never was fully at ease with him. He thought O'Connor "a tip-top fellow, but awfully learned, and sharp, and smooth-tongued."[17] He later wrote in his journal (April 8, 1868):

> It seems to me that one great defect in O'Connor's mind is that he lacks the perception of identity. This shows itself more particularly in his admiration of, and remarks upon, the great poets and authors. What is common to all, he sees clearly enough; but what is peculiar to each, I think, he totally fails to see. Thus Aeschylus and Rabelais, Hugo and Whitman, all awaken the same emotion in his mind, and he applies the same epithets to each.[18]

Burroughs recognized the difference between himself and O'Connor, writing to Myron Benton, "The great trouble with men of your temperament and my temperament, is that we are too reserved, too cautious. We do not get up heat and motion enough. Such men as O'Connor or Victor Hugo err in the other direction. They beat the air wildly. Their writing is a conflagration. . . ."[19] Whitman, friend of both, perceived the differences in their temperaments:

> John never bowls you over with any vivid passion of speech—it is not in him to do it—but he calms and soothes you—takes you out into the open where things are in an amiable mood. John might get real mad—his kettle boil over—but his language would remain conciliatory. William O'Connor under the same excitation would blow fiercely and leave his mark on the landscape.[20]

At another time he said, "John is a placid landscape—William is a landscape in a storm."[21]

Yet it was Burroughs who wrote the first biography of Walt

Whitman. After the storm caused by *The Good Gray Poet*, it was just as well to have a milder presentation in 1867. Whitman himself wrote part of the book and edited the manuscript—understandable since this was Burroughs's first book, and probably was seen as a joint effort. For his description of Walt in Washington, Burroughs quoted some of Piatt's review of *The Good Gray Poet* in the *Ohio State Journal*.[22] *Notes on Walt Whitman as Poet and Person* fulfilled the promise of its title, first interpreting the *Leaves of Grass*, and then giving a biographical sketch of Whitman and a review of *Drum-Taps* as Whitman's latest poetry.

O'Connor promoted the book by writing a review for *The New York Times* (June 30, 1867). Before it appeared, however, he had turned briefly from his preoccupation with Whitman to the defense of another maligned writer. The occasion was one which aroused a good deal of comment and controversy in the newspapers. "Florence Percy" (Elizabeth Akers Allen) had written a sentimental poem entitled "Rock Me to Sleep." It had been published in the *Saturday Evening Post* in 1860 when O'Connor was editor. Beginning "Backward, turn backward, O Time in thy flight," it consisted of six stanzas, all ending with the refrain "Rock me to sleep, mother, rock me to sleep." The Honorable Alexander S. M. Ball, a New Jersey legislator, added nine stanzas to the original poem and claimed the entire poem as his. A friend of his, O. H. Morse of Cherry Valley, New York, published a 72-page pamphlet in support of Ball's authorship. The pamphlet included other verses by Ball to show that he was an accomplished poet. Another friend, Luther R. Marsh of New York City, endorsed his claim.[23]

Newspapers and periodicals took up the controversy, many having been impressed by the arguments of Ball and his friends. The chivalrous O'Connor could not let these lies prevail. He wrote a long article for *The New York Times* on May 27, 1867, entitled, "Who Wrote 'Rock Me to Sleep'? A Review of the Recent Pamphlet of Hon. O. H. Morse." In the article he examines what he considers to be "one of the most extraordinary transactions in the history of current literature." He presents and ridicules all of Ball's arguments, and then from internal evidence—an exegesis of Ball's stanzas compared with Florence Percy's—shows the unpoetic and awkward qualities of the suspect nine stanzas. He ends by turning the tables on Ball by accusing him of having plagiarized a poem of Sarah Helen

Whitman's—"A Still Day in Autumn, 1853." The editor of *The Times* was delighted with the article, and sent O'Connor fifty dollars in payment.

William O'Connor was not content with having demolished Ball in prose. He wrote an elaborate mock-heroic poem in twelve stanzas entitled "The Ballad of Sir Ball," which was published in *The Galaxy* in March 1868. The lady fair was Florence Percy, "with her eyes of pansied blue"; the villain was "Sir Ball, the enchanter curst, whose carols murder joy/For households in the jovial realm of Camden and Amboy." The hero was the bold Sir Doubleyou "the moral foe of wrong;/He heard the lady's injury, he loved the lady's song." The rest of the cast of characters are the donkeys Morse and Marsh and the good Sir Public.

The gallant Sir Doubleyou wins the fray, of course. The devil takes Sir Ball to hell, but Sir Public knows of a more severe punishment to which the villain is consigned:

> . . . let him ride, an endless passenger, on the Camden and Amboy line!
> Let him feel the muscle-destroying racks, the cramps, the jolts, the jars,
> The Spanish Inquisition-for-one of a seat within those cars. . . .
> And never for him the ecstasy that the worst of wretches know,
> When they leave those seats at the terminus, in a blest relief from wo [*sic*].

O'Connor's friends, William Channing and John Burroughs, wrote in praise of the poem, but Walt Whitman's mother held a different view. In a letter to her son on March 24, 1868 she wrote,

> The book for Mary came friday and the galaxy today with the ballad of sir ball i had forgotten all about the piece till i see it and then i had to think where i had heard of it and it came to my mind what piece it was it is signed W i hope nobody will think you wrote it walt.[24]

The Akers-Ball controversy did not end with this poem. Ball, however, because of the article in the *Times*, did write a letter to Sarah Helen Whitman apologizing for his use of her lines in a poem. He does not recollect ever having seen her poem; he had never read her volume of poems, but perhaps he had seen the poem in a newspaper "and the extreme beauty and delicacy of thought impressed me. And years after, most unconsciously, found utterance as my own."25 The *Times* article was answered in the *Tribune* by a supporter of Ball's claim, in six columns on December 31, 1867, signed only with an asterisk.

But with the ballad in *The Galaxy*, O'Connor had had his say about "Rock Me to Sleep"; he went on with his defenses of Whitman. His next pronouncement was his review of Burroughs's *Notes on Walt Whitman as Poet and Person*. In his lengthy review (over 4,000 words) O'Connor gives none of his own opinions of Whitman and *Leaves of Grass*, but stresses John Burroughs's accomplishment in this book, which is the

> first adequate, intelligent and truthful presentation, in an extended sense, either as person or writer, of Mr. Whitman—a man whose fate it has hitherto been, as Mr. Burroughs accurately remarks, "to have his book and his personal character atrociously intercepted from their due audience with the public, whose minds have been plied and preoccupied by detractions and the meanest mis-reports and falsehoods."

O'Connor writes more of Burroughs than of Whitman. He alludes to "the rare charm of the moral quality, the sound-hearted country probity, veracity, personal purity—and general manliness which pervades his every sentence." The book is "permeated with the sense of life out of doors." He quotes extensively from the book, first in describing the countryside in which Whitman grew up, his wholesome ancestry and family, and the poet's appearance, suggesting ideas of "the Beginners, the Adamic men." He goes on to quote what Burroughs has said of *Leaves of Grass*, and then from the writer's appreciation of *Drum-Taps*, with its unusual attitude toward war, and of *Leaves of Grass*, with its conception of the grandness of nature in all its crudeness. He believes Burroughs's book to be "the only modern book which announces with sturdy faith and courage the great canons by which, and only by which, the works of the supreme poets and artists of all ages can be saved from academic condemnation, and in their absolute entirety victoriously explained and vindicated."

By the amount of quotation and relative paucity of comment, O'Connor shows his enthusiastic approval of Burroughs's book, going so far as to say at one point,

> Here, too, is a sentence worthy to be wrought in giant letters of basalt and iron, and blazoned with gold, for the counsel and warning of all artists of every order and degree. It is quietly and simply said, but it belongs to the region of the lightnings: "The highest art is not to express art, but to express life and communicate power."

The review concludes: "Modest as are its form and pretensions, we know of no book since Emerson's first Essays, that deserves to be placed beside it, either for intrinsic worth or power of gracious influence." (Moncure Conway agreed with O'Connor's estimate, thinking it "the best critical work ever produced in this country.")[26]

Burroughs himself was far less confident of his book's power. He was, of course, enthusiastic about his subject, writing to a friend in February 1867, "There is no book in the language projected from a higher water mark of culture than *Leaves of Grass,* or one that implies a greater maturity of the moral and intellectual faculties and perceptions."[27] Nevertheless he wondered whether he had done it justice.

After 500 copies had been printed (100 in one style and 400 in another), he wrote to his friend Myron Benton, "I really hope the *Notes* have got life and enthusiasm in them. I was afraid they were too quiet and tame. I wanted to make a book with warm blood in its veins, and as unruly and revolutionary as possible."[28] This, however, was O'Connor's *forte,* not Burroughs's.

Shortly after O'Connor's review of Burroughs's book was published, he turned to another medium for sharing his appreciation of Whitman—the short story, a form in which he had been successful. The Christmas story, with its formula of having a supernatural element, teaching a moral lesson, and resolving the plot on Christmas Eve, was always in demand by editors for their December or January issues. ("The Ghost," which had been such a story, had just been reissued by Putnam's in book form, with illustrations by Thomas Nast.) O'Connor thought of writing a Christmas story with Walt as the hero.

During the summer of 1867, while Nelly and little Jeannie (who was not well) had escaped the Washington heat by visiting in Rhode Island, O'Connor sat in an attic room in Burroughs's house on Capitol Hill writing furiously after office hours and far into the night. According to Burroughs, he "wrote like a house afire—like Balzac," sustaining himself on tea and tobacco. Burroughs, while hoeing in his garden, occasionally tried to distract him by throwing plums through the open window.[29] The result of O'Connor's efforts was "The Carpenter" which appeared in the newly-revived *Putnam's Monthly Magazine* of January 1868.

The story, following convention, takes place on Christmas Eve in the year "when the armies of Grant and Lee were locked in the death grapple for Richmond." The scene is the home of Elkanah Dyzer, his wife Ruth, and their family—their son John, a veteran of the Union army, his wife Emily and their child Lilian (another child had died) and their youngest son Tom. Two sons were missing in the war, George, a Union soldier of whom his father is proud, and Rupert, their eldest son, a Rebel soldier whom the father has disowned. Their youngest son, Tom, was about to join the army. Also part of the household is the old Negro man-of-all-work, Daniel Snow. Visitors on this Christmas Eve are Fanny Redwood, whom Tom would like to marry, and Michael Faulkner, John's friend who had been Emily's suitor.

Although the family will celebrate Christmas Eve (with neighbors and friends who will arrive later), it is a bad time for Elkanah, who faces ruin. The farm had been left to him by his Uncle Peter, a rich man with humanitarian ideals, who had freed his slaves. He had left his nephew Elkanah the farm, 500 dollars, and two portraits which had been painted by a wanderer ("a loafer" named Simon Tomeny)—one of Peter Dyzer as Judas and the other of Christ as a wanderer. He had told Elkanah never to part with the paintings unless he was in dire straits. This situation had now occurred.

Little Lilian asks, "What *was* Jesus Christ?" to which her grandfather answers, "A mechanic, my dear. What our fine Southern gentlemen call a common mud-sill. A carpenter. God bless him!" Lilian asks whether he will come that evening; she thinks he will, because he is alive, as old Uncle Peter said, he had "grown old and gray walking in the world so many hundred years. . . ."

The stage having been set for the arrival of a mysterious stranger, there is a knock on the door, and a stranger enters. To the readers who knew Whitman there was no mistaking the original model for the stranger:

> He was tall and stalwart, with uncovered head; a brow not large, but full, and seamed with kindly wrinkles; a complexion of rosy cleanness; heavy-lidded, firm blue eyes, which had a steadfast and draining regard; a short, thick, gray beard almost white, and thinly flowing dark-gray hair. His countenance expressed a rude sweetness. . . .

The stranger introduces himself as a wanderer who walks the hospitals, nursing the Union and Rebel soldiers. Elkanah, "feeling a sudden intimacy as of many years, born from his quality of manly love," asks him to stay for the last "jollification" they will be able to enjoy in that house.

In the course of the story the stranger solves all the family's problems, breaking up the incipient love affair between Emily and Faulkner by reminding Emily of her love for her husband and her duties as a mother and introducing Faulkner to a "love passing the love of women." He urges bashful young Tom to declare his love to Fanny; succeeds in saving the farm by finding a treasure in the frame of the old picture, and presents as his Christmas gift the missing sons whom he had nursed in the army hospital. He effects a reconciliation between the father and the son who had served in the Rebel army; then, in the midst of the Christmas Eve celebration with friends and neighbors, he goes off into the night.

Not only was the carpenter easily recognized as Whitman, but there were also many autobiographical details in the story. The name of the father of the family, Elkanah Dyzer, was similar to that of Nelly's grandfather, Elkanah Dyer, who had fought in the Revolutionary War. Emily (a name not unlike *Ellen* or *Nelly*) and her husband John had had two children, one of whom had died (as had the O'Connors' son Philip). The surviving child was a little girl who was lame. (That summer little Jeannie was suffering from a rheumatic inflammation and swelling of the knee joints.) The soldier son who had fought with the Union army was named George, and like Whitman's brother had been wounded at the Battle of Fredericksburg. The uncle who had left the farm and the money to Elkanah was named Peter (the name of William's father). The stranger, modeled after Whitman in looks, speech, and personality, had nursed both brothers—Union and Rebel—in the army hospital, an incident based on one of Whitman's hospital experiences.[30]

There are other possible connections with the lives of William, Nelly, and Walt. The description of the state of Emily's and John's marriage may have been true of the O'Connors' marriage at that time. Nelly's friendship and admiration for Walt may have already been changing to the love which she later expressed in a letter to Walt in 1870.[31] She had also prevented William from leaving his government job to devote his time to writing.

Emily's husband John, upon greeting Michael Faulkner who was once Emily's sweetheart, "was in that uncertain mood in which one, tortured by the deep suspicion that his beloved wife is drifting from him into love with his bosom-friend—as yet suspicious of her only, and unable yet to determine whether the friend is also a just object for doubt, suspends judgment on both in wary scrutiny." O'Connor may have been describing the state of his and Ellen's marriage at the time when he writes:

> There are seasons in a woman's life when her conjugal love, oppressed by the monotony, the commonplace, the humdrum, cold familiarity, the perpetual same intimacy, becomes not dead, but dormant, and existence, void of the old romantic joy, creeps on in weariness and indefinite sad yearning.

Surely Faulkner, although he is not the Whitman character in the story, shared with Whitman the admiration of woman as mother, seeing Emily "with all the added powerful pensive charm of her completed womanliness, the divine dower of the joys and griefs of her maternity." It is interesting to speculate also about Tom's beloved, the beautiful Fanny Redwood. Does Fanny, described as everything that was lovely, bear any relationship to the beguiling "witch" whom O'Connor addressed later in his poem "To Fanny" published in 1871?

Certainly the story served as a vehicle not only for O'Connor's admiration for Whitman and for the expression of the Good Gray Poet's ideas, but also for the expression of O'Connor's views on Abolition and Woman's Rights. Some of these are in the letter left by old Peter Dyzer to his nephew Elkanah:

No Slaves, All Men Are Equal. Pay Wages for your Labour. Vote and Act with Any Party that Aims to Liberate our Bondmen, and make Democracy the Absolute Law of our Country. We must Cut Loose from All the Thinking and Practices of the Old World in Every Respect.

Cherish Womankind. They Should have Representation and Equal Voice in the Government of a Free Country. What Degrades Women injures Men. Mothers are the True Men of Any Land. Women are Men's Equals, and great Mothers are their Superiors. . . .

To reinforce the sentiments of respect for the Negro, O'Connor has the brother George who had escaped from prison helped to safety in Washington by a brave Negro who became a soldier in one of the black regiments.

The reverence for President Lincoln is shown in Elkanah's reaction to the news that the President had pardoned Rupert, the Rebel soldier, at the request of the stranger who had nursed both brothers. He speaks of Lincoln, "the man of all our hearts, . . . the man with millions of haters, who himself calls no man enemy."

Perhaps the most revealing parts of the story are the scenes between Faulkner, Emily's lover, and the stranger, in which O'Connor dramatizes Whitman's ideal of manly love. The twenty-six-year-old Faulkner may be an idealized O'Connor, as he was when he first met Whitman. He was not unlike him in appearance:

Of middle height; slender, sinewy, and elegant, a figure that naturally fell into beautiful and alluring attitudes; with light-brown curling locks, half shading his low, dense, passionate forehead. Brave, sweet, loving, joyous, ardent, amative, proud, generous; well-read, well-bred, proficient in every manly exercise; one who fenced, danced, sang divinely, wrote charming verses, talked brilliantly, had in him the slumbering spells of eloquence; one good at a hunt, a regatta, on a horse, with a rifle, loving all pretty girls lightly and purely, none deeply; very gallant and attentive to old women; friendly to all men, and easily loved by them . . . a Paladin in the bud, but now a perfect squire of dames. . . .

At the carpenter's first sight of Faulkner he calls him "a sweet boy, a born lover." As he gives his hand to each one as he is introduced, the stranger draws Faulkner to his breast, lightly kissing him on the forehead, and saying gently, "My son." "The tender voice, the unusual daring action which sent sweet lightning through Faulkner's veins, left the others with a soft, mysterious thrill." Later the carpenter comes upon Faulkner:

> "I was thinking of you," he said dreamfully, lifting his dark, tender eyes to the carpenter's face as the latter approached him.
> The carpenter put his arm around him, and drew him to his breast. Faulkner, a little faint with emotion, let his head droop upon the stalwart bosom.
> "When I saw you, I loved you," said the gray stranger.
> "And I," returned the young man, looking up with frank affection. "You made me feel the reality of something I thought an abstraction."
> "The love passing the love of women," said the carpenter.
> "The same," answered the youth. "The love of Shakespeare for the unknown, David for Jonathan, John for the Redeemer. The manly love."

Though Faulkner responds to these words, he still is enamored of Emily. John, whose suspicions of his wife had not included suspicion of his friend, finally becomes so jealous of Faulkner that he raises an axe in fury. The stranger stops him and recalls him to his senses. Later the carpenter says he will tell their fortunes if they come in one by one. To Faulkner the carpenter says,

> "Welcome, sweet boy. Welcome thou in whom mixes the perfumed nature of woman with so much of manliness. I greet you, born lover of women!"
> "Born lover of you!" Faulkner replied, blushing coyly, with down-dropped lashes, and drooping into a posture of leopard grace.
> "Lover of Emily Dyzer. Beguiler of a wife. Betrayer of a friend," was the stern, low answer.

The carpenter paints the loathsome picture of what will happen to Faulkner if he persists in his love of Emily. Faulkner promises to ask forgiveness of John and never to see Emily again. As he stood in repentant silence, the carpenter enfolds him in him arms, saying,

All bright and holy fortunes to you, my beloved, my darling. But not for you, with gifts, with eloquence and learning, this life of enervation,—these days of dalliance and idle ease. Awake! Arouse! Go, the apostle of all love and every loving cause. Plant thou, in thy strength and sweetness of nature and fortune, thicker than grass, brighter than flowers, the seeds of truth and liberty and comradeship in America. . . .

After other exhortations, the carpenter concludes, " 'Go; to brows like thine belong every crown—see that thou fail not of the crown of thorns! My son' and, bending, he kissed him on the mouth,—'with this kiss I dedicate you to a manly life.' "

These scenes, which to the modern reader reflect Whitman's homoerotic tendencies, were not considered in any way remarkable by contemporary critics. *Putnam's* paid 280 dollars for the story, and later wanted to issue it as a Christmas book as they had done with "The Ghost." They asked whether the author would consent to change perhaps half a dozen lines "which now disturb the equanimity of very worthy and (perhaps) very stupid people."[32] The lines in question were those which might have been thought to identify the hero with Christ and therefore would cause sensitive people to see "irreverence in the portrait of the Gray Man." George Putnam in another letter thinks the allusion to the carpenter as Christ would offend the audience for the "Christmas book," although he himself feels that "the whole spirit of 'The Carpenter' is so vigorous and healthful and *Christian*, that everybody of sense must be imbued with it, if they only read it in the author's light." Some reviewers had objected to the extravagance of the language, but Putnam felt that "the rollicking extravagant vivid words and outbursts . . . are a matter of taste."[33] Whether O'Connor refused to make changes or not is not known. "The Carpenter" did not appear in book form at that time.

The critical response was varied; the *Boston Commonwealth* (January 11, 1868), quite unmindful that the author had once been on its staff, satirized the plot and deplored the extravagance of the language. "Those familiar with the murdered English of Carlyle and Swinburne may possibly by a great stretch of the imagination, discover the meaning of most of the comparisons and metaphors." The *Southern Opinion* (February 28, 1868) stated that its author is "now quite a pet with the Yankee publick."

An unidentified reviewer says that the story "has been character-ized by almost every epithet in the English language: every quality from sublimity to absurdity, and from sweetness to absolute bosh, has been decided to predominate therein." Yet the reviewer thinks that "the true apotheosis of Walt Whitman in the tale is in the power with which his highest and best teachings come home to us; in the incarnation of the purest and truest spirit of his finest poems." While criticizing the extravagance of language, he praises "the powerful under-current of faith and love, which carries us along on its mighty tide past all the obstructions on the way."[34]

The Nation (December 16, 1867), though finding great faults in the story, says that it is "so true and so powerful, that one cannot but feel very much obliged to him for having written it. Faults and all, it is worth while to get the *Magazine* for the sake of reading it." Yet O'Connor was so upset by the part of *The Nation*'s review which criticized his language that he penned an angry letter in reply.[35] There is no record that it was ever sent.

John Hay was enthusiastic about the story. He wrote from Vienna, "I must thank you, over land and sea, for the pleasure your 'Carpen-ter' has given me. I do not know why, but the instant he came into the firelighted room I knew it was Whitman, before one word of de-scription followed. I am curious to see what people will say of it who dont (*sic*) know him. I think nobody has recently written any thing so bold and so original."[36]

While Hay saw the man Whitman, others thought O'Connor had depicted him as Christ. O'Connor always objected to this. He wrote to Bucke of this matter, "What was attempted in 'The Carpenter' was something different and more subtle, and a phrase like this only does harm, impinging, as it does, on reverential beliefs, and neces-sarily meaning something different to the believer from what it does to you."[37]

O'Connor himself later disparaged his work, saying that haste had spoiled it. "O had I had time and thought to work out that story! We cannot drive Apollo!" he wrote to Stedman.[38] Yet "The Carpenter" has two distinctions in the Whitman canon: It is the first treatment of Walt Whitman as a character in fiction and it became the first and only commercial motion picture to portray the fictional Whitman. "The Carpenter" was made into a two-reel picture by the Vitagraph Company in July 1913.[39] This was done at the instance of Whitman's friend, John H. Johnston, who considered "The Carpenter" the greatest short story ever written, and its author, whom he met only once, in 1869, as "one of the greatest literary men of the century."[40] He suggested the possibility of making it into a motion picture to his friend, the secretary and manager of the Vitagraph Company. The producer promised that it would be announced that the great character in the picture was Walt Whitman, but not only was this not done, but O'Connor was not named as the author; "The Carpenter" appeared as the work of the script writer. Excerpts from this story were later reprinted in Stedman's *Library of American Literature*,[41] and it was one of the stories reprinted in *Three Tales* after O'Connor's death.

The years from 1865 to 1868, beginning with *The Good Gray Poet* and ending with "The Carpenter," were productive ones for O'Connor in his campaign for the appreciation of Whitman and *Leaves of Grass*. It is amazing that while working full-time as a government clerk he was able to produce these two pieces of work, as well as engage in an extensive correspondence with recipients of his pamphlet on both sides of the Atlantic which included long letters of rebuttal to unfavorable critics. In addition he had written lengthy reviews of the Fourth Edition of *Leaves of Grass* and of Burroughs's *Walt Whitman as Poet and Person*, to say nothing of his contribution to the controversy over Florence Percy's poem "Rock Me to Sleep."

Among his letters of rebuttal was one to *The Round Table* (February 16, 1867) entitled " 'C' on Whitman." "C," in writing "The Aldrich-Swinburne Controversy" on January 16, 1867, had suggested, by innuendo, a comparison of Whitman's "To a Common Prostitute" with Catullus's "atrocious Carmen" in *Ad Ipsithillam*. O'Connor is so outraged and shocked that he maintains *The Round Table* would not publish the "Carmen" even in Latin. The contrast is too sharp between a "frank expression of gross lust" by the Roman poet and the "infinitely solemn human voice" raised by the American on behalf of "a being despised and rejected."

Another article of rebuttal was O'Connor's letter to the editor of *The Independent* (November 9, 1867) in which he takes issue with the reviewer of an essay on Walt Whitman by Robert Buchanan, an English poet, for his description of Whitman as a "grotesque, ruffianly-looking loafer" and other personalities both untrue and irrelevant.[42] O'Connor describes Whitman's life and literary accomplishments in the forceful style of *The Good Gray Poet*.

During these two or three highly productive years when O'Connor was writing so much in Whitman's defense, friends continued to come night after night to the O'Connors' to see them and Walt Whitman. William and Jeánnie Channing came for the first time in 1866 and visited frequently thereafter. Their daughter Grace, always a close friend of her cousin Jeannie O'Connor, wrote of those evenings:

> The day existed, for me, to be gotten through with, till it was time to go again to my aunt's and sit there thrilling with (the) thunder and impact of the free display of fireworks of the soul. As never by any chance did all these individualists think alike, there was always some hot discussion or always something for which O'Connor was battling. . . . Whitman produced a new poem, or my uncle outlined a new crushing article of defense; or some generous plan for Whitman's benefit was proposed by someone and eagerly taken up. Campaigns were planned, results were compared and letters drafted; the whole framework of the fame and success of the poet was reared and lovingly laid and built, stone by stone, through those years of nights in the little parlour. None of them had any money; government service was poorly paid; but all had devotion and a perfect faith not merely in the poet but in the cause of letters.[43]

In carrying out these "campaigns," they shared materials. For example, Whitman sent O'Connor a review of *Leaves of Grass* from the *London Leader* (June 30, 1860) to put into *The Good Gray Poet* if he thought it would be helpful.[44] He also wrote much of the biographical part of Burroughs's *Notes on Walt Whitman as Poet and Person*. (It has been said that O'Connor wrote some of the interpretative parts, but there is no record of this.)

There was similar give-and-take in the preparation of the articles and the edition of Whitman's poems which were to spread Whitman's fame in England. In this O'Connor was the prime mover in the United States and the Reverend Moncure Daniel Conway his counterpart in England. Before Conway's efforts there had been two reviews of *Leaves of Grass*, one, already noted, in the London *Leader* and the other in the London *Spectator* (July 4); two reviews of *Drum-Taps*, one in the *London Times* (March 8, 1866) and the other in the London *Review* (June 8, 1866). There had also been an essay by the Orientalist Lord Strangford in which he noted the resemblance of *Leaves of Grass* to ancient Persian poetry (*Pall Mall Gazette*, February 16, 1866).

These were but the first steps in recognition and appreciation of *Leaves of Grass* in England. They were to lead to an English edition of Walt Whitman's poems in which O'Connor played an important role.

NOTES

1. WW, "An Ossianic Night—Dearest Friends," November 1881, in *Prose Works 1892*, I: 283.
2. William Swinton to WDO'C, 27 November 1865 (Feinberg-LC).
3. John Swinton to WDO'C, 11 January 1866 (Feinberg-LC).
4. WDO'C to M. J. Channing, 18 February 1866 (Chamberlin).
5. WDO'C to Church, 24 August 1866 (Perry). This article appeared in *The Galaxy*, 3: 606–15 (1 December 1866). Church had hesitated before accepting Burroughs's review, writing, "I am unable to persuade myself or my associates that there is sufficient public interest in Whitman just at present to justify an article upon him." Letter to O'Connor, 22 September 1866 (Feinberg-LC).
6. *The Galaxy*, vol. 3, p. 605.
7. 15 November 1865.
8. WDO'C to M. J. Channing, 18 February 1866 (Chamberlin).
9. *Prose Works 1892*, p. 713.
10. *Camden*, 2: 164.
11. John T. Trowbridge, *My Own Story* (Boston and New York: Houghton Mifflin and Company, 1904), p. 378.
12. *Prose Works 1892*, p. 712.
13. *Correspondence*, I: 300.
14. (New York: American News Co., 1867). Second ed. (New York: J. S. Redfield, 1871).
15. Barrus, *Comrades*, p. 15.
16. WDO'C to Burroughs, 6 January 1866, *ibid.*, pp. 35–36.
17. Burroughs to Benton, 25 August 1866 (Berg).
18. Barrus, *Journals*, p. 51.
19. Burroughs to Benton, January n.d. 1869 in Barrus, *Comrades*, p. 58.
20. *Camden*, 2: 44.
21. *Ibid.*, 171.
22. Barrus, *Comrades*, p. 11.
23. A copy of Morse's pamphlet with notations in O'Connor's handwriting as well as other materials relating to the controversy are in Feinberg-LC.
24. *Manuscripts, Autograph Letters, First Editions and Portraits of Walt Whitman.* Catalogue of American Art Association/Anderson Galleries. New York, 1936, p. 59.
25. *Providence Journal*, 6 June 1867.
26. Burroughs to Benton, 5 August 1867 (Berg).

27. Burroughs to Benton, 25 February 1867 (Berg).
28. Burroughs to Benton, 19 June 1867 (Berg).
29. Barrus, *Comrades*, p. 49.
30. WW, "Two Brothers, One South, One North," *Specimen Days*, p. 107.
31. 30 November 1870 (Feinberg-LC).
32. Putnam to WDO'C, 21 July 1868 (Feinberg-LC).
33. Putnam to WDO'C, 23 July 1868 (Feinberg-LC).
34. "A New School of Romance," *Beloit College Monthly*, June 1868.
35. 16 December 1867 (Berg).
36. Hay to WDO'C, 8 January 1868 (Brown).
37. WDO'C to Bucke, 10 June 1882 (Feinberg-LC).
38. WDO'C to Stedman, 9 January 1889 (Columbia), a copy sent by Robert Scholnick to the author.
39. Florence B. Freedman, "A Motion Picture 'First' for Whitman: O'Connor's 'The Carpenter,' " *Walt Whitman Review*, 9: 31–33 (June 1963).
40. Charles N. Elliot, *Walt Whitman as Man, Poet and Friend* (Boston: The Gorham Press, 1915), p. 174.
41. Vol. 9, pp. 48–61 (New York: Charles L. Webster & Company, 1889).
42. (Berg).
43. Grace Channing, unpublished memoir (Chamberlin).
44. WDO'C to WW, 19 October 1865 (Feinberg-LC).

CHAPTER XIII

A Sea Change: *Leaves of Grass* In England

ACCEPTANCE OF *Leaves of Grass* in England was important to Walt Whitman and his friends, for the American writers and critics who disparaged the poet's work were among those who praised and imitated English poetry and quoted English critics. Fortunately, an American in England could serve as liaison, Moncure Daniel Conway. He was the first who knew Whitman personally to write about him in England. This was most fitting, for he was among the earliest visitors who had sought him out in Brooklyn after the appearance of the First Edition of *Leaves of Grass*. He had learned of the poems from Emerson, to whom he immediately wrote his impressions of Walt.[1] Conway visited Whitman again two years later. After Conway settled in England, correspondence with O'Connor and Whitman reveals his important role in making Whitman's work known in England. His own writing, his friendships, and his help in launching the Rossetti edition of Whitman's poems were major factors in introducing Whitman abroad. Yet in a letter to O'Connor he modestly wondered whether the poet would remember him.[2]

Moncure Daniel Conway had an interesting history.[3] An unlikely recruit to the Abolition movement, Conway was born in Virginia into a slave-holding Methodist family. Although they were kind to their slaves, always referring to them as "servants" rather than "slaves" and not selling them, they did not approve of their son's anti-slavery stand. He had also departed from his parents' (and his own earlier) religious affiliation, for after having been a Methodist preacher as a young man, he went to Harvard Divinity School and became a Unitarian minister. He was in Boston at the time that the fugitive slave Anthony Burns was sent back to his master in Virginia, and was criticized by his Virginia friends for not having aided the slave's master when he tried to recover his "property."

In the fall of 1854 Conway went to Washington to become minister of the Unitarian Church; there he preached anti-slavery, even though Washington was a slave city. While there he visited the home of Dr. Gamaliel Bailey, editor of the anti-slavery *New Era*, and gave a course of lectures on "The Origins of Words" at Myrtilla Miner's school for free colored girls. In 1860 he became minister of a Unitarian Church in Cincinnati, Ohio, where he edited the Cincinnati *Dial*, the western counterpart of the New England Transcendentalist periodical. The *Dial* of August 1860 contained an article by Conway about Whitman.

In 1863 Conway went to England to try to persuade the English of the justice of the Northern cause. (While there he suggested to the envoy of the Confederacy that the South end the war by freeing the slaves.) He stayed on as the minister of the South Place Religious Society from 1863 to 1884. Before he left the United States his anti-slavery book *The Rejected Stone* was published (1864). While in England he wrote *Testimonies Concerning Slavery* (1864).

During the war he interrupted his stay in England with a visit to the United States. He found that his family's home, the Conway House in Falmouth, Virginia, was being used as a hospital—and that Whitman was visiting wounded soldiers there. Conway later wrote biographies of Emerson, Carlyle, Hawthorne, and Paine, among others. He returned to the United States in 1884, remaining there until his death in 1907.

Correspondence between O'Connor and Conway began with a letter by O'Connor on March 25, 1866[4] which Conway answered on April 24, 1866.[5] O'Connor had sent a copy of *Drum-Taps* which had arrived so laden with fines that Conway had to refuse it. Conway had, however, received copies of *Drum-Taps* and of *The Good Gray Poet* from an American friend. They came in time for him to

include a few quotations from *Drum-Taps* in an article on Walt
Whitman which he was writing for the *Fortnightly Review.* In that
first letter to O'Connor, he suggested that a testimonial with a purse
of money should be arranged for Whitman, and that he would be
glad to subscribe twenty-five dollars. He also asked for some biographical data:

> How did he begin to write? What led to poetry? Did he go to
> school? If I knew enough to produce some interest (personal)
> about him, it might some day serve him. Write to him quoting
> what is proper from my letter at your discretion; ask him to write
> to me about all these things—about himself—to write on paper
> like this and send it to me without prepayment of postage. Who
> knows but it may reach me before my Fortnightly appears.

O'Connor, replying on May 27, stated that Whitman was in need
not of money, but of friends "to reverse the unjust verdict" and "to
secure him his rights as a great poet." As to the adverse American
critics, he wrote that the louse criticizes the lion. Conway's article
was more important than financial support, for "It is not every day in
the year that a magazine is open to us." As for answers to the questions he had posed, O'Connor does not believe that Walt will write
to Conway:

> . . . getting information out of him respecting his career or the
> theory of his poems, that is the eighth labor of Hercules! How-
> ever, by dint of long clinging, and by power and continuity of
> suction equal to that of the devil-fish, as described by Victor
> Hugo in his recent gorgeous and powerful romance, I have some
> items which I will send you. I don't mean to imply that Walt is
> unwilling to divulge, but the thing is to catch him in the mood for
> revelation! He has a curious slowness of delivery.[6]

What O'Connor sent was a manuscript which answers all of these
questions, and gives some facts about Whitman's early life not
known to most readers of *Leaves of Grass.* Entitled "Memoranda," it
was written in the spring of 1866, for it begins: "Walt Whitman is
now 47 years of age. His 47th birthday comes this 31st of May, 1866."
(It seems likely that O'Connor sent this with his letter of May 27.)[7]
The manuscript gives a brief factual account of the poet's ancestry,

parentage, and family and speaks of the influence of Elias Hicks, mentioning that Whitman has prepared a lecture (still in manuscript) about the Quaker preacher.

O'Connor, the Abolitionist, makes much of Whitman's anti-slavery activities. As a writer for the *Brooklyn Eagle* he kept that paper for a long time "against the inclinations of the proprietors, on the side of liberty." Whitman left the paper when the owners "decided to hoist the pro-slavery Democratic flag." O'Connor attributes some of the current hostility against Whitman's writing to his powerful assaults against slavery at that time. O'Connor refers to Whitman's other anti-slavery activities not generally recognized or remembered:

> Alone by himself, and out of his own head solely, he hammered out the theory of the anti-slavery construction of the Constitution, and was considerably surprised when waiting upon Horace Greeley to urge him to adopt that theory, the latter told him that his views had been anticipated by Lysander Spooner. In those early days he attended political meetings as a public speaker in the country places. His first poem was a passionate and fiery cry against the Fugitive Slave law. It is called "Blood Money"—the subject of the first stanzas being the sale by Iscariot of Christ; the application being to the sale of Christ's black brothers in this country under the Fugitive Slave Law.[8]

The "items" Whitman had given O'Connor were incorporated in the letter. O'Connor quotes the poet in saying that Whitman "has felt by years of contact, the hot pulses of populous Manhattan. He has sailed the vast lakes of the north and up and down the mighty Mississippi and Missouri, and down into the Gulf of Mexico, and has traversed [Whitman's notes said 'traveled'] the prairies. These are ever present in his poems, which seem to be impalpably made on their models. During the war, he has lived much with the army, in camp and in hospitals at the front." O'Connor assures Conway that he can rely on the statements in his "pamphlet" (*The Good Gray Poet*).

Perhaps because this is meant for an English audience, O'Connor stresses Whitman's reading, including the work of the philosophers Kant, Hegel, Fichte, Schelling, Leibnitz, and Spinoza. He writes that Whitman understands Greek thought and finds joy in the Greek dramatists. Perhaps to counteract the impression of the "barbaric yawp," O'Connor states that Whitman knows the work on language of the great German philologists, Bopp and Grimm. His wide reading also includes translations from the "Hindu muse." His chief delight, however, is the Bible. "The Women of the Bible he thinks the divinest figures in all the disclosures of genius." O'Connor tells at some length of Whitman's reading of Shakespeare, but refers to occasional disagreements because of O'Connor's "pronounced Delia-Bacon notions of the scope and purport of those dramas." Other books which O'Connor mentions as being among Whitman's favorites are Dante's *Inferno*, Cervantes's *Don Quixote*, the Border Minstrelsy of Walter Scott, George Sand's *Consuelo* (which he rereads every year) and the works of Victor Hugo.

He makes a point of saying that Whitman had not read Emerson's writings until after the publication of the First Edition of *Leaves of Grass*, thus disclaiming any influence of the man who received the *Leaves* so enthusiastically. He writes of Whitman's love of music and art—but emphasizes the fact that "his chief books have been men." He includes a long quotation from a letter Whitman sent him of his views on the current state of poetry in America, and his own aim "to give something to our literature which will be our own."

One statement which Conway later forwarded to Rossetti, and which the latter included in his preface to an English edition of a selection of Whitman's poems, was that Whitman "set out with the determination to avoid making any reflection or criticism on the condition of letters in this country, the compositions of other poets or writers, &c. To do this more effectively—to guard himself from passing the line he drew around his purpose—he wrote on a sheet of paper in large letters: 'MAKE THE WORKS.' "

Although it has been thought that this manuscript of "Memoranda" was prepared by Whitman for O'Connor, the total of Whitman's notes included comprise only sixteen lines of unacknowledged quotation from Whitman and forty-three lines of direct quotation in a manuscript containing 471 lines in all. This can therefore be considered largely O'Connor's own conception of Whitman's life and aims.

In the letter accompanying the "Memoranda," O'Connor gives a summary of Whitman's views and plans. These were taken directly with only a few minor changes from notes sent by the poet to O'Connor for this purpose:

> Passionate Friendship and Love are main elements in his theory. . . . "Enfans D'Adam" celebrates Love and Amativeness. The poems called "Calamus" celebrate Friendship or Adhesiveness.
>
> Pride is another element. It is surcharged throughout with individuality. The State is altogether for the individual.
>
> Modern Democracy is an underlying idea. The vastness and variety of the United States seem always before the poet's eyes.
>
> "Drum Taps" is the expression of the war, . . . the doubts and terrible uncertainty; the perseverance; the smoke and thunder and fierceness of the battle; and yet more, the human interests and sympathies of the struggle. War itself, as such, he does not celebrate. . . . He also comprehends in the plan of his poem, a series of pieces which shall be the expression of the religious or spiritual nature of man.[9]

Conway's article on Whitman appeared in the *Fortnightly Review* in October 1866. In it he wrote of his visits to Whitman in 1855 and 1857, describing his room (with pictures of Bacchus and Silenus) and what Whitman said was his favorite spot for composing poems (a hilltop on which he lay staring at the sky) in terms that did not please O'Connor; the latter did, however, appreciate all that Conway said about the poetry. O'Connor wrote to Conway on February 7, 1867, that he found "no offense" in the article, but that he deprecated "any mention of Walt as an eccentric person, as a rowdy genius, or an oddity or insane person." He does not accuse Conway of doing this, but he felt "a tone, a tinge, a flavor if it. . . ."[10] Whitman expressed his view of the article in a letter to his mother on November 25, 1866: "Mr. Conway's article was about as impudent as it was friendly— quite a mixture of good and bad."[11]

Nevertheless, Conway was to do *Leaves of Grass* a great service by interesting an English publisher in it. Of this project, O'Connor was initiator. In a letter to Conway on December 5, 1866, he wrote: "What would Swinburne's men (Hotten & Co., isn't it?) say about it? Seems to me the courage that prints *Laus Veneris* might dare this. I think it would be a paying enterprise for a British publisher, and I very much wish it could be effected."[12] O'Connor mentions that he is sending half a dozen copies of the new edition (the Fourth Edition, dated 1867, but ready in 1866), one for Conway and the others for distribution, John Burroughs's "masterly critique" from the New

York *Galaxy,* his own article on *Drum-Taps* from the *Times,* and two or three copies of *The Good Gray Poet* to be distributed, one to Swinburne.

In the same letter O'Connor takes issue once again with Lord Strangford's thought (expressed in an article on Walt Whitman in the *Pall Mall Gazette*) that *Leaves of Grass* resembles the Persian poets—a view which Conway supported. "The literary form corresponds to America. The dominant principle of it is liberty. America rives the chains of slaves and the prosodies of poets. . . ." O'Connor was annoyed with Lord Strangford on other accounts as well:

> . . . I consider that he owes a heavy debt of atonement. For my own part, I am utterly at a loss to conceive how such a meaning can be put upon such a book, and not less how a British gentleman could permit himself to couch his notice in such a tone of indecent personal insolence as characterized Lord Strangford's mention of Mr. Whitman.

Conway, pursuing the idea of an English edition, wrote to O'Connor on April 30, 1867, that he had been present at a consultation of Swinburne, Rossetti, and J. C. Hotten, the publisher. They felt that some things in the *Leaves,* as published, would bring a legal prosecution in England, which no publisher would chance.[13] In his reply on May 23, 1867, O'Connor declares himself as totally against any expurgation of *Leaves of Grass:*

> Walt never will consent to it, and if he were willing, I would protest against it myself to my dying day. Far better that the book should go over to the next century, than appear shorn of a single line. There is nothing in it that has not been put there with the most conscientious deliberation, and for purposes deeply religious, if ever there were religious purposes on earth. To excise it would be not only a fatal concession to the vile strictures of the reviewers, but a moral recreancy incapable of any defense which an honest man and writer could offer. If the age is intolerant of art as Shakespeare and Juvenal, as Dante and Ezekiel understood it, let us veil our faces, and wait till a grander age arrives.

In any case, O'Connor feels, after consultation with Ashton (U.S. Assistant Attorney-General) who knows the English law, that no indictment would follow the publication of *Leaves of Grass* in its present form.[14]

Whitman's response to the idea of an English edition was to prepare an introduction for it, to be copied and signed by O'Connor. To the poet, who had written some of his own reviews for the First Edition of the *Leaves*, this would seem expedient and necessary. O'Connor sent this introduction with a copy of *Leaves of Grass*, corrected and revised by Whitman, to Conway. The introduction was not used for the English edition; it remained among Whitman's papers after having been updated several times for possible use.[15]

Conway's letter of acknowledgment shows what was being contemplated at that time:

> The copy suitable for an edition here, should we be able to reach to that, I have and shall keep carefully. When it is achieved it will probably be the result and fruit of more reviewing and discussion. I shall keep my eyes wide open; and the volume with O'Connor's introduction shall come out just as it is. I am not sure but that it will in the end have to be done at our own expense—which I believe would be repaid.[16]

A more favorable opportunity soon presented itself. It would not be necessary for Whitman to publish at his own expense. J. C. Hotten, the publisher whose name O'Connor had suggested to Conway, was willing to undertake the project with William Michael Rossetti to serve as editor and write the introduction.

Whitman knew of Rossetti, brother of the poets Christina and Dante Gabriel, a member of the Pre-Raphaelite Society, an essayist and a critic of art and literature. Rossetti had become acquainted with the First Edition of *Leaves of Grass* through William Bell Scott, poet and sculptor, to whom it had been given by Thomas Dixon, an uneducated cork cutter (just the kind of person which Whitman wanted as his audience).[17] Rossetti later received Whitman's *Drum-Taps* and O'Connor's *The Good Gray Poet* from an American friend, Horace Scudder, who was also a friend of O'Connor and of Conway. Because of his interest in the *Leaves*, Rossetti wrote an article which was printed in *The Chronicle* on July 6, 1867, and reprinted in the *New York Citizen* on August 10. Whitman knew of the article and asked his New York friend Mrs. Abby Price to try to get a few copies of *The Chronicle* for him.[18]

In his article, Rossetti recognized that Whitman has received "much of hard measure in his own America—much rage, much indignation and still more contempt, being mixed in the critical cup presented to be drunk by his lips, themselves far more contemptuous still." He mentions among those enthusiastic about the poet Emerson, Conway, O'Connor, and Burroughs: "Whitman's enthusiasts in America make up in fervor for their paucity, and proclaim their hero to be, beyond all comparison, *the* poet of the epoch."

In talking of Whitman, Rossetti tells of his life and early writings. He discusses Whitman's work, admiring him as "a man of his age, an initiator in the scheme and structure of his writings, and an individual of audacious personal ascendant." Yet he sees Whitman's frankness in ideas and language and certain elements of his style as matters which will prevent his acceptance. The essay is a judicious appraisal, with full consideration of those aspects of Whitman's writings which will interfere with his acceptance, and equal stress on his unique qualities.

Rossetti's balanced article influenced American editors. *The Nation* characterized it as "the most temperate of any we have seen from Whitman's admirers, and all the stronger on that account."[19] Burroughs, himself restrained in his writings, wrote to Conway in August 1867 that *The Round Table* copied the conclusion of the article and completely reversed its verdict of a year ago. "Our cause gains fast. The leaven is working and no mistake."[20]

Conway wrote to Whitman of Hotten's plan to employ Rossetti as editor on October 12, 1867, urging that he take advantage of the opportunity to have his poems published in England with an English editor. He felt that because O'Connor was not known in England, it would be preferable to have an introduction by Rossetti (even though, according to Conway, nothing could equal O'Connor's introduction). Conway reminded Whitman that English publishers actually did not need his consent, nor would they have to pay royalties, for there was no reciprocal law protecting the works of American writers in England nor those of English writers in America. Whitman should therefore consider himself lucky to have a publisher like Hotten who was willing to share the profits with him, as well as an editor of Rossetti's reputation and character.

When Rossetti received Hotten's proposal (he was to receive 25 pounds and 12 copies of the book) he noted in his diary what his principle of selection would be: It would be "to miss out entirely any poem though otherwise fine and unobjectionable, which contains any of his extreme crudities of expression in the way of indecency. I would not expurgate any such poems, but simply exclude them."[21]

Contrary to O'Connor's expectation that Whitman would never agree to any expurgation, the poet did give his consent to some changes in the Preface to the First Edition. In a letter to Conway on November 1, 1867, he wrote:

> I have no objection to his substituting other words—leaving it all to his own tact, &c.—for "onanist," "father-stuff," &c. Briefly I hereby empower him, (since that seems to be the pivotal affair, & since he has the kindness to shape his action so much by my wishes—& since, indeed, the sovereignty of the responsibility is not at all mine in the case,)—to make verbal changes of that sort, wherever, for reasons sufficient to him, he decides that they are indispensable. I would add that it is a question with me whether the introductory essay or prose preface to the first edition is worth printing.[22]

Not long after this (on November 10, 1867) Whitman penned a letter to be sent by O'Connor in the latter's name to Conway. In it he gave his own idea of his book, reiterating O'Connor's idea that the poet is in no way the "rough," the "eccentric," "vagabond," or queer person that some commentators have described; and adding a conception of Whitman and his poems, epitomized in the important words *ensemble* and *modernness*.[23] A few weeks later the poet wrote to Rossetti, supposing that the "reprint intends to avoid any expressed or implied character of being an expurgated edition." He suggests that the title page state: "Walt Whitman's Poems, selected from the American Editions by Wm. M. Rossetti."[24]

Evidently Whitman began to have regrets about the permission to make changes. (It may be surmised that O'Connor's indignation made him change his mind.) On December 3 he wrote saying that he had intended the permission to make verbal alterations to pertain only to a change in some words in the Preface to the First Edition—he had not meant that permission to extend to his poems. He sounds more like O'Connor when he writes:

> I cannot & will not consent of my own volition, to countenance an expurgated edition of my pieces. I have steadily refused to do

so under seductive offers, here in my own country, & must not do so in another country.

He qualifies this comprehensive statement, however:

> . . . if, before the arrival of this letter, you have practically invested in, & accomplished, or partially accomplished any plan, even contrary to this letter, I do not expect you to abandon it, at loss of outlay, &c. but shall *bona fide* consider you blameless if you let it go on, and be carried out, as you may have arranged. It is the question of the authorization of an expurgated edition proceeding from me, that deepest engages me.[25]

He therefore suggests that it would be better in any introduction not to say that the author permitted any expurgation. Later, wanting to reassure Rossetti, he sent a note to O'Connor asking him to include, in his letter to Rossetti, the following remarks:

> I met Mr. Whitman a few evenings since. He has received your letter of December 10th. He duly received the previous ones also, making three letters from you. He is entirely satisfied with your action, & Mr. Hotten's, in regard to the London selection & reprint, and seems pleased with the condition into which that enterprise has been shaped. He spoke with deep appreciation of you and your letters.[26]

The volume when it appeared was entitled *Poems by Walt Whitman*, Selected and Edited by William Michael Rossetti. Under the title was a quotation from Michelangelo in Italian, and below that a drawing of the globe resting on clouds—the design which had been impressed on the front cover of the Third Edition of *Leaves of Grass*. The publisher and date were London: John Camden Hotten, Picadilly, 1868. Facing the title page was a re-engraving of the picture of the poet from the First Edition of *Leaves of Grass*. On the next page were quotations from Swedenborg, Carlyle, and Robespierre.

The text began with a dedicatory letter to William Bell Scott, followed by a "Prefatory Note," in which the editor states his principle of selection (similar to what he had penned in his diary when the publication was first proposed to him):

First, to omit entirely every poem which could with any tolerable fairness be deemed offensive to the feelings of morals or propriety in this peculiarly nervous age, and, second, to include every remaining poem which appeared to me of conspicuous beauty or interest.

He draws for the preface on his own *Fortnightly* article, amplifying some of the points he made there. He relies on Conway for the personal description of the poet, on Burroughs for the biographical material, and on *The Good Gray Poet* for additional biographical and critical material. In his own balanced estimate of Whitman, he admits the poet's faults and shortcomings as he sees them, but stresses his originality and other qualities. He asks his readers to consider the following questions: "Is he powerful? Is he American? Is he new? Is he rousing? Does he feel and make me feel?"

The volume of 403 pages contains Whitman's Preface to the First Edition (with a few changes of words) and about half of the poems of *Leaves of Grass*. While many fine and representative poems are included, the untitled key poem, later called "Walt Whitman" and later still "Song of Myself," is left out, as are the "Calamus" and "Enfans d'Adam" groups. Rossetti arranged the poems in his own way and gave them titles of his own devising. In a postscript he states that Whitman "has had nothing whatever to do with this selection, as to either prompting, guiding, or even ratifying it; except only that he did not prohibit my making two or three verbal omissions in the Prose Preface to *Leaves of Grass*."

There was no comment from O'Connor on the English edition. He probably was annoyed that Whitman had consented to having only a selection of his poems published, and to the changing of some words in the Preface to the First Edition. After O'Connor's initial correspondence with Conway, some of it originating with him and some in which he spoke for Whitman, he seems to have given up his role in the negotiations. Whitman wrote his own letters to Rossetti and to Hotten, the publisher.

Whitman was pleased by his acceptance by the young men of England. "In my own country, so far," he wrote to Conway, "I have received but one long tirade of shallow impudence, mockery, and scurrilous jeers. Only since the English recognition have the skies here lighted up a little." He expressed his willingness for Hotten to sell copies of the English edition in the United States; it turned out later, however, that Hotten was unsuccessful in trying to interest an American publisher in this.[27]

Whitman might have regretted that the first English edition contained only a selection of his poems, and that he had consented to have some words of his Preface to the First Edition changed or omitted, but he could not help being pleased by Rossetti's admiration and advocacy. For his part Rossetti remained a staunch friend of Whitman and his writings. In his last letter before the publication of his edition of the poems, he wrote to Whitman,

> To be honored by your friendship is as great a satisfaction and distinction as my life has presented or ever can present. I respond to it with all my warmth and reverence, and the Atlantic seemed a very small space between us as I read and re-read your letter.[28]

Rossetti showed other evidence of friendship in later years. He paid tribute to Whitman in *Lives of Famous Poets* in 1872 (praising him at the end of an essay on Longfellow). He dedicated an edition of *American Poems* for Moxon's *Popular Poets* to Whitman, had his picture on the frontispiece, and included thirty-two of his poems. In 1876, when there was talk of Whitman's being destitute (leading to publication of controversial articles in the press, one of which O'Connor wrote) Rossetti collected a thousand dollars from distinguished men in England for the purchase of copies of Whitman's Centennial Edition of *Leaves of Grass* and *Two Rivulets.*

Rossetti, while remaining a friend and supporter of Whitman, did not change his mind about the *Leaves.* In what may have been his last statement on the matter, in a letter to Charles N. Elliot, on November 15, 1914, to be included in the latter's book *Walt Whitman as Man, Poet and Friend,* he wrote:

> At the age of 85 I retain unimpaired my love for Walt Whitman & my deep regard for his memory, & my warm admiration of his work in its broad bulk & support—allowing for occasional demur (which I always have entertained) to some points here & there. Whitman is a towering & majestic figure in American & worldwide literature. [29]

O'Connor was understandably not at all happy with Rossetti's edition. While he kept silent in the American press, he wrote his views to

Ferdinand Freiligrath, the German poet, then living in England, who had written in an article of his desire to translate Whitman into German. O'Connor sends him a copy of *Leaves of Grass* (a gift from the poet), Burroughs's book, and his own *Good Gray Poet*, and some other articles about Whitman. He hopes that Freiligrath will translate the entire work into German, and urges him to "use the original edition, and not Mr. Rossetti's selection. Mr. Whitman's friends in this country," he continues, while

> . . . greatly indebted to Mr. Rossetti for what he has done,
> . . . nevertheless must regard his work as essentially cas-
> trated. . . . The long section entitled "Walt Whitman," extraor-
> dinary for its vast elemental power and beauty, is also so vitally
> and intimately related and necessary to the whole, that its omis-
> sion in the Rossetti edition reminds one of our English jokes of
> enacting Hamlet with the part of the hero left out. The change of
> titles, too, is unfortunate, many of Mr. Rossetti's substitutions be-
> ing positive obscurations of the meaning of the pieces, . . .

He suggests that Freiligrath rely for biographical facts upon Burroughs and himself. He does not want him to be misled by Conway "(to whose good will we are deeply indebted)," as quoted by Rossetti. He calls some of Conway's reminiscences of his visits to Walt "an incredible mixture of dream and error."

> the poet's home; the furniture of his room, with the pictures of
> Silenus and Bacchus (wholly imaginary) and . . . that mon-
> strous fable, which I see you have been led to adopt in your article
> in the *Zeitung*, about his lying on his back in the sun at a tempera-
> ture of one hundred degrees Fahrenheit, staring at the noonday
> blaze!

O'Connor goes on to explain the special circumstances under which his *Good Gray Poet* was written, admitting that some passages were inserted for effect.[30]

The Rossetti edition of Walt Whitman's poems led to an interesting friendship and an influential essay. Anne Gilchrist, widow of the biographer of Blake, whose book she completed after her husband's death, read the Rossetti volume and promptly wrote to him: "Since I have read it, I can read no other book; it holds me entirely spellbound, and I go through it again and again with deepening wonder and delight."[31] Rossetti replied, ". . . that glorious man Whitman will one day be known as one of the greatest sons of Earth, a few steps below Shakespeare on the throne of immortality. What a tearing-away of the obscuring veil of use and wont from the visage of man and of life." He defends his leaving out some of the poems, and offers to send her the complete *Leaves of Grass* and a letter that Whitman had sent him on December 3, 1867.[32]

Later Rossetti sent her letter to O'Connor (copied in his own hand, for he wished to keep the lady's identity a secret, and feared that her handwriting might be recognized by someone). Whitman, greatly pleased by her letter, responded to Rossetti in a letter which he hoped Rossetti would show the lady. Under separate cover he sent a photograph of himself for her.[33]

Anne Gilchrist's letters to Rossetti were so eloquent that he suggested that she combine them into an article to be published in the United States, where a woman's praise of Whitman's poetry would be important for his reputation.[34] Rossetti sent her article, "A Woman's Estimate of Walt Whitman," to O'Connor who tried to place it in an American publication. He first approached *The Galaxy*, which had printed Burroughs's review at his request, but the editor declined, although he did say he had gained a high opinion of the lady whose words are quoted. O'Connor finally succeeded in placing it in *The Radical*,[35] a publication of the Radical Club, a Boston group which included many ministers and laymen who were advanced Unitarian and Transcendental thinkers. *The Radical*, which was published from 1865 to 1872, had among its contributors Moncure Conway, Thomas Wentworth Higginson, James Freeman Clarke, and Bronson Alcott. Except for Higginson, all of these were friendly to Whitman. The editors proved their friendship by publishing "An English Woman's Estimate of Walt Whitman," the author's name not given, with an introduction by Rossetti. (Incidentally, Rossetti had given O'Connor permission to alter his introduction if he wished to do so.)[36]

Anne Gilchrist's article pleased O'Connor, for it was completely and unequivocally enthusiastic. Unlike Rossetti in his article and preface, Anne Gilchrist accepted the poet at his own evaluation and interpreted his poems as being pure and moral. Of the language of the poems, she wrote: "the poor old words that have served so many generations for purposes, good, bad, and indifferent, and become warped and blurred in the process, grow young again, regenerate, translucent. . . ." From the woman's point of view she writes of the forbidden subjects:

> It must surely be man's fault, not God's that she has to say to herself, "Soul, look another way—you have no part in this. Motherhood is beautiful, fatherhood is beautiful; but the dawn of fatherhood and motherhood is not beautiful." Do they really think that God is ashamed of what he has made and appointed?

She writes of "Calamus" as "evangel-poems of comrades and of love," and of "Children of Adam"—"these beautiful, despised poems"—as glowing with the "light of a clear, strong faith in God, of an unfathomably deep and tender love for humanity. . . ."[37]

Anne Gilchrist had fallen in love not only with the book but with the man. On first opening Rossetti's edition of Whitman's poetry and seeing the engraving of the author's portrait, she exclaimed: "Here at last is the face of Christ, which the painters have so long sought for."[38] Her first letter to Whitman, on September 3, 1871, was a love letter:

> In May, 1869, came the voice over the *Atlantic* to me—O, the voice of my Mate: it must be so—my love rises up out of the very depths of the grief & tramples upon despair. I can wait—any time, a lifetime, many lifetimes—I can suffer, I can dare, I can learn, grow, toil, but nothing in life or death can tear out of my heart the passionate belief that one day I shall hear that voice say to me, "My Mate. The one I so much want. Bride, Wife, indissoluble eternal!' "[39]

In her third letter (October 23) she was more explicit:

> I am yet young enough to bear thee children, my darling, if God should so bless me. And would yield my life for this cause if it were so appointed, if that were the price for thy having a "perfect child."[40]

Her ardor must have frightened Whitman; he received three letters before he answered her; then on November 3, he wrote in a rather stilted manner:

But I must at least show without further delay that I am not insensible to your love. I too send you my love. And do you feel no disappointment because I now write so briefly. My book is my best letter, my response, my truest explanation of all. In it I have put my body & spirit. You understand this better & fuller & clearer than anyone else. And I too fully & clearly understand the loving letter it has evoked. Enough that there surely exists so beautiful & delicate a relation, accepted by both of us with joy.[41]

Anne Gilchrist was stricken: "Ah, that word 'enough' was like a blow on the breast," she wrote, and reiterated her love for him.[42] She finally realized that she would have to content herself with his friendship, at first through correspondence and later in person. In the early autumn of 1876 she came to Philadelphia with her children, Beatrice, Grace, and Herbert. They were near enough to Camden where Whitman was then living to see him frequently. She stayed until the spring of 1878, when she moved to Boston, and finally left the United States in 1879.

Whitman named her among his "friends of my other soul, my poems" and called her his "noblest woman friend," yet he was never able to reciprocate her emotional response to him.[43]

With his success in placing Anne Gilchrist's article in 1870, O'Connor's labors on Whitman's behalf ceased for a while, although the friendly meetings at the O'Connor home continued until a fateful day two years later when their friendship and the pattern of their lives were interrupted by a shattering quarrel.

Notes

1. 17 September 1855, in Moncure Daniel Conway, *Autobiography: Memories and Experiences* (Boston: Houghton Mifflin, 1904), vol. I, pp. 215–16.
2. See note 10, below.
3. Information based on Conway's autobiography (see note 1 above).
4. (Yale).
5. See note 10 below.
6. Ohio Wesleyan.
7. The ms. is at Yale University.
8. This handwritten memorandum consists of notes by Whitman. (Berg).
9. Fragment of letter in the Dickinson College Library, which appears from internal evidence to have been sent by O'Connor to Conway at this time. Sent to the author by Dickinson College at the suggestion of Charles Feinberg.

10. See Randall H. Waldron, "Walt Whitman's British Connection: Letters of William Douglas O'Connor." *The Papers of the Bibliographical Society of America*, 75, (Third Quarter 1981).
11. *Correspondence*, I: 297.
12. (Yale).
13. (Berg).
14. Three O'Connor letters—27 May 1866, 7 February 1867, 23 May 1867—were published by the American Autograph Shop in *The Book Hunter*, May 1934. They are now at Ohio Wesleyan University.
15. This Introduction in manuscript form was among some papers and letters which Whitman showed to his young friend Horace Traubel on a day in June in 1888. It consisted of four pages in Whitman's handwriting (Morgan Library).
16. Conway to WW, 10 September 1867. *Camden*, 3:267–68.
17. Harold W. Blodgett, *Walt Whitman in England* (Ithaca: Cornell University Press, 1934), pp. 14, 15.
18. 27 July 1867, *Correspondence*, I: 335.
19. Blodgett, *op. cit.*, p. 22.
20. *Ibid.*, p. 22.
21. *Ibid.*, p. 24.
22. *Correspondence*, I: 346–47.
23. *Ibid.*, 347–49.
24. *Ibid.*, 350–51.
25. *Ibid.*, 352–54.
26. *Correspondence*, II:13.
27. *Ibid.*, 16.
28. 16 December 1867. *Camden*, 3:307.
29. (Boston: The Gorham Press, 1915), p. 221.
30. 16 November 1868 (Perry).
31. *Anne Gilchrist: Her Life and Writings*, ed. Herbert H. Gilchrist with prefatory note by William Michael Rossetti, 2nd ed. (London: T. Fisher Unwin, 1887), p. 177.
32. *Ibid.*, pp. 178–79.
33. 9 December 1869, *Correspondence*, II: 91.
34. *Letters of William Michael Rossetti concerning Whitman, Blake, and Shelley to Anne Gilchrist and her son Herbert Gilchrist*, ed. Clarence Gohdes and Paul Franklin Baum (Durham, North Carolina: Duke University Press, 1934), 13 July 1869, p. 28.
35. James Dittart, *The Oxford Companion to American Literature* (London: Oxford University Press, 1941), p. 620.
36. *Letters of Rossetti, op. cit.*, p. 47.
37. *In Re WW*, pp. 41–55.
38. Edward Carpenter, *Days with Walt Whitman, with some Notes on his Life and Work* (London: George Allen & Unwin, Ltd., 1906), p. 17.
39. *Correspondence*, II: 136.
40. Gay Wilson Allen, *The Solitary Singer* (New York: The Macmillan Co., 1955), p. 437.
41. *Correspondence*, II: 140.
42. Allen, *op. cit.*, p. 439.
43. "Going Somewhere," *LG/CRE*, p. 525.

CHAPTER XIV

Decade Of Devotion

FROM 1862 when Walt Whitman came to Washington until 1872 when he and William O'Connor quarreled, William Douglas O'Connor's life was centered in his friendship for and defense of Whitman. The poet, short-story writer, and novelist had been submerged in the plodding government clerk who became his former enthusiastic self when he was with Walt or when he was planning for the defense of *Leaves of Grass*. During the years between 1861, when he finished his story "The Brazen Android," and 1870, he used his facile pen and fervent rhetoric only in defense of Walt Whitman, Elizabeth Akers Allen ("Florence Percy"), Victor Hugo, and his fellow clerks. In a comparable period of time O'Connor had written and published many poems, five short stories, and a novel.

The reasons for O'Connor's abandonment of his earlier interests may lie in his volatile temperament. He was easily elated—and easily cast down; the heights of his appreciation of others were matched by the depths of his self-depreciation.[1] Like Walt, he needed the admiration and love of those about him, but unlike Walt he had no faith in himself. "I have never really written anything except on the spur, or for some occasion: hence nothing of any moment. . . . For years now, I have seemed to be like one whirled along by a strong wind—always in a hurry. . . ."[2]

When he came to Washington to get a government job, his self-esteem was at a low point. His novel *Harrington*, which he had written with high hopes, was wiped out by the failure of Thayer and Eldridge as thoroughly as if it had never been written. The periodical which Thayer and Eldridge contemplated and in which they would have engaged his help was never to be launched. Letters about possible literary employment (to Curtis and Wood) had brought negative answers.[3] He went to Washington burdened by the need to take any kind of job.

O'Connor may have been pleased when he received a temporary clerkship at $1,200 a year, and when it became permanent (in February 1862) at $1,600 a year. It must have been discouraging, however, to remain a clerk of the third class at the same salary until July 1871. The inadequacy of this salary and the way of life it necessitated he described in his report on "The Salaries of Clerks."[4]

The duties of a clerk consisted in taking care of correspondence. All letters were written by hand, and William had to write hundreds of them each week. He would hardly write for pleasure at the end of a day's work, though he could do so when deeply stirred by an injustice suffered by a friend.

William did have some opportunities to leave government service for the literary life he would have preferred. Henry Raymond, editor of *The New York Times*, wrote to him twice about coming to work on his newspaper. On April 2, 1866 he wrote, "I am quite sure you could easily make $3,000 or $3,500 a year & labor much more to your taste than what you are now doing. I should very much like to have the benefit of your pen in the *Times*." The following month Raymond wrote, "I have been really hard at work . . . trying to put a little more life and variety into the *Times*. If I knew better your taste and readiness in paragraphing—I would not hesitate to make a bid for your pen. Your head is full of information and you tell it tersely & sharply. If you can write on several topics—men, books, and things,—as readily as you talk you could earn here more than there. I appreciate fully your wish for a *certain* income; chance writing is very unsatisfactory & unsafe. I wish you were in a position to *try your hand* a little in writing for a newspaper."[5]

William did not completely give up the idea. A year later he came to New York to see Raymond about writing for the *Times*. (On this trip to New York he met Walt's mother, who was much taken with him.)[6] He must have been sorely tempted to take his chances with the *Times*, especially since he was so unhappy with his job, and according to Raymond, might earn much more than his salary as a government clerk. Grace Channing gives as the reason for his reluctance Nelly's need for security; a steady income, however small, meant too much to her to risk losing it. According to Grace Channing, her Aunt Nelly was

an exceptional and extraordinary woman, and the very last a man of imagination or genius should have married. It is enough to say of her that while she made an incomparable hostess and was the understanding friend of all the brilliant circle which nightly adorned her house, her conscientious attitude towards life, as it affected her, was that one should not give up a certainty for an uncertainty. She was expressly and particularly framed to see life from the opposite standpoint of O'Connor and to quietly and unviolently frustrate every attempt of his native talent. She was the best stifler of self-expression in others I have ever known. Against the calm rock of her opposition, the great waves of his aspirations beat in vain. They ought to have separated as quickly as possible. But that was the last thing my aunt would have thought of, and the pride of the Irishman kept O'Connor chained to an office chair. . . . Outside the family she passed in later years for a saint. Inside the family *this* passed for a joke. We loved her, but we appraised her more justly. I never heard her raise her voice; the smile rarely left her lips; but against her quiet inflexibility armies might be shattered. . . .

Grace Channing wrote that when the offers came from Raymond, "O'Connor met that smiling steadfastness of opposition. 'It was not wise to risk a certainty for an uncertainty,' to abandon office life for literature. Poor lady. He stayed, but I think he never forgave it; that then and there the marriage ended in all that counted."[7]

With coldness between him and his wife, how much more Walt's friendship meant to William—and to Nelly too. No need for him to suffer resentment or for her to take refuge in self-righteousness when all could be forgotten in the excitement of Walt's presence, in emotional and intellectual group discussions, and in Nelly's and William's joint desire for Walt's success.

They were also one in their love for little Jeannie and in their concern for her health. During the summer of 1867, just after William had refused Raymond's offer, Jeannie was quite ill; tuberculosis was suspected, and she had swelling of the knee joints which caused lameness.[8] The affectionate portrayal of the lame child Lilian in

"The Carpenter," the story which William wrote that summer, shows his love for his daughter.

Depressed by what he saw as the death-knell of his own ambitions as a writer and finding little warmth in his marriage, it is not surprising that William should have thought that the best use of his talent would be in service to Walt, whose genius and destiny were, in his eyes, glorious. At O'Connor's urging, the editor of *The Galaxy* not only published Burroughs's review of *Drum-Taps* but also later accepted one of Whitman's poems and two of his essays.[9] When John R. Gilmore, about to embark on the publication of a new magazine, the *Continental Monthly*, wrote in October 1866, asking O'Connor to become one of his contributors, he answered:

> I am sadly immersed in official cares here but I will endeavor to do what I can for you. . . . You tell me you mean to allow "the utmost freedom of speech." I therefore venture to ask if you will admit, from me, an article on my friend Walt Whitman's "Leaves of Grass." You know, probably, since everybody seems to know, what I think of that work. I regard the critical notice it has received as the literary disgrace of the century.[10]

Later that month O'Connor acknowledged Gilmore's reply, saying, "You answer me very kindly and properly. I will endeavor to do what I can for you."[11] There is no record, however, of any contribution of O'Connor or of Whitman in the *Continental*.

After O'Connor helped to place Anne Gilchrist's essay on Walt Whitman in *The Radical* in 1870, he was not to write on the poet's behalf for another six years. Perhaps he felt that with the recognition in England of Whitman's poetry there was no further need of his efforts. Perhaps the periodicals here had done all they wanted to do for the poet. Or, as seems likely, he was somewhat disillusioned by Whitman's acceptance of the changes in the English edition of words in the Preface and the elimination of many poems. Even the title, *Leaves of Grass*, was not to be found there.

When O'Connor next attacked an enemy in a periodical it was not in defense of Whitman but of Victor Hugo, and the writer whom he attacked was John Burroughs, Whitman's friend and his. O'Connor, who Trowbridge said could have been "our American Hugo,"[12] greatly admired the French author. Burroughs had had an article in

Appleton's Journal, "More About Nature and the Poets," on September 10, 1870. O'Connor's rejoinder was published on November 5.[13] Robert Carter, editor of *Appleton's*, called it "very long for the subject, & very frantic in parts," but accepted it nevertheless.[14]

In his opening paragraphs O'Connor speaks of the

> strain of hostility toward that heroic cycle of composition which shames our poor literary sand-grown scrub with its vast and dazzling sheaves of masterpieces. Your essayist is no exception, though, from one whose gift of sympathy and insight enables him to perceive the cosmical grandeur of Walt Whitman's poetry, I should have expected something like a corresponding apprehension of the writings of the illustrious Frenchman.

In taking issue with Burroughs, O'Connor states that Hugo sees "not beautiful Nature merely, but cosmical Nature as well." He closes with a slash at Burroughs:

> To criticize Victor Hugo in such a strain, if it does not betoken a singular unacquaintance with his writings, certainly shows a total lack of insight regarding them; while to style their lofty and glowing pictures and interpretations of things "a sort of mad-dog Nature," is simply to lose truth in epigram, and epigram in absurdity.

In addition to this published article on Hugo, O'Connor had written a very long reply (over 3,000 words) to an unfavorable review in *The Nation* of "L'Homme Qui Rit" on December 9, 1866. That periodical, always unfriendly to O'Connor and Whitman, did not publish his rejoinder. O'Connor also translated a few of Hugo's poems, which are to be found among his papers, together with other material about Hugo. O'Connor revealed the depth of his admiration for Hugo in a letter to Stedman on April 23, 1876.[15] This letter reveals also O'Connor's conception of his relationship to Whitman—which he flatly denies was one of "discipleship."

> Champion, yes—with all my might, to my utter-most ability; but "disciple," no. Nor can I see that Walt has any "disciples" among the group that defends him and his book. John Burroughs comes nearer that than any of us, but I couldn't admit it, even of him. Indeed, my dear, you can't fail to notice that Walt had founded no

school, as, for example, Victor Hugo has; nor can you fail to see that all our writing for him is in a strictly *defensive* tone. If, therefore, we young men *defend* him, solely, against attacks we think not only unjust but outrageous; almost always doing it, with expressed reservations or qualifications as to his art or doctrines (sometimes injurious, as admissions—witness Dowden's, Buchanan's, Sanborn's, etc.) and never, *in any case*, imitating his methods of expression, or adopting more than is reasonable, his views; you can't possibly justly call us "Disciples," any more than you could Ruskin for his perfectly "judgmatical," unbiased, and confirmed, defence of Turner; or Boccaccio for his passionate vindication of Dante; or the poet of the Shakespeare Sonnets for his lavish praise of Spenser. We simply recognize in Walt a poet of vast genius; different obviously, in kind and degree from other respected poets of our time; and with an aim and scheme, avowedly loftier; and after he has undergone ten years of the most determined and terrific abuse and ill treatment, culminating in his ignominious dismissal from a public office, and has been, for all that decade, as you ought to recollect, almost wholly without defense, we begin a movement, commencing with my pamphlet, strenuously resisting the attempt to crowd him down. We are, therefore, simply his champions, and no more. For my own part, I am far more a "disciple" of Lord Bacon's, (you know I think he is Shakespeare) and my sense of his supremacy is just tremendous; and Victor Hugo, though I don't allow him greater than Walt, is certainly far nearer to my sympathies, individually, as a poet; so that I could far more justly be called a "disciple" of either than of W.W.

Years later, O'Connor again linked Hugo and Whitman:

. . . France, as in the magic mirror of Agrippa, in all the horror and grandeur of the feudal past, the revolutionary combat and anguish of the present, the superb promise of the future, and in the supreme glory of compassion which streams from the poet's mighty heart, lives in the poetry, the drama, the romance of the illustrious Victor Hugo; but in what poem have all the things which make up the show of a people's life appeared with such comprehensive and vivid reality, such national distinctiveness and such strength of charm, as in *Leaves of Grass*? . . .[16]

At the time that O'Connor's article on Victor Hugo appeared, he wrote a poem that was very different in spirit, that seemed, indeed,

to hark back to the work of "Aramis" in youthful lightness of spirit—
"To Fanny," accepted by the *Atlantic Monthly* on November 1,
1870 and published in February 1871. In sending the proof, William
Dean Howells, the editor, wrote, "Your poem, which I liked so much
in Ms., is even more charming in print. . . . Be so good as to verify
all your outlandish proper names; otherwise I shall have an endless
job doing it."[17]

It would appear from this poem that William had found a new
love, or at least had become infatuated with a charming young lady.
That she was a real person is attested by John Burroughs who said to
his friend and biographer, Clara Barrus, " 'Fanny' will be aghast at
the images she has caused to arise in his fertile brain."[18] Her identity,
however, is unknown.

"To Fanny" is a captivating poem of intricate rhymes and fantastic images. In it O'Connor displays vast erudition with sparkling fan-
tasy and humor. Under the title appear the words *Allegretto
Capriccioso*—and so it would have to be read, even without this
direction. The poem, which fills eight pages of the *Atlantic Monthly*,
begins with the two-line stanza:

> Fanny, it's my belief
> You're the work of a witch and a thief!

The poem goes on to elaborate what kind of witch she was *not*;

> Not such a witch as revealed his doom in the war
> To the king, by the ghost, in the dwelling at hilled En Dor;
> Or stalked in Thrace, wrinkled, austere, acerb,
> With brazen sickle cropping the moonlit herb;
> Nor she, against the abyss of the night descried,
> Throned on the ragged rock on the mountainside,—
> The invoker of carnage, black, with fire-eyed glare,
> Grand in the depths of the livid and trembling air.

Unlike all the wicked witches of the past, the witch who was the
creator of Fanny is a

> little witch-Queen of May,
> Funny and fair and good . . .
> a maid of honor to Cupid god
> . . . a fairy girl of the period,

> Foreign to horror and melancholy,
> And guiltless of any uncanny proceeding.
> Fond, to be sure, of the latest fashion;
> Silks and laces and gems her passion:
> Fond as well of the flower-bright lawn,
> Bluebird, spring-time, star, and dawn.
> And as for a broomstick, there you can trust her:
> My lady, indeed, as it might be presumed,
> Wouldn't mount upon less than peacock-plumed,
> Ivory-handled parlor duster!

As for the thief who had something to do with Fanny's creation, he is unlike all the wicked thieves of history and legend. He is a "little minikin thief," who

> . . . could steal with sweet dexterity
> The honey bag from the rapiered bee,
> Quicker than you can say to me,
> Honorificabilitudinity!
> He could steal the lash from the eye of a star,
> Or the sparkle out of the heart of a spar;
> He could steal the fame from a conqueror's name,
> And shame and blame from a noble aim,
> Next to impossible feats, I claim.
> Naught you might guard with Solomon's seal,
> Or dog or police, but he could steal;
> Steal as surely as high desire.
> Eagle ambition and hope like fire,
> Beauty and health and the heart for strife,
> And the glory and perfume and grace of life,
> Are stolen, and vainly sought when gone,
> By a Government office in Washington.

(This was surely a sad commentary on what its author thought of his job.)

The thief and the witch joined to produce the lovely lady: The thief stole camellias from a grand conservatory;

> The bright witch, smiling and debonair,
> Sat, and charmed in the magic night,
> The petals into a lady white,—
> Glowing white and fair.
> Still they bloom, brilliant and fresh,

In your camellia flesh;
They are the splendor and grace
Of your japonica face;
And the glossy camellia leaves are seen
In the dress you wear of silken green.

The thief then stole the wild, white rose, of whose perfume her
face was molded, the amber halo of the moon for her hair, and the
geranium and the pomegranate for her lips.

Seeing you, O young Eve-dressed-well!
Grace-diabolical! Peri-belle!
A-la-mode angel! Siren-child!
Dandy-dryad!—enrapt, beguiled,
I feel at the time of your origin,
That the witch and the thief were themselves mixed in!

The poem ends with the prophecy that the time will come when
among the lovers she has bewitched,

One in turn bewitches you,
And another heart secures
By completely stealing yours!

"To Fanny" had a mixed reception. O'Connor kept cuttings of
several reviews, not all identified.[19] One called the poem "a brilliant
and fantastic piece of versification; every line of it worth reading,
and much of it worth studying. It is in itself a bewitching bit of
witchcraft." The *Evening Transcript* (January 17, 1871) reprinted
one of the passages of this "long and rather remarkable poem."
Another unidentified review, however, speaks of O'Connor's lines
"which we think we have never seen equalled in worthless and offensive absurdity by any contribution to any magazine."

The *Leavenworth* (Kansas) *Times* was most laudatory; its author
was obviously a friend who dissents from the adverse criticisms the
poem has received: He says, in part: "He uses the vast learning his
mind is stored with perfectly, and writes with a fancy and grace no
American poet has equalled. Shelley would have given the author of
some of the stanzas in 'Fanny' a most brotherly greeting." Nevertheless, the reviewer closes with the suggestion that O'Connor go back
to writing prose, such as his successful *The Good Gray Poet*.

Osgood and Company, publishers of the *Atlantic*, sent a check for $100 in payment for "To Fanny";[20] and it must have been clear to the author that he could never make his fortune by writing. An excerpt from "To Fanny" was published in Volume 9 of Stedman's *Library of American Literature*, so that it became one of O'Connor's writings to be widely known at that time.

Whether or not Nelly knew that there was a "Fanny" who had captivated her husband, she surely knew that her marriage "had ended in all that counted."[21] In the month that "To Fanny" was accepted by the *Atlantic Monthly*, but before it was published, she turned to Walt Whitman for emotional sustenance. She expressed her love for him in the following letter (quoted verbatim and with the original punctuation):

Providence, R.I.
Nov. 20th 1870.

Dear Walt,

My very dear friend—It is good to feel so assured of one's love as not to need to express it, & it is very good to know that one's love is never doubted or questioned, & for these reasons it is I am sure that we do not write to each other. I always know that you know that I love you all the time, even though we should never meet again, my feeling could never change, and I am *sure* that you know it as well as I do. I do flatter myself too, that *you* care for *me*,—not as I love you, because you are great and strong, and more sufficient unto yourself than any woman can be,—besides you have the great outflow of your pen which saves you from the need of personal love as one feels it who has no such resource. You could not afford to love other than as the Gods love; that is to love *every body*, but no one enough to be made unhappy, or to lose your balance. You know that Hector Tyndale was always preaching that to us, to be like the Gods.   But however it is with you—it is very good sometimes for me to try to tell those that are very dear to me how I like them.   And ever since I left home I have had it in my heart to write you,—but it has been postponed, waiting for the more fitting time. It is only when I am away from you that I am conscious of how deeply you have influenced my life, my thoughts, my feelings, my views—*myself* in fact, in every way, you seem to have permeated my whole being. And knowing you as intimately as I do I find myself constantly wondering and thinking how such or such a thing seems to you, what your ideas are in relation to this or that.

I find too, that the estimate in which persons hold you is a sort of test of them to me all the time. My friend Mrs. Mitchell with whom I was at Nantucket, said to me one day, "I see plainly that if I am to remain in your good graces, I am to come to the knowledge and love of your friend Walt Whitman," she said that she could see that I made it a test in some sort.

Every where, as usual, I find some who ask me about you, & who want to hear of you. I have enjoyed very much reading the "Passage to India" the other I lent as soon as it came and it has not yet been returned. Thank you for both. I shall have to scold you for some portion of the arrangement—but that I will reserve till I see you. I always feel refreshed and stronger for reading your poems, they seem so sane, so sweet, so human and healthy. But more than all your poems, more than all you ever can write, *you* are to me; yet they were very much to me before I knew you. It is good to have my love for them rounded by knowing you, and finding my feeling and thought about you justified. I have sometimes suffered very deeply, but I feel that I have been dealt very kindly by, and had more than fullest compensation in the great privilege of knowing you, and being permitted to be with you as I have.

I hope that the good angels who take care of us will for long, long yet spare us to each other. And you must be very good and come often to see us. You must not neglect the golden opportunity of letting me love you and see you all that is possible. I think that I must have been very good at some time to have deserved such a blessing.

Very soon I hope to see you now, very soon, till then good by. Jeannie sends much love to you, so does my sister Jeannie. My Jeannie has grown to be a tall girl, & is very graceful sometimes in her manner, as you used often to tell me that she would be. She is quite womanly about some things. She longs to be at home, though she enjoys her cousins.

I, too, quite long to be with you all. Soon I shall be. (D.V.) Good by.

With love ever—
Your affectionate
Nelly

I came near forgetting to send you a letter which I cut from a Boston paper on purpose to send you. It is the account of the death of those persons who were overtaken by the snow storm in the mountains. The diary is to me very touching, the simple manly, unflinching tone of what that dying man wrote is to me very noble, I can't read it once without the tears blinding my eyes. It is such a scene, he alone in that mountain pass with no hope of escape and the snow falling in fearful quantities. It is one of the *loneliest* pictures that I ever conceived. As I read it I thought of you.

Good by again.
With love Nelly.[22]

Walt Whitman's reaction to this letter is not known, nor was there any reference to it by William O'Connor. If he had seen it, in his own bitter and frustrated mood, might it have been one of the sparks that ignited the quarrel? Or would he have accepted Nelly's love for Walt as the poet's due? The quarrel, which seemed to spring full-blown in 1872, may have had its roots several years earlier.

NOTES

1. Whitman: "Poor O'Connor! He had 'em.' [the blues] Would get 'em in the most violent way . . . it was constitutional with him." *Camden*, 5: 165. See also *Camden*, 6: 456. O'Connor himself had noted: "I am so self-distrustful, self-accusing, self-depreciating, that praise, if it is intelligent, often has a good tonic effect on me. I say, if it is intelligent, for I have often been terribly upset and cast down by being extolled ridiculously." WDO'C to Burroughs, 15 May 1876 (*Comrades*, p. 131).
2. WDO'C to Bucke, 26 August 1880 (Feinberg-LC).
3. Curtis to WDO'C, 17 February 1860 (Harvard). WDO'C to Wood, 17 February 1860 (Historical Society of Pennsylvania.).
4. (Feinberg-LC).
5. Raymond to WDO'C, 2 April 1886, and 6 May 1866 (Berg).
6. WW to WDO'C, 5 May 1867, *Correspondence* I: 328–29. For O'Connor's feeling about Mrs. Whitman as "Madonna grown old," see *Camden*, 3:522.
7. Grace Channing, unpublished memoir (Chamberlin).
8. WDO'C to Piatt, 18 June 1867 (Historical and Philosophical Society of Ohio).
9. Poem: "A Carol of Harvest for 1867" (later called "The Return of the Heroes"), *Galaxy*, September 1867. Essays: "Democracy" (December 1867); "Personalism" (May 1867).
10. WDO'C to Gilmore, 13 October 1866 (Johns Hopkins).
11. WDO'C to Gilmore, 26 October 1866 (Johns Hopkins).
12. John Townsend Trowbridge, *My Own Story* (Boston and New York: Houghton Mifflin and Company, 1904), p. 375.
13. "Victor Hugo's 'Nature,' " *Appleton's Journal*, 4: 550–52 (5 November 1870).
14. Carter to WDO'C, 19 September 1870 (Feinberg-LC).

15. (Columbia.) I am indebted to Robert Scholnick for sending me a copy of this letter. One evidence of O'Connor's criticism of Whitman is in reference to a Whitman article in the *North American Review:* "I only wish the style was a little clearer. I like better your earlier manner, so free from sub-clauses, involutions, parentheses—so direct and simple. In this country, in this age, when the necessity is upon us of addressing the whole people, and not the college professors or bookmen merely, I set extreme value upon communication." *Camden,* 2: 14.

16. "Mr. O'Connor's Letter," in R. M. Bucke, M.D., *Walt Whitman* (Philadelphia: David McKay, 1883), p. 97.

17. Howells to WDO'C, 2 December 1870 (Feinberg-LC).

18. Clara Barrus Scrapbook (from David Goodale).

19. (Feinberg-LC).

20. (Feinberg-LC).

21. Grace Channing, *op. cit.*

22. (Feinberg-LC). This letter was first published in full by William White in *The Long-Islander,* 25 May 1967, Sec. 2, p. 6.

CHAPTER XV

Night Of
Dissolution

THE "FAINT clews and indirections"[1] pointing to a rift between Walt and William were not known—or at least not mentioned—by the loyal group which continued to meet with the old enthusiasm. The months in 1872 which preceded the climactic quarrel seemed to be carefree and happy. In January, William, Nelly, and their daughter Jeannie took a trip to Cuba as the guests of the owner of the Atlantic Mail Steamship Company.[2] (Throughout the years they had taken their vacations separately, Nelly and Jeannie often visiting the Channings during the summer when William was at work, and William visiting them at other times.)

In May 1872 Nelly, William, Walt, and John Burroughs all went on a picnic together, at the invitation of Dr. Frank Baker of the Smithsonian Institution. In the invitation the ladies, among them May Cole (the future Mrs. Baker) and Nelly O'Connor, were given the names *Hepatica*, *Spring Beauty*, and *Arbutus*. The men, among them John Burroughs, Walt Whitman, Colonel Stone, William O'Connor, and Frank Baker, were prosaically called *Lunch Consumers*. The invitation contained quotations from Shakespeare, Emerson, and Whitman—the last reading,

> Now I see the secret of the making of the best persons
> Is to grow in the open air, and to eat and sleep with earth.[3]

Later that year the break came. The approximate date could not have been earlier than August 1872 because Whitman was away from Washington during July. (On July 9 he applied for an extension of two weeks of his leave of absence from work.) On July 19, he wrote to Charles Eldridge, replying sympathetically to the news of William and his family who were all feeling ill, and assuring Nelly, "I shall return next week, & then I shall surely come to the house, & see you & all."[4] The quarrel may have occurred after his return, for in a letter to his mother on August 27, Walt tells her that Mrs. O'Connor has called upon him, but says nothing of William.[5] It seems more likely, however, that it happened in December when other provocations occurred. The argument which caused the break, according to John Burroughs in later reminiscences, had to do with Negro suffrage and Sumner's policies, with William, a fiery Abolitionist, feeling that the Negroes should exercise their vote immediately, and with Walt, always lukewarm about this issue, thinking that their enfranchisement should be a slow process.[6]

Bliss Perry, who years later interviewed Nelly and others in preparing his biography of Walt Whitman, wrote that the original cause was "a trivial though violent difference of opinion over the merits of Sumner's reconstruction legislation, which Walt had attacked and O'Connor defended till both men lost their tempers."[7] In Bliss Perry's notes of his talk with Nelly he wrote, "The story of their quarrel on the Civil Rights Bill is not to be published." This remark is followed by these notes:

> O'Connor and Whitman had a strong argument over the Civil Rights Bill. In these discussions both indulged in such strong personalities that Mrs. O'Connor was always afraid that something would be said which would never be forgotten. Whitman rather enjoyed stirring O'Connor up. He did not realize that Mr. O'C. cared any more than he did about these things, but Mr. O'C. was very sensitive and many things hurt. . . . It puzzles her to hear it said so often that he (Walt) never raised his voice in argument. This was so very different from her experience and certainly was not true of Whitman when she knew him.[8]

In her "Personal Recollections of Walt Whitman" which appeared in the *Atlantic Monthly* in June 1907, Nelly (then Mrs. Calder) wrote that the quarrel concerned the Fifteenth Amendment and took place in 1871,[9] but that hardly seems likely in view of the letters and the picnic of a later date.

John Burroughs, talking to Clara Barrus about a contemplated essay on O'Connor, said of the estrangement, "They were in the habit of goring each other like two bulls (in argument) and at that time Walt was, I guess, rather brutal and insulting. He took his hat & went home in a pet. When they met on the street the next day, Walt put out his hand, but William shied around him & went on. The iron had entered his soul."[10]

In a review of O'Connor's posthumously published *Three Tales*, Myron Benton, John Burroughs's friend, wrote: "There was a certain feather-edge to O'Connor's temperament, of which manifestation was in taking umbrage at some fancied offense on Whitman's part. This severed the intercourse; but even after the break he would, on occasion, in public print, fly chivalrously to his defense."[11]

If the quarrel took place in August,[12] the immediate spark that ignited it could have been a petition from a group of Negroes asking Sumner how to cast their votes in the election (Grant versus Greeley) and Sumner's answer favoring Greeley, both of which were published in the *New York Tribune* on July 31, 1872. This could have given rise to a serious disagreement between William, who was always devoted to Sumner, and Walt, not so impressed by him, and completely opposed to Greeley.

A more plausible date is December 1872. (There is little Whitman correspondence between August and December, and no letters in which there is any mention of Nelly or William.) There was an occasion for possible contention in December involving Sumner, who had returned from a visit to England and France on November 29. He attended the Senate for sixteen days ending December 18, when he left because of illness, not to return until March 1873. During those days he pressed without avail for his Civil Rights Bill which he had introduced in January 1872. This was a measure to secure equality of civil rights to the colored people, to prohibit discrimination against them by common carriers of passengers, by proprietors of theatres and inns, managers of schools, of cemeteries and of churches, and discrimination against their serving as jurors in any courts, state or national. Sumner had also proposed a bill to enforce equality in the schools of the District of Columbia.

An argument centering on Sumner would therefore have ranged from Civil Rights and educational equality to the Franco-Prussian War (in which Sumner had favored United States neutrality and opposed our shipping arms to France.) Another issue, which might have been meant by "Sumner's policies," was his proposal to erase from the Army Register the battles of the Civil War in order to help reconciliation between North and South. He made this proposal to the Senate on December 18, 1872—and was promptly censured officially by the Massachusetts legislature for having done so.

Knowing O'Connor's Abolitionist background, one may easily see that he would support Sumner's views on the Negro question. In addition, personal loyalty would reinforce this support. As early as 1860 O'Connor had included favorable mention of Charles Sumner in his novel *Harrington*. The publishers, Thayer and Eldridge, had sent a copy to Sumner with the request that he write an opinion of it for their use.[13] In 1861 Sumner was among those who sponsored O'Connor in his application for a government job when he came to Washington.[14]

That this friendship continued is revealed in two unpublished letters from Wendell Phillips to O'Connor:[15] On February 21, 1871 Phillips wrote that he was sorry to have missed O'Connor at Sumner's:

> Your visit was not lost—it came most opportunely. Sumner was not only pleased, but soothed & comforted by it. He spoke of it several times—& enlarged to Schurz and Boutwell on the pleasure he has in your talk. Sometime I'll tell your wife the warm compliments he paid you as always giving him great satisfaction in comparing views.
>
> So be glad you give a sick man, racked with pain, an easy hour & something especially pleasant to think of. . . .

After Sumner's death, Phillips wrote again in the same vein:

> By the by, did you know how kindly the Senator always spoke of you? with what hearty appreciation? Very shortly before his death he held forth on your curious learning & genius—& was moved almost to tears telling me of a visit you had then lately made him with consoling words & thoughtful kindness—you reached his heart—hard to be done but there was one—& beside a scholarly appreciation there was warm brotherly grateful regard—

Whitman knew, however, that Sumner could not accept his sympathy with the South:

I knew Sumner. I had spent a good deal of time in the South, off and on. Sumner seemed to know about it—once suggested that I should give him my impressions of Southern life and character. I went to Sumner but he would not stand for me—not a damned bit of it. My view of the South was a little bit favorable—this seemed to irritate him: he would not have it so: stormed, stormed, would not yield a point. I have no doubt there is just as much chivalry, consideration, of its own kind, north here as south—in expressing some approbation of the southern social spirit I did not intend to accuse Yankeedom. But Sumner would not have the applause on any terms—cast it out of court.[16]

Nor was Sumner among those who appreciated Whitman's poetry: "Sumner said to William once: 'Whitman would have been all right if he'd only written Democratic Vistas.' Phillips, too, it seems, told somebody that Leaves of Grass was a mistake."[17] In view of these opinions O'Connor's whole-souled championship of Sumner and his ideas and Whitman's opposition could easily have provoked a quarrel.

Most of Whitman's biographers referred to the quarrel, but none knew why the estrangement seemed irrevocable. The key circumstance of the quarrel was not revealed until 1965, when an unpublished memoir by William's niece, Grace Ellery Channing, came to light.[18] Grace, who was a writer, had wanted to write a biography of her adored uncle and made notes in preparation. Her notes begin:

No just biography of a great man can be written perhaps until those closely associated with him in life are gone. Not because time is needed for true perspective, but because the truth about any life is certain to wound somebody's susceptibilities rather brutally. . . .

For this reason Grace Channing would not have wanted to publish her biography or even a biographical sketch while her Aunt Nelly was alive. Her appraisal of her aunt's nature and personality, given earlier, would account for her reticence; but even more cogent was her account of the quarrel. It is set in a framework of her reminiscences of the two protagonists and the circle that surrounded them, among them LeBarnes, a lawyer, Edmund C. Stedman, the editor and writer, Hector Tyndale, Hubley Ashton, and George Bacon ("Aramis's" old friend "Athos"). Grace writes:

> . . . but all the rest were frankly subsidiary to the two friends, the two brilliant figures of Whitman and O'Connor, and to their deaths judgment was divided in the circle as to the relative greatness of the two.
>
> If the apple had been left for us children to award, there would have been no contest: Whitman had no chance beside that chevalier, the gallant Irishman. . . . Even Whitman's striking appearance (I used to think he looked like an amiable lion) suffered by comparision, in our eyes, with O'Connor's dark beauty. And he had none of my uncle's charm for childhood. One sat on his knee and allowed him to stroke one's curls, but always with an eye to wriggling away if D'Artagnan peeked at one from around the door—as he was very likely to do. His beautiful voice, low, rich, sonorous, musical . . . was charm enough. The poet sat and smiled upon the frolic—but he did not frolic himself. There was nothing of the Celt in Whitman and nothing of the courtier. O'Connor combined all things—and yet I never thought of him except as the most American thing I knew. . . .
>
> . . . I have known most of the great men of my own generation and not a few of this. . . . Against the background of them all flashes the brilliant . . . and now tragic figure, of the incomparable Irishman.

Of the talk that went on in the little parlor night after night, and the quarrel that ended it, Grace wrote:

> Conversation cannot have gone beyond that—before or since. It was not the Brahminical cult but the Olympian. One sign of it was the laughter; I have never heard such gaicty, such arrows of wit struck everywhere, and nothing and nobody was exempt. Governments, creeds, and civilizations were dealt with without remorse. Nothing that man had ever done or might attempt to do was left untouched. It was there I learned the boundless spaces of thought,—what a free mind means. Science, art, government, ethics, cultural values. And it was not one night—but every. . . .
>
> I thrilled and sometimes trembled, as the heavy artillery rolled over me, but always it broke at last in laughter and the tolerance of great minds. —Always until once. I remember one night my fa-

ther saying on our way home to my mother, "Well, what an evening; did you ever hear anything so wonderful in your life?" And her reply, "Too wonderful; some day the word too much will be spoken."

And suddenly,—with no warning, the end came: we were not to go to my uncle's house that night, that was all I knew. What I did not know was—that we were never to go again, in the old way. What had happened? The knowledge of what had happened came to me very slowly. The word too much had been spoken— and I had not even been aware of it,—it was so indistinguishably like other words. Naturally our elders tended to minimize it to us: perhaps they doubtless honestly hoped it would all blow over. I was under the impression for years that the difference between Whitman and O'Connor had been concerning the Franco-Prussian War. It was, according to my aunt who should have known, about Sumner's war policies. No more than that. But only those who had heard language exhausted over a mere Baconian difference, or the relative merits of two writers or two statesmen, could understand how easily the possible point could be over-stepped, and once over-stepped how final it must be.

Probably my mother was right; no group of people could continue forever to play with high explosives without a casualty. And given the magnitude of the two involved, it was bound to be a fatality as well. Whitman was arrogant; my uncle was proud as he was generous. He had literally spent himself upon Whitman; something the latter said outraged him. Whitman rose and took his hat and departed. My aunt took his part. Whereupon my uncle took his hat and departed. (Opinion was all divided. My parents, who remained warm friends with both combatants always, insisted that the poet had passed the permissible limits in his host's house.)

To me—it was the end of the world. What must it have been to them? Personally I believe it was the beginning of the end for both. It was like depriving them at a blow of the air they breathed, the nourishment by which they subsisted. All that circle on which Whitman leaned spiritually—. . . .

Whitman himself may have come to feel so, for some time after, meeting O'Connor on the street he held out his hand. O'Connor made him a low bow and passed on. *His heart and his home had been broken and he was in no mood to forgive. That was the end.* He (O'Connor) never returned except long after. . . . But with strict consonance with his conception of duty, his untouched pay envelope was delivered to my aunt every month. He lived on the narrow earnings he could make outside, only years afterward, when his pay was increased, retaining a few hundreds for himself.

Grace's account makes it clear that Whitman and O'Connor could not be reconciled after the quarrel, not because of its intensity but because it had caused the breaking up of O'Connor's home. Nelly's love letter to Walt, if William had seen it, may have added fuel to the fire when she agreed with Walt in the argument.

That O'Connor could not bring himself to shed any light on either the quarrel or the reconciliation is expressed in a letter to Burroughs:

It is better that Walt and I should not meet. But I have no feeling for him but affection and sorrow, and there never has been any time when I would have let harm I could prevent come to him or his belongings. You speak of "neglect," but this English testimonial grew from me, and I have always done what I could, though quietly. As for my letter in the "Tribune," it is, as service, just nothing, and nothing should be based upon it.

It is an awkward subject to write about, and I hope you will keep what I have said to yourself. The trouble between us I have never circulated, but it has been used against me by others, as reconciliation would be, and the matter is better as it is. Walt and I know our own feelings for each other, which is the best on my part, as I think it is on his; and here I rest. On reflection, you will agree with me, especially when you bear in mind that the interference of others gives the matter a complicated premise. Say nothing to any one.[19]

O'Connor's desire for secrecy was evidently adhered to by his friends. Charles Eldridge, planning to write reminiscences of Walt Whitman—which never appeared—wrote to Burroughs on March 7, 1896:

Of course I shall have to practice a degree of reticence about some matters. . . . For instance, how shall I treat that matter of his quarrel with William? Shall I ignore it, or just allude to it, or give all the details? These are just three courses open to me. What do you advise? Please think it over and let me know when you can find time to write to me.[20]

Burroughs's answer is not known, but Eldridge refers to it in his reply of April 4, 1896: "I was glad to hear what you thought about the quarrel of William and Walt, in regard to its treatment by me in my reminiscences. I shall undoubtly follow your advice, and will probably send you the whole manuscript for criticism and suggestion before I publish anything."[21]

How Whitman felt about the quarrel during the years of estrangement is not known. Years later he recognized and appreciated O'Connor's point of view on politics, saying to Horace Traubel:

> At that time, for the first two or three years of the War, O'Connor was warm, earnest, eager, passionate, warrior-like for the anti-slavery idea—immersed, sucked in, in a way that would have offended the deep and wise Emerson. This in some ways served to keep us apart—though not really apart—(superficially apart): I can easily see now that I was a great deal more repelled by that sentiment—by that devotion—in William—(for with him it was the profoundest moral devotion)—than was justified. With these latter-day confirmations of William's balance, of his choice, of his masterly decisions—the fruit of later eventuations—the later succession of events—there has come to me some self-regret—some suspicion that I was extreme, at least too lethargic, in my withdrawals from William's magnificent enthusiasm. Years have added lustre to the O'Connor of that day: some things I did not see then I see now. After all I may have been tainted a bit, just a little bit, with the New York feeling with regard to anti-slavery; yet I have been anti-slavery always—was then and am now, and to all and any other slaveries, too, black or white, mental or physical.[22]

Nelly, too, finally arrived at the opinion that William had been the injured one in the quarrel. Her sister, Jeannie Channing, when visiting Nelly almost two years after William's death, wrote to her daughter Grace:

> She [Nelly] had a letter from Dr. Bucke yesterday. He had expected to be here in May but will probably have to go to England instead. She said she was very sorry as she particularly wanted him to meet me, and especially on account of wanting him to hear from me the account of the beginning of the quarrel between Walt and W.D. And said again her "feeling is changed about it."

Jeannie Channing adds tartly:

> But why did she have to wait until Wm. had died to learn this. I think—always did—& so did your father that Walt grossly insulted your Uncle Wm. and in a house where he was the guest & your Uncle Wm. made no reply when Walt walked up in front of him & pointed his finger almost in Uncle W.D.'s face, said his say and walked out of the house.
>
> Until now I never heard anything but blame of your Uncle Wm. for the whole of it. I mean until this winter.[23]

It is difficult to assess the effect of the quarrel and estrangement on Walt Whitman and his poetry. In the case of the severance of close bonds between other men of letters such as those between Melville and Hawthorne, and between Conrad and Ford Madox Hueffer (Ford Madox Ford), a change in their writings can be traced to the break in these key relationships.[24] With Walt Whitman the quarrel was followed so closely by an attack of paralysis (and soon after that by other personal tragedies) that the quarrel cannot be isolated as a cause of a decline in poetic power. Yet it may be a major factor.

Grace Channing refers to the possible effect in her memoir:

> I am naturally alive to the tragedy of my uncle's side—but [*sic*] I suspect he really suffered the more, as a person. But I have often speculated on the quality of the disaster to Whitman. There was no replacing that little society: brains like those could not be duplicated—not those brains. There was no other D'Artagnan on the horizon. And those who had not taken sides, but remained mourning friends of both, could do nothing. They suffered enough. The interest of the world, however, is the effect on the poet. All that made his ambient was suddenly removed, and he must have suffered in the knowledge of the domestic tragedy. The kindling contact with other minds to which he had been so long accustomed—the special critical appreciation of his friend and champion, the loss of the next thing to home—must have profoundly affected anyone like Whitman—a man capable of great affection and a poet.
>
> He broke quickly after this and moved away. . . .

According to Whitman, his physician, Dr. Drinkard, diagnosed the attack of paralysis as the result of "the emotional disturbances to which I was subjected at that time."[25] Surely the chief disturbance at that time was the fight with O'Connor and the rift that ensued. Another break in the circle came when John Burroughs resigned from his government job at the end of December and moved back to New York State.[26] There is no hint that his moving away was connected with the quarrel—he had spoken three years earlier of his thought of resigning—but it may well be that the peace-loving, calm Burroughs was upset by the situation. During the spring Burroughs visited several times when in Washington to see about selling his house, but the almost daily companionship was gone.

Nelly O'Connor and Ursula Burroughs visited Walt during his illness, but they could not make up for the absence of their husbands. In Walt's correspondence with his mother, almost every letter contained something about a visit from Nelly. He wrote that, although at first he saw very few of his many callers, Nelly was among them. One day he wrote, "As I write Mrs. O'Connor is sitting here in the room, mending some stockings &c for me—she has brought me some nice roast apple in a tumbler." About a week later he wrote that she brought a basket of nice things. When he was able to go out, Nelly "convoyed" him, and one day Mrs. Burroughs took him out for a carriage ride. In his letter of March 21 he writes that Mrs. O'Connor has come in—"the first time in three days," which indicates that her visits had been almost daily ones.[27] When the doctor was considering some form of electric battery therapy, Nelly asked her brother-in-law, Dr. William Channing, who was both a physician and an inventor, to send Walt some material on this. On March 19 he sent a copy of the treatise on medical electricity he had written in 1849, and warned that electricity must not be used "while there is *existing lesion* of the brain or nerve centers." It might induce congestion, apoplexy or convulsions.[28] This type of treatment was postponed.

Walt's paralytic stroke was followed quickly by two other blows—the death of Martha, his brother Jeff's wife of whom he was very fond, on February 19, and the death of his beloved mother on May 23. During 1873 and 1874 Whitman began to write his reminiscences of the war years for the *Daily Graphic*; at first entitled "Tis But Ten Years Since," they later were called "Memoranda During the War." The six installments were published between January and March 1874. Nine years earlier O'Connor had written to Whitman about writing just such a book:

I got the Times with your long letter about the Hospital experiences, which I read with a swelling heart and wet eyes. It was very great and touching to me. I think I could mount the tribune for you on that and speak speech which jets fire and drops tears. Only it filled me with infinite regrets that there is not a book from you, embodying these rich and sad experiences. It would be sure of immortality. No history of our times would ever be written without it, if written with that wealth of living details you could crowd into it. Indeed it would itself be history.[29]

Later "Memoranda During the War" became part of "Two Rivulets" in the 1876 Centennial Edition, and was also issued as a separate book. As he prepared these reminiscences, did Whitman remember the words of his lost friend?

During this period of illness, loneliness, and discouragement Whitman wrote a poem in which he expressed his feelings through the image of a dying redwood tree. He had become familiar with the idea of death; early in 1874 he wrote to Nelly O'Connor: "Death has been much in my quiet thoughts & musings now for many months."[30]

In a poem he wrote at this time, "Prayer of Columbus," he identifies with the aging, ill Columbus, writing to Nelly, "As I see it now I shouldn't wonder if I have unconsciously put a sort of autobiographical dash in it—."[31] He portrays Columbus as "old, poor and paralyzed." The poem begins:

A batter'd, wreck'd old man,
Thrown on this savage shore, far, far from home,
Pent by the sea and dark rebellious brows, twelve dreary months,
I take my way along the island's edge,
Venting a heavy heart.

Despite his loneliness and illness Whitman retained his vision of the future, not only for nature and the world, but also for himself and his poems. He began to work on the Centennial Edition of *Leaves of Grass*. The quarrel, his illness, and his loneliness had combined to weaken his physical and his poetic power, but they had not destroyed him.

The effect of the quarrel on O'Connor is also difficult to assess, because it was followed immediately by the breakup of his home.

Not only was Walt no longer part of his life; there was no parlor to be the setting of the gatherings of old. Whatever his resentment against Nelly, he probably missed her, and he certainly missed the daily companionship of his beloved daughter Jeannie. (When she was older she frequently came to see him at his office.) Others sought him out at the Treasury Building and enjoyed his brilliant conversation—but there was no substitute for Walt and the old circle.

For Nelly these must have been difficult years. She may have thought she was only being fair in siding with Walt in the argument. Years later she wrote, "Unfortunately I have the gift of seeing both sides, being able to put myself in the other fellow's place, which makes me sometimes, as William once said angrily, 'no better than an enemy.' "[32]

Nelly, who loved having a house, had struggled throughout the years, living in two rooms when they first came to Washington. In 1868 they occupied half the house that John Burroughs built on V Street. (It was at this house that Walt began to have Sunday breakfasts at the Burroughses'.) Nelly and Ursula Burroughs did not get along very well, and the arrangement soon ended. (The misunderstandings continued; when Burroughs was abroad in 1871, he wrote to his wife: ". . . sorry you have been sick, and that you and William's family did not get along well. But let it pass.")[33]

After leaving the Burroughs home in 1868, Nelly and William had rented a little house at 1015 O Street—all for themselves—and Nelly was very happy with it. After the quarrel she had her house and William's salary for rent and other expenses. How hollow the "security" she had longed for must have seemed to her now!

The lonely O'Connor found some companionship and recreation in a club called The Gymnasium (dues one dollar per month) of which the president in 1873 was William C. Wood and the secretary Charles Eldridge. O'Connor was on the board of directors.[34] The Gymnasium had not only athletic equipment, but also a reading room with journals and newspapers. Since it was open until 10 P.M. it may have filled some of the empty evenings. In 1873 The Gymnasium issued a small, attractive pamphlet consisting of a 2,000-word essay by O'Connor on the importance of athletic activity. The essay, which begins with the Greeks, goes on to the age of chivalry, the influence of Rousseau, and the modern European practice. He cannot resist quoting Lord Bacon: " 'There is no disease that may not be cured, as there is no disease that may not be prevented, by gymnastics'—a remark the force and reach of which are only beginning to be perceived through the labors and writings of the great Swedish gymnasiarch, Ling."[35] It might have been appropriate to have quoted Whitman—but not in 1873 when the wound was still fresh.

O'Connor continued his interest in The Gymnasium. A folded leaflet in 1877 lists his name as Vice-President, with Wood still president and Eldridge secretary. The first page consisted of a humorous poem by O'Connor called "The Hermit" and an amusing drawing (one of the few examples of his art extant).[36]

At this time O'Connor may have derived some satisfaction from the fact that his government work was appreciated. From 1872 on he rose in rank and his responsibilities increased. On July 3, 1873, eighteen members of the staff petitioned that he be made Chief Clerk, and this was done on July 14. In January 1874 he was transferred temporarily to the office of the Secretary of the Treasury, with the salary of $2,000 per year. By July of that year, however, his salary was reduced to $1,800 because of a reduction in appropriations by Congress. In March 1875 he was assigned to the Customs Division of the Secretary's office, and within two weeks he was advised to report to Mr. S. I. Kimball, principal clerk of the Revenue Division of the Secretary's office. He became librarian of the Treasury Department, a position for which he was very well suited. In 1878 he was appointed Assistant General Superintendent of the Life-Saving Service at a salary of $2,500 per year, in which post he stayed for the rest of his life.[37] During these years O'Connor's reports, vivid though they were, surely could not have satisfied his urge to create.

Not having the need to write on behalf of Whitman, O'Connor should have seized the opportunity to write poems and stories, but he could not do so. He did submit two poems to Howells of the *Atlantic Monthly*, one in 1873 and another in 1874. There is no record of their titles or whether they were old or newly written. Howells, an old friend, sent friendly rejections: "Don't give up because I give up your poem. Perhaps my lyric moods are past, but this seems a trifle too indefinite," and a year later, "Not quite, but very near indeed. Let me see something else from the same machine.—I hope it won't abolish *your* handwriting."[38]

O'Connor was evidently not stirred to write again until he was needed as a defender, this time of the memory of Edgar Allan Poe; in his essay on Poe he stubbornly insisted on including favorable comment on Whitman—though they were still estranged—and by so doing sacrificed an opportunity to have his essay published.[39]

NOTES

1. WW, "When I read the book—the biography famous." *LG/CRE*, p. 8.
2. WW in letter to Rossetti, 30 January 1872, says O'Connor, wife and daughter are on a month's pleasure trip to Cuba. *Camden*, 4:61. Atlantic Steamship Co. to W.D.O'C, 15 January 1872 (Feinberg-LC).
3. Barrus, *Comrades*, p. 72.
4. *Correspondence*, II: 181–82.
5. *Correspondence*, II: 183.
6. Barrus: *Life and Letters* vol. I, p. 132.
7. Bliss Perry, *Walt Whitman. His Life and Work* (Boston and New York: Houghton, Mifflin Co., 1906) p. 212.
8. Copy of notes sent by David Goodale to the author.
9. Vol. 99, no. 6, p. 833.
10. Barrus, *Comrades*, p. 96.
11. *Atlantic Monthly*, 17: 184 (February 1892).
12. Suggested by Jerome Loving, *Walt Whitman's Champion: William Douglas O'Connor* (College Station, Texas: Texas A&M University Press, 1978), p. 95.
13. Sumner's copy of *Harrington* in the Harvard Library contains this letter dated 12 November 1860 (Harvard).
14. (General Services Administration).
15. (Feinberg-LC).
16. *Camden*, 1: 258.
17. *Camden*, 4:199.
18. (Chamberlin).
19. 4 May 1876 (Doheny Collection, at St. John's Seminary).
20. (Berg).
21. (Berg).
22. *Camden*, 3:75–76.
23. 31 December 1890 (Chamberlin).
24. Bernard C. Meyer, "Some Reflections on the Contribution of Psychoanalysis to Biography," *Psychoanalysis and Contemporary Science*, 1: 373–91 (1972). Dr. Louis Linn called my attention to this article. Edwin Haviland Miller, *Melville* (New York: George Braziller, Inc., 1975), "A Bond . . . Passing the Love of Woman," passim.
25. *Camden*, 4:472.
26. *Correspondence*, II: 208.
27. *Correspondence*, II: 193–95, 196, 205.
28. (Feinberg-LC).
29. 30 December 1864 (Feinberg-LC).
30. *Correspondence*, II: 268.
31. *Ibid.*, 272.

32. Ellen O'Connor Calder to Horace Traubel, 2 November 1906 (Feinberg-LC).
33. 28 October 1871, in Barrus, *Life and Letters*, p. 152.
34. Listed on inside title page of brochure, "The Washington Gymnasium," published in Washington by McGill & Witheron, 1873 (C. J. Furness to David Goodale to the author).
35. *Ibid.*, p. 9.
36. See note 34 above.
37. Notice from Treasury Department, 29 June 1878 (Goodale to author).
38. (Feinberg-LC).
39. WDO'C to SHW, fragment, n.d. (Feinberg-LC).

CHAPTER **XVI**

"The Time To Defend A Friend"

"THE TIME to defend a friend is when you have quarreled with him," O'Connor told his niece Grace Channing in explanation of his championship of Whitman during the period when they were estranged.[1] His first opportunity came in 1875. The occasion was the publication of a memorial volume to mark the reburial of Poe's remains and the dedication of a monument to him in Baltimore. The idea for the monument had originated with the Public School Teachers' Association of Richmond, Virginia in 1865. When the monument was ready, a public ceremony was held on November 17, 1875, to which many poets were invited—but only Walt Whitman came.[2]

A record of the ceremony has been preserved in the Whitman canon in an article in the *Washington Star* which has been attributed to Whitman himself.[3] The article was headed "Walt Whitman at the Poe Funeral." Under the subhead of "Conspicuous Absence of the Popular Poets" the article read:

> Being in Washington on a visit at the time, "the old gray" went over to Baltimore, and though ill from paralysis, consented to hobble up and silently take a seat on the platform, but refused to make any speech, saying: I have felt a strong impulse to come over and be here to-day myself in memory of Poe, which I have

266

obey'd, but not the slightest impulse to make a speech, which, my
dear friends, must also be obey'd.

Later, in an informal group, Whitman gave his views on Poe.[4]
At this time, Whitman sent Nelly a note:

> Tuesday, 9th Nov. 11 A.M.
>
> Dear Nelly,
>
> I am in Washington, stopping at Mr. & Mrs. Nash's L. st. south
> east, Navy Yard—am middling well, for me—shall be in pretty
> sure up to 10 A.M. & from 2 to 3 P.M. Am so fixed that it is very con-
> venient for my friends to call—Love to you.
>
> Walt W[5]

It has been said that at the Poe ceremonies O'Connor and Whitman saw, but did not greet, each other.[6] Nevertheless, William insisted that due credit—even homage—be given to Whitman for having been the only poet who appeared to do honor to Poe's memory.
Asked to contribute an essay to a memorial volume being prepared
by Miss Sarah Sigourney Rice in connection with the ceremonies,
O'Connor insisted upon including an encomium on Whitman.
He sent his article first to Sarah Helen Whitman, adopted all her
suggestions "except one,"[7] and sent it on to Miss Rice, who did not
want her volume compromised by the inclusion of a reference to
Whitman. Sarah Helen Whitman was inclined to agree, saying of
Miss Rice,

> She wants the rose without its thorns, it seems—the play of Ham-
> let with the part of Hamlet left out.—Well, I can hardly wonder.
> She says the article impressed her as a golden summer sunset,
> overhung with stormy clouds—and would like apparently to have
> the electricity drawn out of them. . . .
> I cannot advise you to pare down your magnus Apollo who
> certainly stands alone to the confusion of the other gods of the
> nineteenth century. I can't advise you to do it—but I can't help
> *wishing* that you *would.*
> If I thought you would consent to omit a few aggressive words
> about the recusant poets who were invited but didn't go, and
> didn't send polite answers,— to omit these things from the article

as published in the memorial and reprinted as it now stands *after-wards*, I should be *so glad*. You see that you are throwing down a gauntlet in the midst of a funeral service, as it were, beside an open grave. I dimly felt this all through but the splendid eloquence of your rhetoric silenced my misgivings.[8]

But William was adamant. In May, Miss Rice wrote that she hoped that he would not be too uncompromising and that she would still be able to include his letter.[9] In November, Helen consoled him with:

Certainly this feeble attempt at diplomacy is the coolest thing I ever read.

The book is evidently intended for the *hour* & the place—a Baltimore annual—only this & nothing more.

I am glad that your noble essay is not in it.[10]

Although Mrs. Whitman criticized the memorial volume when it appeared, she still hoped that O'Connor's letter might appear in a future edition.

In a letter to Mrs. Whitman of which a fragment remains, O'Connor wrote exasperatedly about Miss Rice,

. . . doesn't know *savoir faire*, which is a noble art and almost exclusively confined to "the d—d yankees." One thing Miss Rice ought to do. She ought to engage not to publish—*never*—my *ms.*, *which was written for that book and time*, should not now appear, and cannot, as a whole, without appearing ridiculous. If she would engage never to publish it to me, I would consent to her keeping the *ms.* for her private delectation, and as a souvenir, etc. Then I could feel like really using whatever in it is not ephemeral or for the occasion. But, you see, she still contemplates its publication, which shall never take place with my consent *now*, and if it takes place without my consent will be outrageous.

What you said to her was admirable, and I wonder she could resist you. You don't know how it comforts my lonely mind to know that you like what I wrote about Poe in that *ms.* All the rest is overstated, effusive, and only justified by the generous desire to make the most of a rather poor and inadequate occasion.[11]

The fight to recover the manuscript did not end with the deaths of Mrs. Whitman and O'Connor. Nelly (then Mrs. Albert Calder) in going over William's papers, found only the rough draft, and had her secretary write to Horace Traubel, one of Whitman executors, on April 18, 1893, asking him to obtain the manuscript from Mrs. Rice.[12]

The unpublished article was in the form of a letter to Miss Rice. The excerpt preserved comprises pages 5 to 23 of O'Connor's manuscript written in his own hand.[13] (The beginning is in another's handwriting.) After describing the scene of the memorial meeting and the gathering at the monument, he writes of Whitman's presence:

> . . . no judgment worth notice will deny sufficient noble celebrity the platform up whose stairs we saw slowly limp our loftiest poet, broken with his hospital service to the wounded and dying of both sides in the war, and grand in his age and infirmity, like a crippled eagle, *The Good Gray Poet*—he, at least, loyal to the spirit of the old free-masonry of letters, and paying with his presence his share in the honors the literary class of Europe never neglects to offer its illustrious dead. Whatever they may say here, the Old World, where his name lives in the light from Copenhagen to London, will not find lacking in the proper literary dignity, an occasion graced by the great and venerable presence of Walt Whitman. Where MacGregor sits, is the head of the table!

O'Connor calls James Russell Lowell's interpretation of Poe's sufferings "a shallow judgment." It is the nature of society that

> explains the doom of messiahs and the anguished lives of the geniuses. A phrase you will hear among the roughs, . . . expresses the social destiny evolved for one like Edgar Poe: *The one the others are down on.* Why should they not be down upon one like him: He was proud, superior, solitary; he had the courage of his opinions; he disdained fools and despised knaves; he felt and showed acerbity and scorn for things imperfect and base in art and life; . . . he was unpurchasable, undissuadable; he was original; he endowed literature with fresh thought and glorious imaginings, cast in novel forms, always an offence to mediocrities and bane of the convention and routine; he had conscience, honor, moral purity, spiritual reverence, deep religious feeling,—shown everywhere in his sombre and starry pages; he was disinterested, romantic, simple, chivalrous, guileless, truthful, sensitive, loving; . . . Necessarily, he had many bitter enemies. No doubt, also,

> he had friends, but this, alas! for one made like him, was perhaps
> only another reason for his misfortunes. We often suffer no less
> from the sad fatuity of friends than the enmity of foes.

Despite his disappointment about his contribution to the Edgar Allan Poe Memorial Volume, O'Connor planned another defense of Poe in answer to Fairfield's attack in the *Library Table*. He began to collect material about Poe, placing it in a scrapbook and a notebook which Nelly later presented to Brown University Library. The notes indicate some of the points he wanted to make in answer to Poe's critics, including Stoddard, "whose failure in literature is his sole qualification for criticism."[14] This article was never written.

Although still estranged from Whitman, O'Connor again seized the opportunity to defend him when it presented itself. An article in the *West Jersey Press* on January 26, 1876 (written by Whitman himself), entitled "Walt Whitman's Actual American Position" and describing the neglect of American publishers and the poet's poverty, aroused sympathy in England and controversy in the American press.[15]

English writers had not lost interest in Whitman. Standish O'Grady (under his pen name Arthur Clive) had a flattering article "Walt Whitman, the Poet of Joy" in the *Gentleman's Magazine* of December 1875. In it he stresses an aspect of Whitman's work which had not been presented in earlier essays—the contrast of Whitman's joyous spirit with the melancholy undertones of the English poets from Byron on. To support his thesis, he gives pages of evidence from Whitman's writings, declaring, "He expresses more than happiness, he expresses exultation. . . . It is no longer a mean thing to be a man. From a hundred points he comes back always to this, that man is great and glorious, not little and contemptible."

O'Grady explores Whitman's ideal of "manly love" with more explicitness and admiration than his other critics and defenders had done. (In this Burroughs felt that Clive had "turned new and deep ground.")[16] He considers Whitman a mystic as well as a poet, "who looks at this world with the wondering freshness of a child, and to the world beyond with the gaze of a seer."

In the same month that "Walt Whitman, Poet of Joy" appeared, an article by Peter Bayne attacking Whitman was published in the English *Contemporary Review*. Burroughs noted that the latter, being hostile, was reprinted in the United States; the former was not.[17] The American press seemed eager to echo the British press especially when it was inimical to Whitman or made what they thought were unfounded claims for him. Therefore the *West Jersey Press* article, picked up by the English, stirred up controversy in America—a literary tempest that was probably good for Whitman in the long run.

The controversy came at the time that Whitman had just published the two-volume Centennial Edition (also known as the Author's Edition) which he planned to sell at ten dollars the set. Having printed the books himself, he did not have a publisher to handle the commercial aspects of the sale. As in the past he had to be his own press agent and salesman. It is not surprising that he sent copies of the *West Jersey Press* article to friends abroad, including William Michael Rossetti, who in turn had excerpts from the article printed in the *Athenaeum*. The Scottish poet, Robert Buchanan, in a letter to the London *Daily News*, attacked the American writers and critics for their neglect of their greatest poet. This was reported in the *New York Times* the following day, and the controversy began.

The *New York Tribune*, under the editorship of Whitelaw Reid, had always been friendly to Whitman, but early in March Bayard Taylor, a well-known poet and novelist, joined the editorial staff and launched an attack on Whitman and his British sympathizers. During the month of March 1876 he wrote four editorials in this vein. In one of them he took the British writers, and especially Buchanan, to task for talking of the American writers' neglect of Whitman. He stated that when Whitman was ousted by Secretary Harlan, it was the American writers with Edmund C. Stedman at their head, who quickly saw to it that he got another position. To this Stedman responded, placing the credit where it belonged: "If anybody was especially prominent in behalf of the 'good gray poet,' it certainly was his brilliant and impetuous friend, Mr. William D. O'Connor, the devoted adherent who at the time gave him that title—and the credit should be placed where it belongs." Stedman also refuted Buchanan's allegations of neglect, saying that American authors have a sincere regard for Whitman and would surely help him if help were needed.[18]

This favorable mention of O'Connor brought him into the fray—possibly prodded by a "kind telegram" from Stedman to which he referred in a letter.[19] Stedman offered to help place O'Connor's defense of Whitman in the *Tribune*. While O'Connor was writing it, the *Tribune* printed a lengthy, well-reasoned article by John Burroughs entitled "Walt Whitman's Poetry: An Estimate of Its Value." He had sent his article on March 30, but it was not presented until April 13, having been held until the day after an adverse article by Taylor entitled, "American vs. English Criticism."

Burroughs writes of Whitman's influence upon him, of the British artists and critics who accept him and of those who dissent. He praises Whitman's power:

> . . . sweet poets, elegant poets, learned, correct, beautiful poets, are not rare in our age, but powerful poets, poets who can confront and compel the gigantic materialism of our times and land, and who by dint of native inward force can rise above the poetic and literary consciousness with which the very atmosphere is rotten, are rare, and, it seems, are misunderstood when they come. . . .

As to the charge of formlessness leveled at Whitman's writing, Burroughs says,

> It is a kind of disloyalty to Nature to say Whitman has no form. He has not form as a house, or a shield, or a heart, or a molder's pattern, or a sonnet of Hood's, or a dainty bit of verse by Longfellow has form; but he has form as a tree, a river, the clouds, a cataract, a flash of lightning, or any vital and progressive thing has form, and this is all the form he aims at.

In regard to the start of the controversy—Whitman's condition—he knows that it is true that he is poor and in feeble health.

O'Connor liked Burroughs's letter; he thought his "quiet believing style, free from passion or the glitter of rhetoric, and giving one the sense of simple eyesight," so effective that he almost gave up the idea of writing something himself.[20] The article in the *Tribune* of April 12, however, convinced him that "this gallant Bayard was bent on making war," and he joined the battle.[21]

In the same letter to Burroughs O'Connor was able to indulge in satire which he could not include in his *Tribune* article if he expected it to get past Taylor into print. Of Bayard Taylor and his groups, he wrote,

They go to their "scratch-my-back" club, which is called "The Century," and their tickle-my-elbow club, which is called "The Lotos," and they read each other their little essays and their less verses, and they call each other gods and geniuses, and they concoct their epigrams and epithets, and arrange who shall be written up and who down, and police Parnassus generally. Among them this gent of whom Park Benjamin made Humboldt say that he had "travelled more and seen less than anyone living," is a conspicuity. He is called Bayard by way of emphasis, I suppose, because he has both reproach and fear, and Taylor because he is the ninth part of a man. . . .

O'Connor's letter to the *Tribune*, entitled "Walt Whitman, Is He Persecuted?" appeared on April 22, 1876. In it he considers, and refutes, the arguments advanced by Bayard Taylor in his essays of March 28 and March 30. Of Whitman's condition, O'Connor wrote plainly, "He is old, even less with years than noble service; his labors and emotions in the hospitals of the war have left him paralyzed; and he lives, wholly without personal means, in the humble dwelling of a relative." He resents Taylor's remarks discrediting Buchanan's proposal that copies of the new edition of *Leaves of Grass* should be purchased by friends in England—"an assistance and a homage which the case fully justifies." He also resents the London correspondent of the *Tribune*, Smalley, who characterized such purchases as "charity" and "alms." (G. W. Smalley, the London correspondent of the *Tribune*, was later characterized by Whitman's friend, William Sloane Kennedy, in *The Fight of A Book for the World*, as "our pompous Tory and self-constituted newspaper minister-plenipotentiary to England.")

O'Connor satirizes the allusions to Whitman's dress, "the small and stale old slurs and figments of the imagination invented twenty years ago," which have "the vague and grotesque intention to make him at once criminal and ridiculous." He answers the *Tribune*'s criticism of Whitman's use of Emerson's private letter with a telling blow: "It was originally published in the *Tribune*, and at the importunate and protracted solicitation of the editor."

To the charge that *Leaves of Grass* is not fit to be "read under the evening lamp," O'Connor rejoins that this is not the criterion by which great books should be judged. Besides he has often heard it "read aloud . . . 'under the evening lamp,' and in very high and pure society too; . . ." He mentions the appreciation of the *Leaves* by a woman, "as spiritually noble in mind and soul as she is beautiful in person, and whose position in society equals the best in London," which she had expressed in the article "An Englishwoman's Estimate of Walt Whitman" in the Boston *Radical*.

O'Connor disputes the opinion that American authors were indignant at Whitman's dismissal. Stedman, whom he never knew "to be second in any good work when he could be first," did not have the opportunity to help as he was not even in Washington at the time. The only defenders were Henry J. Raymond, Frank B. Sanborn, and Richard Hinton. As an instance of American authors' neglect and opprobrium of Whitman, he cites the New England authors who discouraged an English visitor from presenting a letter of introduction to Whitman, saying he "was nothing but a low, New York rowdy" and "a common street blackguard."

He does not go into the theory and poetry of *Leaves of Grass* (Burroughs having covered that excellently), stating only that he is writing not out of "the bias of friendship," for his regard for the work antedated by several years his acquaintance with the author.

> It was morning in the world to me when I first read those mighty pages, and felt to my inmost soul the vast charm of their sealike lines and superb imagination; and today, after many years have passed, I never open the book without receiving again that supreme impression of its wild delicacy and splendor. To all its wondrous recreation of the actual orb of things gross and delicate; its consummate art of selection and coordination; the grand felicity of its apt and agreeing rhythmus, like the copious and unequal pouring of the breakers upon the sands; and the sublime and living beauty interfused with the whole—it appears that many are insensible. . . .

He sees that many are insensible also to the "gorgeous and lofty sanctus of so great a poet, in prose and verse, as Victor Hugo." He concludes by asking "whether the man by whom New York and our country in this age will one day be chiefly remembered, as England lives in the memory of Shakespeare, is to languish away his few remaining years in neglect and poverty at Camden! . . ." Is it only death, he asks, that "will open to him the gates of a good fame . . . ?"

Bayard Taylor drew the sting from O'Connor's article by publishing in the same issue his editorial entitled "Intellectual Convexity," in which he satirizes "disciples" in general and Whitman's "disciples" in particular. "All that relates to the master expands into colossal proportions in the atmosphere of his cloudy greatness. A cranberry from his hand becomes a huge Hesperidian apple; he smiles, and there is morning in the world. . . ."

Taylor especially disputes Burroughs's and O'Connor's praises of Whitman and censure of American critics, writers and publishers. Of the formlessness of Whitman's writings, which Burroughs said represented Nature, he writes:

> Sculpture represented by a huge mass of clay, with scattered attempts at shaping fingers or noses! Architecture turning her back on the finished temple, and proudly pointing to her unhewn blocks! Music setting gigantic wind-harps (untuned) in her halls and squelching Beethoven! Pages of catalogued objects silencing the perfect pentameters of Milton!

He writes with a certain admiration of other authors who had their contributions to magazines returned and did not "whine" about it! "Hawthorne was ignored during his best years, Emerson abused and ridiculed, and their friends never dreamed of imagining a conspiracy against them. No man in this country had ever been so constantly advertized by his disciples as Walt Whitman."

He ends with a final blow at the "disciples": "If their master's new venture should fail, they will be chiefly to blame. He has wisely held himself aloof from their aggressive championship; and we heartily commend the silence and apparent indifference of 'the good gray poet' to the imitation of his good green friends." (Whitman's "aloofness" can be questioned in the light of the fact that he had started the movement with his own anonymous article in the *West Jersey Press*.)

O'Connor would have enjoyed answering Taylor, but he could only sputter in letters to Burroughs and to Stedman. He knew that the *Tribune* had said its last word on the subject of Whitman for a while. Taylor's publication of "Intellectual Convexity" in the same issue as O'Connor's "Walt Whitman: Is He Persecuted?" was its way of ending the controversy.

O'Connor was named as Whitman's admirer in an article by the poet Nora Perry, which appeared on the same day as "Walt Whitman: Is He Persecuted?" and "Intellectual Convexity." In "A Few Words About Walt Whitman" in *Appleton's Journal*,[22] she mentions his admirers, beginning with Emerson and including the English poets and critics and "our own William O'Connor." She quotes extensively from Anne Gilchrist's essay, and, although she is less enthusiastic than Whitman's other admirers, states that she is confident that his purpose is noble. The following month John Holland, editor of *Scribner's*, wrote against Whitman under the pen name, "Timothy Titcomb," which led O'Connor to satirize him in a letter to Burroughs as "Tittlebat Titmouse."[23] George William Curtis had something to say about the matter in the June *Harper's* "Editor's Easy Chair." When O'Connor saw this announced in the *Tribune* he thought he was going "to catch it." After the article appeared, O'Connor's old friendship for Curtis did not prevent him from poking fun at him in a letter to Burroughs:

> My disappointment is ludicrous. The artificial mountain in Brooklyn park has labored, and produced a toy mouse. We haven't even a living animal, when I expected at least a carnivorous though elegant and well-conducted jabberwock! O George William! How are the mighty fallen! Absolutely, his contribution is nothing but a dilution of Bayard Taylor's editorials—and resembles excellent mutton broth made by boiling, without condiment, the shadow of a sheep's trotter.[24]

In the balance of this letter O'Connor gives advice to Burroughs that is much calmer and more judicious than the principles by which he himself had been guided in all his writings about Whitman. Perhaps the estrangement, while not diminishing his admiration for *Leaves of Grass*, had given him the opportunity to plan a campaign coolly and with an eye to the utimate aim of having Whitman accepted. He begins by advising Burroughs to take adverse criticism of Stedman out of his essay "The Flight of the Eagle," since Stedman is friendly to Whitman. In general he directs that the practice of Whitman's friends should be to avoid naming any other poets "except for very grave and definite reason."

The better way, I think, is to accept, to admire, to extol, all the poets as far as consistent with truth, but to discriminate between them and a poet like Walt; and to insist, in the strongest manner, that he is, with all possible respect and cordial appreciation of them and their uses, something different and greater, both in his ambition and achievement. This seems to me a position at once just, generous, and impregnable. You think of it.

He goes on to state his own conception of literary art:

My own general feeling is that art is a firmament, in which there are constellations as well as stars; in which one star differs from another in glory, but all are stellar; and in which even the star-dust and nebulae and the transient meteors, are respectable and perform their worthy offices. . . .

He returns to the old dream of having a magazine of their own. "What a chance there is for a superb review, political, social, artistic, and literary, such as this country has never dreamed of. . . ." If they only could win the Havana lottery! Such a review, called at various times "The Pathfinder" or "The Open Road," had long been the subject of hopeful planning by O'Connor and other friends of the poet.[25] At first it was thought of as a vehicle for the presentation of Whitman's poems and a forum for their defense at a time when most of the existing periodicals were closed to him. Later, O'Connor thought of it in broader terms.[26]

In order to earn money for such a periodical and to supplement his meagre income, O'Connor worked on various inventions, undoubtedly spurred by the example of his brother-in-law, William Channing, who had patented two inventions—the first an electric fire-alarm system (1865) which he gave to the City of Boston, and the second a portable electro-magnetic telegraph (1877). In the late 1870s he was at work on a ship-railway to transport ships by land between the two coasts. He asked O'Connor's help in finding out in Washington about its possible adoption. O'Connor referred to his inventions in several letters: When he was corresponding with Rossetti about an English edition of Whitman's poems, he apologized for his delay in answering a letter: "I have just recently hit upon a new method of making cast steel in a very short time and at a very low price—an invention, as you may imagine, of extreme value."[27]

Almost three years later, the invention had not yet succeeded when Anne Gilchrist asked about it in a letter to Walt Whitman. More than a decade later, O'Connor wrote to Sarah Helen Whitman that he had a patent upon application, but he did not say what it was: "If I am successful with it, I should be able to do more for you than my house of bondage, and all my cares and sorrows, have hitherto allowed." He adds that he has "toiled terribly"; his hair has gone very gray and his walk is lame. He has suffered much from rheumatism for the past year. He signs the letter incongruously "Ariel," an "Ariel" now aging and lame.[28]

Although O'Connor was not able to help Sarah Helen Whitman financially, he did help with the complete edition of her poems, first suggesting that she undertake such a project, and later, after her death in 1878, helping William Channing, who was her executor, decide upon the arrangement of her poems and in other ways assisting in editing the volume, which was published by Osgood and Company of Boston in 1879.

In asking for O'Connor's help, Channing wrote that in Helen's last conversation with Jeannie Channing she had spoken of "O'Connor's literary judgement and critical capacity as greater than that of any person she knew" and that she had "constantly referred to him questions about her poems and accepted his suggestions about them." William Channing felt that O'Connor knew her poems better than anyone living. Indeed, he knew most of them by heart. Mrs. Whitman had kept hundreds of O'Connor's letters which Channing returned to O'Connor.[29] Few of them survived among O'Connor's papers.

Helen's death on June 27, 1878, ended a friendship in which he was still the "morning star" of the early years in Providence. It was the closing of a chapter in his life. Only a few days later, on June 29, 1878, he was promoted to the position of Assistant General Superintendent of the Life-Saving Service at a salary of $2500 a year. On his former salary, which he had continued to send to Nelly, he had had to borrow money. With the increase in salary, he was able to support Nelly and Jeannie as before, while retaining more money for himself.

Nevertheless, he did not give up the idea of becoming an inventor. In writing to Channing about the latter's plan for a ship-railway, he asked about an idea of his which he would like to convey to Edison:

Would, or would not a horseshoe of asbestos—say defibrinated and then compressed into form—serve better than carbonized pasteboard for Edison's purposes in electric lighting? If it would, I would like to make the suggestion to the wizard, but don't know enough about electricity to be sure that the suggestion wouldn't be asinine.[30]

This proved to be unfeasible.

At that time O'Connor was also experimenting with mucilage, trying to make the special kind that the revenue stamp required. In this too he was unsuccessful.[31] John Burroughs wrote in a note to Clara Barrus: "O'Connor experimented a good deal with chemicals. He had no scientific training or knowledge, but had a dream of sudden wealth by some discovery. He pottered about, but I never could find out what it was all about. Nothing ever came of it."[32]

After William's death Nelly wrote to Walt that she was left with very little, William having put money into "mostly worthless *inventions* that are good for nothing but to swallow up good money."[33] The failure of the invention of a method of making cast steel may have contributed to the frustration William felt at the time of the quarrel with Walt.

Unsuccessful in his inventions and separated from Walt Whitman, O'Connor used his talents only in connection with his job. In 1878 a bill to organize the Life-Saving Service, which had been established in 1871, was presented to Congress. It was opposed by a bill to transfer the Service to the Department of the Navy. In connection with the ensuing debate, O'Connor wrote a request to the Honorable Charles Older, Secretary of the Treasury, protesting the transfer.[34] Whether he wrote this to be sent in his own name or to be signed by others is not known, for the manuscript is not signed.

In the letter O'Connor cited incidents in which the Life-Saving Service could have helped, but the Navy was powerless. As a result a number of lives had been lost. Life-Saving operations require special knowledge: brick-gunnery, "the art of firing lines over distant and unsteady hulls, walling in the breakers, . . . the depth setting up of hoses and holding lines," and other skills which the Navy lacked. Whether because of this letter or for other reasons, the Life-Saving Service was not transferred to the Department of the Navy; O'Connor remained as Assistant General Superintendent. Among his duties was conducting the entire correspondence of the Service, amounting to about a thousand letters a month—all written by hand. Some years later, when he left his position because of illness, the work had to be given to three or four people.[35]

One element of his work did give him the opportunity to do some writing which had elements of creativity. This was the preparation of the Annual Reports of the Life-Saving Service. This arduous task consisted of summarizing and coordinating reports from over 200 life-saving stations of the property and lives imperiled, saved, or lost within their operations. In his annual reports O'Connor described in detail those wrecks in which there was loss of life. The project of publishing these narratives (twenty-five in all) was initiated by Nelly in 1891. She asked Kimball for copies of the reports from 1878 to 1889. Charles Eldridge undertook to select and edit the appropriate excerpts, and had almost completed the work when he died in 1903. The story had come full circle; Eldridge who had published *Harrington* in 1860 also participated in the preparation of O'Connor's book—the posthumous *Heroes of the Storm*.

Sumner I. Kimball in the introduction to that volume praised O'Connor and his Annual Reports:

> The labor of preparing a volume of this character involves an amount of patient application verging upon drudgery, and is liable in unskillful hands to impart a shade of dullness to the pages. No such defect ever marred Mr. O'Connor's work. Up to the year 1889 most of the accounts of shipwrecks involving the loss of life, are from his pen. . . . The most romantic sea tales of fiction are no more absorbing, and yet there is not in them a word of exaggeration, and participants in the scenes described have often and invariably pronounced them absolutely correct.

O'Connor's contemporaries expressed diverse views of his devoting his talent to the work of the Life-Saving Service. Journalist Rebecca Harding Davis thought that this work was O'Connor's salvation:

> After the war was over, he took a brief for Bacon vs. Shakespeare, and became one of the Pfaff crowd of Bohemians, a hater of orthodoxy, a dabbler in all kinds of heresies. He made Walt

Whitman an idol, and sang paeans to the Good Gray Poet with his whole being.

William O'Connor, however, calmed down in his later years, and under the guardianship of Sumner Kimball found a place in the Life-Saving Service. Nobody could be long factitious in the atmosphere of that sane, noble department of the government. O'Connor did much quiet good work in it before he left the world.[36]

The novelist John Trowbridge differed:

He had turned aside from literature, in which we who knew him in the flower of his youthful promise had believed him destined to excel, and entered a department of the government,—one of those vast mausoleums in which so many talents, small and great, have been buried, and brave ambitions have turned quietly to dust. His first employment was in the Treasury. . . . When O'Connor left the Treasury it was to enter the Lighthouse Board, where he became head clerk, and sat like a spider in the midst of his web, a coast light at the end of each invisible line, hundreds of thousands of miles away. In those useful radiations the beams of his genius became too deeply immersed to shine otherwise than fitfully in what I always deemed his proper sphere. . . . The most eloquent of pens became subdued to the daily routine of office drudgery. . . .[37]

A renewal of his friendship with Walt might have relieved the drudgery, but O'Connor's defense of the poet in 1876 did not lead to a reconciliation. In conversations with the artist Herbert Gilchrist (son of Anne Gilchrist), which he recorded in his notebook of 1876 and 1877, Whitman said, in talking of Burroughs:

He is just the same as when I first saw him—always the same— not like some of my friends very thick at first and then fall off. . . . O'Connor he was an old friend until—we had some argument in which I let some hard words drop. I thought no more about it but he hasnt [sic] forgiven me. (Here Mr. Whitman seemed moved.) Mr. O'Connor is Irish, a quick temper etc.[38]

Despite these words of regret Whitman made no direct overtures of friendship to O'Connor, and O'Connor, aside from his defenses of the poet, remained silent. Perhaps reconciliation might have occurred earlier than it did if there had not been physical distance between them. If Whitman had continued to live in Washington, chance encounters might have led to an earlier renewal of friendship. But early in 1873 the ailing poet went to live in Camden, New Jersey, with his brother George and sister-in-law Louisa. He stayed in that city, later living in a small house of his own, until his death in 1892.

During the years after the quarrel O'Connor's life must have been dreary. No great cause inspired him to attack or defense. No "Fanny" appeared to move him to writing poetry. Living apart from Nelly and his daughter Jeannie, in the austere manner which his finances dictated, without the sun of Walt's presence, there was little to do but throw himself into his government work. In August 1873, in a loving letter to his daughter Jeannie, then staying with the Channings near Newport, Rhode Island, he wrote, "I have half the feeling of being in jail and the other half of being dead." He tempers the statement with the half-humorous, "This is exhilarating, and does not promote letter-writing."[39]

O'Connor's first published writing after the *Tribune* letters in 1876 was an account of the history of the Life-Saving Service for *Appleton's Encyclopedia of the Year 1878*. It is a comprehensive article illustrated with engravings of men and equipment.

O'Connor would have agreed with Trowbridge that his talents were being wasted. He also began to be plagued by poor health. Because of the night work his eyes began to fail, and he suffered from rheumatism. As he approached his fiftieth year, he could hardly have imagined that he would be called on to promote Whitman's fame and to defend *Leaves of Grass* again.

NOTES

1. Grace Channing, unpublished memoir (Chamberlin).
2. Jerome Loving, *Walt Whitman's Champion: William Douglas O'Connor* (College Station, Texas: Texas A&M University Press, 1978), p. 105.
3. Gay Wilson Allen, *The Solitary Singer* (New York: The Macmillan Company, 1955), p. 468.
4. WW, *Prose Works 1892*, I: 230–33.
5. *Correspondence*, II: 342–43.

6. Henry Bryan Binns, *A Life of Walt Whitman* (London: Methuen & Co., 1905), p. 258.
7. WDO'C to S. H. Whitman, 5 March 1876 (Brown).
8. S. H. W. to WDO'C, 20 March 1876 (Feinberg-LC).
9. Rice to WDO'C, May n.d. 1876 (copy sent by Gertrude Traubel to author.)
10. S. H. W. to WDO'C, 24 November 1876 (Feinberg-LC).
11. WDO'C to S. H. W., fragment, n.d. (Feinberg-LC).
12. Copy sent by Gertrude Traubel to author.
13. (Berg).
14. (Brown).
15. A full account of this controversy may be found in Robert Scholnick, "The Selling of the 'Author's Edition': Whitman, O'Connor and the *West Jersey Press* Affair," *Walt Whitman Review*, 23: 3–23 (March 1977).
16. Burroughs to Dowden, 10 April 1876, in Barrus, *Comrades*, p.140 f.
17. *Ibid.*
18. E. C. Stedman, "Walt Whitman's Clerkship," *New York Tribune*, 31 March 1876.
19. WDO'C to Stedman, 31 March 1876 (Feinberg-LC).
20. WDO'C to Burroughs, 4 May 1876 (Doheny Collection-St. Johns Seminary) Carmillo, California.
21. *Ibid.*
22. 22 April 1876.
23. See note 20 above.
24. 15 May 1876, in Barrus, *Notebooks*.
25. Eldridge to Burroughs, 10 May 1892 (Berg).
26. WDO'C to Burroughs, 12 July 1882, in Barrus, *Comrades*, p. 320, and Lafcadio Hearn to WDO'C, March (n.d.) 1884, in Elizabeth Bisland, *The Life and Letters of Lafcadio Hearn* (Boston and New York: Houghton Mifflin Company, 1906), p. 317.
27. 28 August 1869, in *Rossetti Papers, 1862–1870, A Compilation* by William Michael Rossetti (New York: Charles Scribner's Sons, 1903), p. 459.
28. 20 May 1878 (Brown).
29. Dr. W. F. Channing to C. Fiske Harris, Esq., 23 August 1878 (Brown).
30. 11 March 1880 (Chamberlin).
31. WDO'C to Dr. W. F. Channing, 18 August 1879 and 19 February 1880 (Chamberlin).
32. Note by Barrus on what Burroughs had told her (Barrus Scrapbook), p. 235.
33. 3 August 1889 (Feinberg-LC).
34. MS in O'Connor's handwriting (Syracuse).
35. WW described O'Connor's work in the Signal Service as that of "the one who does all the work for the fellow who wears all the ornaments." *Camden* 1: 179, 19 May 1888.
36. Rebecca Harding Davis, *Bits of Gossip* (Boston and New York: Houghton Mifflin Company, 1904), pp. 214–15.
37. John T. Trowbridge, *My Own Story* etc. (Boston and New York: Houghton Mifflin Company, 1904), pp. 373–75.
38. (Pennsylvania).
39. (Feinberg-LC).

CHAPTER XVII

Reconciliation:
"Word Over All,
Beautiful As The Sky"[1]

RECONCILIATION BETWEEN Whitman and O'Connor, openly desired by their friends, and probably secretly by themselves, occurred in 1882, ten years after the quarrel. It was initiated by a new friend, Dr. Richard Maurice Bucke, prompted first by a projected biograghy of Whitman and later by a new and powerful threat to *Leaves of Grass.*

Dr. Bucke, the best educated of Whitman's close friends up to this time, was a physician and author. In 1879 he dedicated his book, *Man's Moral Nature*, to Whitman, writing,

> I dedicate this book to the man who inspired it—to the man of all men past and present that I have known has the most exalted moral nature—to Walt Whitman.[2]

Bucke was probably drawn to the *Leaves* because of his own mysticism and love of nature. Born in England and brought to Canada as an infant, he had spent his youth in the mining fields of western United States. During a winter expedition in the Sierras, the cold was so severe that his companion froze to death, and he himself had to have one foot and part of the other amputated. Despite this he went on to study medicine at McGill University and later in England

and France. He became an alienist (the word used much as psychiatrist is today), and was head of the London, Ontario Asylum for the Insane. His views and practices in the treatment of the insane were far ahead of those of his time.[3] He may have been drawn to Whitman's writings not only because of the poet's love of nature, but also because of his inclusion of all people in his celebration of humanity. Bucke's book, *Cosmic Consciousness*, published in 1901 (after Whitman's death) tells of Whitman's spiritual experiences.[4]

Bucke's first letter to Walt Whitman was written on December 19, 1870. He had read and admired *Leaves of Grass* in Rossetti's 1868 edition, and then had borrowed a copy of the 1855 edition and bought the 1867 edition. He wrote asking to buy two copies of *Leaves of Grass* and one copy each of *Passage to India* and *Democratic Vistas*. Although this was his first communication with the poet, he did not hesitate to affirm that he had compared "Song of Myself" in the editions of 1855 and 1867 and much preferred the earlier version.[5]

In the fall of 1877 Bucke came to the United States to view the Centennial Exhibition (still in progress). He visited Walt Whitman in Camden, New Jersey. Bucke felt on meeting the poet "a sort of spiritual intoxication" which remained with him for some time.[6] On his return to Canada, Bucke lectured on Whitman in Sarnia and London, Ontario. This started a controversy in Canada; one of the newspapers charged Bucke with "digging up from the gutter a book stained with filth." Undeterred by this, Bucke persuaded a London, Ontario bookseller to advertise *Leaves of Grass* with his own list, obtaining copies from Bucke as needed.[7]

To promote the sales of *Leaves of Grass* was not enough. Bucke wanted to write a biography of Whitman, and in a letter to him on January 19, 1880 asked him to write a sketch of his "interior life— especially in relation to the conception and elaboration of *Leaves of Grass*."[8] In lieu of fulfilling this request, Whitman recommended some books for him to read. Bucke responded on February 3 that he had read Burroughs, O'Connor, and Gilchrist, but "What I specially want just now is new facts about the man—both bearing on his inward and outward life. . . ." Whitman did not comply.[9]

Seeking further information about Whitman, Bucke sent a form letter to friends and acquaintances of the poet; he called it "casting a net."[10] Among the recipients was Ellen O'Connor, who wrote:

> I thought I should have time to write my reminiscences of Walt for
> you. . . . I will, however, put into shape for you the one thought
> that always from the day I first read a line of Walt Whitman
> pressed upon me, the certainty that none but a good and pure man
> would dare to write and publish what he did.[11]

Other letters, such as those from Mrs. Helen Price and Thomas A.
Gere, which Bucke included in his book, may have come in response
to this form letter.

Thinking that he could get more information from Whitman if he
saw him again, and eager to be with the poet, Bucke invited him to
visit him and his family in Canada. By late spring of 1880 this became possible. It was Walt's first trip to another country. He arrived
in London, Ontario, on June 4, 1880, having stopped to see Niagara
Falls on the way. During his four-month visit he and Dr. Bucke took
a trip down the St. Lawrence and up the Saguenay Rivers. While
they were together, Bucke discussed his projected biography with
Whitman, who for some reason was not enthusiastic about the
idea.[12] He capitulated, however, to the point of writing his own account of his birthplace and antecedents, which comprise the first
twenty-four pages of Bucke's book. It may have been at this time
that Whitman suggested that O'Connor's *The Good Gray Poet* be
reprinted in the biography with an introductory letter to bring it up
to date.[13] Bucke and O'Connor began corresponding. Bucke wrote
on July 1, 1880 enclosing a clipping from a newspaper which he
thought would be of interest to O'Connor if he was planning to rewrite and enlarge "The Carpenter." He also expressed interest in
O'Connor's other writings.[14]

O'Connor, beset by office work and suffering from failing eyesight, did not answer until August 26. He expressed his usual disparagement of his own work:

> I hope you failed to get "Harrington." It is monstrously crude,
> and was written, under contract, in a terrible hurry. Like "The
> Carpenter," haste spoiled it. After the second feat of this sort, I
> made up my mind never to write anything to order, or in a hurry
> again. It's the slow brew makes the great malt, the English brew-
> ers say.[15]

An exchange of letters followed, dealing mostly with an article by
Stedman which both disliked.[16] Bucke had written an answer and

sent it to the papers; when it was not accepted, he agreed with O'Connor that they should drop the matter, since there was some good in Stedman's article. They also agreed that Bucke's book should include *The Good Gray Poet*. Bucke asked O'Connor to write a prefatory letter, of which the chief object would be to state his present opinion of Whitman. (William F. Channing had expressed a desire to reprint *The Good Gray Poet*, but O'Connor preferred that it be in Bucke's projected volume.)[17]

In his reply on June 21, 1881 O'Connor promises to send the pamphlet and the introductory letter within a month. He expresses misgivings about the value of *The Good Gray Poet*.

> It has so decidedly the tone of being provoked by an occasion, as indeed it was—that I feel it is useless to perpetuate it, not to mention its crudeness.

In the same letter he suggests that Bucke get Whitman to tell him the story of his dismissal by Harlan as Judge Otto had told it to him. He mentions that he (O'Connor) had told all the circumstances in his article, "Walt Whitman: Is He Persecuted?" in *The Tribune* in 1876.[18]

In his reply Bucke wrote of *The Good Gray Poet*,

> You rate the work altogether too low. Certainly it was written for an occasion, but that occasion, and (if I am not mistaken) the "Good Gray Poet" which it called forth, will live in the minds of men for many a long year. . . . If all of my book should have the merit of this part of the appendix to it I should feel confident of its future.[19]

Because of pressure of work and ill health, O'Connor did not send the copy of *The Good Gray Poet* until December 13, 1881, and delayed writing the introductory letter. After waiting for a while, and wanting to spare O'Connor the extra burden of writing an additional letter, Bucke altered his plan for the book so as to get along without it. By the time O'Connor received a letter to that effect, however, he had written a great deal of the letter at fever heat, and wanted it to be included. Bucke was delighted.

The introduction was finally sent on February 24, 1882, with the charge that Bucke not alter a single word, "for I have composed it with an eye to proportion, and to strike out anything would be to mar that effect."[20] On the other hand Bucke could leave it out entirely if he wished. This Bucke had no intention of doing: "It is immense, and is just what was wanted to help my attempt."[21] He does wish, however, to leave out the text of Emerson's letter, since that appears elsewhere in the biography. O'Connor would not consent to this, urging that it was needed where he had placed it—in direct refutation to one of the critics, Clarence Cook. Bucke acquiesced. "Your placability about my MS. is simply delightful," wrote O'Connor.[22] Walt Whitman, who saw O'Connor's contributions to the book before publication, made no corrections (although he did suggest changes in other parts of the biography), urging only the excision of two lines on the last page of The. Good Gray Poet.[23] Although O'Connor had been dubious about those very lines, he refused to eliminate them, because they had been criticized when the book came out and he did not wish to seem to be capitulating to his critics.[24]

Far from being the short letter which was requested, O'Connor's introductory letter took up twenty-five pages of the book, with The Good Gray Poet taking up thirty-five. It is written in the same tone of attack and defense as the pamphlet which it introduced. Although the content is different, it is a sustained polemic, meant to arouse as well as to inform. O'Connor restates the circumstances of the Harlan dismissal, adding some facts which he learned after the publication of The Good Gray Poet, and answers those critics who received the 1881 edition of the Leaves with disdain and censure. He concludes with an encomium of the Leaves, equal in enthusiasm to his earlier appraisal, but with new insights and interpretations.

His new ammunition against Secretary Harlan consisted of the fact that the book on which the action was based had been stolen from Whitman's desk and replaced without the knowledge of its owner:

> Who was it that edged along the shadowy passages of the huge building from the Secretary's apartment—that quietly slipped down the dim stairway—that crept, crawled, stole, sneaked into the deserted room of his illustrious fellow-officer—that tiptoed up to the vacant desk—that put a furtive hand into the private drawer and drew out the private volume—that glided back with it to the office of the Secretary? When the hours of gloating were

over, and the building was darker and dimmer under its few fu-
nereal gaslights, turned murkily low, who crept back down the
dead-house corridors and stairways, with a volume in his hand, to
the earlier visited apartment, stealthily replaced the volume in the
desk, and softly slunk away? Was it Tartuffe disguised as Ami-
nadab Sleek, or was it the rampant God Priapus masquerading as
Paul Pry?[25]

In the same vein of satire and diatribe, O'Connor attacks the critics, "our literary ku klux." (O'Connor enjoyed his own rhetoric, writing to Bucke that he had gone through the critics like a "scythed
chariot.")[26] He takes up the criticisms of the 1881 edition, among
them those of the *New York Times*, the *Atlantic Monthly*, and *The
Nation*. He names Bayard Taylor, Thomas Wentworth Higginson,
and Clarence Cook, answering each of them at some length. He is
especially angry at Higginson's disparagement of Whitman for having served in the hospitals instead of at the front. (Higginson had
been colonel of the first colored regiment.) To O'Connor Higginson
was far from the "Dear Preceptor" of Emily Dickinson. O'Connor
trades insults with Higginson:

> I also beg leave to tell him, since he brings personalities into
> fashion, that Walt Whitman's work of comfort and charity beside
> the cots of Union and rebel soldiers, will last as long and stand as
> fair, as the military bungling which distinguished this clergyman
> turned colonel, and evoked such agonized curses from his com-
> manding officer at Port Royal. Better be a good nurse like Walt
> Whitman, than a nondescript warrior like the Rev. Col. Higgin-
> son.

The main part of O'Connor's refutation of the critics is devoted to
Clarence Cook who, in writing of the 1881 *Leaves* in *The Inter-
national Review*, stated that the *Leaves* are derived from Emerson,
that Whitman's use of the Emerson letter in his second edition was a
"breach of confidence," and that Emerson was shocked at the
Leaves.
In rebuttal O'Connor prints Emerson's letter in full and disputes
the opinion that Emerson repudiated the *Leaves*. Cook had attributed to Emerson the statement, "Strange that a man with the brain of
a god should have the snout of a hog." This was not said by Emerson,

according to O'Connor, but was a *mot* of E. P. Whipple in about the year 1855.

> It was reported to me, with great glee, fresh from his lips, by one of his dear friends, who afterwards ran away with the trust funds and beggared the widow and the orphan—a natural consequence of his delight in such sarcasms.

O'Connor goes on with a quotation from De Quincey: "The habit of murder inevitably leads to procrastination and Sabbath-breaking," and adds, "A man who admires Mr. Whipple's wit may be expected, sooner or later, to make off with the cash of the community."

In answer to Cook's calling the poem destitute of beauty and proportion, O'Connor cites Ruskin's admiration of the *Leaves*. To Cook's assertion that the book's worst fault is its lack of humor, O'Connor asserts that "we do not split our sides over the Book of Isaiah."

As to the allegation that *Leaves of Grass* lacks taste, he retorts,

> . . . there are only ten baskets of taste let down from heaven for each generation, and he (Cook) and nimble men like him have always got them all, which is the reason why none of the great geniuses in poetry ever had any, from Aristophanes to Molière, or from Aeschylus to Victor Hugo.

He concludes by asserting that, contrary to Cook's statement that Whitman "is as ignorant of society as a Digger Indian," the poet is considered a perfect gentleman in the best society. (O'Connor noted also that those paragraphs which were favorable to *Leaves of Grass* in Cook's article had been left out in the *Tribune's* reprint.)

The last third of O'Connor's letter is devoted to his appraisal of the greatness and uniqueness of *Leaves of Grass*. "It is the first poetic work in the English language since Shakespeare . . . that sounds the trumpet for a new advance; that is not merely original but ab-original . . . that is, in its theory and purpose, a new departure. . . ." O'Connor reviews the great poets since Shakespeare, praising them but indicating their shortcomings: The early promise of Burns, Keats, Shelley and Byron was unfulfilled because of their untimely deaths. He praises the early Tennyson, but deplores his having learned that "kind hearts are less than coronets, and simple faith than Norman blood."

In American literature there "has not appeared a single racy specimen." The only possible exception, though in a minor key, is "the weird and lovely lyric verse of Edgar Poe, perfectly distinctive, shrining a strange mythology of personal love and sorrow, and having its roots in certain parts of our southern life." But poetry such as his only influences; it does not emancipate or lead. He names Longfellow, Emerson, and Bryant as poets whose work has many virtues, but does not "smack of any particular soil."

He goes back to Shakespeare for the "last full signal for a great march, for an exodus out of old conventions, old dogmas, old ideas, old theories. . . ." He goes on to explore the nature of Shakespeare's new departure, comparing him with the Greek dramatists. (Here he takes issue with Walt Whitman, feeling that Whitman gives too much weight to the historical plays, deriving from them the idea that Shakespeare was the poet of feudalism. This is the only adverse criticism of Whitman in the letter.)

In his feelings about *Leaves of Grass*, however, there is no wavering from the superlative. He terms *Leaves of Grass* "the poem of embodiment. It indicates the august kosmic (*sic*) fact of numberless material entities held in cohesion by spirit, which in time loosens and departs." Other poets, such as Rabelais, have celebrated the body alone, or as Shelley, the spirit alone, "like the dream of the soul remembered in a dream." But the *Leaves* is "the strongest, amplest, most definite projection of the incarnate soul—the human creature, male or female—the female equal to the male—the being, dual and unitary at once, like the globe of two hemispheres. . . ."

This being is heir to an

> omnific personal destiny which is alike the destiny of each and all; governed through all the nature by the egoistic pride, and by love and the necessity for love, as by two paramount vital springs; conscious at the summit of the highest knowledge of the eternal mystery in which all beings must remain to each, and of the eternal mystery one must be to one's self; and, from that lofty summit, joyous, haughty, transfigured in the sense of the democratic constitution of the Universe, in which all between the worm and the god are equal, being all organically necessary to the whole, and of

which perpetual ascension, perpetual transfer and promotion, is the law. . . .

In *Leaves of Grass*, O'Connor asserts, Whitman has expressed the representative man and woman of this country. Other poets, such as Homer, Juvenal, Rabelais, and Hugo, have portrayed the people of their time—

> But in what poem have all the things which make up the show of a people's life appeared with such comprehensive and vivid reality, such national distinctiveness and such strength of charm, as in *Leaves of Grass*? Above all, the wonder of it is, to me, the marvel that what was thought commonplace and prosaic is restored in the book to the superbest poetry by the revelation of its intrinsic significance—by the establishment of its mystical relation.

Of the poems of the war for the Union, he says that "they alone of all the song born from that struggle are the true key."

He concludes the text of his letter with the statement,

> . . . to have conceived and written *Leaves of Grass*—to have been of the old heroic strain of which such books alone are born— to have surcharged the pages with their world of noble and passionate life—to have done all this, to have dared all this, to have suffered for all this—is to be the true brother of Shakespeare.

Between the time of O'Connor's completion of the material for Bucke's book and the book's publication there occurred another crisis in the reception of *Leaves of Grass*—one in which the barrier between O'Connor and Whitman was finally completely swept away. The episode began auspiciously with an offer to Whitman from Osgood and Company of Boston to become the publishers of a new edition of *Leaves of Grass*. This was the first commercial publishing house to have made such an offer since Thayer and Eldridge had done so more than twenty years earlier.

Osgood's interest in the *Leaves* had been stimulated by John Boyle O'Reilly, an Irish-born novelist, poet and editor whom Whitman later linked with O'Connor as both belonging to the "tempest class: Ardent Irish natures—clean, clear, afire with ideals of justice—willing, eager, anytime to live or die for justice." And again,

"If you take a pinch of the best Irish salt, you get the best salt of the earth."[27]

O'Reilly wrote to Whitman of Osgood's offer, and the poet wrote his acceptance on the back of the letter, describing his plan for the volume: In addition to some thirty pages of new pieces, the main changes would be in the arrangement of the poems—the *ensemble*. He gives his prospective publishers fair warning that "the old pieces, the *sexuality* odes, about which the original row was started and kept up so long, are all retained, and must go in the same as ever."[28]

After another exchange of letters Whitman sent the revised *Leaves of Grass* to Osgood and Company on May 28, 1881, and the contract was signed in June.[29] In September Whitman went to Boston to see the book through the press—a stay made memorable by his visits to Concord where he saw the aging Emerson and was well received by him and others of the Concord group. Copies of the Osgood edition began to circulate in the United States and in England (where it was distributed by David Bogue, after having been declined by Trübner & Co.).

In the meantime Bucke sent the manuscript of the biography to Whitman who made a number of corrections, writing,

> Without explaining each particular point of elision or addition, I will only say that I am convinced if you accept and print this copy as now arranged, you will bless your stars afterward—(printed in the old shape it would have turned out ill, and in very many things would probably have been unendorsed by you, as it certainly would be by me.)
>
> The character you give me is not a true one in the main—I am by no means that benevolent, equable, happy creature you portray—but let that pass. I have left it as you wrote.

He added some words of praise: "There is enough to make a very creditable, serviceable book—a permanent storehouse of many biographic, personal & other things, and of your glowing and penetrating criticism."[30]

When Bucke's *Walt Whitman* came out, Whitman wrote to O'Connor:

> Taken together the Introductory Letter and the GGP are so tremendous & vehement, so beautiful & orbic in themselves—so

fitting for the body of the volume (almost its heart & lungs)—so
honest & subtle, as well as stupendous a eulogy & dissertation, on
L of G, & on certain primary & spinal literary laws—so assuring a
pedestal for my future fame—& as here printed so satisfactory in
their type style & paragraphing &c. *as they stand* that any change
in those particulars would be worse than unnecessary—would be
fatuous—[31]

O'Connor was pleased by this wholehearted acceptance as proof of
the truth of his work. He wrote to his niece, Grace Channing, "Of
course as Walt saw my Ms. in proof, and could have corrected any
misunderstanding of his doctrine, the fact that it came to me without
a word of suggested alteration, seems evidence of my accuracy."[32]

Despite Whitman's favorable opinion of Bucke's *Walt Whitman*
and Osgood and Company's expressed interest in publishing it, its
fate was tied to that of the new edition of the *Leaves* which soon
encountered opposition. The Osgood edition of *Leaves of Grass*,
published in November 1881, had been out but four months when an
adversary to freedom in letters struck a blow against it. On March 1,
1882 Oliver Stevens, the Boston District Attorney, wrote to Osgood
and Company, "We are of the opinion that this book is such a book
as brings it within the provision of the public Statutes respecting
obscene literature and suggest the propriety of withdrawing the
same from circulation and suppressing the editions thereof."[33]

The publishers promptly forwarded this letter to Whitman asking
his consent to withdraw the present edition and substitute an edition
lacking the "obnoxious features." Eager to have his book distributed, and thinking that the proposed revision would comprise not
more than about ten lines and a half-dozen words and phrases to be
left out, Whitman consented to making some changes, though he
stated that he was not afraid of the District Attorney's threat. The
poet's suggested revisions were of words and phrases in "I Sing the
Body Electric," "A Woman Waits for Me," and "Spontaneous Me."

This compromise was not all acceptable. The passages which the
District Attorney wanted changed included three poems to be excised completely—"A Woman Waits for Me," "Dalliance of Eagles,"
and "To a Common Prostitute." In addition there were twenty-two
other citations involving more than a hundred and fifty lines.[34]
Whitman was no longer in the mood to compromise. "The list,

whole and several, is rejected by me, and will not be thought of under any circumstances."[35] For emphasis, he sent a copy of *Leaves of Grass* with the changes he had in mind. They appeared on only four pages. He urged that the book be reissued with only those changes.

A week later Osgood and Company wrote, "We do not think the official mind will be satisfied," and demanded the elimination of "A Woman Waits for Me" and "To a Common Prostitute."[36] But Whitman was now obdurate. The publishers and the poet made arrangements for the termination of their contract. Osgood and Company returned the plates and sent the royalties then due on April 22, 1882. This ended the second Boston publication of *Leaves of Grass*. The poet had conducted the business arrangements with calm attention to detail, displaying no anger over the matter. He wrote to Burroughs that he would try to publish it himself: "in some respects shall like it just as well."[37]

Whitman's calm and matter-of-fact reaction was not shared by O'Connor, who was as aroused by this new injustice as he had been by Harlan's dismissal of Whitman seventeen years earlier. He wrote to Burroughs:

> I have just been thunderstruck by a letter from Bucke telling me that Osgood, under a threat from the District Attorney at Boston, Sanger, had stopped the publication of Walt's book, I don't let the grass grow under my feet when an outrage of this kind is committed—one which makes Harlan's insignificant—and I am going to make the District Attorney regret that he was ever born, if I can compass it.

When this challenge came O'Connor was an exhausted warrior, worn by overwork and illness, and with a pen that had grown accustomed to writing letters and reports, not literary essays. Nevertheless he rose to the occasion. As soon as he received Bucke's letter describing what had happened, O'Connor flew downstairs with *Leaves of Grass* in his hand to the Solicitor of the Treasury Kenneth Raynor, and "for two hours to him and Robinson (the Assistant Solicitor) and Barton (the law clerk) I gave the District Attorney unlimited volcano." After hearing him read and expound the poems, they agreed that it was an outrage. He immediately went down to see

Brewster, the Attorney General, but was temporarily stopped in his efforts by Brewster's absence. He planned to see him upon his return.[38]

It turned out that O'Connor had selected the wrong target. He learned later that the true culprit was Oliver Stevens, the Massachusetts State District Attorney, acting, not under federal statutes, but under those of the State of Massachusetts. The Attorney General of the United States, therefore, had no jurisdiction in the matter.

O'Connor's first overture to Whitman since the quarrel followed this incident. He wrote directly to get information about the poet's relations with Osgood and Company.[39] Whitman answered the letter on May 3, 1882, enclosing a "budget" of material (twelve items in all) and asking that it be sent on to Bucke. Four days later he sent O'Connor a brief synopsis of his dealings with Osgood and Company, discreetly leaving out the fact that he had been willing at one point to make a few changes.

As to the prime mover in the suppression, Whitman had learned from Ben Ticknor of Osgood and Company that the affair "originated from State Attorney General Mr. Marston, who (at the instigation of certain parties) peremptorily instructed the Boston District Attorney Stevens to proceed against L of G." Whitman asserted that he was not angry at the publishers. "Marston is the target for you," he wrote to O'Connor.[40]

O'Connor was not the only friend of Whitman who did not share the poet's calm acceptance of the withdrawal of Osgood and Company. The first published attack on Oliver Stevens was by Bucke. It appeared as a letter to the editor in the *Springfield* (Mass.) *Republican* on May 23, and dwelt upon the essential morality of *Leaves of Grass*. Yet even if the book were one "in which sensual pleasures were pictured and praised for their own sake, or in which some of the fundamental principles of morality were attacked, it would still be wrong, inexpedient, and contrary to the spirit of the age and country to suppress it by legal interference." In *Leaves of Grass*, however, the author's "whole crime . . . is that he believes in the grandeur and goodness of humanity in all its parts and relations; that he, being himself pure, sees that man is so in his essential nature . . . that his parts and all his functions are well made and divinely appointed. . . ."

Bucke's letter seems to be an answer not only to Oliver Stevens, but also to the reviewers of the new edition, one of whom had referred to the "slop-bucket of Walt Whitman," and said, ". . . The chief question raised by this publication is whether anybody—even a poet—ought to take off his trousers in the market-place." The review concluded: "The gross materialism of his verses represents art in its last degradation rather than in its rude infancy."

On May 22, 1882, the *New York Tribune* published a factual account of what had happened between Osgood and Company and Walt Whitman, saying that Oliver Stevens had acted under the direction of State Attorney General Marston. The *Tribune* ended with a statement made by the poet to someone who had visited him in Camden to the effect that the settlement with the publishers had been satisfactory, and that "the Attorney General's action was only another buffet, but no more serious than any previous obstacle." The same issue of the *Tribune* contained a summary of a speech, entitled, "Mr. Collyer's Tribute to Emerson," in which no mention was made of Emerson's attitude toward *Leaves of Grass*.

Three days later, O'Connor's article, entitled "Suppressing Walt Whitman" and subtitled (probably by the editorial staff) "Raising a New 'Barbaric Yawp' Over the Roofs of the World/Red-Hot and Dead Earnest" appeared. It begins: "Sir: I have just learned the details of an outrage so signal in its character and so sinister in its bearings as to become, in my judgment, a matter of the widest public concern."

O'Connor tells of the first edition of *Leaves of Grass* which met with the "censures of the small" but with the approbation of Emerson and other writers and scholars in America and in England. "Finally after twenty-five years of combat, darkened by frequent acts of persecution, and involving bitter suffering to the author," the book was published by Osgood and Company, which withdrew as publishers after the intervention of the District Attorney. "Mr. District Attorney triumphed; and for the first time, I believe, in the history of this country, an honest book, the work of a man of great admitted genius, has been suppressed by an officer of the law."

O'Connor then describes eight of the offending passages and poems, showing their nobility and sublimity. He does not name the remaining fourteen passages, but states that they were all part of the first edition of the *Leaves* which was endorsed by Emerson, "our man of deepest insight, our man of holiest heart." It is ironic that the suppression happened in the very month of the death of Emerson,

> when the old landscape we New England men and women love saddens into an immense vacancy, as if Monadnock had sunk silently below the horizon—in the very month when the heavens open to receive our noblest citizen—the pentecostal book he had covered with his glowing eulogy is suppressed by law! . . . Fit souvenir: to make stalk against the bright horizons around that grave the spectre of the black Puritan!—Happy thought—to complete Concord with a reminiscence of Gallows Hill!

In a tone reminiscent of his early story, "Loss and Gain: A Tale of Lynn," he declares that Osgood and Company, instead of falling "into the category of hucksters whose business cannot afford a conscience," should have fought the District Attorney. Stevens is now the peril of Shakespeare and the Bible. In this connection O'Connor brings in for the first time a name which was to become a symbol of the suppression of literature—Anthony Comstock: "Even his bolder and brassier ally in this holy war, Mr. Anthony Comstock,—even he tempers valor with discretion for the nonce, and says 'he will not prosecute the publishers of the classics unless they specially advertise them.' "

In his conclusion O'Connor promises to persist in his attack upon Oliver Stevens. He will never let it be forgotten that

> Massachusetts has a District Attorney, named Oliver Stevens, true to the blood of Mather, faithful to the darkest traditions, who wrenched the law from its purpose to crush and extinguish "the most extraordinary piece of wit and wisdom America has yet contributed"—the sanest, the largest, the most splendid and enduring literary product which the Celto-Saxon race has given the age. Let this fame console him even in the sad event of his being expelled from the office Concord and Harvard may say he has disgraced and polluted!

This eloquent—even extravagant—letter brought praise to O'Connor from John Hay, among others. Hay wrote from Cleveland, Ohio, that he felt he could pardon the folly of Oliver Stevens for having touched off this "splendid" letter. He agreed that Osgood and Company should not have given up the publication just because "a super-serviceable official threatened to give him a magnificent advertisement gratis."[41]

O'Connor responded enthusiastically: "My Dear John Hay: You are an angel boy!" He writes of other letters of congratulation, and adds: "Wish us well in the fight we are entering. It is a great cause—fifty years hence people will say so. I only wish I were free of this wretched office life, that I might do my champion's devoir more freely."[42]

It was Whitman's letter that meant the most, of course. He wrote on May 28, "I like the big letter of May 25 the more I have read it—I think it will never die—."[43] Yet Whitman's own words were used to contradict O'Connor. The Reverend John W. Chadwick, a Unitarian minister, in a letter to the *Tribune* published on May 28, writes that, although he believes that Whitman "has not written a line that was not pure and high in its *intention*," O'Connor is wrong in saying that Emerson never qualified in any way his enthusiastic response to *Leaves of Grass*. His proof came from Whitman himself. In an article published in *The Critic* on December 3, 1881, Whitman had written:

> Up and down this breadth by Beacon st., between these same old elms, I walked for two hours, of a bright, sharp February midday twenty-one years ago with Emerson, then in his prime, keen, physically and morally magnetic, arm'd at every point, and when he chose, wielding the emotional just as well as the intellectual. During those two hours he was the talker and I the listener. It was an argument-statement, reconnoitering, review, attack, and pressing home, (like an army corps in order, artillery, cavalry, infantry,) of all that could be said against that part (and a main part) in the construction of my poems, "Children of Adam." More precious than gold to me that dissertation—it afforded me, ever after, this strange and paradoxical lesson; each point of E.'s statement was unanswerable, no judge's charge ever more complete or convincing, I could never hear the points better put—and then I felt down in my soul the clear and unmistakable conviction to disobey all, and pursue my own way. "What have you got to say then to such things?" said E., pausing in conclusion. "Only that while I can't answer them at all, I feel more settled than ever to adhere to

my own theory, and exemplify it," was my candid response. Whereupon we went and had a good dinner at the American House. And thenceforward I never waver'd or was touch'd with qualms, (as I confess I had been two or three times before).

Here was O'Connor contraverted by Whitman himself! What a dilemma for a champion! Whitman must have felt guilty, for he sent the Chadwick letter to O'Connor on the day it appeared, and after congratulating O'Connor on his letter of May 25, continued with an explanation of the Emerson affair. He wrote:

> I am glad the Rev. Mr. Chadwick appears with his *Tribune* letter to you today (as enclosed) for the fine chance it affords to ventilate the real account and true inwardness of the Emerson talk on the Common in 1860—& I at once send you the best synopsis of it I can recall—quite—quite certainly the same in amount as I told you while it was fresh in my memory—the which with hasty scrib- blings on my relations with Emerson—I hope (working in as from yourself) you will incorporate in your answer to *Tribune*.[44]

Enclosed were some twenty-two lines, which he suggested might be quoted by O'Connor "as extracted from a late letter to you from me." Two days later Whitman wrote again, giving more details about Emerson's relations with him, stressing that Emerson's objec- tions to the "Children of Adam" poems "sprang exclusively from conventional and what may be called the usual technical literary considerations."[45]

O'Connor's answer to the Reverend Mr. Chadwick appeared in the *Tribune* on June 18, 1882, under the title and subtitle: "Emerson and Whitman: Mr. O'Connor Replies to the Rev. Mr. Chadwick— The Concord Philosopher's Love for the 'Good Gray Poet'—All That Could Be Said, Not All That Has Been Said—Dynamite and Anthropophagy." O'Connor charges that the Reverend Mr. Chad- wick called him a liar with respect to what he had written about Emerson and Whitman. In his response O'Connor cites evidence of Emerson's continued friendship and regard for Whitman. (Among evidences of friendship and regard, he fails to mention the letters of recommendation which Emerson gave Whitman to present to Sal- mon P. Chase and Charles Sumner when he was job hunting in

Washington in 1862. Perhaps he had never known of them, or he and Whitman had both forgotten about them.)

In a letter to Burroughs, O'Connor wrote that he thought his answer to Chadwick "quite composed in tone,"[46] even though he had characterized Chadwick's arsenal as "a toy gun loaded with a single green pea," and his fortification as "a cobweb Gibraltar." O'Connor had closed his article by saying, "For less than he has done to me, the good cannibals have eaten many a missionary." He also stated to Burroughs that the article had cost him "severe labor." Since a large part of the letter had been supplied by Whitman, the labor probably was caused by his effort to keep his invective on the safe side of being libelous.

The *Tribune*, in its attempt to be even-handed, published a diatribe against Whitman, signed "Sigma," on the very day that O'Connor's "Emerson and Whitman" appeared. (Later O'Connor indentified *Sigma* as Stoddard.)[47] The article was headed: "Judging the Case on Its Merits," with the subhead, "The Mistake of Trying to Reform Society by Abolishing Clothes—Emerson's Qualification of His Approval of Whitman."

The tenor of the argument is that, while the lawyers will decide whether *Leaves of Grass* falls into the category of obscene literature as defined by the statute, there is no doubt that the *Leaves* is "a glorification of the animal man, who is exhibited to us—regardless of sex—*in puris naturabilis*. Mr. Whitman writes out for us minute anatomic catalogues of 'bodily organs' and calls them 'poems.' " *Sigma* lists writers who were thought to be most candid, such as Montaigne and Rousseau, who nevertheless kept certain reticences. He calls Whitman "the apostle of the unclean." Even though it may suit his inclination to go naked, "civilized mankind yet retain a marked prejudice in favor of clothes." He ends by stating that Emerson did later qualify the approval expressed in his 1855 letter.

O'Connor did not attempt to answer *Sigma*. He may have been discouraged by a letter from Whitelaw Reid of the *Tribune* who wrote that, even though he admired O'Connor's letter of May 25, "For my own part, I really wish that Whitman had left some of the ranker things out."[48] He may also have been put off by Whitman's thought that *Sigma* might have been "some crafty friend who takes the mask of foe."[49]

A different view of O'Connor's championship was taken by Anne Gilchrist, who thought he made too much of Emerson's endorsement. (She could not have known that Whitman himself was the source of much of O'Connor's reply to Chadwick.) She wrote to John Burroughs:

> I agree with you in wishing Mr. O'Connor would not lay so much stress on the Emerson affair; but not quite for the same reason as you. I think (though I admire and reverence Emerson as much as you, or any American) that its importance is immensely overrated. No man, however eminent, can make or mar another's fame. If Emerson recognized greatness in Walt Whitman, so much the better for Emerson; to himself the chief benefit. Walt Whitman has to abide longer and severer tests. Time is the arbiter. . . .

Of *Sigma* she wrote: "Honi soit qui mal y pense." She considers it a sweeping misstatement to say that *Leaves of Grass* is mainly a celebration of the body. That theme occupies no more than thirty pages out of three hundred. "I am the poet of the soul" is emphasized throughout. Anne Gilchrist suggests that Burroughs may send any part of her letter to the *Tribune* for publication, but he evidently did not do so.[50]

O'Connor in the meantime turned his attention to trying to ferret out the prime mover in the Osgood suppression. In attacking Oliver Stevens he had hoped to "smoke out" Marston. In this he failed. He then wrote to a friend, E. B. Foote, asking him to try to find out from Benjamin Tucker whether he could identify the culprit.[51] Benjamin Tucker was then on the editorial staff of the Boston *Globe*, as well as being the editor of *Liberty*, a radical publication. He was a philosophical anarchist, opposed to violence, a translator of Proudhon, former editor of *The Word* and of *The Radical Review*. In his publication, *Liberty*, he later printed the works of George Bernard Shaw.

Tucker wrote to Whitman early in the controversy (on May 25) urging that *Leaves of Grass* be published in Boston, where it had been "struck down." If he had the means to do so, he would gladly "put the book on the market, advertised as the suppressed edition, and invite the authorities to dispute my right to do so." If Whitman could not find someone to publish the book, he would gladly sign himself as the publisher and go to jail if necessary.[52] Whitman did not need to avail himself of this offer, since he found commercial publishers for the new edition—Rees, Welsh and Company of Philadelphia. Tucker did advertise the book in Boston in *Liberty* (on July 22), writing that it could be procured from him.

To O'Connor's inquiry about who was responsible for the suppression, Tucker responded that the culprit was not Oliver Stevens (whom he considered to be "philosophically, politically, and instinctively a democrat") but Marston, whom he characterized as a "legal shyster of much shrewdness but no depth, an unscrupulous and tricky politician, and physically a huge, gross, bull-necked sensualist." He also quoted Stevens as having said that he received a complaint from an agent of the New England Society for the Suppression of Vice, who in turn was a mere tool of Anthony Comstock.[53]

Whitman evidently appreciated Tucker's efforts on his behalf: When O'Connor wrote in 1883 that he had sent a copy of Bucke's *Walt Whitman* to Tucker, the poet was pleased, writing "He is a good friend."[54] Although Tucker admired Whitman, he did not hesitate to criticize him when he thought him wrong. In 1888 when Whitman wrote a poem eulogizing the German Emperor Wilhelm as a "faithful shepherd" Tucker criticized him in *Liberty* in a biting article entitled "Cases of Lamentable Longevity." He later wrote to O'Connor, "I was sorry to have to be so severe on Whitman, but I wrote deliberately, meaning every word. Seldom have I been so pained and disappointed as by his eulogy of that cursed despot, Wilhelm."[55] O'Connor agreed with Tucker. "O'Connor, too, fell, afoul of me for my emperor piece," Whitman remarked. "Why that piece almost threatened to create a split in the church! O'Connor is quite as radical as Tucker, though much less interested in political study. . . ."[56]

At the time of the suppression of the Osgood edition, however, there was no "split in the church." Tucker was wholeheartedly helping O'Connor to find the culprit. O'Connor agreed that the villain was Marston. He asked Tucker, "Who was it roused him from that day's enjoyment of *The Lustful Turk* or *The Adventures of the Little French Bedstead* and set him to hunt the great book Emerson and Concord praised?"[57]

Soon another defender rose to test the suppression. George Chainey, a former minister who had come to feel that more attention should be paid to this world, published an essay on Whitman, called "Keep Off the Grass" in his journal, *This World* (with "one world at a time" as his motto and subtitle). To placate his fearful printer, he had the poem "To a Common Prostitute" printed separately to be sent as an enclosure. He then asked Postmaster Tobey to rule upon it before mailing. Tobey refused to do so until he had the approval of Oliver Stevens, the District Attorney, who in turn felt that the matter should be referred to the United States Postmaster General.

Upon hearing of this, O'Connor immediately got in touch with Chainey (whom he had not known previously) to ascertain the facts. Then he enlisted the aid of Colonel Robert Ingersoll, called "the great agnostic," who was a lawyer, orator, lecturer, and statesman. After practicing law in Illinois, Ingersoll had served as colonel of the 11th Illinois volunteer cavalry regiment. Later he was Attorney General of Illinois, and might have become governor of that state had it not been for his outspoken agnosticism. He came to Washington in 1879, where he pursued his career as lecturer and writer. O'Connor chose well, for Ingersoll was highly regarded in Washington.

An exultant O'Connor was able to write to Whitman on July 7 that the Postmaster General had reversed the action on Chainey's publication, ruling that *Leaves of Grass* must pass unmolested through the mails, that a book, generally accepted by the public, admitted into libraries and accepted by the literary class, cannot be brought under the operation of the statutes respecting taboo matter. ". . . We owe this victory to the tact, bonhomie, energy and gallantry of Ingersoll, who put the case to the Department in the best manner possible."[58] Whitman appreciated Ingersoll and said of him, "He is always a marvel of a man to me—a sort of child man who is honest with himself; who acts out according to his nature—is on the square—has neither false reserve nor false parade."[59] (Ingersoll remained a good friend. In November 1890, he lectured on Whitman, sending the proceeds of $900 to the poet, and later delivered a memorable eulogy at Whitman's funeral.)

Despite the ruling of the Postmaster General, Boston's postmaster, Tobey, did not act to release the bags of copies of *This World*. They were finally dispatched, without orders, by the "honorable audacity" of a subordinate.[60] Tobey was not to escape O'Connor's wrath.

He sent the *Tribune* a tirade entitled "Tobey or Not Tobey" characterizing the postmaster's words, tones, looks and demeanor as

> sleek, sanctimonious and oleaginous. . . . If superimposing one miracle upon another, the prophet Jonah could have absorbed the whale that had previously swallowed him, he would not have been a completer interfusion of sanctity and oil than was embodied in the suave saint of the Boston mailbags on that Holy Thursday.

Summarizing the actions of Stevens, Comstock, and Tobey, O'Connor concludes that Tobey ought to be removed from his office.

The *Tribune* refused this article. O'Connor did not seem disturbed—perhaps because he planned to gather all his articles about the 1882 suppression of *Leaves of Grass* into a pamphlet—a plan which Whitman encouraged. This was not done; "Tobey or Not Tobey" was not published until after O'Connor and Whitman were both dead, when it appeared in *The Conservator*, Horace Traubel's periodical.

Undeterred, O'Connor's next attack was against the instigator of the suppression—Anthony Comstock, whose role in the suppression he had first learned of from Tucker. (Comstock had not denied his part in the affair when the Boston press had written of it.)

In Anthony Comstock, O'Connor had selected a formidable antagonist, experienced in laying snares for the writers and publishers of works he thought salacious. Comstock had begun his career as a reformer of morals in 1871, when he was twenty-seven years old, by founding the Society for the Suppression of Vice. Within two years he was instrumental in having the Postal Law of 1873 passed, which prohibited the use of the mails for sending obscene material. He became a special agent of the Post Office Department and Secretary of the Society for the Suppression of Vice. His inability to distinguish between obscenity and good literature led him to act in later years against many excellent works, among them George Bernard Shaw's play, "Mrs. Warren's Profession." This caused Shaw to coin the term "comstockery" which became part of the English language.

Comstock boasted that he had caused fifteen suicides among the purveyors of obscenity—but he did not make Whitman or O'Connor cringe. O'Connor's response to his attack was "Mr. Comstock as Cato the Censor" which appeared in the *Tribune* on August 27, 1882. This was subtitled merely, "Another letter from William D. O'Connor." The first line was an excellent opening salvo: "Mr. Anthony Comstock's hostility to the nude, appears to extend even to the naked truth." This sentence had been pruned by the editor, possibly out of fear of libel; O'Connor had written: "Mr. Anthony Comstock's hostility to the nude, of which an illustrious example was his famous prosecution of three unfortunate women whom he had hired to dance for him, for over an hour, without clothing, in a New York brothel, appears to extend even to the naked truth."

O'Connor accused Comstock of having veiled "in deceptive and elusive terms" the truth that *Leaves of Grass* could go through the mails, just as ". . . any book, belonging to the day-lit realm of letters, published openly by a reputable publisher, recognized by the literary class, admitted into libraries, discussed by reviews, accepted under any conditions by the general public, will not be excluded from the mails." (Comstock had hinted otherwise to the *Tribune* reporter.) This, O'Connor reminded his readers, was the principle under which the post office authorities had allowed Boccaccio's *Decameron* to go through the mails. Similarly, *Leaves of Grass* is also "under the aegis of the eagle . . . safe from being hawked at and slain by any mousing owl of the Vice Society. If Mr. Comstock doubts it, let him whet his beak and try."

O'Connor cites, as he had done in his previous writings, prominent clergymen and authors in the United States and abroad who had appreciated *Leaves of Grass*. Notwithstanding all these praises, Comstock had threatened to act against the *Leaves*. O'Connor ends with a threat of his own:

> So long as Mr. Comstock chooses to confine his industry to the removal of the stuff which Dutch and English lust produces and calls French, so long as he limits his energies to cleaning out the bawdy fiction, the lascivious engravings, the filthy devices of the lecher and abortionist, all may be well with him. But let him dare to throw into his night-cart that pearl of great price, the book of any honest author, let him venture to carry out his wicked menace in regard to the work of the good gray poet, and he will quickly find himself the centre of a tornado which will only pass to leave the United States Post Office without its scavenger.

When there was no answer from Comstock, O'Connor exulted in a letter to Whitman: "Comstock takes the dare! He cowers like a kicked spaniel, and does not venture to carry out his threat. I thought my letter would have the effect of making him cautious."[61] In the same letter, O'Connor tells Whitman of his attack on Tobey, the Boston postmaster, which he has sent to the *Tribune*. "It is gay and stinging, until near the close, when it rises and darkens into righteous anger."

Comstock was not silenced; he bided his time. In October 1882, he caused the arrest of someone who printed two of the questioned poems from *Leaves of Grass*. This was Ezra H. Heywood, a radical reformer who had been active in the anti-slavery movement, but who, unlike O'Connor and Whitman, espoused the theory of Free Love. In his journal, *The Word*, he published "To a Common Prostitute" and "A Woman Waits for Me." He also put *Leaves of Grass* on his trade list.

Comstock rose to the bait and had him arrested. Perhaps he thought he was safer in this maneuver than he had been with Reverend George Chainey, since Heywood had served a term in jail because of one of his publications, though he had later been exonerated and released.

On October 27 O'Connor wrote to Whitman that the notice of Heywood's arrest made his blood boil: "All this is damnable. I don't like Heywood's ways, and I don't like the Free-Love theories at all, but he has his rights, which these devils trample on."[62] Whitman answered that there must be some mistake. Had not the Chainey affair settled the matter of mailing *Leaves of Grass*?

A week later Heywood wrote to Whitman, introducing himself and telling of his career. He had been interested in *Leaves of Grass* ever since the edition of 1860 had appeared. As to Comstock, he described some of the ruses and impersonations Comstock had used in order to obtain evidence, including the episode described by O'Connor in the opening sentence of "Anthony Comstock as Cato the Censor." (This was the part that had been cut by the *Tribune*.) He referred to Tucker's advertisement of the *Leaves* in *Liberty*, stating that if Comstock succeeded in having *him* convicted, he would undoubtedly proceed against Tucker.[63]

Fortunately Heywood did not ask for Whitman's support—only for ideas or suggestions from him or his "immediate comrades."

Whitman wrote of this to O'Connor: "(As to the vehement action of the Free religious & lover folk, in their conventions, papers, &c. in my favor—and even proceedings like these of Heywood—I see nothing better for myself or friends to do than quietly stand aside & let it go on) . . ."[64]

Heywood's trial took place on November 26, but the verdict was not given until the following April. Whitman then wrote to O'Connor: "The Judge peremptorily ruled out the L of G slips part of the indictment—(which ruling was received with applause,) and H was afterwards on the remaining part or parts acquitted."[65]

This action indicated that *Leaves of Grass* was no longer in danger. The Rees, Welsh edition sold out quickly. Later the firm was taken over by David McKay, who published subsequent editions during the poet's lifetime. David McKay also published Bucke's *Walt Whitman* (copyrighted by O'Connor) in 1883. The following year an English edition of Bucke's biography appeared, printed in Glasgow by Wilson and McCormick, with a supplement by Edward Dowden about English critics of Walt Whitman. A second English edition was published in 1888.

With the publication of Bucke's biography containing *The Good Gray Poet* and "Mr. O'Connor's Letter," O'Connor's "champion's devoir" for Walt Whitman was finished. He soon had occasion to resume the advocate's role on behalf of William Francis Channing. His next published piece was "Some Nails for a Coffin," in the *Tribune* on February 11, 1883. In it he refuted the claim made by a historian, Charles C. Coffin, in his book *The Building of a Nation*, that Moses G. Farmer (the author's brother-in-law) had invented the electric fire-alarm. In fact it had been invented by William Channing, who had presented it as a gift to the city of Boston. (Farmer had been his assistant.) O'Connor contraverts Coffin's claim with evidence that includes quotations from Farmer himself. O'Connor's array of facts and tone of irony should have silenced Coffin, but the *Tribune* published a rejoinder from him on February 21 and a letter from O'Connor five days later, entitled "The Fire-Alarm Controversy," which ended the dispute. Brief and matter-of-fact, these letters were quite different from the letters written in defense of Whitman.

The bond of friendship between O'Connor and Whitman was now strong, and they exchanged letters and cards frequently until O'Connor's final illness. O'Connor's joy in the resumption of friendship, however, could not offset the sadness caused by a personal tragedy which clouded his remaining years.

NOTES

1. LG/CRE, p. 321.
2. Published by G. P. Putnam's Sons, New York.
3. "Twenty-five Years Ago," account of Bucke's experiences in the Sierras, *Overland Monthly*, November and December 1857, vol. 1, series 2, June 1883, 553–60. Richard Maurice Bucke, "Catalogue to the Exhibition, Canadian Medical Association and Canadian Psychiatric Association Annual Meetings, June 10–14, 1963, Toronto."
4. Bucke, *Cosmic Consciousness* (Philadelphia: Innes & Sons, 1901). Slightly revised version, New York: E.P. Dutton, 1923.
5. (Feinberg-LC).
6. Bucke, "Memories of Walt Whitman," *Walt Whitman Fellowship Papers*, 6 (September 1894).
7. Bucke to WW, 18 March 1880: Artem Lozynsky, *The Letters of Dr. Richard Maurice Bucke to Walt Whitman* (Detroit: Wayne State University Press, 1977) p. 7.
8. (The John Rylands Library, Manchester, England).
9. (The John Rylands Library, Manchester, England).
10. Bucke to WDO'C, 27 June 1881 (Perry).
11. 31 October 1881 (Perry).
12. Edward Carpenter, *Days with Walt Whitman* (London: George Allen & Unwin, Ltd., 1906), pp. 36–37.
13. "It was Walt's idea asking you to do it and I know he will be glad to have it done." Bucke to WDO'C, 22 December 1881 (University of Texas Library).
14. (Feinberg-LC).
15. (Feinberg-LC).
16. (Feinberg-LC).
17. WDO'C to Bucke, 29 July 1882 (Feinberg-LC).
18. (Brown).
19. 27 June 1881. From unpublished paper presented by Henry S. Saunders, "Bucke and O'Connor as seen through their letters." Whitman Fellowship Meeting in New York, 31 May 1915.
20. (Feinberg-LC).
21. Bucke to WDO'C, 28 February 1882 (Feinberg-LC).
22. 13 March 1882 (LC). Although publication of Bucke's book seemed imminent when these letters were written, the book did not appear until the summer of the following year, the original publishers, Osgood and Company, having turned it down when they dropped their interest in the new edition of *Leaves of Grass*.
23. WW to Bucke, 7 February 1882, *Correspondence*, III: 266–67.
24. WDO'C to WW, 20 February 1883, *Camden*, 1:351.
25. "Introductory Letter to the Good Gray Poet," in Richard Maurice Bucke, *Walt Whitman* (Philadelphia: David McKay, 1883), pp. 73–98.

26. 24 February 1882 (Feinberg-LC).
27. *Camden*, 2:37–38.
28. WW to Osgood, 8 May 1881, *Correspondence*, III: 224.
29. *Prose Works*, I: 278–82.
30. 7 February 1882, *Correspondence*, III: 266–67 and n. 12.
31. 31 March 1883, *Correspondence*, III: 336.
32. Unpublished letter, 8 October 1883 (Chamberlin).
33. *Correspondence*, III: 267, n. 16.
34. *Correspondence*, III: 270, n. 22.
35. WW to Osgood, 29 March 1882, *Correspondence*, III: 270–71.
36. *Ibid.*
37. 28 April 1882, *Correspondence*, III: 274.
38. WDO'C to Burroughs, 28 April 1882 (Feinberg-LC).
39. The O'Connor letter initiating their correspondence is apparently lost.
40. 17 May 1882, *Correspondence*, III: 279.
41. 27 May 1882 (Brown).
42. 8 June 1882 (Brown).
43. *Correspondence*, III: 285.
44. *Ibid.*
45. *Correspondence*, III: 287.
46. 4 June 1882. Among copies of letters given by Clara Barrus to Clifton J. Furness
    (author of *Walt Whitman's Workshop*) to David Goodale to the author.
47. WDO'C to WW, 29 June 1882, (Feinberg-LC).
48. 27 May 1882.
49. WW to WDO'C, 18 June 1882, *Correspondence*, III: 292.
50. 28 July 1882, in Barrus, *Comrades*, pp. 220–21.
51. Tucker to WDO'C, 4 July 1882 (Feinberg-LC). For more information about
    Tucker, see Charles A. Madison, *Critics and Crusaders* (New York: Henry
    Holt and Company, 1947–1948), pp. 194–214.
52. Tucker to WW, *Camden*, 2: 253–54.
53. See note 51 above.
54. 29 August 1883, *Correspondence*, III: 349.
55. 15 April 1888 (Feinberg-LC).
56. *Camden*, 1:58.
57. WDO'C to Tucker, 6 July 1882 (Pennsylvania).
58. (Feinberg-LC).
59. *Camden*, 2:32.
60. "Tobey or Not Tobey" (Feinberg-LC).
61. 20 September 1882 (Feinberg-LC).
62. (Yale).
63. 5 November 1882 (Berg).
64. 12 November 1882, *Correspondence*, III: 314.
65. 14 April 1883, *Correspondence*, III: 338.

CHAPTER **XVIII**

"Still In Our Ashes Live Their Wonted Fires" [1]

THE CHIEF tragedy in William O'Connor's life was the death of his daughter Jean on May 5, 1883 at the age of twenty-five. [2] The exhilaration of the preceding year, with his renewed championship of *Leaves of Grass* and friendship with Walt Whitman, gave way to depression. Now all the triumphs turned to ashes.

Jean's loss was devastating to him. She had always been her father's daughter, sharing his love of learning, his interests and his humor. [3] Jean had not inherited her father's good looks; the doll-like prettiness of early childhood was later changed by the thick-lensed eyeglasses she had to wear because of nearsightedness. Yet she was attractive. Her golden hair "in immense quantities" reached below her waist; her brown eyes often had "an imp of mischief in them," and her sparkling humor made her "so full of color and impetuosity that no one ever thought of her as colorless." [4] Although she liked to wear clothes of coachman's drab that she thought went well with her hair, on one occasion when she "received" with a friend, Mrs. James, her costume was "an elegant garnet-satin-finish silk dress with two basques—one of velvet and the other of silk—to wear with it, and a little bonnet of cream white felt satin and feathers. . . ." [5]

The separation of her parents when she was fourteen years old had affected Jean profoundly. Her adored father was no longer part

311

of the household, although she saw him frequently and was sure of his love for her. The atmosphere of her home had changed. Not only was her father absent, but also "the amiable lion,"[6] as Grace had termed Walt Whitman, came no more. Only Charles Eldridge of the nightly gatherings visited occasionally. Whitman fell ill and Nelly visited him, but did not take Jean along. Nelly was unhappy, bitterly self-righteous.

It was not until nine years after the quarrel that Jean permitted herself to hint at the situation even to her cousin Grace, with whom she kept up a lively correspondence. Grace was about to visit; Jean warned her: "You know what you come to in coming here and so I am hoping you won't be homesick. . . . We have just finished the first dinner as a family for four months which I have been anticipating for some time but it was vain of me to imagine that the dinner would be an event." It would seem that Jean herself was homesick for the home she used to have.

In the same letter Jean indirectly revealed another reaction to the separation. She was writing to Grace about ideas she had about a free kindergarten which she hoped to establish for poor black children. (Grace had founded a similar free kindergarten for poor children in Providence.) Jean proposed the idea of having fathers' meetings. Commenting on the fact that the fathers are usually left out, she wrote: "The father is a more important element than the mother in the happiness of the family. . . . It is quite time to recognize the father as an important factor in the happiness or unhappiness of the world."

In a later letter Jean was more explicit:

> You know doubtless much of the state of affairs which exists between my father and my mother, but don't know how I have felt about it in times past or how wretchedly unhappy I have allowed myself to be. I think it is my own discontent which I have overcome and that I have learned to look at my own surroundings differently. You may be assured else that I could not write these lines—the first I have ever written.

Jean's unhappiness was increased because she did not get along well with her mother who was very exacting about housekeeping and behavior. Jean had two sides to her personality. Like her father she could be witty, fun-loving, and sociable (as revealed in her letters to Grace). Like him also, she could be moody and impatient. This is the side of her that her mother often saw and complained about. On one such occasion her cousin Molly (Grace's older sister) was visiting just after Jean had quarreled with one of her beaux, Jack Knowles. Jean confided what had happened to Molly but not to her mother, who found Jean irritable for no reason that she could see. Molly was sorry for her long-suffering Aunt Nelly.[7] She was the only Channing, however, who sympathized with Nelly. Although they were William's relatives only by marriage, Jeannie, William and Grace Channing commiserated with William and Jean, and thought Nelly impossible to live with.

One of Nelly's failings may have been the lack of a sense of humor. She was bright, but serious. She could hardly have considered the time well spent when young Jean drew up the constitution of a secret society which bound its members to use only oaths and epithets which came from Shakespeare because contemporary oaths were so colorless. To the constitution (complete with the appropriate "whereases") was appended a long glossary of Shakespearean oaths (some of them written in French).

Jean's letters to Grace were filled with lightness and humor. She referred to a rather effusive Mrs. Kane as Sugar Kane, and called Charles Eldridge "the bright, the free, the ever-gay." She even joked about her illness. On one occasion she wrote to Grace that her mother had gone to call the doctor from the nearest phone, which happened to be in an undertaking establishment, and reported to Jean that the undertaker's wife had asked about Jean's health in what seemed to be professional anticipation. At another time Jean wrote that her mother suspected that she had a quick consumption, "and not of victuals either."

Despite recurring illnesses, Jean was interested in social life, inquiring often about the young people of their acquaintance in Rhode Island, and envying one young man who had an opportunity to study at the Massachusetts Institute of Technology. She wrote about her own social life in Washington. On one occasion a young man in the Treasury Department took her for an eight-mile ride on the "sociable"—a double tricycle—and at another time to the bike races.

On the more serious side, Jean studied music, piano and violin. She wrote of how her mother scolded when the piano lesson did not go well (and this when she was twenty-three years old). She also wrote of "torturing" the violin. She shared her father's talent in art, for she wrote of sketching while on vacation, and at the age of twenty-two got a job as a draftsman in the office of Page and Gray. (Her father often dropped in to see her at the office.)

Jean took a keen interest in her father's championship of Whitman. She wrote to Grace of his disappointment when Whitman undercut his articles in the *Tribune* with a published memorandum which indicated that Emerson had qualified his endorsement of *Leaves of Grass*. Jean understood her father's need for appreciation and support, asking Grace to write to him expressing her admiration of his articles on Whitman. She followed her father's interest in the Baconian controversy; her last gift to him was a copy of Spedding's *Evenings with a Reviewer, or Macauley and Bacon*, a refutation of Macauley's essay on Bacon.

In a family of hero-worshippers Jean chose as the object of her devotion Susan B. Anthony.[8] Sharing her parents' interest in the Woman's Rights movement, Jean attended six of the nine sessions of the Woman's Rights Convention in Washington in January 1882. She especially liked the address of Phoebe Cozzens on "The Monopoly of Sex." At that time she talked with Mrs. Stanton and with "dear, good Susan Anthony." In June of that year she visited Miss Anthony who was not feeling well.

Jean also shared her mother's interest in the education of the poor. She had visited Miss Walker, whose home was in a section of Washington where poor blacks lived, and learned from her of the plight of children who came from poor and even criminal homes. She decided to start a free kindergarten and wrote to Grace about financing the project as well as about curriculum. Here she offered some of her ideas, such as the teaching of certain handicrafts to all, reading to those who were ready for it, and the need for fathers' meetings, referred to earlier.

Miss Walker offered to house the kindergarten for the first year. After that it was hoped that the Unitarian Church might take over the support. Jean approached the Reverend Rush Shippen, but failed to persuade him to do so. She might have persevered, but the kindergarten idea had to be dropped when Jean became very ill.

Jean had always been beset by illness, from rheumatism when she was small (portrayed by her father in little Emily's lameness in his story "The Carpenter") to measles when she was sixteen. She suffered from frequent headaches and pain throughout her life—conditions which she tried to conceal or make light of.

Four years before her death she wrote to Grace:

> I don't believe in inflicting my miseries even on the people who love me best and I do sincerely try to wear a bright face and keep my mind in accord with it. But I am very human and therefore very weak and my physical suffering makes me weaker still, for I do suffer. Yes, no one realizes how much, and how much of the time I am in acute pain, but that is a thing that I am to learn to bear and conceal and I think I am learning to conceal it from those who see me.

Two years later she wrote that she didn't know whether she could get through without "a grand smashup." And yet she lived, always ailing, for almost another year and a half. Nelly, too, was often ailing, but she lived to be eighty-three. She was perhaps more worried about Jean's and her own health because of the death of her brothers and her father when she was young.

Jean's final illness was variously diagnosed, by one doctor as involving the spleen and stomach, and by another as lung disease. Still another said that her lungs and bronchial tubes were clear. When her illness failed to respond to treatment, she went to the Channings in Providence, Rhode Island, to be taken care of. There were several advantages. Her Uncle William was a physician (although he did not practice medicine) and she was always happy with her understanding Aunt Jeannie and her cousins, Molly, Grace, and Harold.

William O'Connor came to the Channings on March 10 to spend his vacation with his daughter. When he left on April 1 he had no idea of how ill she was. When she died, on May 5, her mother was with her.

William Channing, knowing what a blow Jean's death would be to her father, immediately set out for Washington so as to tell him the sad news in person and be with him when Jean's body arrived. While he was on his way, a funeral service was held in Providence. Nelly turned to Grace for comfort, holding her hand as the lid was lowered on the coffin, saying, "This is the hardest of all." Charles Eldridge had come to the Channings, and it was he who made arrangements to have the body transported by rail to Washington. Nelly, Jeannie, and Charles accompanied the body to Washington, where they were met by William Channing and William O'Connor. Jean was buried at Oak Hill Cemetery that afternoon; William's colleagues at the Life-Saving Service sent a "broken column" of white flowers with purple immortelles at the top.

The funeral was over by 6 P.M. Both Jeannie and William Channing wrote descriptions of the day to their daughters, softening the bleak mood with allusions to the flowers and shrubs in full bloom. Less than two hours after the funeral was over her father wrote to Grace, "Your Aunt Nell is talking to your mother as brightly apparently as ever," and ". . . your mother got through all this without extreme fatigue." Evidently the sisters were emulating the New England reserve with which their mother had met the death of her sons and her husband. There was no mention of William O'Connor's presence at the house in the Channings' letters. Evidently he and Charles Eldridge had left the cemetery to mourn together.

The effect of Jean's death on the Channings was profound. Not only had they lost one dear to them, but Grace, who had shared her room with Jean and had nursed her every day after work, contracted tuberculosis. Her father urged her to close her school for a week or so. (He would pay her salary as soon as he got some money.) He begged her not to be "so fatally perverse as poor dear Jean," but Grace went on as before and became very ill. The family was advised that they must move to a more favorable climate if Grace was to survive. They moved first to Florida and later to Pasadena, California, where they remained. There William O'Connor came to be cared for by the Channings in February 1887, and from there Grace and Harold Channing went to visit the O'Connors in 1888. Jeannie did not come to see her sister until 1890, after William O'Connor's death. Charles Eldridge eventually settled in California.

As for Nelly, since Jean's death did not bring about a reconciliation with William, her life went on much as before. For her the main change had come more than ten years earlier when she and William had separated. At that time, although she undoubtedly suffered loneliness and hurt, her self-righteousness (described by her sister Jeannie in later years) probably sustained her. She could maintain the rented house on O Street, since she received William's unopened pay envelope every month, but her home was no longer the salon it had been. Although Walt was still her friend, his illness prevented him from coming to see her. She used to go to see him and bring him delicacies but this was quite different from basking in the radiance of a poet surrounded by a circle of friends. The Channings with whom she used to exchange visits were far away in California. Only the faithful Charles Eldridge continued to visit as long as he was in Washington.

Nelly's home was undoubtedly more peaceful; the volatile William—so enthusiastic, so despairing, so unpredictable—was no longer there. Her equally volatile daughter Jean probably kept things stirred up a little; Jean's activities and moods brought forth scoldings, while her frequent illness was a cause of worry and concern. Fortunately Nelly could escape her loneliness and worry by continuing to engage in the activities which had always occupied her. She maintained the social and political interests which had begun in her youth and never abated. One of these was the Woman's Rights movement; in 1879 she was vice-president of the Washington branch and attended the National Convention in Buffalo. Nelly also served on the Board of the Homeopathic Hospital, and was proud that there were other women on the Board as well.

The work which took most of her spare time, however, was a continuation of her concern for the Negro and for education which had been influenced by Dr. Gamaliel Bailey and the Abolitionists who used to visit his home, and which later had found expression in her work for Garrison's *Liberator*. Now she was able to combine these interests in a practical and important way through her involvement with Myrtilla Miner and the school which she had founded in Washington for the education of free Negro girls.

In 1851, when Ellen Tarr had been part of the Bailey household, Myrtilla Miner had just established her school. Coming from a poor family in western New York State, Myrtilla had had to struggle against poverty and ill health to attain an education. Although she had the early advantage of having the district school housed in her home, with her aunt as teacher, and later of having the library there, she had to work hard to gain higher education which gave her the credentials to become a teacher. She saw education as the means for advancement of the free Negro. In establishing her school in pro-slavery Washington, she had to face community antagonism. (One of the supporters of her school, Dr. L. Gale, was dismissed from his post in the Patent Office because of his help to the school.) During its early years the school had to move several times. When Miss Miner finally acquired a permanent school building, rowdies threw rocks and arsonists set fire to it. It was only after passersby saw Miss Miner and her assistant practicing target shooting that the harassment ceased.

Financing the school was a difficult task. Miss Miner was constantly trying to raise funds. One of her chief benefactors was Harriet Beecher Stowe who gave her one thousand dollars from the royalties of *Uncle Tom's Cabin*. Miss Miner often had to leave the school to go on fund-raising expeditions. At one time when she was away one of her assistants ran the school; at other times Horace Mann's wife, Mary Peabody Mann, and his sister, Rebecca Mann, took her place.

During the years when Nelly was in Boston and Philadelphia, she undoubtedly heard of Miss Miner through mutual friends who were helping her in her fund-raising activities. In Boston Miss Miner was helped by Dr. William Channing who took her to call on the Reverend James Freeman Clarke; in Providence she stayed with Paulina Wright Davis. In 1859 Nelly sent regards to Miss Miner from Philadelphia through a friend in Washington.

When the O'Connors settled in Washington, Myrtilla Miner was away, having gone to California in order to restore her health and to interest people in the West in her endeavors. Although the school was closed, its supporters in Washington, including Nelly, continued to work for it. In 1863 Congress passed an act to incorporate The Institution for the Education of Colored Youth. The legislation was due chiefly to the efforts of Senator Henry Wilson who later became Vice-President of the United States. One of the incorporators was Mrs. Nancy Johnson. It was to her home in Washington that Myrtilla Miner, having met with a serious accident in California, returned in December 1864—ten days before her death on December 17. During that time, Nelly O'Connor came to see her every day, taking care of her correspondence, learning about her life, and discussing her plans for the future of the school. From that time on Nelly was deeply involved with the school.

Notwithstanding its incorporation in 1863, the school remained closed until 1871 when it became part of Howard University, the

Miner funds supporting a preparatory and a normal (teacher-training) division. Four years later the trustees of the Miner Fund (of whom Ellen O'Connor was one) decided that the fund could best serve the intentions of its founder by becoming independent. A new building was dedicated in 1877 by the Reverend William Henry Channing; Frederick Douglass spoke at the exercises. Two years later this school (the Miner Normal School) became part of the District of Columbia School System, with some administrative functions to be performed by the trustees of the Miner School. George P. Baker and Ellen O'Connor served as representatives of the Fund.

Among Nelly's duties was the grading of examinations for entrance to the school. Jean O'Connor wrote to her cousin Grace about "Mama's school affairs. . . . Tonight she examined the examination papers of the candidates for the next year. There are nineteen who have passed."

Nelly's greatest contribution, however, was a book, written after Jean's death, about the founder of the school: *Myrtilla Miner: A Memoir*, which was published by Houghton Mifflin and Company in 1885.[9] In preparing the book, Nelly wrote to relatives, friends, students and coworkers of Miss Miner, and drew on her correspondence and school records. Hers was a straightforward narrative without embellishments, which proved to be a moving tribute to a remarkable woman.

After Jean's death Nelly's absorption in the book must have helped to fill her empty hours. Soon after it was published William, whose health had been steadily failing, returned home to be cared for by her.

Like any writer, Nelly was interested in the reception of her work. She wrote to Edmund Clarence Stedman to thank him for a notice in the *Tribune*.[10] He answered in a letter to William on January 7-8, 1886, asking him to tell Nelly that the notice was not his, but was probably written by Ellen Mackay Hutchinson, who was his co-editor of the *Library of American Literature*.[11] His sending the message through William is the first indication in William's correspondence that he had returned home.

Although it seems likely that Nelly would have sent a copy of the book to Walt Whitman, he never thought of her as a writer. More than two years after its publication, in praising her to Horace Traubel, Walt said: "Superb woman—without shams, brags—just a woman. Ellen does not write: that gives her more time to get on with the essentials of life."[12]

As for William, after Jean's death he was lonely, mournful, and ill. The tragedy had not brought him and his wife together. They left the cemetery separately and were not to be reconciled for another two years. During Jean's illness the separation had not seemed so complete, for William came daily to see her and the family dined together. Now there was no longer any reason to visit the house on O Street.

There was some consolation in the fact that he and Walt were friends again; the poet, however, no longer needed his championship. The 1882 furor, in which O'Connor had played a leading role, had resulted in a good sale of the new edition of *Leaves of Grass*; indeed it was said that it had sold out in a day. Periodicals, such as *Harper's*, were now receptive to Whitman's poems.

William and Walt's friendship was expressed in letters to each other and to mutual friends, but they did not see each other until three years after their first exchange of letters. The distance between Washington, D.C. and Camden, New Jersey, was not great when measured in miles, but formidable in view of the illness of the two friends. Perhaps, too, they did not wish to blur the memories of their younger and more vigorous selves by superimposing images of lameness and wrinkles. In addition, William felt chained to his office desk.

It was not until William had to be away from Washington for reasons of health that he was able to visit Walt. In 1885, after spending some time with Dr. Bucke in Canada, and stopping in Buffalo, New York, to be examined by two doctors, William went to Camden, New Jersey, at the end of September and spent a few days with Walt. It was their first time together since their quarrel in 1872.

William reported in a letter to Bucke:

> I was a good deal shocked when I saw him, not only in his having aged so much and grown feeble, but to see his eyes dreadfully inflamed. He anticipates going blind, but I don't give in to that, and I think rather talked him out of it. . . . I had a ride in the famous buggy! It is a big thing. Very satisfactory.[13]

Walt must have been equally shocked by the sight of William who described himself upon his arrival home as "dreadfully tired, legless, backless, brainless."[14] William was to see Walt only once more—a few years later.

During the years of loneliness, declining health and slow recovery from the tragedy of Jean's death, William was heartened by correspondence with a young writer to whom he could be both friend and mentor. In February 1883 William admired an editorial on Gustave Doré in the *New Orleans Times-Democrat*. Upon inquiry he learned that the writer was Lafcadio Hearn. They corresponded from February 1883 to March 1887. These letters are quite different from those which O'Connor and Whitman exchanged, for they deal with many writers, whereas the longer correspondence with Whitman mentioned other writers only in connection with Whitman and his work.

Lafcadio Hearn was born in 1850 in Greece on the island of Santa Maura, called Levkas or Lefcado, from which his name derived. His mother was Greek and his father Irish. He had a cosmopolitan background, having spent his growing-up and school years in Ireland, Wales, and France. At nineteen he arrived in New York City, alone, penniless, and with one eye blinded as the result of a school accident. He was a sorry figure. Unable to find a job in New York he went on to Cincinnati, where he became a journalist. In 1879 he moved to New Orleans, where he wrote for the *Times-Democrat*.

At the outset of their acquaintance, O'Connor wrote to the editor of *Harper's Magazine*, praising the younger writer. Later Hearn wrote of O'Connor as the person who had first introduced him to *Harper's*, which later published many of his stories.[15]

Among the writers whom they discussed in their letters were Gautier (whose short stories Hearn had translated), Hugo, whom Hearn criticized adversely despite O'Connor's high regard for him, and Edwin and Matthew Arnold, about whom they agreed, admiring Edwin Arnold, author of *The Light of Asia*, and disliking the more famous Matthew Arnold, whom Hearn called "one of the colossal humbugs of the century: a fifth-rate poet and unutterably dreary essayist;—a sort of philosophical hermaphrodite, yet lacking even the grace of the androgyne. . . ."[16]

The correspondence was interrupted by Jean's illness and death.

O'Connor's letter about her death, Hearn wrote,[17] filled him "with that sympathy which, in certain sad moments expresses itself only by a silent and earnest pressure of the hand—because any utterance would sound strangely hollow, like an echo in some vast dim emptiness."

After receiving copies of O'Connor's *Tribune* letters, the Life-Saving Reports and *The Good Gray Poet*, Hearn praised the letters as having been written "in a fashion realizing my long-cherished dream of English in splendid Latin attire." These writings led Hearn to give at some length his thoughts about Whitman. He had always secretly admired the poet, but could not praise him in the ordinary newspaper "whose proprietors always tell you to remember that their paper 'goes into respectable families.' " His admiration, however, fell short of O'Connor's enthusiastic praise: "Whitman is indeed a Titanic voice; but it seems to me the voice of the giant beneath the volcano—half-stifled, half-uttered,—roaring betimes because articulation is impossible." He does admire O'Connor's work on Whitman's behalf: "Whatever you do to defend, to elevate his work you do for the literature of the future, for the cause of poetical liberty, for the cause of mental freedom."

Hearn and O'Connor never met. Hearn tried to discern O'Connor's character and personality from his handwriting, thinking he must be large, strong, and keen, with "a disposition as level and even as the hand you write."[18] How O'Connor set him right about his disposition is not known, but it may well be that Hearn's conception of O'Connor's appearance was corrected by a photograph sent by O'Connor.

Hearn sympathized with O'Connor in his illness, having himself suffered "the same causes, the same symptoms—in every particular."[19] Pressure of work prevented O'Connor from taking his advice about moving to a warm climate and spending a few months or weeks at the seashore.

When O'Connor sent him *Hamlet's Note-Book*, Hearn confessed that he knew little about Elizabethan literature; nevertheless he wrote an editorial about the book in the *Times-Democrat*.

In his last letter to O'Connor, Hearn wrote that he was about to go to Martinique, the West Indies, as a correspondent for *Harper's*. He stayed two years, returning in the year of O'Connor's death. The following year Hearn went to Japan, where he married a Japanese lady of a Samurai family, adopted Japanese citizenship and a Japanese name—Yakumu Koizimi.

Hearn's books were very popular in the United States. Of O'Connor, who had seen his early promise and had encouraged him, he wrote to a friend named McDonald, "Is it only Irish or Latin people who make friends for friendship's sake?"[20]

The illness which O'Connor described to Hearn became worse, until it necessitated a great change in his life. He had to return home to be cared for by his wife. This step was subject to differing interpretations. Adelaide Johnson, a sculptor who was doing a portrait head of John Burroughs, recorded their conversation (as she did that of all her sitters) in her journal in 1904: "Today we spoke of the O'Connors whom he knew well,—he said William spent his evenings out. I said yes, he kept another establishment until he was helpless, then came upon Mrs. O'Connor to be cared for. He (Burroughs) felt it was an outrage, though evidently fond of O'Connor, and said they should have separated properly if that was so, which course meets with my views."[21]

Grace Channing thought that his return was a boon to Nelly: "Years later he was stricken with paralysis and died under his own roof. I have always thought that this was hard on him, but it was a great consolation to my aunt."[22] Nelly may, indeed, have felt vindicated by the fact that William had to come back to her to be cared for.

O'Connor's ailments had begun with poor eyesight in 1879. He wrote to Bucke: "My eyes, like an eagle's all my life till within two years, have given way under the night work and the abominable worry of office life, until I cannot in decent prudence use them at all at night now."[23]

His eyesight never returned to its earlier keenness. Other ailments followed. At the time of Jean's death he suffered from rheumatism. During that year and the following one he wrote of being tired and feeble. In September 1885 the doctor, "Looking very ominous at the state of my back, head and spinal column" did not want him to write even a short letter. Nevertheless, during all that time (and for several years thereafter) he continued to work in the Life-Saving Service, at one time in spite of a "terrible back, which they blister severely, and legs of weakness, and pain in the back of my head if I do much of anything."[24]

His health continued to deteriorate—and he continued to seek a cure. In February, 1887 he went to the home of the Channings in Pasadena, California. Not being able to travel alone, he was accompanied by Charles Eldridge, who wrote that it was a serious undertaking to take so sick a man three thousand miles by railroad, and that William was very ill when he arrived at the Channings.[25] He stayed with the Channings until July, appreciating their loving concern, but realizing that his physical condition did not improve. Shortly before leaving California he wrote to Dr. Bucke: "The doctors keep telling me that I shall get well. These nervous breakdowns require time for recovery. At present, I am worse than when I came—more helpless, feeble, weak-headed, and I can't walk without aid."[26]

After he returned to Washington, his niece Grace wrote how much she missed him. His answer describes his mood and physical state when he was with the Channings:

> I was under my worst conditions and aspects, and it seemed to me that I must have been a perfect eyesore; an ill-kept, ill-kempt, bizarre, old, fat and crippled monster; the bogy of the piazza, and as stupid as a half-witted owl! Verily, I should have thought you would have been glad that I was gone. But you were not. I marvel![27]

In Washington O'Connor helped the Channings to find a purchaser for a Gilbert Stuart portrait of George Washington which William Channing had inherited from his mother.[28] Known as the Gibbs-Channing-Avery portrait, it now hangs in the Metropolitan Museum in New York City.

Although William was no better when he came home, he was still hopeful of finding a cure. In the summer of 1887 he went to Bar Harbor, Maine, to try a method developed by Dr. Kinnear. He even went with the doctor to St. Johns, New Brunswick, Canada, so as not to interrupt the treatment. After Dr. Kinnear's treatment, which consisted of cold and hot applications to relieve the congestion in the spine, William's paralysis was better, but he still suffered severe spinal pain. He apologized to Grace for writing of his illness, saying, "Every sick man is a scoundrel, and I feel like nothing less than a convict, and shrink from the incongruity of unrolling my malady before you."[29]

His illness did not prevent him from writing long, affectionate letters to Grace, who seems in some measure to have filled the void left by Jean's death. He addressed her as Gracie-Gay, and advised her on literary matters. Grace, who was to go on to become a professional writer, adored her brilliant uncle. In 1887 she planned to produce a calendar consisting of appropriate quotations from *Leaves of Grass*, which was to be illustrated by Charles Stetson, an artist, who later became her husband. When Whitman failed to respond to her letter requesting permission, William excused his negligence as due to failing health and his resultant inability to make decisions.

William and Walt were deeply concerned about each other's health. While William was in California Walt wrote to William Channing, that "many an anxious and loving thought is wafted thither on his account."[30] On his way back to Washington after Dr. Kinnear's treatment, William again stopped in Camden to visit Walt, spending the day and evening of October 18, 1887 with him.[31] They talked of many things, and William presented him with a photograph of himself—Walt's favorite. This was the last meeting of the two old friends. During the ensuing year and a half of William's life they exchanged letters frequently, Nelly taking over the correspondence with postcards about William's health after he ceased writing. All the letters exchanged between Bucke, Burroughs, Eldridge, and Whitman during William's last months contain reports about O'Connor's condition.

O'Connor suffered a new kind of attack on January 16, 1888. At the dinner table he suddenly felt a "still-mindedness" and lost consciousness for five hours. When he recovered to find Nelly and two doctors at his side, he found that he could not speak, but was able to write a few words. After an hour his power of speech returned. The doctors said that he had broken a small vessel in the brain and had had a touch of apoplexy—and that another such attack would cause his death.[32]

In June he wrote to Dr. Bucke of the "torpor—the perfect narcolepsis" that has weighed on him for weeks. Yet in the same letter he discusses the new book on the Baconian controversy—Ignatius Donnelly's *The Great Cryptogram*—which had met with adverse reviews: "I am going to try to write an answer to Donnelly's reviewers, if I can only manage to pick up enough health to do it. . . ."[33]

Despite his own illness, he sent a check of twenty-five dollars to a fund being raised for Whitman, and refused to permit Bucke to return his check. At this time his eyelid was paralyzed, causing the eye to close (ptosis). In October he had to refuse a request from Gilder of *The Critic* to write an essay on Whitman's last days (assuming that the poet could not sustain life much longer). O'Connor referred this task to Dr. Bucke.[34]

Yet there was another claim upon Whitman's champion which O'Connor could not refuse to honor. It had seemed for some time that the poet was close to death. During the summer of 1888 his friends were concerned about having a proper funeral when that sad event occurred. In mid-July Bucke wrote to O'Connor that the executors appointed in Walt's will—Horace Traubel, Thomas Harned, and he—had agreed that it would not be appropriate to ask a clergyman to conduct the services; they preferred to have the words of a good friend. John Burroughs, their first choice, upon being invited, even urged, by Traubel and himself, had declined, saying that the state of his health and his feelings would make it impossible. He suggested burying Walt in silence, or if the others did not agree to that, to have Bucke speak. Bucke, however, thought that silence on the part of the poet's friends would be considered disgraceful now and in the future. Although willing to speak, "just as I would be willing to sacrifice all I have or even my life if it was required in this cause," Bucke thought that it would be unwise to have someone who was "not even an American" speak at Walt's funeral. They had hesitated to ask O'Connor, who was himself very ill at this time, but Bucke now did so; "the very fact of its being hard will make your act all the more gracious and memorable."[35]

The program, as planned and sent by Bucke to O'Connor, was as follows:

1. A short address (this ought to be given by Burroughs or yourself but he declines and we have not dared—in your state of health—to ask you). I should propose now to ask Col. Ingersoll to make this.
2. The five pages of "The Good Gray Poet," 39 to 43, read by yourself with such slight verbal alterations as may suggest itself to you.
3. The "Death Carol" to be sung, as proposed by Traubel.
4. As the body is lowered into the grave Mr. Clifford to recite

such verses from the Psalms, New Testament and Leaves of Grass as may seem to him fittest.

5. Address by myself.

My idea further would be that the *whole service* should be as quickly as possible thereafter, printed as a pamphlet and sold and distributed as broadly as possible.

O'Connor replied promptly:

> I have been so much in Walt's life—loved him so—fought for him early and long—that I should feel it my greatest calamity if I could not do all I can to honor his grave. It is not with me a question of its being *hard* to speak at his funeral, but only a question of its being possible. If I am able to stand, if I am able to articulate, I should be and I must be there. . . .[36]

O'Connor approves of the program, with the exception of reading from *The Good Gray Poet*. He doubts whether that would be in keeping. He thinks it would be good to have Colonel Ingersoll speak. "He greatly admires 'Leaves of Grass,' and is noble-hearted and truly Western. I only wish that his mind had a greater affirmative quality, and received more from the book he so values."

He sympathizes with John Burroughs; "He *could* not speak. It would break his heart in two. I feel now as if the effort would break mine, but, if I can, I must make it."

Almost two months later Bucke sent O'Connor the final program:

1. Address by Ingersoll
2. Death Carol—Cauffman
3. Address—O'Connor
4. Verses—Clifford
5. Address—Richard M. Bucke

Walt rallied after that bout of illness, but his life was despaired of again in the following December. In the meantime some people had expressed opposition to having friends speak at the funeral services. Bucke wrote to O'Connor:

> How *could* we take the body of the grandest man of the 19th Century to its grave, bury it and come away as if we had buried a

criminal or an animal? Again how could we have him buried by a clergyman with the ordinary services, stultifying his lifelong teaching and our own feelings and convictions?[37]

The friends went on with their plans for the funeral services. Whitman's health improved, and he lived on for more than three years. It was O'Connor, thirteen years his junior, who preceded him in death in May 1889. Whitman's funeral service took place at Harleigh Cemetery, Camden, New Jersey, on March 30, 1892.

During 1888 and 1889 O'Connor's health continued to decline. In the fall of 1888 his spirits were lightened by a visit from Grace Channing and her younger brother Harold, then nineteen and a half years old. Harold was to spend the winter with the O'Connors in Washington, studying mathematics and science. Grace came to help him plan his program and, of course, to see her ailing uncle. In one letter to her parents Grace wrote that Uncle William had come home ill and exhausted from the office, then rallied and conversed as brilliantly as ever for three hours.

After Grace left, Harold stayed on, complaining in his letters home about Aunt Nelly's exacting ways.[38] Considering that she had become set in her ways while living alone, and now had the care of an invalid, she could hardly be blamed for her lack of flexibility in accommodating to another person in the house—and a young man at that.

During the year 1888 William and Walt frequently exchanged letters and postcards, each inquiring about the other's health and telling of his own. The last missive William wrote was a postcard on December 9, 1888, in which he thanked Walt for sending him *November Boughs* and told him that he had deeply enjoyed Walt's reminiscences of the elder Booth. William wrote that Booth and Rachel were the only "vast" actors he had ever seen.[39] After December 9 Nelly took over William's side of the correspondence.

In the early spring of 1889 Horace Traubel, Whitman's young Camden friend, went with Dr. Bucke to visit O'Connor. He had known and admired Walt Whitman ever since the poet had come to live in Camden, New Jersey, when Horace was only fourteen years old. As a boy he was a visitor and messenger; as a young man, editorial assistant, companion—almost a surrogate son. Horace had heard a great deal about "the grand O'Connor." Indeed Whitman said, "All my friends, all those who cherish me, all the people who really know me and my work, consider, include, love, admire William."[40]

In March 1888 Traubel, then twenty-nine years old, had begun to keep a daily record of Walt's conversation, his state of health, his visitors, together with copies of letters and memorabilia which the poet would fish out of a pile of papers to share with him. This record (later published in six volumes, but not yet complete)—*With Walt Whitman in Camden*—is the source of much that is known of the poet's last years, and a great deal (through the letters and his comments) of his earlier life. The account of the visit to William O'Connor on March 2, 1889 and of the succeeding days, tells in detail of the memorable encounter between the aging and the young devotees of the poet.

In January 1889 William, suffering from increasing weakness, paralysis, eye trouble, and a mood verging on despair, had applied for and received a leave of absence from his job. As March approached, with the inauguration of a new administration, William feared that he might lose his job. Donnelly, who had political power, wrote on his behalf to the new Secretary of the Treasury, William Windom, praising O'Connor and asking that the new Secretary not permit him to be dismissed from his job.[41]

On leave from his job, and assured that he would not be dismissed, William finally, ironically, had the leisure to write which he had vainly sought all his life, but lacked the strength to do so. Nevertheless he continued against great odds to work on *Mr. Donnelly's Reviewers*. He received the first (incomplete) set of proofs only three weeks before his death. By early May he had completed all of them. Like the dying Cyrano, he did not permit his plume to be lowered, although his armor was rusted and his rapier blunt.

At the two-story brick house on O Street, Bucke and Traubel were welcomed by Nelly, whose manner was restrained and composed.[42] They were escorted to William's upstairs bedroom, where they saw a stout, pale man with lustreless eyes. "Well, here I am," said O'Connor, "or rather, here are my remains." He described his most recent attack: "One bright morning about six weeks ago the Department woke up and found itself deprived of its right arm."

As he talked with his visitors, his cheeks gained color and his eyes flashed. Horace especially noticed his musical voice and his hands, almost as beautiful as Whitman's. In looking at Horace, William became his old animated self. Turning to Nelly he said, "Here he is, Nelly! See him: he is the youth in our story—its poetry, its prophecy, made visible."

When Bucke went downstairs to meet William's doctor, with Nelly following, William reached out his hands, embraced and kissed Horace and drew him close. "Now I'm happier!" he said. "Thank God you didn't come too late! Thank God! thank God!" After Bucke and Nelly rejoined them, they talked for more than two hours, with no hint of tiredness on William's part. Of Victor Hugo, whose photograph Horace had noticed downstairs, William said, "I call Hugo the Walt Whitman of France; Hugo has more culture, but they are innately related."

Of Whitman's work they discussed *November Boughs*, with O'Connor wishing that he had written even more about the elder Booth. He also suggested that Walt should publish his "comrade letters." (When this was reported to Walt, he said, "It might be done, but not by me. I would not be the best one for such a delicate task.")

They talked of Whitman's friends and supporters: of Burroughs, who O'Connor thought had cooled toward him, though he had been enthusiastic about *The Good Gray Poet* when it appeared; of Stedman, whose change toward fuller appreciation of Whitman O'Connor thought he had influenced; of Ingersoll, who had called Walt a child of nature—the sweetest born of our day, "the inheritor of the infinite childhoods of all the past."

The visitors showed William a very favorable article by Gabriel Sarazin, which Walt ranked next to O'Connor's letters (by which he meant *The Good Gray Poet* and the "Introductory Letter" in Bucke's book). With Whitman the O'Connor letters always came first.

They talked of the old days in Washington, before Traubel and Bucke had known Whitman. Horace wondered how Walt had avoided breaking down. "By not working hard," William answered. "He would come in of a morning, sit down, work like a steam engine for an hour or so, then throw himself back in his chair, yawn, stretch himself, pick up his hat, and go out. . . ." Yet "if he had been any other sort of fellow we should never have had Leaves of Grass." O'Connor remarked on how different his own temperament was: ". . . the Irish in me won't do for me what the Dutch in Walt does for him."

Buoyed by the conversation, William began making plans for the future; he would make a collection of Whitman photographs, something he had long wanted to do, as soon as he "got about" again. In parting William said that their visit had not been an invasion; it had been an illumination, and Nelly, waiting at the bottom of the stairs, said: "It has all been beautiful; he will carry it with him into the next world."

In the next two months William became weaker, but he continued to work on the proofsheets of *Mr. Donnelly's Reviewers* until shortly before his death. According to Nelly, his mind was clear, except for brief periods immediately following attacks. He thought lovingly of Donnelly and his work until his last hours, and even when his mind was wandering he thought of Walt. Awakening from a dream he asked Nelly whether Walt had gone. She answered that he had not been there, but when William repeated the question, she said, "Yes, he has gone."

William died on May 9, 1889; the cause of death given on the death certificate was cerebral-spinal sclerosis, and the duration of his last illness as four years. During those years he had often spoken of his "gelatine legs"[43] and increasing paralysis. In Bucke's opinion, O'Connor had locomotor ataxia.[44]

On the day of William's death, Walt wrote to Nelly, "Have been sitting here some time thinking of Wm—am deeply depress'd by y'r card of yesterday—but keep up hope. . . ."[45]

Nelly's card was then on its way:

> The sad end is come. William passed peacefully to rest at 2 A.M. this day. He failed very much the last week, & more on Sunday and from that day on.
> It is sad because he so wanted to get well, & to the last thought he was going to recover.
> But he lies now, the image of perfect rest and peace, & more beautiful than I ever saw him, & looks as he did when I knew him first so long ago, & the late loss of flesh in the face has brought back the very look of youth.[46]

On the following day, when Walt received the sad news, his first words were, "Poor Nelly, poor Nelly," and later, "Poor O'Connor! Poor Nelly! Poor me!"[47] He sent brief and similar notes to Burroughs, Bucke, and William Sloane Kennedy: "Our dear friend O'Connor died peacefully at 2 A.M. yesterday."[48] All three answered, each offering consolation in his own way:

Burroughs wrote in part, ". . . it is sad to me that he has left behind him no work or book that at all expresses the measure of his great powers."[49]

Bucke expressed the same thought: "My great regret is that with his magnificent abilities he should have done so comparatively little to keep his name alive. However he will be long remembered—if for nothing else—for the "Good Gray Poet". . . ."[50]

One note which Walt penned on that sad day seems strange. To Thomas Harned he wrote, "Tom: If you will, fill the brown bottle with sherry for me, and the small white bottle with cognac. My dear friend O'Connor is dead."[51] Harned wrote in his notebook, "Judge Garrison was passing my office at the time, and I showed him the card. He said, 'I wonder if the old man is going to have a wake?' "[52]

The note is easily explained. Harned used to supply Whitman with wine. (The large bottle held eight ounces and the small six.) When Walt ran out of wine he was in the habit of sending Eddie Wilkins, the young man who took care of him, to Harned with the empty bottle and a note telling what he would like to have. He had probably written the note when he learned of William's death and added that terse sentence before Eddie left.

During the days of William's illness and at the time of his death, Walt often spoke of him to Horace Traubel, showing some of his old letters and commenting appreciatively and sadly:

> The grand fellow . . . O'Connor was a chosen knight—a picked man. Like the Arthurian heroes, true as steel, chivalric to the bone, high in hope and intention. What the knights were in chivalry, O'Connor was in literary action. He had an ideal so high—a human, literary, social, moral, religious, aspiration so pure—a passion for right, justice, the race, so intense—a disdain for mere literary craft and skill so overwhelming—he seemed out of place in the modern world, its so often mean ambitions. A cat in a strange garret indeed. The grand O'Connor! Who can take his place today? Who can take his place for me?[53]

He spoke of William's writings. Of "The Carpenter" he said the character was meant for him, "though drawn with O'Connor's vehement, impressive Elizabethan pen—with exaggerated lines—not halting or lame at all in its testimony."[54] He thought William's work was "all a great ship under full sail, proudly sailing whatever seas. . . .[55]

On May 10 William O'Connor was buried at Oak Hill Cemetery in Washington, D.C.[56] As part of the funeral service, held at the O'Connor home with only his most intimate friends present, the Reverend Rush Shippen, minister of the Unitarian Church, read the conclusion of William's story, "The Ghost"—the farewell letter of the poet George Feval to his friend Dr. Renton:

> In the name of the Saviour, I charge you, be true and tender to mankind. Come out from Babylon into manhood, and live and labor for the fallen, the neglected, the suffering and the poor. Lover of arts, customs, laws, institutions, and forms of society, love these things only as they help mankind! With stern love, overturn them, or help to overturn them, when they become cruel to a single—the humblest—human being. In the world's scale, social position, influence, public power, the applause of majorities, heaps of funded gold, services rendered to creeds, codes, sects, parties, or federations,—they weigh weight; but in God's scale—remember!—on the day of hope, remember!—your least service to humanity outweighs them all.

While awaiting word about the funeral, Walt wrote to John Burroughs, ". . . our dear friend is buried & all has gone like tracks on the shore by sea waves washed away passing."[57] Later that month friends joined in the celebration of Walt's seventieth birthday. John Burroughs spoke of the old Washington days, and of O'Connor, "whose presence among you today, as I knew him then, would be like music and banners."[58]

NOTES

1. WDO'C to Bucke, 2 December 1883 (LC). Quoted from Thomas Gray's "Elegy Written in a Country Churchyard": "E'en in our ashes live their wonted fires."
2. The account of Jean O'Connor and of her mother Ellen (Nelly) in this chapter is based on the Channing family letters which were in the possession of the late Katharine Beecher Stetson Chamberlin of Pasadena, California. Many were copied for and sent to the author by David Goodale, and others by Mrs.

Chamberlin. The letters are from Jean O'Connor to her cousin Grace Ellery Channing (from 1879 to 1883); from Grace to her mother, Mary Jane (Jeannie) Channing, and from William F. Channing (Grace's father) to her. Letters to and from other people will not be noted separately. The originals of these letters are now in the Library of Congress, presented by Charles Feinberg.

3. Stedman to WDO'C, 4 December 1883 (Feinberg-LC). "I have heard from Mrs. O'Connor, and from others, of your daughter; how much she was like you, and how thoroughly you lived in and *understood* each other."

4. Grace Channing to her stepdaughter, Katharine Stetson (later Chamberlin) describing Jean for a portrait that Katharine was planning to paint. The portrait was never finished (Chamberlin).

5. Mary (Mollie) Channing to her sister Grace, 24 February 1881 (Chamberlin).

6. Grace Channing, unpublished memoir, quoted in Florence B. Freedman, "New Light on an Old Quarrel: Walt Whitman and William Douglas O'Connor 1872," *Walt Whitman Review*, 9: 36 (June 1965).

7. (Chamberlin).

8. Sara M. Algeo, "Equal Suffrage Notes," *Providence Daily Journal*, 23 July 1911. WDO'C admired Phillips; Nelly, Garrison.

9. Facsimile Edition (New York: Arno Press and *The New York Times*, 1969). Introduction by Florence B. Freedman.

10. 15 December 1885 (Columbia).

11. (Feinberg-LC).

12. *Camden*, 1:350.

13. 3 October 1885 (Barrus Collection).

14. *Ibid.*

15. Hearn to Mitchell McDonald, February (n.d.) 1899, in Elizabeth Bisland, *The Life and Letters of Lafcadio Hearn*, 2 vols. (Boston and New York: Houghton Mifflin Company, 1906), vol. II, p. 432.

16. *Ibid.*, vol. 1, p. 318.

17. The following quotations are from a letter, August 1883, *ibid.*, pp. 270–74.

18. *Ibid.*, p. 340.

19. *Ibid.*, pp. 365–66.

20. See note 16 above. After O'Connor's death Hearn wrote to Grace Channing (n.d.), "Your letter brings back to me . . . the meaning of so many kind things done, and kind words said in my behalf by your uncle" (Chamberlin).

21. Unpublished MS (LC). This was called to my attention by C. Carroll Hollis, then at the Library of Congress.

22. Grace Channing, unpublished memoir (Chamberlin).

23. 21 June 1881 (Brown).

24. WDO'C to Burroughs, 19 September 1885.

25. Eldridge to WW, 11 February 1887. Barrus, *Comrades*, pp. 262–63.

26. 2 July 1887 (Feinberg-LC).

27. WDO'C to G. Channing, 20 September 1887 (Chamberlin).

28. Note from K. B. S. Chamberlin to author.

29. See note 28 above.

30. 4 July 1887, *Correspondence*, IV: 106.

31. WW to Burroughs, 26 October 1887, *Correspondence*, IV: 128.

32. WDO'C to G. Channing, 9 February 1888 (Chamberlin).

33. 6 June 1888 (LC).

34. WDO'C to Bucke, 30 October 1888 (Barrus Collection).

35. Bucke to WDO'C, 15 July 1888 (Feinberg-LC). See also, Florence B. Freedman, "Walt Whitman's First Funeral," *Walt Whitman Review*, 27: 132–34 (September 1981).
36. WDO'C to Bucke, 19 July 1888 (Barrus Collection).
37. 18 December 1888 (Barrus Collection).
38. (Chamberlin).
39. (Feinberg-LC).
40. *Camden*, 4:277.
41. Copy of Donnelly's letter sent to O'Connor, 4 March 1899 (Feinberg-LC).
42. *Camden*, 4:252–63.
43. Eldridge to WDO'C, 10 August 1885 (Berg).
44. *Camden*, 2:439–40. Whitman talking to Traubel, 6 October 1888: ". . . we regard it as a sort of secret . . . there was silence on both sides. Bucke . . . is an austere investigator who is not to be fooled." For a recent interpretation of the medical symptoms, see Jerome Loving, *Walt Whitman's Champion: William Douglas O'Connor* (College Station, Texas: Texas A&M University Press, 1978), p. 143, n. 19. The dictionary definition of locomotive ataxia: "tabes dorsalis, syphilis of the spinal cord and its appendages, characterized by shooting pains and other sensory disturbances, and, in the later stages, by loss of control over the muscular movement, mainly in walking, and by paralysis."
45. *Correspondence*, IV: 334.
46. Ellen O'Connor to WW, 9 May 1889 (Feinberg-LC).
47. *Camden*, 5:161, 162.
48. *Correspondence*, IV: 335.
49. Burroughs to WW, 11 May 1889 (Feinberg-LC).
50. Bucke to WW, 13 May 1889, in Artem Lozynsky, ed., *The Letters of Dr. Richard Maurice Bucke to Walt Whitman*, (Detroit: Wayne State University Press, 1977), p. 125.
51. 10 May 1889 (Feinberg-LC).
52. Thomas Harned's notebook, shown to the author by his son, Professor Herbert Harned of Yale University.
53. *Camden*, 5:165 ff.
54. *Ibid.*, 364.
55. *Ibid.*, 373.
56. The account of the funeral service is from the Washington *Post*, 12 May 1889.
57. *Correspondence*, IV: 338.
58. *The Critic*, 8 June 1889.

CHAPTER XIX

"To Keep Green The Memory . . ."[1]

"WILLIAM WILL die with a hurrah on his lips," said Walt. "He'll never know he's dead," Horace Traubel replied. "He'll be so busy with resurrection day."[2]

A kind of resurrection came with the obituaries, which told of his "beautiful traits, which much endeared him to his friends," of his charm as a conversationalist, his loyalty to Whitman, his defense of the Baconians, and his eloquent reports for the Life-Saving Service. Yet they contained a note of regret because of his unfulfilled literary promise. A writer in the *Springfield* (Ohio) *Republican* spoke of him as "a remarkable man, who was more than his fame, though that is considerable, as it is peculiar." He went on to say that "few men of so striking quality and capacity in literature have left less behind them to be remembered by." The article listed among his publications *Harrington, The Good Gray Poet*, "The Ghost," *Hamlet's Note-Book*, and the letters in defense of Whitman in 1882; it left out his other letters, other stories, and poems.[3]

The *New York Daily Tribune*, which had published his letters in 1876 and 1882, printed a dispatch from Washington:

> The death in this city on Thursday night of William Douglas O'Connor was a severe loss to a large circle of devoted friends in Washington, who loved him for his gentle and noble traits, and will be sincerely regretted by thousands of men and women who

had learned to admire his character as exhibited in his honest and excellent literary work.

The obituary continued with a resumé of O'Connor's life and writings.[4]

The Critic of May 18 printed what Whitman thought was a "rather tame" obituary, after having refused one by Horace Traubel.[5] The *Washington Post*, however, was laudatory:

> He was a man of exceptionally strong characteristics, and to his friends was genial and open-hearted. One of the most charming conversationalists of the day, he was always a most welcome guest at all social gatherings, and had it not been for his strong aversion to courting popularity, he would have been one of the best-known men of the community.[6]

Mr. Donnelly's Reviewers, O'Connor's answer to the critics of *The Great Cryptogram*, appearing two weeks after the death of its author, began with a memorial note praising O'Connor's work for the Life-Saving Service and his powerful contributions to the Bacon-Shakespeare controversy. (It does not mention his other writings, even those about Whitman.) The memorial note concludes with remarks by Mr. Henry Latchford of *The Chicago Evening Journal* about O'Connor's personal qualities:

> He always had something delightful to say on any subject. . . . I had heard O'Connor spoken of in Dublin, London, Paris and Boston as "a spirit finely touched." It is almost impossible to describe the charm of his presence, his character, his voice, grey eyes, silken yellow hair and his wonderful conversation. But it is possible for those of us who knew him to say that when so much high endeavor, such a splendid intellect, such wide sympathies, and such a gentle voice have been embodied in one human being, the death of this rare person means that "there has passed away a glory from the earth."

Critiques of *Mr. Donnelly's Reviewers* were in part obituaries. As with *Hamlet's Note-Book*, reviewers were not likely to react favorably to a book which criticized them, yet they spoke well of the author. An extensive review in *Poet-Lore* admitted the inadequacies of some reviewers, explained them as due to the exigencies of their craft, praised other reviewers, and in a closing paragraph lauded O'Connor:

> As for Mr. O'Connor, whose recent death is just cause for lament, one cannot but sympathize somewhat with his brilliant and most readable attack upon the men whom [*sic*] he thinks are to blame for the sudden popular downfall of a theory he had long held at heart. He is said to be the only man who ever read all of Delia Bacon's book. He was a single-handed champion of a theory which, in her person and in his, has both interest and pathos. He had made its most witty and attractive defense in times past, and the palpable hit he has made against some of "Mr. Donnelly's Reviewers" in this, his posthumous work, places it, with his "Hamlet's Note-Book," as an uncommonly valiant and clever piece of controversial writing.[7]

Liberty contained a paragraph of praise:

> William Douglas O'Connor, the author of the "Good Gray Poet," whom Liberty counted with pride among its warmest friends, is dead. The world of letters loses in him one of its grandest and most unique personalities. Mr. O'Connor was a student, a scholar, a passionate lover of art, and took no part in practical affairs. But the few short productions of his pen will yet be recognized as the ornament and glory of English polemical literature. Some day the conspiracy of the "paltry and venomous swarm" of literary hypocrites and prudes, poisoners and blackguards, will be put down by public intelligence, and then Mr. O'Connor's defense of Walt Whitman will be ranked higher than the "Provincial Letters."[8]

Two months later *Liberty* published a much longer article by Horace Traubel which Walt thought "strong and fine."[9] In it Traubel deplored the fact that O'Connor had never received the recognition accorded many lesser men. He described him as a man "with a pen never trifling in its brilliance, and an impetuosity never mistaken in its aim, with the divine gift of *advocate* crowning all else. . . ."[10]

Traubel had written a similar appreciation which was published in *Unity* on June 29, 1889. Here he stressed the value of O'Connor's work on behalf of *Leaves of Grass*:

To some who approached O'Connor, and passed into the spell of his wonderful speech, it was a mystery that, given such vast capacity, the written evidence of it, where expression with pen came as easy as with tongue, should have been so meagre. However the one fact is to be explained, the other fact remains, that what he has written of Walt Whitman alone entitle [*sic*] and will give him immortality.

In writing of O'Connor's books on the Bacon-Shakespeare controversy, Traubel says:

> . . . I do not expect O'Connor to go into history on the wings of these writings. After this controversy shall have been forgotten or otherwise settled, the tremendous and timely power of his defense of Walt Whitman, who through future years is to stand in the foremost ranks of great world characters, will be cherished and will subdue criticism.[11]

Walt, of course, appreciated these lines as well as the praise of O'Connor. In response to Traubel's statement that some people thought the article too strong, he replied, "Well, why should we not be strong in discussing a strong man? And especially with us—knowing him so well—how could strong words be avoided?"[12]

In using the words "we" and "us," Whitman may have indicated that he had helped to write the article. Whether this was so or not, Traubel had certainly expressed Whitman's sentiments. Walt wanted more to be written about William. He said he himself would like to write about him, "only to relieve my fullness."[13] He suggested to Bucke that he include additional *Leaves of Grass* letters by O'Connor in any future printings of his *Walt Whitman*.[14] He urged Traubel to write more fully on O'Connor, deploring the fact that Eldridge, from whom he could get much information, was far away in California. "Yet it ought to be done," he added. "I even want to do it myself."[15]

Walt was glad to see that Volume 9 of Stedman's *Library of American Literature* included the writings of O'Connor, as well as those of Burroughs.[16]

Articles about O'Connor appeared in both Johnson's and Appleton's encyclopedias in the year of his death. Another appreciative account appeared in the annual report of the Life-Saving Service of that year, calling his death "one of the saddest cases on the death-roll of the year." Before giving a summary of his accomplishments, both in literature and in the Life-Saving Service, the writer paid a personal tribute:

> The stroke was peculiarly painful to all who had ever enjoyed the privilege of his personal friendship, because to them his death was not only the extinguishment of a shining light, but the departure of a singularly delightful and loving companion. Few persons, and none but those most truly constituted of gentleness and grace, have held their friends by such strong yet tender cords as he.

These praises and the concern of Walt and other friends must have pleased Nelly, but could hardly help to solve her problem—for she had been left very little to live on. She blamed William for having squandered money on his inventions and for having been too generous to needy friends. If only the people who owed him money would repay it to her, she would not have worried so about daily expenses! In writing to Walt about her predicament, she tried to be philosophical but the bitterness showed: ". . . I did so plead with William, always, to try with me to buy a little, little house, so that we might have a home; but it was not to be, & so must be right."[17]

Knowing of her financial straits, Sumner Kimball, William's superior at the Life-Saving Service, would have liked to have given her a position in his department, but Civil Service laws precluded that. He did promise (with eventual success) to get her a job in the newly established Census Bureau.

Nelly began to find some solace in spiritualism. Her sister Jeannie wrote tartly: "She has had no end of communication from Uncle William (isn't it too much when you know how he felt?) and he and Jean direct her life and guide her. She did not let them do it in life anyway."[18] Nelly acknowledged that William had not believed in spiritualism, but insisted "he is glad enough to come back now."[19]

Nelly wrote to Walt that she had seen William in a dream, looking as he had in the old days in L Street. As to Walt, "I have had several very *vivid* dreams of you. So distinct that all the next day I feel as if I had been with you; I wonder whether my 'astral body' went to you, or yours came to me. . . ."[20]

Perhaps it was that remark which caused Dr. Bucke (to whom

Walt had rather hesitantly sent the letter) to have what he thought was an excellent idea—that Nelly and Walt should now marry each other. Nelly would have a home and Walt would have someone to take care of him.[21] Nelly, however, worn out by the care of one invalid, and herself ailing (her weight was down to ninety-five pounds), was no longer the Nelly of the 1870 love letter to Walt, and the poet was his usual cautious self. Both refused the suggestion, Walt saying to Traubel: ". . . Doctor's last letter was written in a terrible strain: he proposes to me that, Mrs. O'Connor having no place (of) her own now—nothing to do—that we somehow set up a bargain—that she keep house for me—that we go into alliance—get spliced. I wrote the Doctor at once, explaining why I thought it was impossible, or at least unlikely."[22]

What Whitman had written was, "—your letter ab't Mrs. O'C rec'd—doubt whether it w'd suit her—such a plan—am not mov'd to it favorably—Most things are bad enough with me, but I am blessed thankful they are no worse & that I get along as well as I do—am getting along better than you suppose—"[23]

Nelly wrote nothing about Bucke's suggestion to Walt and set about making other plans. She accepted the invitation of a friend to spend the summer with her in North Perry, Maine. In no hurry to get back to her lonely life in Washington when the summer ended, she visited a friend on Nantucket Island, her nephew Charles Legge in Boston, and other nieces and nephews in that vicinity. She then went to Philadelphia, where she stayed with friends for a few days, and was able to cross to Camden and visit Walt on November 13 and 16. When she returned to Washington, she was not able to occupy her house which was being repaired. When she could live in it again, she found it difficult to meet her expenses. With the job in the Census Bureau not yet available, she took two young girls to board with her for six weeks until their school term ended.[24] She also resubmitted William's story, "The Brazen Android," which had been accepted by the *Atlantic Monthly* and then withdrawn by its author in 1861. It was published in April and May 1891.

Perhaps because she felt some guilt at having hampered William's career as a writer, Nelly decided to have the seven short stories he had written published in book form. She wrote to Walt, asking him to write an introduction to the book, which he gladly consented to do.[25] Houghton, Mifflin & Company, decided to publish only three of the stories. The book, entitled *Three Tales* ("The Ghost," "The Brazen Android," and "The Carpenter"), appeared in 1892.

By 1891 Nelly's financial situation had improved a little. The *Atlantic Monthly* paid her $300 for "The Brazen Android," a few people who owed money to William paid the interest and promised to pay the principal soon, and she began to work for the Census Bureau. Her salary was sixty dollars a month.[26] Her sister Jeannie came to visit her in the fall of 1890 and stayed through the spring of 1891—her first visit since the Channings had left the East after Jean O'Connor's death. (The Channings had met with financial reverses, and Nelly wanted to keep the house so as to provide a home for them if they needed it, in gratitude for all that they had done for Jean and William. This proved not to be necessary, as the Channings were able to remain in Pasadena.) Jeannie offered to pay for her board, but Nelly refused. Jeannie did help by sewing for Nelly.

When Nelly had to give up her house, a friend, Miss Emily Howland (who had been one of the volunteer teachers at the Miner School) offered Nelly the use of her house, rent-free and tax-free, since she had to be away from Washington for a time. This was a boon, for the house (at 112 M Street, N.W.) was a very short distance from the Census Bureau. Nelly was unhappy, however, for the house was not to her liking and her work was both difficult and temporary.[27]

Communing with William's spirit seemed to have brought Nelly closer to understanding and appreciating him. She wrote to Walt, acknowledging receipt of his preface to *Three Tales*:

> I know that you & I feel more & more tender & growing love for dear William, & all his noble and generous qualities show out to me by contrast, all the time. I don't find others like him, tho' I have nothing to complain of: & have warm & loyal friends.[28]

Among her friends was Albert Calder, a widower from Providence, Rhode Island, with whom Nelly and the Channings had been acquainted for many years. (He had known Jeannie Channing as far back as 1847.)[29] Calder was a successful business man with a large house in Providence. In the spring of 1891 Calder often called on Nelly and Jeannie, but his daughters seemed reluctant to come. When Nelly left "visiting cards" for them (a social custom which called for a visit in return) they failed to respond immediately, although they had carriages at their disposal. They did come, however, after several weeks had passed.[30]

Albert Calder's attentions to Nelly caused her family to wonder whether he would propose to her. The letters which the Channings exchanged with each other were less than complimentary to Nelly. Jeannie quoted their sister Martha Legge as saying, "I hope she will never marry anyone for she never would make a tolerably comfortable home for any man."[31]

William Channing held a more balanced view:

> What I wish to express is my hearty approval, provided that she will not worry him too much. He is too good and generous a man to be nagged. Perhaps they will fit and help each other. She was *not* a helpmate for William O'Connor and her marriage with him ought not to count. . . . I sincerely sympathize with Nell and give her my best wishes. . . . I believe in all helps to love at all times.[32]

Not only Mr. Calder but other friends and acquaintances held opinions of Nelly quite different from those of her family. They thought her wonderfully brave after her husband's death, sweet and generous—a veritable saint. Her sister loyally said nothing to disturb these favorable views. Friends watched the progress of the romance. In June 1891 Jeannie denied that her sister and Albert Calder were engaged to be married. They had come to another kind of understanding, however, which Nelly wanted to keep quiet. Refusing to go to his house as a guest, Nelly had accepted the position of housekeeper. She was wondering how she would manage a house with four servants, and he was worried about whether his offer of compensation would be generous enough. When they agreed upon terms, which were generous, Nelly bought a new wardrobe, for she knew that in Providence she would have a busy social life.

Nelly went to live in the Calder house at 34 Benefit Street on October 2, 1891. On November 19 she wrote to Walt, "I am getting used to my new abode. I ought to get well, for my cares are not heavy, & the people are kind."[33]

Nelly was to remain in this abode, not as housekeeper, but as the lady of the house. She and Albert Calder were married on March 22, 1892.[34] As Mrs. Albert Calder she was quite different from Mrs. William O'Connor. With a husband who adored her, no money worries, a house such as she had longed for, and four servants to abide by her rules and cater to what her sister Jeannie had called her "little, finical, petty punctilios"[35] she could be a paragon of a wife and a perfect hostess.

While in Providence Nelly continued to be concerned about Walt's health. She was grateful to Horace Traubel and his wife Anne for keeping her informed about his condition. On December 29, 1891 she wrote to Dr. Bucke, "If Walt can at all understand, will you give him my *love*? I know he has thought of me for on Christmas morning, *no*, the morning after Christmas, he *came* to me. I never have seen him more plainly than I did then."[36] (Her intuition was correct, for Walt, who had been very ill, rallied on Christmas morning, and spoke to John Burroughs about Nelly.) Walt died on March 26, 1892, four days after Nelly's marriage to Albert Calder. Unable to attend the funeral services, she sent a letter.[37]

Nelly's happiness in her marriage had a beneficial effect on her personality. Her sister Jeannie, whose illness prompted a visit from Nelly in the spring of 1894, wrote about the change to her daughter Grace: "She is devoted to Mr. Calder & is I believe a very happy woman in that tie, so very much improved by her happiness."[38] During her visit to California, Nelly stayed for a while with Jeannie's older daughter, insisting on paying generously for her board, and giving her some money as a gift for Jeannie.[39] (The two sisters were not to see each other again, for Jeannie died in 1897 after a long illness.)

Not long after Nelly's visit to Jeannie, Grace had a chance to observe the change for herself: "This afternoon I made a call on Aunty and Mr. Calder, who were in their perennially blooming state," she wrote home. "Certainly I never saw two people who took more comfort apparently in one another and surrounding circumstances. It is very agreeable."[40]

In Providence Nelly continued to busy herself with sorting William's letters, manuscripts, and notes. She had begun this effort shortly after his death and continued it while she remained in Washington. There were many boxes of materials; she had discarded a great deal that she thought was insignificant. The Whitman material she had forwarded to Dr. Bucke, offering to him and to Walt O'Connor's manuscripts and books.[41] After her marriage, Nelly was able to hire a secretary to help her with her work and her correspondence.[42] This was especially helpful when Nelly had an accident and was not able to write for a while. Nelly continued to try to have William's works printed or reprinted. Among these were the sketches of rescues at sea which had been part of the annual reports of the Life-Saving Service written by William.

Horace Traubel had agreed to make the selection with the help of Lieutenant Walker of the Service. (Nelly wanted Horace to have the royalties if the book was published.) When Horace was too busy to undertake the task, Charles Eldridge consented to do so, reading through the voluminous reports and selecting suitable sketches to be published. It seemed fitting that Eldridge, the publisher of *Harrington* in 1860, should perform this service for his friend thirty years later. He selected the twenty-five sketches to be included in *Heroes of the Storm*, but died before the book was published by Houghton, Mifflin & Company in 1904.

The introduction to *Heroes of the Storm* by Sumner I. Kimball, General Superintendent of the Life-Saving Service, gave a brief sketch of O'Connor's life and accomplishments and a personal appreciation of his character and personality and of his work for the Service:

> To say that his wonderful imagination was his most brilliant quality would be to do him wrong, unless the opinion were duly qualified with the statement that his mind was thoroughly logical and his perceptions were extremely acute. His reason was as powerful as his fancy. He could argue as clearly as he could paint a picture, either with words or colors.

Of his work for the Life-Saving Service, Kimball wrote that all the accounts of shipwreck involving the loss of life were written by O'Connor: "The appearance of the Annual Reports containing these narratives attracted wide attention, and the demand for the volumes became so great that larger editions were necessary to meet it. The interest in the service thus stimulated by Mr. O'Connor's work largely contributed to its early development and aided in its subsequent prosperity and success."

Kimball ends his Introduction:

> Mr. O'Connor's death, in May, 1889, was a serious loss to the Life-Saving Service, as well as an inexpressible bereavement to his friends. He was a singularly delightful and lovable companion,

most truly constituted of gentleness and grace, always distinguished by a bearing that never lacked dignity, nor yet suggested coldness. To those to whom it was given to be his associates in his later days, he manifested an uncomplaining endurance of physical suffering which only the more clearly exhibited and, perhaps, intensified the amiable qualities which through life so much endeared him to all who knew him well.

Although books *by* O'Connor appeared, the book *about* him was not written, even though Whitman, Eldridge, Traubel, and Grace Channing (who had become a professional writer) had expressed an interest in writing it. Several articles by O'Connor which had been rejected during his lifetime were published: after Whitman's death his executors, Horace L. Traubel, Richard Maurice Bucke, and Thomas B. Harned, included an article by O'Connor in their volume *In Re Walt Whitman* published by David McKay of Philadelphia in 1893. "The Good Gray Poet: Supplemental" had been sent by O'Connor to the *Boston Transcript* on January 23, 1866, but not published. A sequel to his pamphlet *The Good Gray Poet*, it was an answer to the *Transcript*'s review which, while praising O'Connor (though deploring his lack of calm), did not see Secretary Harlan's action as reprehensible.

O'Connor in his response displayed the same vehemence as he had in the pamphlet: He explains that in attacking Harlan he was speaking for "the interests of intellectual liberty and the rights of authors in this age":

> It is an age when the dark spirit, born of the narrow mind and rotten heart, which so often compelled the richest and boldest meanings of the great literature of medieval Europe to skulk in enigma and innuendo, and which followed thought everywhere with the rack, the fagot and the axe, no longer fronts its victims in the robes of the inquisitor or the bloody jerkin of the torturer, but wears the respectable black coat of the dull divine or the office-jacket of the ass reviewer.

He cites the effect of these strictures on the fortunes of many bold writers, as well as on the work of those who conformed. Typical is his appraisal of Thackeray:

> Look at Thackeray, born a giant satirist, gifted with the divine power to make villains tremble; the charmed circle of convention

is drawn around him; he shrinks under the fatal magic to a burly pigmy; drops the tremendous knout of great satire for a gentleman's riding whip; flinches, spares, moderates; never strikes any vices, any crimes, that one may not decently name, though these are the worst; turns away from the dreadful massed miseries and wrongs and shames of England; becomes a beater of dogs not merely dead, but rotten, like the Georges—a beater of poodle lords and wiffet flunkeys—but a sparer of the huge, powerful, cruel, bloody bull dog—British government and society; and, at last, when all is done, is nothing but the admirable, melancholy bloody torso that might have been the English Juvenal.

Another rejected article, "Tobey or Not Tobey? That Is the Question," written in the midst of the 1882 controversy and submitted to the *Tribune* on September 16, 1882, appeared in the *Conservator* on September 7, 1896. Following this, several articles about O'Connor appeared in the *Conservator*: William Sloane Kennedy, who had joined the Whitman circle in the 1880s when he was on the editorial staff of the *Saturday Evening Post* in Philadelphia, wrote of O'Connor in "To Keep Green the Memory of a Gallant Man" in October 1896: "O'Connor was a born Paladin of struggling causes. He championed Mrs. Pott and Donnelly from sympathy and because he liked a fight; and his impetuosity finally won over Walt Whitman in the weakness of his later years." The words "because he liked a fight" drew an answer from George A. Bacon, who retorted, "Indeed! he defended them from deepest conviction."[43] In January and February Kennedy returned with "William Shakespeare Begs Leave to Be," in which he satirically applied the Baconian argument to the unschooled Walt Whitman, deducing that Emerson was the real author of *Leaves of Grass*. The following month Ellen O'Connor Calder joined the argument with "William Douglas O'Connor's Award to Bacon," stating that O'Connor had been a Baconian when they met and that his defense of Mrs. Pott and Donnelly sprang not from love of a fight but from conviction.

Nelly's blissful second marriage ended with Albert Calder's death on May 24, 1899 at the age of seventy-three. He left her an annuity which enabled her to live in comfort. She moved to 306 Hope Street in Providence where she lived until her death in 1913.

Ellen O'Connor Calder continued to be a source of information about Whitman's Washington days. Bliss Perry, the Harvard professor who was the first of the second generation of Whitman biographers (those who had not known him personally), consulted her, took notes, and incorporated much of what she told him in his *Walt Whitman*, published in 1906. (He acknowledges her having supplied him with Whitman-O'Connor letters, but does not mention his interviews with her.)[44] He urged her to have the correspondence published in the *Atlantic Monthly*. This she did not do, but she wrote an article, "Personal Recollections of Walt Whitman," which was published in the *Atlantic Monthly* in June 1907. (She sent the manuscript to Bliss Perry in advance of publication so as to help him with his book.)

In her last years Nelly was something of a celebrity in Providence, not only because of her friendship with Walt Whitman, but also because of her anti-slavery and woman's rights activities. An interview with Nelly, entitled "The Soldier's Friend Was Walt Whitman," was published in the *Providence Journal*,[45] and another, entitled "Equal Suffrage Notes" by Sara Algeo, was published in the same paper on July 23, 1911. This told of Nelly's life and of her friendship and acquaintance with that "remarkable group of equal suffragists, numbering among them such women as Susan B. Anthony, Elizabeth Cady Stanton, Julia Ward Howe, Harriet Beecher Stowe, Isabella Beecher Hooker, Lucy Stone, and others." Algeo writes that Mrs. Calder met Harriet Beecher Stowe at the home of Dr. Gamaliel Bailey in Washington, and quotes a letter (not very significant) which she received from Harriet Beecher Stowe in 1856. The letter concludes, "Tell me about our William." Algeo mentions that Mrs. Calder had just prepared an introduction for a reprint of *The Good Gray Poet* to be published in Canada. This reprint, with her introduction, though planned by her in correspondence with Quoin House, a Canadian publishing firm, did not appear until 1927, when it was issued in a limited edition by Henry S. Saunders of Toronto, Canada.

In her introduction, Nelly quoted Whitman's preface to O'Connor's *Three Tales* in full and told of the Washington days. She concluded with some remarks about the reception of the "Vindication," and a description of its author's appearance:

> I do not think that the "Vindication" raised a ripple. A few personal friends cared very much; but people in general are not interested in authors, and at that time the thing uppermost in the minds of the people was the war. But we need not be surprised that the

"Good Gray Poet" caused no stir, we have only to remember how new thoughts, ideas and utterances have always been received,— accepted by a few and rejected or treated with indifference by the multitude. One cultivated man feared lest Mr. O'Connor was endangering his own position by such a fearless vindication of his friend, but of course no such reason could ever influence him.

While Mr. O'Connor was a fairly good subject for the photographer, I know of no picture of him that does him justice. His face was one of uncommon beauty, and his blue eyes full of expression. He had brown hair, and a very fair complexion. When he was animated his face grew radiant. His head was noticeably large and dome-like. He was of medium height and slender in youth, but inclined to stoutness in his later years.

Whitman's preface to O'Connor's *Three Tales*, which he valued enough to include in his *Complete Prose Works* (1892), was his only published tribute to a friend. In it he described O'Connor as "gallant, handsome, gay-hearted, fine-voiced, glowing-eyed . . . and the most welcome company in the world . . . a first-class orator . . . (of) a power and persuasiveness beyond any man's else . . . a critic, . . . deeper than any . . . (who) knew all and welcomed all sorts of great *genre* literature, all lands and times from all writers and artists" who "kept an idiosyncracy and identity of his own very marked, and without a special tinge or color from any source. . . ."[46]

The glowing Preface expressed the poet's feeling without enumerating what O'Connor had done for him. The student of O'Connor's life realizes that O'Connor gave Whitman a sense of place and destiny and his home to be a meeting place for a circle of literary friends and appreciators, as well as the realization that there were often depths of meaning in his poems that their creator was unaware of. O'Connor was a champion without being a disciple. He built powerful defenses in *The Good Gray Poet*, in his review in *The Times*, the *Tribune* articles in 1876 and 1882, and his contributions to Bucke's *Walt Whitman*. He proposed and fostered Rossetti's English edition, and arranged for the publication of Anne Gilchrist's "A Woman's Estimate of Walt Whitman." Yet he dared to criticize lines in *Leaves of Grass* as well as whole poems such as "The Dead Emperor." He maintained his principles and honor in the quarrel and its aftermath.

In his life of grueling work, separation from his wife and home, deep personal tragedy, and in his later years, painful illness, O'Connor maintained the chivalric ideals of his youth.

With the passage of time, Whitman attained the place in American and world literature to which O'Connor had assigned him, while his defender remained a one-dimensional figure, known only because of his connection with Whitman, and sometimes disparaged for what was judged to be his excessive zeal.

Yet a study of O'Connor's life affirms Whitman's own words:

O'Connor was a chosen knight—a picked man. Like the Arthurian heroes, true as steel, chivalric to the bone, high in hope and intention. What the knights were to chivalry, O'Connor was in literary action.[47]

NOTES

1. Part of the title of an article by William Sloane Kennedy in *The Conservator* VII: 116–18 (October 1896). (*The Conservator*, a monthly magazine founded by Horace Traubel in 1890 and edited by him until his death in 1919, while not the journal of O'Connor's dreams, did publish articles relating to Whitman and showed the influence of the poet. It reflected also the socialism of Horace Traubel, who was a follower of Eugene V. Debs.)
2. *Camden*, 2:176.
3. 16 May 1889.
4. 14 May 1889.
5. *Camden* 5:313. Whitman went on to say: "what the Critic wants—what the American now seems to want—is . . . anything that is pale, colorless, vapid. . . . "
6. *Washington Post*, 12 May 1889.
7. *Poet Lore*, August 1889, pp. 384–88.
8. *Liberty*, 1 July 1889. The editor was Benjamin Tucker.
9. *Camden*, 5:492.
10. *Liberty*, 7 September 1889, vol. 6, pp. 5 ff.
11. A copy with Traubel's own inked corrections sent to the author by Gertrude Traubel.
12. *Camden*, 5:334.
13. *Ibid.*, 169.
14. *Ibid.*, 177. Whitman wanted O'Connor's great letters preserved and so suggested placing them in an appendix of a reprint.
15. *Ibid.*, 177.
16. WW to Burroughs, 30 September 1889, *Correspondence*, IV: 337–38.
17. Ellen O'Connor to WW, 3 July 1889 (Feinberg-LC).
18. M. J. Channing to G. Channing, 2 April 1891 (Chamberlin).
19. M. J. Channing to G. Channing, 6 July 1891 (Chamberlin).

20. 3 July 1889, *Correspondence*, IV: 353 n.
21. Artem Lozynsky, ed., *The Letters of Dr. Richard Maurice Bucke to Walt Whitman* (Detroit: Wayne State University Press, 1977), p. 134.
22. *Camden*, 5: 366.
23. 13 July 1889, *Correspondence*, IV: 356.
24. Channing family letters (Chamberlin).
25. WW to Ellen O'Connor, 21 September 1890, *Correspondence*, V: 90.
26. Channing family letters (Chamberlin).
27. M. J. Channing to G. Channing, 7 November 1890 (Chamberlin).
28. 5 October 1890 (Feinberg-LC).
29. M. J. Channing to G. Channing, 8 February 1893 (Chamberlin).
30. Channing family letters (Chamberlin).
31. M. J. Channing to G. Channing, 9 May 1891 (Chamberlin).
32. Channing family letters (Chamberlin).
33. (Feinberg-LC).
34. Wedding announcement (Feinberg-LC).
35. M. J. Channing to G. Channing, 12 April 1894 (Chamberlin).
36. (Feinberg-LC).
37. Ellen O'C. Calder to Traubel (Feinberg-LC).
38. Channing family letters (Chamberlin).
39. Channing family letters (Chamberlin).
40. Channing family letters (Chamberlin).
41. Ellen O'C. Calder to Bucke, 13 February 1891 (Feinberg-LC).
42. In the spring of 1893, letters from Ellen O'C. Calder to Traubel were written by K. H. Austin, who served as her secretary at that time.
43. William Sloane Kennedy also wrote a study of Whitman for the *Californian*, vol. 3, pp. 149–58: *Reminiscences of Walt Whitman* (covering the period from Dr. Bucke's book to Whitman's death), published by David McKay; *The Fight of a Book for the World* (West Yarmouth, Mass.: Stonecroft Press, 1926).
44. Bliss Perry, *Walt Whitman: His Life and Work* (Boston and New York: Houghton Mifflin Company, 1906), p. 149, n. 1.
45. Undated. Found among Ellen O'C. Calder's papers.
46. For complete text of Preface, see Appendix A.
47. *Camden*, 5: 165.

Appendix A

WALT WHITMAN'S TRIBUTE
TO WILLIAM DOUGLAS O'CONNOR:
The Preface to O'Connor's
Posthumously Printed *Three Tales*[1]

A HASTY memorandum, not particularly for Preface to the following tales, but to put on record my respect and affection for as sane, beautiful, cute, tolerant, loving, candid and free and fair-intentioned a nature as ever vivified our race.

In Boston, 1860, I first met William Douglas O'Connor.° As I saw and knew him then, in his twenty-ninth year, and for twenty-five further years, he was a gallant, handsome, gay-hearted, fine-voiced, glowing-eyed man; lithe-moving on his feet, of healthy and magnetic atmosphere and presence, and the most welcome company in the world. He was a thorough-going anti-slavery believer, speaker and writer (doctrinaire), and though I took a fancy to him from the first, I remember I feared his ardent abolitionism,—was afraid it would probably keep us apart. (I was a decided and outspoken anti-slavery believer myself, then and always; but shied from the extremists, the red-hot fellows of those times.) O'Connor was then correcting the proofs of "Harrington," an eloquent and fiery novel he had written, and which was printed just before the commencement of the Secession War. He was already married, the father of two fine little children, and was personally and intellectually the most attractive man I had ever met. Last of '62 I found myself led towards the war-field—went to Washington City (to become absorbed in the armies, and in the big hospitals, and to get work in one of the Departments)—and there I met and resumed friendship, and found warm hospitality from O'Connor and his New England wife. [They had just lost by death their little child-boy Philip; and O'C. was yet feeling serious about it. The youngster had been vaccinated against the threatening of small-pox which alarm'd the city; but somehow it led to worse results than it was intended to ward off—or at any rate O'C. thought that proved the cause of the little boy's death. He had one child left, a fine bright little daughter, and

---

°Born January 2, 1832. When grown, lived several years in Boston, and edited journals and magazines there; went about 1861 to Washington, D.C., and became a U.S. clerk, first in the Lighthouse Bureau and then in the U.S. Life-Saving Service, in which branch he was Assistant Superintendent for many years,—sickened in 1887,—died there at Washington, May 9, 1889.

a great comfort to her parents. (Dear Jeannie! She grew up a most accomplish'd and superior young woman—declined in health and died about 1881.)][2]

On through to '73 I saw and talked with O'Connor almost daily. I had soon got employment, first for a short time in the Indian Bureau (in the Interior Department), and then for a long while in the Attorney General's office. The Secession War, with its tide of varying fortunes, excitements—President Lincoln and the daily sight of him, the doings in Congress and at the State capitals, the news from the fields and campaigns, and from foreign governments, with a hundred matters, occurrences, personalities—(Greeley, Wendell Phillips, the parties, the Abolitionists, etc.)—were the subjects of our talk and discussion. I am not sure, from what I heard then, but O'Connor was cut out for a first-class orator or public speaker or forensic advocate. No audience or jury could have stood out against him. He had a power and sharp-cut faculty of statement and persuasiveness beyond any man's else. I know it well, for I have felt it many a time. If not as orator, his forte was as critic, newer, deeper than any; also, as literary author. One of his traits was that while he knew all, and welcomed all sorts of great *genre* literature, all lands and times, from all writers and artists, and not only tolerated each, and defended every attacked literary person with a skill and heart-catholicism that I never saw equaled,—invariably advocated or excused them,—he kept an idiosyncrasy and identity of his own very marked, and without special tinge or color from any source. He always applauded the masters, whence and whoever. I remember his special defenses of Byron, Burns, Poe, Rabelais, Victor Hugo, George Sand, and others. There was always a little touch of pensive cadence in his superb voice; and I think there was something of the same sadness in his temperament and nature,—perhaps, too, in his literary structure. But he was a very buoyant, jovial, good-natured companion.

NOTES

1. Eager to promote the sale of *Three Tales* on 25 November 1890 Whitman sent a postcard to the Editor of *The Critic*, requesting an announcement of O'Connor's forthcoming book and mentioning his preface. *The Critic* complied with a sentence at the end of a long paragraph about Whitman in its issue of 29 November 1890. The postcard is presented in facsimile with explanatory material by William White, "An Unpublished Letter to *The Critic*," *Walt Whitman Review* 27 (June 1981), back cover.
2. The material in brackets appeared in Walt Whitman's original ms. but was deleted at Nelly's request. Whitman was mistaken in the date of Jeannie's death which occurred on 5 May 1883.

APPENDIX B

WILLIAM DOUGLAS O'CONNOR AND WALT WHITMAN:
An Exchange of Letters

William Douglas O'Connor to Walt Whitman[1]

Washington, D.C., December 30, 1864.

Dear Walt:

I have been constantly hoping to have you here again and now begin to see something more than a glimmer of fruition. Ashton has spoken (at my instigation) to Mr. Otto the Assistant Secretary of the Department of the Interior in your behalf, and Mr. Otto says that if you will write a letter of application to the Secretary of the Interior, he will endeavor to put you on.

Now, dear Walt, do this without delay. The object of your writing the letter is to get a specimen of your hand. Pick out, then, a good pen and write as fairly as you can a letter formally applying for a clerkship. Then enclose a *copy* of this letter to Ashton, so that he can follow it in to the Secretary. The *first* letter you will, of course, mail to the Secretary direct.

Do this as soon as you can. We shall fetch it this time. I have every confidence that you will get a good and an easy berth, a regular income, &c, leaving you time to attend to the soldiers, to your poems, &c,—in a word, what Archimedes wanted, a place on which to rest the lever.

I shall wait anxiously to hear that you have sent on the letters. I've been thinking of you constantly for months and have been doing everything I could to secure you a foothold here. For a long time, deceived (I must think) by Swinton's pretensions to influence and by his profuse promises, I hoped to get you either one of the New York State Agency Assistantships or the place of an Assistant Librarian in the Congress Library (the latter would be really a sinecure if the right one was got). But who follows Swinton follows a will-of-the-wisp and though I followed him remorselessly every blessed day, for several weeks, and gave him neither rest nor peace, as the saying is, I got nothing except promises. Since I gave him up, I have been badgering Ashton, who is a man of another sort, as what he has done shows. The difficulty was to get the right thing. He secured me some little time ago a place in the Post Office for you, but I declined it, because I thought it was not the proper place for you. I think a desk in the Interior would be first-rate.

354

I told Ashton that there was nothing I would not do for him if he would carry this affair to a safe conclusion. He has been very good and anxious in your behalf. He would have given you a desk in his own office if a vacancy had occurred as was expected.

Don't forget to do as I tell you immediately.

I never answered your letter of September 11th, but, dear Walt, I always think of you, though I write so seldom and so badly. You are never forgotten. I read your poems often, I get their meaning more and more, I stand up for them and you, I expound, define, defend, vindicate, justify them and you with all the heart and head that I have whenever occasion demands.

I got the Times with your long letter about the Hospital experiences, which I read with a swelling heart and wet eyes. It was very great and touching to me. I think I could mount the tribune for you on that and speak speech which jets fire and drops tears. Only it filled me with infinite regrets that there is not a book from you, embodying these rich sad experiences. It would be sure of immortality. No history of our times would ever be written without it, if written with that wealth of living details you could crowd into it. Indeed it would itself be history.

I saw your letter about the prisoners. It was as just as powerful. I have been hearing for a fortnight past that it is the Secretary of War's "policy" which prevents exchange, and if this is true, I pray from my heart of hearts that it never may be forgotten against him. Reddest murder is white to an act like this and its folly is equal to its crime. It would be demonism of another kind indeed than the Southerners', yet as bad, perhaps worse, because sprung from calculation rather than hatred.

Such things make one sicken of the world.

I write this letter at intervals between the press of office work, which has driven upon me in spasms today, but pretty severely when it did come. Any incoherences in it, you may refer to the obfusticated state which such hurryings have induced in me.

Farewell, dear Walt. I hope to hear from you very soon. We are all tolerably well at home. Eldridge comes every evening. We often talk of you. On Christmas you were wanted to make the dinner at home perfect. We all spoke of you. On Thanksgiving it was the same. At dinner that day I said "I wish"—and stopped. "What?"—said Nellie. "*I* know," chirped little Jeannie, "he wishes Walt was here." Which was true—that *was* the unuttered wish.

Let me hear soon.

Your loving W. D. O'Connor

Walt Whitman, Esq.

Walt Whitman to William Douglas O'Connor[2]

To William D. O'Connor
Address: Wm D O'Connor   Light House Board
Treasury Department   Washington DC.
Postmark: New York   Jan 6.

Brooklyn   January 6 1865

Dear friend

Your welcome letter of December 30 came safe. I have written & sent my application to Mr. Otto, & also a few lines to Mr Ashton, with a copy of it. I am most desirous to get the appointment, as enclosing, with the rest of the points, my attentions to the soldiers & to my poems, as you intimate.

It may be Drum-Taps may come out this winter, yet, (in the way, I have mentioned in times past). It is in a state to put right through, a perfect copy being ready for the printers—I feel at last, & for the first time without any demur, that I am satisfied with it—content to have it go to the world verbatim & punctuation. It is in my opinion superior to Leaves of Grass—certainly more perfect as a work of art, being adjusted in all its proportions, & its passion having the indispensable merit that though to the ordinary reader let loose with wildest abandon, the true artist can see it is yet under control. But I am perhaps mainly satisfied with Drum-Taps because it delivers my ambition of the task that has haunted me, namely, to express in a poem (& in the way I like, which is not at all by directly stating it) the pending action of this *Time & Land we swim in*, with all their large conflicting fluctuations of despair & hope, the shiftings, masses, & the whirl & deafening din, (yet over all, as by invisible hand, a definite purport & idea)—with the unprecedented anguish of wounded & suffering, the beautiful young men, in wholesale death & agony, everything sometimes as if in blood color, & dripping blood. The book is therefore unprecedently sad, (as these days are, are they not?)—but it also has the blast of the trumpet, & the drum pounds & whirrs in it, & then an undertone of sweetest comradeship & human love, threading its steady thread inside the chaos, & heard at every lull & interstice thereof—truly also it has clear notes of faith & triumph.

Drum-Taps has none of the perturbations of Leaves of Grass. I am satisfied with Leaves of Grass (by far the most of it) as expressing what was intended, namely, to express by sharp-cut self assertion, *One's-Self* & also, or may be still more, to map out, to throw together for American use, a gigantic embryo or skeleton of Personality, fit for the West, for native models—but there are a few things I shall carefully eliminate in the next issue, & a few more I shall considerably change.

I see I have said I consider Drum-Taps superior to Leaves of Grass. I probably mean as a piece of wit, & from the more simple & winning nature of the subject, & also because I have in it only succeeded to my satisfaction in removing all superfluity from it, verbal superfluity I mean. I delight to make a poem where I feel clear that not a word but is indispensable part thereof & of my meaning.

Still Leaves of Grass is dear to me, always dearest to me, as my first born, as daughter of my life's first hopes, doubts, & the putting in form of those days' efforts & aspirations—true, I see now, with some things in it I should not put in if I were to write now, but yet I shall certainly let them stand, even if but for proofs of phases passed away—

Mother & all home are well as usual. Not a word for over three months from my brother George—the probabilities are most gloomy. I see the Howells now & then. I am well, but need to leave here—need a change. If you see Miss Howard tell her Jesse Mullery has been to see me—came yesterday & has just left this forenoon. He talked of nothing but her. His life is saved, & he will have tolerably good strength & health, at least for present. His address is Ward 7, Centre st. Hospital, Newark New Jersey. I was up at Mrs Price's the other night. She is better this winter. Mrs. Paulina Wright Davis is stopping with her this winter. I have sent a paper with sketch of Hospital Visits to Dr Wm F Channing. I cannot forgive myself for not acknowledging his assistance for the Hospitals, by letter at the time. I send you another paper also, as you might like it. I take it by a line in your letter that Charles Eldridge has not gone to Boston. I have been reading the strange articles from the Richmond press. A thousand Satans baffled, with terror, hatred, malignant squirming, appear in every paragraph. Little California is playing around me as I finish, & has been for half an hour. Love to dear Nelly & Jeannie & all.

Walt Whitman

NOTES

1. (Feinberg-LC).
2. *Correspondence*, I: 246–48. Of the more than 2700 letters written by Whitman and collected in the *Correspondence* edited by Edwin Haviland Miller, this letter to O'Connor is the only "literary" letter, the only one expressing in depth his own feelings and intentions in his poetry.

Bibliography

Bibliography of William Douglas O'Connor*

1. "Shadow on the Wall." Boston *Weekly Museum*, December 22, 1849.
2. "Mabel." Providence *Journal*, September 23, 1851.
3. "About the Goblet." Providence *Journal*, October 16, 1851.
4. "To the City Fathers." Providence *Journal*, October 28, 1851.
5. "To Athos." Providence *Journal*, November 25, 1851.
6. "Aves." Providence *Journal*, December 20, 1851.
7. "The North Star." Providence *Journal*, January 22, 1852.
8. "A Valentine." *The Carpet Bag*, May 15, 1852.
9. Review of *The Howadji in Syria*, by George William Curtis. Providence *Journal*, June 5, 1852.
10. "The Lost Land." *The Carpet Bag*, August 23, 1852. Providence *Journal*, October 1, 1852. Reprinted in *Mercantile Library Reporter* 2 (December 1855), 15.
11. "A Midsummer Night's Dream. To Katie." Providence *Journal*, October 9, 1852. Reprinted in *The Carpet Bag*, October 30, 1852.
12. "Resurgamus." Providence *Journal*, September 23, 1853.
13. "The Sword of Mauley." *Harper's Monthly Magazine* 8 (January 1854), 239–48.
14. "Alma Mater." Boston *Commonwealth*, March 31, 1854.
15. "The Grotesque." *Mercantile Library Reporter* 2 (December 1854), 19–22.
16. "Loss and Gain: A Tale of Lynn." *Harper's Monthly Magazine* 10 (December 1854), 82–99.
17. "To Jeannie, with a copy of Poems of Thomas Hood." *Una*, July 1855.
18. "What Cheer?" *Putnam's Monthly Magazine* 6 (July 1855), 8–24.
19. "The Knocker." *Harper's Monthly Magazine* 12 (December 1855), 57–73.
20. "The Ghost." *Putnam's Monthly Magazine* 7 (January 1856), 20–40. Published in book form, with two illustrations by Thomas Nast, by G. P. Putnam and Son, 1867; by Houghton Mifflin in *Little Classics*. Without authorization, with the title "The Colonel's Story" by "Beadle of the Dime Novel." (WDO'C to Stedman, 9 January 1889.) It was one of O'Connor's *Three Tales*, Houghton Mifflin and Company, 1892.
21. "The New Year." *Mercantile Library Reporter* 2 (January 1856), 17–21.

---

*Starred titles have been reprinted in Jerome Loving's *Walt Whitman's Champion: William Douglas O'Connor*. College Station and London, Texas A & M University Press, 1978.

22. "Chivalry." *Mercantile Library Reporter* 2 (March 1856), 57–60. "Chivalry." *Saturday Evening Post*, October 11, 1856.
23. "Address of the Carriers of the Saturday Evening Post to their Patrons." *Saturday Evening Post*, January 1, 1857.
24. "Shakespeare." *Saturday Evening Post*, April 11, 1857.
25. "The Shakespeare Question." *Saturday Evening Post*, May 30, 1857.
26. "The Humours of Criticism." *Saturday Evening Post*, September 19, 1857.
27. "Address of the Carriers of the Saturday Evening Post to their Patrons." *Saturday Evening Post*, January 1, 1858.
28. "Woman's Rights." *Saturday Evening Post*, February 18, 1860.
29. *Harrington: A Story of True Love*. Boston: Thayer and Eldridge, 1860.
30. "Salaries of Clerks." Memorandum presented to Congress, February 1865.
° 31. *The Good Gray Poet: A Vindication*. New York: Bunce & Huntington, 1866. Reprinted with slight revisions in Richard Maurice Bucke, *Walt Whitman* (1883), pp. 99–130, and in a limited edition by Henry S. Saunders, Toronto, Canada, 1927 (with an introduction by Ellen M. O'Connor Calder.)
32. "Letter to the Editor." *Round Table*, February 3, 1866. Reprinted in Richard Maurice Bucke, *Walt Whitman* (1883), pp. 131–32.
33. "Earl Mord." *Galaxy* 2 (December 1, 1866), 605.
34. "Walt Whitman." New York *Times*, December 2, 1866.
35. " 'C' on Walt Whitman." *Round Table*, February 16, 1867.
36. "Who Wrote 'Rock Me to Sleep?' " New York *Times*, May 27, 1867.
37. "Walt Whitman." New York *Times*, June 30, 1867. Review of John Burroughs, *Notes on Walt Whitman as Poet and Person* (1867).
38. "To the Editor of the *Independent*." November 9, 1867.
39. Letter to *The Nation* (never sent), December 16, 1867.
40. "The Carpenter." *Putnam's Monthly Magazine*, New Series (1 January 1868), 55–90.
41. "The Ballad of Sir Ball." *Galaxy* 5 (March 1868), 328–33.
42. "Victor Hugo's 'Nature.' " *Appleton's Journal* 4 (5 November 1870), 550–52.
43. "To Fanny." *Atlantic Monthly* 27 (February 1871), 161–69.
° 44. "Walt Whitman: Is He Persecuted?" New York *Tribune*, April 22, 1876.
45. "The Hermit." Illustrated poem in the membership leaflet of the Gymnasium, 1877.
46. "The United States Life-Saving Service." *Appleton's Cyclopedia*. New York: D. Appleton's, 1878.
° 47. "Suppressing Walt Whitman." New York *Tribune*, May 27, 1882.
° 48. "Emerson and Whitman." New York *Tribune*, June 18, 1882.
° 49. "Mr. Comstock as Cato the Censor." New York *Tribune*, August 27, 1882.
50. "Mr. O'Connor's Letter" (Introductory letter to *The Good Gray Poet*). In Richard Maurice Bucke, *Walt Whitman* (1883), pp. 73–98. Published in England in 1884 and 1888.
51. "Some Nails for a Coffin." New York *Tribune*, February 11, 1883.
52. "The Fire Alarm Controversy." New York *Tribune*, February 20, 1883.
53. "Ignatius Donnelly." *Appleton's Cyclopedia*. New York: D. Appleton's, 1885.

54. *Hamlet's Note-Book*. Boston: Houghton, 1886.
55. *Mr. Donnelly's Reviewers*. Chicago: Bedford, Clarke & Co., 1889.
56. Selections from *Harrington*, "The Carpenter," and "To Fanny," in *A Library of American Literature*, ed. Edmund C. Stedman (New York: 1889), vol. 9, pp. 48–61.
57. "The Brazen Android." *Atlantic Monthly* 62 (April 1891), 433–54, and (May 1891), 577–600.
58. *Three Tales*. Preface by Walt Whitman. Boston: Houghton Mifflin Company, 1892. Contains "The Ghost," "The Brazen Android," and "The Carpenter."
59. "*The Good Gray Poet*: Supplemental." Submitted to the Boston *Transcript* with the date of January 23, 1866; not printed there. In Horace Traubel et al., *In Re Walt Whitman*. Philadelphia: David McKay, 1893 (pp. 139–57).
60. "Tobey or Not Tobey? That is the Question." Submitted to the New York *Tribune* with the date of September 16, 1882; never printed. In *The Conservator*, September 7, 1896 (pp. 99–102).
61. *Heroes of the Storm*. (Selected Accounts of Rescue Operations by the Life Saving Bureau.) Introduced and edited by Sumner I. Kimball. Boston: Houghton Mifflin Company, 1904.

Bibliography of Ellen M. O'Connor Calder

1. *Myrtilla Miner: A Memoir*. Boston and New York: Houghton Mifflin Co., 1885. [Facsimile Edition (New York: Arno Press and *The New York Times*, 1969). Introduction by Florence B. Freedman.]
2. "William Douglas O'Connor's Award to Bacon." *The Conservator*, VIII, March 7, 1897.
3. "William O'Connor and Walt Whitman." *The Conservator*, XVII, May 1906, p. 42.
4. Introduction to *The Good Gray Poet* (Toronto, Canada) Henry S. Saunders, 1927.
5. "Personal Recollections of Walt Whitman." *Atlantic Monthly* (June 1907), pp. 825–34.

INDEX

Abolition movement, 3, 57, 58, 59, 77, 79, 101, 219, 251, 307, 348
Adams, John Quincy, 112, 114
"Address of the Carriers of the Saturday Evening Post to their Patrons" (O'Connor), 93–4
Akers-Ball controversy, 204–6. *See also* Allen, Elizabeth Akers
Akers, Paul, 93
Alcott, Bronson, 59, 140, 179, 200, 233
Alcott, Louisa May, 140
Aldrich, Thomas Bailey, 47, 140
Algeo, Sara, 348
Allen, Elizabeth Akers (pseud. Florence Percy), 7, 92–3, 139, 204, 206
American Feminists (Riegel), 85
Andrews, Stephen Pearl, 145, 147
Anthony, Susan B., 60–1, 62, 147, 314
Appleton's Encyclopedia, 117, 339
Appleton's Journal, 241, 276
"Aramis." *See* O'Connor, William Douglas
Arnold, Edwin, 321
Arnold, George, 140
Arnold, Matthew, 185, 187–8, 321
Ashton, J. Hubley, 87, 128, 157, 167, 168–70, 174, 180, 225
Athenaeum, 271
"Athos." *See* Bacon, George A.
Atlantic Monthly, 90, 119, 121, 128, 243, 246, 251, 263, 341, 342, 348
Attucks, Crispus, 111

Bacon, Delia, 64, 65–7, 68, 110. *See also* Baconian theory
Bacon, Francis, 115, 116
Bacon, George A. ("Athos"), 13, 17, 255, 347
Bacon, Theodore, 69, 70
Baconian theory, 70, 71, 73, 135, 242, 280, 314, 325, 339, 347
Bailey, Gamaliel, 57, 79, 127, 220, 317
Baker, Frank, 133, 250
Baldwin, John Denison, 38, 90
Ball, Alexander S.M. *See* Akers-Ball controversy
"Ballad of Sir Ball, The" (O'Connor), 205
Balzac, Honore, 208

Barrus, Clara, 243, 251, 279
Bayne, Peter, 270
Beecher, Catherine, 65, 66
Benton, John, 120
Benton, Myron, 8, 203, 207, 252
Blake, William, 232
Booth, Junius Brutus, 328, 330
Boston, 11–2, 34, 41, 77
Boston Commonwealth, 13, 27, 40, 90, 116, 213
Boston Daily Evening Voice, 192
Boston Transcript, 193, 195, 245, 346
Boston Weekly Voice, 137
Boston Wide World, 120
"Brazen Android, The" (O'Connor), 91, 121–3, 237, 341
Brigham, Johnson, 172, 173
Brisbane, Albert, 133, 148. *See also* Fourierism
Brook Farm, 16
Brooklyn Eagle, 171, 222
Brown, John, 94–5, 101, 105, 136
Bryant, William Cullen, 291
Buchanan, Robert, 215, 242, 271, 273
Bucke, Richard Maurice, 214, 258, 320, 323, 324, 346; and Canadian controversy, 284; as matchmaker, 340–1; and O'Connor, 286, 320, 329, 332; and Stevens, 296–7; and Whitman, 283, 285–7, 326–8
Bunce and Huntington, 186, 187
Burns, Anthony, 81, 220
Burns, Robert, 179, 188, 290
Burroughs, John, 257–8, 275, 301, 302; and O'Connor, 72, 205, 240–1, 243, 251–2, 279, 323, 330, 332–3; in Washington, 133–4, 154, 260, 262; and Whitman, 133, 165, 197, 224, 227, 230, 232, 241, 270, 272, 285, 295, 326, 344
Burroughs, Ursula, 133, 260, 262
Byron, George Gordon, 270, 290

" 'C' on Whitman" (O'Connor), 215
Calder, Albert, 342–3, 347
Calder, Ellen Tarr O'Connor, 148, 348; and O'Connor's writings, 280, 345, 348–9; in

361